2

WITHDRAWN

RUSSIAN RESEARCH CENTER STUDIES, 90

Published under the auspices of the
Davis Center for Russian Studies,
Harvard University

Mikhail Bulgakov

The Early Years

Edythe C. Haber

HARVARD UNIVERSITY PRESS

Cambridge, Massachusetts

London, England · 1998

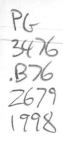
Library of Congress Cataloging-in-Publication Data

Haber, Edythe C.
Mikhail Bulgakov : the early years / Edythe C. Haber.
p.   cm. — (Russian Research Center studies ; 90)
Includes bibliographical references and index.
ISBN 0-674-57418-4
1. Bulgakov, Mikhail Afanas'evich, 1891–1940.
2. Authors, Russian—20th century—Biography.
3. Autobiography in literature.
I. Title.   II. Series.
PG3476.B78Z679   1998
891.7'84209—dc21
[B]   97-42403

Contents

Preface

At the sunset hour on a cold, wintry day in 1967, two citizens (of whom I was one) appeared in Schoenhof's, the Cambridge, Massachusetts, foreign language bookstore. While we were exchanging some unholy academic gossip, there suddenly appeared before us on a shelf a "diabolical" apparition: the recently published *Master and Margarita,* clothed in a forbidding gray cover. One cannot, of course, compare this commonplace occurrence to the fateful encounter that opens *The Master and Margarita*—which my own beginning rather lamely apes—yet Bulgakov transformed my life almost as totally as the devil did those of the Moscow literati he came upon at Patriarch's Pond. The principal scholarly result of our meeting that winter day is this book. But before I turn to my main subject, I feel compelled by recent circumstances to describe the writer's role in my personal life.

It was to do research on Bulgakov that I went to Moscow in the fall of 1977. There I led the double life so familiar to exchange students and scholars during the late Brezhnev years: in the daytime I spent long hours in Moscow's Lenin Library and in the evenings partook of the still semi-illicit pleasures offered by Moscow's artistic-intellectual circles. One of my acquaintances, who stood out for his wit, vitality, and warmth, for a kind of subversive mischievousness (legacy of Woland and his retinue?) that often took the place of overt political protest in these circles, was Timur Djordjadze, a Georgian theater director studying and working in Moscow. Timur and I fell in love and in February 1978 were married. The following day I had to leave the Soviet Union, but I returned later in the year.

Timur and I lived in Moscow until April 1980, when we left for the United States. It was then that I finally began to work seriously on my book, although still fitfully, what with the demands of teaching and a commuting marriage. If things nevertheless gradually moved forward, it was due largely to Timur's unfailing encouragement—not only his moral support but also his constant acts of love and devotion, both large and small: doing all the cooking, dishwashing, and laundry; almost all the commuting; cutting my hair; sewing my clothes; and much, much more.

In 1992, Timur began to suffer from severe back pain, and in the autumn—exactly fifteen years after our romance had begun in Moscow—he was diagnosed with lung cancer, which had metastasized to his spine. For about two years he struggled with the disease, suffering unendurable pain. Timur died in August 1994, thus not living to see the completion of the book that had first brought us together.

As I look back at my time with Timur, I am struck by the correspondences with Bulgakov's life and that of the Master. We, like the Master and Margarita, first met on the street (Timur had been sent out by a mutual friend to meet me at a trolley stop), and our romance was also at first clandestine, although for political, not marital, reasons. We too went through a forced separation when I returned to America but were happily reunited in our own apartment in Moscow. When Timur's act of marrying a foreigner brought his heretofore highly promising theatrical career to a halt, we, like the Master and Margarita, flew off from Moscow—although not astride a devilish steed but on an Aeroflot jet—and headed for America, not the next world.

The strongest sense of connection between our marital life and Bulgakov's, however, was in the way it ended: the long and tormenting illness, which tapped the deepest reserves of love and devotion between husband and wife, and the premature deaths of rare and gifted men at approximately the same age (forty-nine). It would be the height of presumption, of course, to compare my book to Bulgakov's great novel, and yet my modest contribution to literary scholarship is as inextricably interwoven into my life with Timur as was *The Master and Margarita* into Bulgakov's with his third wife, Elena Sergeevna. It is therefore with undying love and longing that I dedicate this book to Timur.

A second person to whom I would like to pay final respects here is Lyubov Evgenievna Belozerskaya, Bulgakov's second wife, with whom I developed a close tie while in Moscow. I remember sitting weekly over tea in the apartment she shared equally with her cats and Bulgakov memorabilia, as she reminisced about her early life, pointed out with characteristic indignation the latest misrepresentation of Bulgakov in the press, or—far more rarely—recommended some article for its accuracy and erudition. By creating a vivid sense of the places and people surrounding Bulgakov in the 1920s, Lyubov Evgenievna contributed much to my understanding of the man and the time.

As an almost pathological loner when it comes to writing, I must accept sole responsibility for any shortcomings in the study that follows. Many of its good points, however, have been enhanced by the help of a few people. I want to express special thanks to Donald Fanger for his scrupulous reading of two versions of my manuscript—particularly for his unsparing but very constructive critique of the earlier version. Some of the others who, at various stages, have generously offered good advice and shared their knowledge are M. O. Chudakova, L. A. Gladkovskaya, Vladimir Lakshin, Ellendea Proffer, Vsevolod Setchkarev, Richard Sheldon, M. N. Sotskova, Anatoly Smelyansky, and Aleksei Vitkovsky.

I would also like to acknowledge financial and/or research support from the following institutions: the International Research and Exchanges Board; the American Council of Learned Societies; the W. Averell Harriman Institute for Advanced Studies of the Soviet Union at Columbia University; my home institution, the University of Massachusetts in Boston; and most of all the Kathryn W. and Shelby Cullom Davis Center for Russian Studies at Harvard University, without whose encouragement over so many years—and without the material and moral support at the end—this project could not have come to fruition.

Much thanks goes as well to George and Sandra Langworth for technical help at a very critical time. I am also very grateful to Margaretta Fulton and Erin Wilson Burns at Harvard University Press for their frequent help and good advice and to my thoughtful and meticulous editors at ESNE, Elaine L. Kehoe and Susannah Noel. Last but very far from least I want to thank my late mother, Jennie Haber, and my sisters and brother-in-law, Clara Haber, Zelda Haber, and William Halsey, for their unfailing love and support.

Note on Transliteration

Russian names of people and places are transliterated according to the Library of Congress system with the following modifications in the interest of readability: (1) standard English forms of places and well-known people are used (Moscow, Leo Tolstoy); (2) in the text soft signs are omitted (Igor), whereas in the notes they are indicated (Igor'); (3) *-ii* and *-yi* are replaced by *-y* (Gorky, Bely); (4) *y* is used instead of *i* to represent a y-glide or soft consonant before an *a* or *u* (Yury, Tanya).

Russian titles in the notes and occasional Russian words in the text are spelled according to the unmodified Library of Congress system. The exceptions are words with a standard English form (glasnost, intelligentsia).

Abbreviations

Editions of Bulgakov's Works

Izb. pr. = *Izbrannye proizvedeniia v dvukh tomakh* (Selected works in two volumes). Ed. Lidiya Yanovskaya, 2 vols. Kiev: Dnipro, 1989.

Sob. soch.(A) = *Sobranie sochinenii*, vols. 1–4, 8. Ed. Ellendea Proffer. Ann Arbor, Mich.: Ardis, 1982–1988.

Sob. soch.(M) = *Sobranie sochinenii v piati tomakh* (Collected works in five volumes), 5 vols. Moscow: Khudozhestvennaia literatura, 1989–1990.

Sob. Soch. (1995) = *Sobranie sochinenii v desiati tomakh* (Collected works in ten volumes), vols. 1–3. Ed. Viktor Petelin. 10 vols. Moscow: Golos, 1995.

Periodicals

IAN	*Izvestiia Akademii Nauk*
Lg	*Literaturnaia gazeta*
Lo	*Literaturnoe obozrenie*
Nm	*Novyi mir*
RÉS	*Revue des Études Slaves*
Rl	*Russkaia literatura*
RLJ	*Russian Literature Journal*
RLT	*Russian Literature Triquarterly*
RR	*Russian Review*
SEEJ	*Slavic and East European Journal*
SR	*Slavic Review*
TKDA	*Trudy Kievskoi Dukhovnoi Akademii*
Vl	*Voprosy literatury*

MIKHAIL BULGAKOV

Introduction

The Bulgakov Phenomenon

In the broad field of Russian letters in the USSR I was the one and only literary wolf. I was advised to dye my fur. Absurd advice. You can dye a wolf, clip a wolf—he still doesn't look like a poodle.

MIKHAIL BULGAKOV, LETTER TO JOSEPH STALIN, MAY 30, 1931

This excerpt from one of several letters Bulgakov wrote to Stalin and other political figures during the last decade of his life tells much about the writer: his boldness at a time of great vulnerability, his disarming humor in response to an exceedingly grave situation. Also of importance here is the use of the past tense, for the writer, having been "pursued for several years according to the rules of literary ambush," now announces that he is "no longer a wolf, not a literary man . . . He has fallen silent."[1]

Bulgakov, of course, was far from the only writer hounded into silence during the so-called proletarian episode in Russian literature, from 1928–1932.[2] Yet he—although allowed in a limited way to manifest his "wolfish" nature during the relatively tolerant NEP period—had been singled out from the very beginning of the Soviet period as a particular class enemy, one who, in the words of the prominent proletarian critic, Leopold Averbakh, did "not even disguise himself in the colors of a fellow traveler."[3] Bulgakov, in fact, in a 1930 letter to the Soviet government, actually agreed with his enemies, declaring their judgment that his works "cannot exist in the USSR . . . ABSOLUTELY RIGHT" (5:445).

The writer gave as a fundamental reason for his impermissibility his "persistent depiction of the Russian intelligentsia as the best segment in our country" (5:447). He uses the slippery term *intelligentsia* here to denote

1

that fragile layer of Russian educated society, shattered by revolution, in which the old civilization—its culture, traditions, civility—had made its home. His faithfulness to that old world had led him not only to portray sympathetically *intelligenty* in the anti-Bolshevik camp but also to direct his trenchant satire against those whom the Communists championed—the masses—who, in his view, were threatening to uproot the delicate blooms of prerevolutionary Russian civilization. No matter what the times demanded, he could not force himself to portray what he calls the "terrifying traits of my people" (5:446) as exemplary features of a noble Communist proletariat.

It is hardly surprising therefore that by early 1929 Bulgakov's works had entirely disappeared from both print and the stage.[4] In 1930, to be sure, after a telephone call from Stalin, he was given a post at the Moscow Art Theater (the deeply suspicious Stalin evidently preferring avowed wolves to those he perceived as wolves in poodles' clothing),[5] but in the decade that followed Bulgakov's name nevertheless sank into obscurity. There it remained for over a quarter of a century after his death in 1940, until the publication of his extraordinary novel, *The Master and Margarita*, in 1966–1967.

The trajectory that the writer's reputation has followed since the appearance of *The Master and Margarita* closely parallels the cataclysmic social and political changes in Russia over those years. During the Brezhnev era, he lived the shadowy life of the so-called partially rehabilitated: he was published from time to time, but in very small press runs; his critics, while producing some very valuable studies, were forced to operate within very tight ideological constraints. Beneath this frozen surface, however, *The Master and Margarita*—as rollicking entertainment and complex ethical-religious exploration, as tender romance and cruel satire—enjoyed an extraordinarily broad and fervent following. People could recite whole passages by heart, while short, aphoristic citations had become a part of daily speech.

This hidden adulation exploded into the open during the glasnost period. It has taken many forms, among which are the following: the Moscow apartment house where Bulgakov spent his first Moscow years (and in which the devils in *The Master and Margarita* took up residence) after having become a virtual shrine—its walls covered with Bulgakovian graffiti—has resently been made into a museum; annual festivals have been held in the writer's honor; restaurants and cafés bear the names of his characters; the post-Soviet nouveaux riches have held their own Satan's Ball, admission price $100.[6] Not only does Bulgakov now enjoy immense popular renown, moreover; he has also gained the official recognition that eluded him throughout his life and for many years after his death. In the past decade or so volume after volume of his works have come out. These have been accompanied by an immense outpouring of critical and biographical works of the most varied scope and quality, from scholarly investigations of the first magnitude (most notably M. O. Chudakova's massive biography)[7] to the works of amateur sleuths, seeking out "Bulgakov places" and forgotten texts published in obscure periodicals.[8] In general Bulgakov is now as fulsomely praised as he was once excessively censured—and at times by the same critics. He is called (to cite a few random examples) not merely a "great writer" *(velikii pisatel')* but a "supremely great writer" *(velichaishii pisatel')* who has "become the stuff of legend."[9] A Bulgakov Prize has even been established, and by none other than the Moscow writers whose forebears had in crueler political times so mercilessly persecuted the Master—and Bulgakov himself.[10]

In the topsy-turvy world of post-Soviet society, it is perhaps inevitable that the writer has also gained some dubious political and ideological allies, that some on the far right extol him for the very reasons he had once been maligned: as a retrograde White Guardist and monarchist. There are those, indeed, who have gone so far as to attribute to him—on very tenuous evidence and despite much counterevidence—their own extreme Great Russian chauvinism and anti-Semitism.[11] Thus, the attempt to make the "literary wolf" into a poodle—to confine him within ideological bounds, although now of the right rather than the left—persists.

It stands to reason that, after all the furor surrounding Bulgakov, Russian readers have grown rather satiated in the last few years. As one observer writes: "Today Bulgakov's novels are no longer included on best seller lists . . . But they will probably be read through the ages."[12] However, this descent from the status of superstardom, which had been accompanied by unquestioning adoration and overheated polemics, should prove a good thing for scholarship, allowing for a more dispassionate and balanced examination of the writer's life and, especially, his works. This is not to say, of course, that a good many significant and insightful studies, both biographical and critical, have not already appeared (and I will acknowledge my debt to them in the appropriate places). Some of Bulgakov's best critics have also offered flashes of deep insight into recurring motifs in his works

(Chudakova and Smelyansky immediately come to mind).[13] Yet on the whole critical works so far have been either too broadly or too narrowly focused (overviews of life and works, articles on a single work) to permit a sustained exploration of underlying patterns, which originate in Bulgakov's first writings and take their final form in *The Master and Margarita*. By concentrating here on the early years I hope to do just this: to probe to the very roots of Bulgakov's creative life and follow from there both the diverging branches of his literary production and their hidden interconnectedness.

The Fictional Life

My emphasis throughout this study is on the narrative prose, although I also discuss some of the plays in greater or lesser detail when relevant to the lines I trace. In general the writer's biography, so exhaustively examined in recent years, plays a subordinate role to literary interpretation. The exception is the first chapter, which recounts Bulgakov's earliest life (until the end of the Civil War) in some detail. The reason for this is twofold: the considerable influence the cultural and ethical values of his formative years had on his writings and the centrality of the Civil War to the writer's serious works of the twenties. Familiarity with the actual events allows one to place in clearer perspective the transformations they underwent in Bulgakov's successive fictions.

Part I deals with Bulgakov's early biography and his serious prose of the twenties. Most of these works, set in the years immediately surrounding the Civil War and reflecting to a greater or lesser degree the author's own experiences, belong to the category of autobiographical fiction. This mode, in which the writer, however fictionalized, appears as an actor in the text, raises in especially acute form the "cursed" question of the relationship of art and life. As Genette remarks on Proust: "Each example from the *Recherche* can produce . . . an endless discussion between the reading of the novel as fiction and a reading of the same novel as autobiography."[14] This "inherent duality," which Jane Gary Harris finds in all autobiographies,[15] is reflected in my own approach. On the one hand, I recognize the fictionality of the texts and resist the temptation, to which others have at times succumbed, of treating the early prose as raw material to reconstruct the biography. Rather, I approach even the earliest works as complex aesthetic entities, whose full significance can be culled only by examining the interrelated artistic means the writer uses to convey his vision: his narrative strategies, style, imagery, and plot structures, among other things.

I do, however, diverge from the great authorities of my student days— the Russian formalists and American New Critics (who have in other ways taught me so much)—in that I do not treat the relationship between the writer and the heroes he created in his own image as beyond the bounds of literary study.[16] For although one cannot facilely equate the author's experiences and emotions with those of his surrogates in the texts—especially given Bulgakov's ever-present irony—I take it as a given that the literary personae's moral and psychological conflicts as they evolve from work to work reflect, on a deeper and less literal level, the author's own. I approach the totality of the early autobiographical fiction as a kind of macrotext, tracing repeating and evolving motifs to construct what Zholkovsky calls the "poetic world" of the author.[17] This macrotext, if read in order of the dates of publication, unfolds, oddly, in a roughly reverse chronological order: *Notes on the Cuff* (1922–1923), which describes the immediate *post–* Civil War period; the Civil War writings (1922–1925); and *Notes of a Young Doctor* and "Morphine" (1925–1927), which depict a time shortly *before* the protagonist's involvement in the Civil War. By following this backward plotline, however, one witnesses a psychological-moral *progression,* the writer repeatedly remolding his past self until he arrives at a persona that allows him to transcend that past, both in his life and his writings. One has here the interpenetration of the literary and "real" selves, noted by Gusdorf: "Confession of the past . . . effects a true creation of self by the self. Under guise of presenting myself as I was, I exercise a sort of right to recover possession of my existence now and later."[18]

My focus on the autobiographical hero (or, as I often call him, the authorial persona) not only serves an extraliterary purpose—greater insight into the author's inner life—but is also justified by the very nature of the texts. In most of Bulgakov's serious early prose—the shorter works, certainly—the protagonist occupies an absolutely central position, the plot typically revolving around the confrontation of the frightened and solitary intellectual hero with some inimical force: the violent Cossacks in the Civil War works; the ignorant peasants—and death itself—in *Notes of a Young Doctor;* hostile critics and fellow writers in *Notes on the Cuff.* My concentration on social and ethical issues is also justified by the texts, for the hero's encounters take place largely on an ideological plane, his personal life, except in *The White Guard,* playing a marginal role. Even those aspects of the protagonist's life that do come into play—his home, family, profession, his native city, Kiev—become ideologized, are elevated to the generalized plane of tradition, culture, and enlightenment. Such focus on the hero's inner life, moreover, is considered by some theorists a defining characteristic of autobiographical fiction, which emphasizes the "moral dimension," is concerned primarily "with inward problems and struggles," and "centres on a spiritual problem."[19] Bulgakov, indeed, fits well Howarth's description of "poetic" autobiographers: "'difficult' men, given to intellectual brooding and sharp critical dissent," who, like Rembrandt and Van Gogh, "continue to revise their self-portraits" while engaged in "the *poetic* act of continuing self-study."[20]

Concentration on self is also apparent in the few works I treat in Part I that contain no obvious referents to the author's biography but whose heroes are placed in plot configurations and face moral choices similar to those of the authorial personae ("The Khan's Fire," "The Raid," *Flight*). These can be called autobiographical only as Spengemann applies the term to such works as *The Scarlet Letter*, where the author creates characters who, although externally unlike him, represent aspects of his own self. The language is "*allegorical* in that whatever the explicit, sensible referent of any linguistic figure may be, its ultimate and principal referent is always the ungraspable self."[21] In the search for self, indeed, Bulgakov at times distributes its features among several characters ("The Raid," "Morphine," *Heart of a Dog*). Like the Dickens of *David Copperfield*, as Spengemann describes him, he thus finds "in his past experiences not the tangled root-system of a single self, but the seeds of many separate selves, . . . brought together upon a fictive stage."[22]

In Part II of my study, I turn to the satiric works written between 1922 and 1926. These fall into two categories: the large body of feuilletons and stories Bulgakov published in the periodical press (primarily in the newspapers *Nakanune* and *Gudok*) and his three novellas—*The Diaboliad, The Fatal Eggs,* and *Heart of a Dog*. The shift from the serious to the comic is accompanied by a movement both forward in time, from the revolutionary period to the Soviet Union of the 1920s, and outward in perspective, from the spiritual trials of the autobiographical hero to a portrayal of the new society. Nevertheless, it proved illuminating to examine the satire against the background of the serious prose. The connection was most obvious in the few short pieces where the embattled authorial persona appears, his "foe" now the benighted and violent cohabitants of his Moscow communal apartment. I raise the possibility, indeed, of an interaction between the past and present selves of the Civil War prose and the satire, written concurrently: that the development of a relatively strong persona in the latter— himself a reflection of Bulgakov's tenacious struggle for existence in Soviet Moscow—contributes to the rehabilitation of the former. Here one finds another component of the complex interrelations of past and present, art and life, which Gusdorf finds characteristic of autobiography: "Temporal perspectives . . . seem to be telescoped together and to interpenetrate one another; they commune in that self-knowledge that regroups personal being above and beyond its own time limits."[23]

In the far greater number of satiric pieces where the autobiographical hero is not present, focus shifts to the other pole in the ideological confrontation—inimical forces of the new world. These I define by distilling repeated themes, plot patterns, and character types from the immense quantity of short pieces, thus constructing Bulgakov's *Soviet* "poetic world." Here there is no fictionalized persona to combat the negative phenomena, but they are far more effectively countered by the sharp-tongued narrator (Bulgakov's remaining surrogate in the text) and by the often castigating plot resolution—justice meted out by the author himself as demiurge of the fictional world he has created.

Finally, I turn to Bulgakov's most significant satires of the 1920s, the three novellas, in which the blend of the fantastic and quotidian, which reaches its fullest realization in *The Master and Margarita*, appears for the first time. Here, as in the serious prose, the protagonists are again at the very center of the narratives. They are not, strictly speaking, authorial personae, although, as solitary men associated with the old world, battling against hostile forces of the new, they conform to Spengemann's looser definition of the autobiographical. More precisely, the novella's heroes are linked to unfulfilled versions of self—as functionary, scientist, doctor— abandoned when Bulgakov became a writer. By revealing the underlying ideological and ethical flaws inherent in these rejected alternatives and their hidden links to the diabolical new system, the author implicitly justifies his decision to abandon his other potential selves in the name of literature.

Throughout my analysis I point out the thematic and formal kernels of the later writings, especially of *The Master and Margarita*, in the early prose. In the conclusion I further abstract the constant though evolving pattern apparent in the early works and show its final permutation—and transcendence—in *The Master and Margarita*. I thus approach Bulgakov's masterpiece not through an extrinsic exploration of its relation to the religious-philosophic-literary tradition, as many scholars (including myself) have done before, but through the internal evolution of the writings. Thus my study promises, by closely scrutinizing some of Bulgakov's works, to illuminate the whole.

PART

I

Early Life and
Later Reflections

The Earliest Years

Prehistory

By his own account, Mikhail Bulgakov wrote his first short story when he was seven years old. Entitled "The Adventures of Svetlan," it began: "There was a large field below." The angle of vision is explained by the fact that the hero is on horseback.[1] It would be foolhardy, of course, to attribute too much significance to this childish effort, especially since its author thereafter abandoned creative writing altogether until his fifth year in school; that is, until he was about fifteen. Nevertheless, if only by coincidence, what he tells us about this piece of juvenilia provides a good starting point for an exploration of Bulgakov the writer.

Of note, first of all, is the emphasis placed on the particular point of view of the hero, his unique perspective from atop his horse. Such individual perceptions, Bulgakov complained, were not allowed in his school compositions, and therefore, although well written, "this was bad writing from a generally human point of view, false—on standard [*kazennye*] themes."[2] If Bulgakov could not manifest his individuality in his schoolwork, it was expressed, as the writer Konstantin Paustovsky, a fellow student, recalls, in his boyish yarns and pranks. These subjected the dull real world to fantastic changes: "He transformed school customs we had learned by heart into a world of improbable events and persons . . . By the tricks he thought up, Bulgakov moved the people around him from their real world out to the very edge of another world of almost fantastic exaggeration."[3] This juvenile trait of "interweaving reality and fantasy in the most unexpected but internally justified forms" continues, as Paustovsky rightly saw, in Bulgakov's writings.[4]

The other significant point about the future writer's first story is that it was a knightly tale, that is, a type of adventure story. That he was attracted from early childhood to adventure fiction was no doubt symptomatic of his character as a whole, for the future writer was a lively and combative boy. Paustovsky describes a yearly battle at the school between the two groups into which each class was divided: the rich, aristocratic "block-heads" on the one hand, and the sons of the "intelligentsia, of middle-class officials, of Jews, and of Poles" on the other. The second group always won, and "in the front ranks of the conquerors was a high school student with a perky, turned-up nose—the future writer Mikhail Bulgakov. He tore into the fighting at the most dangerous places. Victory always followed him, and crowned him with a golden wreath of his own disordered hair."[5]

A love of adventure, not surprisingly, influenced Bulgakov's early reading preferences. He recalls that when, at the age of nine, he first read *Dead Souls* by his favorite writer, Nikolai Gogol, he regarded it as an adventure novel. Later he combined an interest in the Russian satirist, Saltykov-Shchedrin, with one in the American writer of adventure tales, James Fenimore Cooper.[6] This intertwining of adventure fiction and satiric comedy is also significant, for in the adventures of the schoolboy Misha Bulgakov his sharp and ready tongue was arguably his most deadly weapon. Paustovsky remembers "his impetuous liveliness, his merciless tongue which everyone feared, and the sense of determination and strength which could be felt in every word he spoke."[7] Comments survive from various victims of his cutting wit, from the school inspector Bodyansky ("You have a venomous eye and a malicious [*vrednyi*] tongue") to his landlord's daughter ("Mikhail Afanasievich liked making fun of people, he enjoyed being ironical and sarcastic").[8]

Only one more step was required for Bulgakov to wield the same verbal weapon, combined with his fantastic vision, in his writings. Indeed many of his mature works are a kind of battlefield. While in the Civil War writings the hero is literally called upon to oppose the dark forces of violence and death, in the satiric works it is the writer's venomous pen that fights ignorance and sham. Bulgakov in fact applied to himself the following description of E. T. A. Hoffmann: "He transforms literature into a battle tower, from which as an artist he metes out satiric punishment against all that is deformed in the real world."[9]

It is important to add, however, that Bulgakov did not agree with others' views of his youthful aggressiveness. He insisted that he was shy as a boy, a trait that remained with him in his adult life, although he concealed the fact. He described to a friend an encounter in the Moscow of the twenties with a former schoolmate, now a writer (most likely Paustovsky), who recollected how the young Misha terrorized the teachers with his tongue. Bulgakov protested that he remembered no such thing, that all he was doing was "defending his independence."[10] He added, however, that there certainly were conflicts with the authorities, a problem that was to plague him all his life. Bulgakov's remarks imply that his seeming aggressiveness as a boy actually stemmed from inner uncertainty. Fearful that his "independence" would be sacrificed to the standardized curriculum and discipline of school, he chose to defend it by taking the offensive. A similar boldness from a position of weakness, also in defense of his independence, was later manifested in Bulgakov's dealings with the Soviet state. Moreover, the theme of the fearful man called upon to act courageously in order to preserve his self-esteem runs through the writer's works, from his earliest Civil War stories to *The Master and Margarita*.

Behind the mocking exterior of the satirist it is not difficult to discern the moralist, for the practice of satire presumes an implicit moral standard against which the subject is measured and found wanting. Moral principles were in fact deeply instilled in Bulgakov by his parents, especially by his father, Afanasy Ivanovich (1859–1907), a professor of church history at the Kiev Ecclesiastical Academy. The son of a poor village priest, the elder Bulgakov constantly emphasized in his writings the paramount importance of traditional moral and spiritual values, which he saw subject to ever-fiercer attack in the modern world.[11] A fundamental way of countering the onslaught, he believed, was through education, which, he insisted, must have a moral basis. Since his eldest son, Mikhail, received his earliest education at home, having begun formal schooling only in his ninth year,[12] his father most likely put his pedagogical ideas into practice on him: "If the child's soul is not prepared from the very first years of life to perceive and master even elementary scientific knowledge, children are capable from practically the first days of their lives of cultivating good habits, of developing good feelings . . . The distinction between good and evil, an arousal of love of good and hatred of evil, . . . —these are the cornerstones that should form the foundation of 'educational' [*prosvetitel'nyi*] activity."[13]

Even more important for Bulgakov's further development was his father's general commitment to spiritual values. In the seemingly endless debate between those Russian thinkers who advocate the Western materialist-rationalist model for Russia and those who support the eternal spirituality associated with Orthodox Christianity, Afanasy Ivanovich unequivocally came out on the side of the latter. Throughout his writings, within the most various contexts, he emphasized the importance of the "otherworldly, supernatural element" in human life,[14] warning of the baleful influence of mindless material advancement.

Afanasy Ivanovich died of a kidney ailment in 1907, when Mikhail was only sixteen years old, and his mother later remarried. Her second husband, Ivan Pavlovich Voskresensky, a doctor, brought a very different worldview into the life of the Bulgakov children, reinforced in Mikhail's case by his own medical studies. Of greatest significance were the theories of Darwin, which, together with Nietzschean philosophy, so fashionable at the time, served to undermine Bulgakov's traditional religious upbringing. Thus Bulgakov's sister Nadezhda later commented on a 1910 entry in her diary: "Misha did not fast that year. It seems he definitely resolved the question of religious belief for himself—nonbelief. He is captivated by Darwin. He finds support in Ivan Pavlovich." And in the winter of 1912–1913, she gave the following description of her brother: "Unbridled Satanic pride, . . . pride heightened by the consciousness of his own exceptional nature, an aversion to the ordinary way of life—the Philistine, and hence: the rights to egoism." She later explained: "We were reading Nietzsche at the time and discussing him; Nietzsche fired the imagination of callow [neokrepshaia] youth."[15]

Despite this abandonment of his father's beliefs, the image of the elder Bulgakov always remained with his son. As the writer remarked approximately twenty years after his father's death: "The image of a lamp with a green shade has special meaning for me . . . It arose from my childhood impressions—the image of my father writing at his desk."[16] The image of the thinker at his desk was one Bulgakov readily adopted for himself. Even before he became a professional writer, in a letter to a friend in 1916 or 1917, he contrasted the daily trials of his medical profession to "the lofty pleasure of mental labor, in the deep solitude of night, far from noise and people."[17] The nocturnal picture of the creative intellectual at work, typically illuminated by a lamp with a green shade (which later appears numerous times in Bulgakov's works), is thus one in which the writer and his father merge.

The rejection of his father's religious convictions, moreover, proved neither total nor permanent. By 1923 an entry in Bulgakov's diary indicates that he could not sustain his youthful atheism and Nietzscheanism: "Perhaps the strong and bold don't need him [God], but for the likes of me it is easier to live with the thought of him . . . that is why I place my hope in God."[18] And after a few years, in the late 1920s, he began immersing himself in his father's spiritual world, studying the Gospels and collecting other religious works with which Afanasy Ivanovich would have been familiar.[19] That he also turned to his father for artistic sustenance is clear from his comment that Afanasy Ivanovich's image "should be the starting point for another work that I am contemplating."[20] This work has generally been assumed to be *The Master and Margarita*.[21] Indeed, with its scholarly and creative hero engaged at his desk in the lone quest for spiritual truth, with its assertion of the superiority of the spiritual realm (in which, however, the superhuman, "Nietzschean" Woland and the meek, loving Yeshua coexist),[22] it is a fitting tribute to Afanasy Ivanovich.

The individualism and independence that were Bulgakov's outstanding traits from his earliest days did not make of him a very docile schoolboy. Indeed, in his years at the First Kiev Gymnasium, where he enrolled in 1901, he proved, on the whole, an indifferent student, who upon graduation was given the highest grade in only two subjects: Scriptures and geography.[23] Nevertheless, this school, one of the best of its type in prerevolutionary Russia, left "very rich impressions," as Bulgakov later remarked,[24] and at least a few of its gifted teachers, chosen from among the professors at Kiev University and the Polytechnical Institute,[25] might have helped cultivate his unique gifts.

Most intriguing is the possible influence of the philosophy teacher, Georgy Ivanovich Chelpanov, a well-known philosopher and psychologist, who in 1907 left Kiev for Moscow University and was later to found the Moscow Psychological Institute. Renowned as a teacher, he "propagandized the consistent and fundamental teaching of philosophy at various stages of education, from the gymnasium to the university."[26] Among his writings are *Brain and Soul* (termed rather extravagantly by Zenkovsky "the best critique of metaphysical materialism not only in Russian but in world literature")[27] and a textbook, *Introduction to Philosophy*, based upon his course of lectures at Kiev University.[28]

In both these books, Chelpanov carries on a spirited polemic against materialism and what he calls "naive realism." Borrowing from the findings of contemporary science as well as from philosophers such as Kant and Schopenhauer, he gradually chips away at the materialists' facile assumptions, finally reaching the conclusion that *"spirit has the more undoubted existence"* than matter, that, indeed, "all existing things are formed from the spiritual."[29] Thus, Chelpanov's ideas might have provided Bulgakov with the first philosophical underpinnings for that belief in the primacy of the spiritual already instilled by his father.

For all of Bulgakov's love and admiration of his father, there is no question that his mother, Varvara Mikhailovna (née Pokrovskaya) (1869–1922), was the dominant spirit in the family, all the more so since she outlived her husband by fifteen years. Bulgakov's sister Nadezhda described her mother as "an exceptional woman, with a strong will, energetic, bold, resourceful during life's difficult moments."[30] When she was left a widow in 1907, with few resources and seven children, two nephews, and a niece in her care, all of these qualities came into play. She was compelled to return to work, first as a teacher, then as treasurer of the Froebel Society for Furthering the Cause of Education.[31] Varvara Mikhailovna could reportedly be very strict when necessary to maintain order in her large, unruly household.[32] For the most part, however, she took pains to provide an atmosphere of informal gaiety and broad culture for her children. Nadezhda recalls: "The family was large, merry, full of the joy of life and love of life."[33] The landlord's daughter relates how Varvara Mikhailovna "arranged *jours fixes*—something like receptions on a particular day—on Saturdays. Masses of young people gathered."[34] Paustovsky tells how from the Bulgakov apartment "sounds of a piano and even of a piercing French horn, the voices of young people, scampering and laughter, arguments and singing, could constantly be heard."[35]

The art form that especially united the Bulgakov family was music. Nadezhda comments: "Father played the violin. Mother was an excellent pianist. Our sister Vera, after graduating from school, sang in the Koshits Choir. Our sister Varya . . . studied piano at the conservatory . . . The younger brothers—Nikolai and Ivan—participated in the school orchestra."[36] She adds that, while Mikhail did not study music formally, he had a fine, soft baritone. This family passion for music left a permanent mark on the writer, and musical motifs play an important role in his writings. He commented years later: "The need to listen to music is very characteristic of me. One might say that I worship good music. It aids creativity."[37]

The Bulgakov family also shared a love of the theater and took full advantage of the rich theatrical life in Kiev. Mikhail especially loved the opera, with its merging of theater and music. According to his sister, he saw

Faust no fewer than fifty-one times during his student years.[38] Other particular favorites were *Aida, La Traviata,* Wagner's *Walküre,* and the overture to *Ruslan and Lyudmila.*[39] Indeed, Mikhail's first dream of an artistic career, which arose when he was still at school, was to become a singer.[40]

But Bulgakov's true artistic calling, of course, lay elsewhere. After his first effort at the age of seven, he began writing again when he was about fifteen. These early "humoresques," as he called them,[41] were a natural outgrowth of the stories and games he fabricated for his schoolmates and for family celebrations. As one friend recalled: "Misha was a constant participant in all family name day celebrations. Wherever Misha was, jokes, laughter, merriment, and wit invariably ruled . . . A game of charades turned into small theatrical performances . . . Aside from that, he wrote impromptu short stories, which aroused unrestrained merriment and laughter."[42] During these early days, Bulgakov's artistic efforts were protean. In addition to stories and plays, he wrote satiric verse, sketched caricatures, and acted in his own theatrical productions.[43]

While none of this juvenilia has survived, traces of two of these early writings remained in the memory of Nadezhda. The first is a play, and it shows how the future writer—probably under the influence of Gogol—already combined the everyday and the macabre:

> Their stepfather, a doctor, went to see a patient in Zhitomir by auto-coach [*na dilizhanse-avtomobile*], which at that time had only just begun to be widespread, were strange, didn't instill confidence—and they really weren't perfected. He went by automobile on the advice of his brother. And it was suggested to his brother . . . by the devil himself. Naturally the coach broke down along the way. He had to complete the rest of his trip by cart. And when, late at night, their stepfather reached his destination and knocked, a head peered out and said, 'He's dead.'[44]

The second story, written, Nadezhda recalls, in about 1912–1913, was entitled "The Fiery Serpent." It was "about an alcoholic who drank himself to the point of delirium tremens and perished during an attack: he was strangled (or burned) by a serpent (a hallucination), which had crawled into his room." What was apparently a later variant of the story, called "The Green Serpent," survived until 1921 when, Nadezhda says, Mikhail burned it.[45]

It is interesting that the pathological images in this early effort continued to exert a strong hold on Bulgakov's imagination. Abnormal mental states accompanied by hallucinations appear, for example, in "The Red Crown" (1922) and "Morphine" (1927), while giant serpents wreak death and destruction at the end of *The Fatal Eggs* (1925).[46] Most strikingly, however, the images of unbalanced psyche, destroying monster, and fire again come together in *The Master and Margarita*. There the mentally ill Master feels at night as if "an octopus with very long and cold tentacles was crawling through the window." And on the night of his breakdown, he "woke up from the sensation that the octopus was there . . . It suddenly seemed to [him] that the autumn darkness would knock out the glass, would pour into the room, and [he] would choke in it as in ink" (5:142–143). While the Master himself does not burn like the hero of the "Fiery Serpent," he proceeds to destroy—by fire—what gives his life its special worth, his novel on Pontius Pilate.

Bulgakov early recognized his calling, and as far back as 1912 told Nadezhda: "Now you'll see. I'll be a writer."[47] A literary profession was not, however, realistic for the eldest son from a large family of modest means, and by the time he uttered these words he was already a medical student at Kiev University. His choice of a career is usually attributed to the influence of his two maternal uncles and his mother's second husband, all of whom were doctors.[48] Bulgakov himself explained that he chose medicine because "brilliant work always attracted me. A doctor's work seemed brilliant to me." [49] Its brilliance, to be sure, was not especially apparent to him during his years at the university, which he compared unfavorably to the gymnasium.[50] Nevertheless, after a rather shaky beginning (he had to repeat his second year, due to the distraction of courting his first wife),[51] Bulgakov did very well and in 1916 received the degree of "doctor with highest honors" (*"lekar' s otlichiem"*).[52]

In 1913 Bulgakov married Tatyana (nicknamed Tasya) Lappa, the daughter of an official from Saratov and niece of his mother's friend.[53] Bulgakov's mother opposed the early marriage,[54] and hindsight suggests with some justification, for it was to end in divorce approximately a decade later. Tasya's recollections of their early days, however, vividly recreate an atmosphere of youthful gaiety and insouciance, which was to disappear all too soon from the couple's life: "Kiev was a merry city at that time, there were open cafés right on the streets, lots of people . . . In general [Mikhail's] attitude toward money was: if there's money, you have to use it up at once. If we were down to our last ruble and a smart cabman was standing nearby—we would take a seat and drive off. Or one of us would say: 'I want so much to take a ride in an auto!'—and the other would say right off—'So what's the problem—let's go!'"[55]

Bulgakov himself left a nostalgic reminiscence of the Kiev of his youth: "But those were legendary times, times when a carefree young generation lived in the gardens of the most beautiful city of our Homeland. At that time certainty was born in the hearts of that generation that its entire life would pass in white, quietly, peacefully, dawns, sunsets, the Dnieper, Kreshchatik, sunny streets in the summer, and in the winter large-flaked, caressing snow, not cold or harsh…" He adds ruefully: "…And it turned out to be just the opposite. The legendary times were broken off, and suddenly, and menacingly, history came" ("Kiev-Town," 2:307).[56]

History

History, in fact, arrived shortly after Bulgakov's marriage, with the outbreak of the First World War in 1914. The coming years of war, revolution, and civil war were to shatter the serene life of the writer's childhood and youth. And yet, unlike many Russian writers, from Sergei Aksakov to Vladimir Nabokov, Bulgakov never attempted, except in isolated passages such as the one quoted above, to recreate the lost "legendary" past in his works. It was precisely the coming of dreaded history—its clash with the old world and threat to the old image of self—that jarred him into becoming a professional writer and provided the subject for most of his serious early works.

Because of the autobiographical nature of Bulgakov's writings, there has been a tendency, at least until recently, to borrow freely from them to reconstruct his life of this early period. Their fictional nature makes this a risky business, however, and I will follow the more cautious procedure of first establishing the indubitable facts of the writer's life. It will then remain to examine the transformation of fact into successive fictions.

In the summer of 1914 the young Bulgakovs were in Tasya's native Saratov when they learned of the outbreak of the war. Tasya's mother organized a hospital, where Mikhail practiced medicine, perhaps for the first time. Later, while still studying at the university, he worked at a military hospital in Kiev, and, immediately upon graduation in 1916, he left for the southwest front, where he served as a Red Cross volunteer. Tasya soon followed him and worked as a nurse, "held the legs which [Mikhail] amputated," as she recalled.[57] In September Bulgakov was mobilized, but, rather than serving the war effort directly, he was dispatched to a *zemstvo* hospital. (Recent medical school graduates were regularly sent to replace experienced doctors who were serving at the front.)[58]

Bulgakov worked almost exactly a year, until September 1917, as head—and only—doctor at a remote rural hospital in the village of Nikolskoe, Smolensk province. The tiny village—Tasya recalls that it "wasn't even a village, but an estate" with a "half-ruined manor house"—was a full day's journey along muddy roads to the nearest town. The inexperienced doctor was called upon almost immediately to perform medical feats for which he felt woefully unprepared. Tasya remembers that during their first days at Nikolskoe a woman in labor was brought to the hospital "in terrible pain, of course; the baby was coming out wrong. I searched for the necessary places in the medical textbook and Mikhail left her, looked [in the book], told me what to search for."[59] Such medical emergencies occurred repeatedly during Bulgakov's stay at Nikolskoe, above and beyond the endless stream of more routine procedures he was called upon to perform. The certificate he received upon leaving states that during his year there he saw 15,361 patients and carried out an impressive array of operations. The certificate evaluates him highly as an "energetic and tireless worker in the *zemstvo* field."[60]

In September 1917, Bulgakov was transferred to the district town of Vyazma to become head of the infectious and venereological department of the *zemstvo* hospital there. (Because of the prevalence of syphilis in Nikolskoe, he had decided to specialize in venereology.) Compared to Nikolskoe, Vyazma was a bustling metropolis, and Bulgakov's work was easier there, because he was part of a well-equipped hospital with a large staff. During his six months in the town, he continued to work impressively, his certificate upon departure noting that he "carried out his duties irreproachably."[61]

Bulgakov could thus be justly proud of his accomplishments as a *zemstvo* doctor, but the experience brought with it feelings of disillusionment, both with the world surrounding him and with himself. He felt profoundly alienated and lonely in his primitive surroundings, and in a letter to a friend he expressed dismay at the "grasping [*kulatskaia*] and callous nature" of his peasant patients. He went on to contrast his life to the civilized pleasures of town: "You pass before my mental gaze in dinner jacket and starched shirt front, treading upon the feet of the first rows of the orchestra, while I..."[62]

There are indications of other reasons for Bulgakov's unhappiness at this time. First of all, he apparently felt growing frustration because his exhausting medical practice was preventing him from pursuing his dreamed-of career as a writer. He later expressed regret that he hadn't begun writing four years earlier than he actually did, that is, in 1916, before his stay at Nikolskoe.[63] Tasya recalls that Bulgakov actually was working on a story then, but her added comment suggests another source of anguish for her husband—his belief that she was incapable of sharing in his creative life: "He was concealing [his writing], or he thought I was a fool and didn't understand anything about literature."[64]

Bulgakov's feelings of loneliness and alienation may have accounted, at least in part, for his addiction to morphine, which began at Nikolskoe. Many years later Tasya revealed that he was an addict for approximately a year, after having taken morphine as a painkiller. He conquered his dependency only after their return to Kiev, when Tasya's refusal to continue to get morphine for him finally cured him.[65] This addiction—the subject of a later story, "Morphine"—would in all probability have planted the first seeds of the self-doubt that were to burgeon during the Civil War years.

In any case, Bulgakov's unhappiness continued in Vyazma. He wrote Nadezhda in December 1917: "I am again drudging away in Vyazma, I again work in an atmosphere hateful to me, amidst hateful people. My surroundings are so repulsive to me that I live in total isolation . . . My only comfort is work and reading in the evening" (5:389–390). Such feelings were no doubt intensified by the fact that he was stuck in this backwater during the cataclysmic events of 1917. In the same letter to Nadezhda he wrote of his longing to "go to Moscow or Kiev, where, although life is coming to a halt, it is still proceeding" (5:390).

He actually had been in Moscow earlier that month, in an unsuccessful attempt to get a medical discharge.[66] It was then that Bulgakov caught his first glimpse of the ravages of the Civil War. His observation of the behavior of the unbridled masses could only have reinforced his less than sanguine view of the common people gained at Nikolskoe:

Recently, on my trip to Moscow and Saratov, I was compelled to see with my own eyes what I would not like to see again.

I saw gray crowds, whooping and swearing vilely, smashing the glass in trains, I saw them smashing people. I saw ruined and scorched houses in Moscow . . . obtuse and bestial faces . . .

I saw crowds besieging the entrances of seized and locked banks, hungry lines by shops, I saw hunted and pitiful officers, I saw the pages of newspapers, where they write, essentially, about one thing: about blood, which is flowing in the south and in the west and in the east. I saw everything with my own eyes and understood once and for all what had happened. (5:390)[67]

Bulgakov's anxiety and dread of mass violence must have been exacerbated by his awareness of the danger to which his family in Kiev was subjected during the revolutionary days. One incident in particular left such a deep impression that he later adapted it for the plot of one of his first published works. On October 25, 1917, the Military Engineering School where Nikolai Bulgakov was studying was cut off from the rest of the city, and Varvara Mikhailovna became so worried that she decided to go there. While Nikolai was accompanying her home, they were caught in cross fire near the Konstantinovsky Infantry School and lay on the ground near the wall for "a terrible hour: machine guns and rifle shots were rattling, bullets were clattering against the wall, and were then joined by the crashing of shells." [68] Mother and son managed to run back to the Engineering School, and later that night, together with seven other people, Varvara Mikhailovna made her way home in what she describes as an "eerie and fantastic voyage in pitch darkness, in fog, through some ravines and gullies, through impassable, sticky mud, in single file, in total silence, the men with revolvers in their hands." [69] She reached home safely, but Kolya had to spend two more nights in the school before a Ukrainian Republic was proclaimed and fighting ended.

After this incident Bulgakov was not to remain away from his family for long. In February 1918, he went again to Moscow and this time succeeded in getting his military discharge. Soon after he and Tasya returned to Kiev.

The Ukrainian capital was a particularly tumultuous place during the Civil War, the political-ideological struggle exacerbated by the national question and foreign intervention. As Bulgakov wrote in "Kiev-Town": "According to the calculation of Kievans, they had eighteen coups; some freight-train [*teplushechie*] memoirists number them at twelve. I can report precisely that there were fourteen of them, of which I personally lived through ten" (2:305).

By the time the Bulgakovs returned to Kiev in late February or early March of 1918,[70] several changes had already taken place. The Central Rada, a Ukrainian nationalist government, which had ruled since the overthrow of the tsar, had been toppled by the Bolsheviks in February 1918. The Bolsheviks' stay proved short-lived, however, and when the Bulgakovs arrived in Kiev, the Germans, in conformance with the Brest-Litovsk peace treaty, were occupying the city and had reinstated the Rada, ostensibly in the interests of an independent Ukraine, but in fact with the aim of making the area a virtual German satellite. The Germans soon grew dissatisfied with the left-leaning Rada, however, and threw their support behind the more conservative Pavel Skoropadsky, who, adopting the obsolete royal title of hetman, came to power in late April. In general Skoropadsky's Ukrainianism took a rather external and theatrical form; he actually had close ties to the highest circles in imperial Russia, the bulk of his support coming from local Russians, such as the Bulgakovs, who feared more extreme Ukrainian nationalists.[71]

During the reign of the hetman Kiev was an island of peace and plenty in a tumultuous sea of war and revolution. However fragile this situation would prove to be, it coincided with Bulgakov's desire to return to his old life. He and Tasya moved back to the family apartment at 13 Andreevsky Slope, and the lively home life resumed. The landlord's daughter recalls how the house at this time was noisy and merry, always full of guests, who "sang, drank, always talked at once, trying to outshout one another."[72] At the same time, Mikhail tried to further his medical career, opening a private practice as venereologist in the apartment. After seeing patients, he often spent evenings writing. In the roughly one and one-half years spent in Kiev, four manuscripts were produced, of which only the titles survive: "The Green Serpent," apparently a reworking of the early "Fiery Serpent"; "Jottings of a *Zemstvo* Doctor," the earliest draft of *Notes of a Young Doctor*; "The Ailment"; and "The First Bloom."[73]

Bulgakov's attempt to return to the past was, of course, thwarted by the merciless movement of history. The Skoropadsky regime was never popular with the Ukrainian masses, and when the Germans, defeated in the World War, withdrew on December 14, 1918, the hetmanate was easily toppled by more extreme Ukrainian nationalists, led by Simon Petlyura. Bulgakov and his two brothers served—Mikhail as a doctor—among the few units of young, poorly trained troops that staged the unsuccessful defense of the hetmanate (initially unaware that the hetman himself had escaped with the Germans). As the writer told his friend: "On December 14 I was on the streets of Kiev. I experienced something close to what happens in the novel [*The White Guard*]."[74]

It is likely, in fact, that some of the more melodramatic events of the novel are fictional. What is certain is that the writer witnessed the debacle, and when he found out that Skoropadsky and other leaders had deserted, leaving their followers to perish, he abandoned the fray and went home. Tasya remembers her husband's deep disillusionment, how he "returned by cab, said that everything was unready, the generals had betrayed them, had abandoned everything and left." In the meantime, the two younger brothers remained in the gymnasium, one of the gathering points for the hetman's army. Trapped by the Petlyurites, they both later succeeded in returning home.[75]

And so the reality of combat proved far from the chivalric-adventure model instilled in Bulgakov by his childhood reading and games. The good—the idealistic young defenders of the hetman—did not conquer, as in the make-believe battles, but stood powerless before approaching evil. Bulgakov's personal sense of impotence, moreover, may well have been augmented by his inability to save his brothers, still in danger after he had arrived home safely.

That Bulgakov regarded the Petlyurites as the embodiment of evil—as the horrifying "heart of darkness" of the revolution—is obvious from his writings. The callous peasantry of Nikolskoe, the anarchic mob that had filled him with horror during his trip to Moscow, he now saw running amok in his beloved Kiev. As he wrote in the story, "I Killed": "The mind cannot grasp what Petlyura's troops did in Kiev . . . Pogroms were in full swing every minute, they killed someone daily, giving preference to the Jews, naturally. They requisitioned things, automobiles sped around the city, and inside them were men with pointed red gallooned caps on top of their fur hats. The cannons didn't stop roaring in the distance for a single hour during the last days. Both day and night" (2:650–651).

During the final days of Petlyura's one and one-half month rule, Bulgakov was mobilized by his army as a doctor. He was with the troops on the night of February 2, 1919, when they made their last stand against the approaching Bolsheviks. He witnessed atrocities, one in particular—a Cossack chief beating a Jew to death with a ramrod—filling him with such horror and guilt at his own inability to intervene that he returned to the episode obsessively in his Civil War writings. Later that night, Bulgakov succeeded in deserting as the troops were retreating from the city. Tasya recollects how he arrived home at one o'clock that morning: "He was very pale . . . , totally beside himself, trembling all over. He told us: they were taking him with all the others from the city, they had crossed the bridge, farther on there were pillars or columns . . . He lagged behind, dashed behind a pillar—and they didn't notice him." After this experience Bulgakov fell ill and ran a high temperature. Tasya says that it was probably nerves. He definitely was not wounded.[76]

In his writings, Bulgakov's heroes generally welcome the coming of the Bolsheviks—which may not be the case of simple expediency it at first appears. With his deep dread of the Petlyurites' anarchic destructiveness, he perhaps felt that the Bolsheviks' reputed iron discipline was precisely what the circumstances warranted.[77] Whatever he might have felt before the occupation, however, his views apparently soon changed drastically. Under the Bolsheviks, indeed, the situation grew so risky for the Bulgakov family that, according to Tasya, she, Mikhail, and three of his brothers and sisters hid in the forest in the summer of 1919. They had reason to avoid the attention of the new authorities, because class or professional affiliation alone was sufficient cause for arrest and even execution, and among those affected were acquaintances of the Bulgakovs.[78]

The terror experienced by the city's bourgeoisie is vividly conveyed in a recently discovered article signed Mikh. B. and attributed to Bulgakov, which was published in Kiev soon after the Bolsheviks' departure. The reporter describes the mass killings carried out by the Cheka (the Soviet secret police), tells how victims were forced to lie down naked on a cellar floor, which was "all covered with puddles of human blood, spattered with brains, with human liver and bile," and how they were shot point-blank, "disfigured beyond recognition."[79] Lending credence to the attribution of the article to Bulgakov is an early version of the ending of *The White Guard,* in which the hero, dreaming that the Cheka is after him, muses that "the most terrible thing in the world is the Cheka."[80]

The Bolsheviks retreated from Kiev in September 1919, after the city was attacked almost simultaneously by two mutually hostile forces: Petlyura's troops and Denikin's White Russian army. The latter was soon to take exclusive control. It was probably soon after this that Bulgakov left with the Whites for the Caucasus city of Vladikavkaz. Less than a month later Tasya joined him, and after a short period the couple was sent to the nearby city of Grozny, where Mikhail was assigned to a first-aid detachment.[81]

The question of whether Bulgakov joined the Whites voluntarily or was mobilized was a ticklish one during the Soviet period, because the former would imply support for the ideological foe.[82] The issue, however, has become moot, since recent revelations in any case leave no doubt as to where his sympathies lay. Thus, in an article that appeared in a Grozny newspaper in November 1919, "Prospects for the Future"—Bulgakov's first published work found thus far—he writes: "The heroes of the Volunteer Army are ripping the Russian land from Trotsky's hands inch by inch . . . everyone is passionately awaiting the liberation of the country."[83] And during an interrogation by the OGPU (the secret police) in 1926, Bulgakov responded with startling directness to a question about his loyalties in Vladikavkaz: "My sympathies were wholly on the side of the Whites, whose retreat I regarded with horror and bewilderment."[84]

If Bulgakov's support of the Whites was unambiguous, this does not imply that he entirely absolved them from the guilt that besmirched their foes. Thus, Yanovskaya hypothesizes that he witnessed atrocities in Grozny similar to those depicted in his story, "The Red Crown," and his play, *Flight.*[85] Whether or not this occurred, Bulgakov's horror at the "terrible road" the Whites had been following and the retribution that was bound to ensue sound clearly in "Prospects for the Future": "The madness of the last two years has thrust us onto a terrible road and there is no halt, no respite for us. We have begun to drink the cup of punishment and we shall drink it to the dregs."[86]

Literature

It was in the Caucasus that Bulgakov finally decided to become a professional writer. He recalled the circumstance: "One night in 1919, in late autumn, while riding on a broken-down train, to the light of a candle stuck in a kerosene bottle, I wrote my first little story. In the city the train dragged me to I brought the story to a newspaper office. It was printed there. Later they printed several feuilletons."[87] The city in question was apparently Grozny, where "Prospects for the Future" was published.[88]

Bulgakov's decision to publish did not in itself represent a sharp break in his life. He had, after all, been writing since adolescence, and publication was only the natural outcome of a long process. A more radical change took place a little later, in early 1920, when he decided to give up medicine. In his comments to his friend, Pavel Popov, he described how and precisely when this occurred: "I experienced a mental crisis [*dushevnyi perelom*] on February 15, 1920, when I gave up medicine forever and devoted myself to literature."[89] While the exact nature of this "mental crisis" is uncertain, the disillusionment resulting from his Civil War experiences provides reason enough for Bulgakov's growing psychological malaise in early 1920. During the successive mobilizations to which his medical profession had made him particularly susceptible, he had not, after all, lived up to the heroic ideals of his childhood imaginings. On the contrary, he had turned into a veritable pawn, helplessly shuttled from one side of the conflict to the other, a witness to atrocities he could in no way prevent. Because he was unable to become a valiant hero on the field of battle, Bulgakov perhaps felt all the more attracted to the verbal weapons of literature, which he had brandished with some skill since childhood.

An additional source of intense anxiety at this time was the news that both his younger brothers, Nikolai and Ivan, had disappeared from Kiev and their whereabouts were unknown.[90] This was especially troubling to Bulgakov as the eldest son in a fatherless family, who felt special responsibility for his younger siblings.[91] Indeed, his first published fictional work of which anything is known, the story "A Tribute of Delight" ("Dan' voskhish-cheniia"), is a response to the disappearance of his brothers.[92] Based upon the incident of October 1917, when his mother and Nikolai were almost killed in revolutionary fighting, only three fragments, sent by the author to his sister Vera, survive. In the first, Nikolai, "his eyes sparkling with laughter," sings the same song later sung by Nikolka Turbin in *The White Guard* and *Days of the Turbins*: "Hello, vacationers, hello, vacationers,/ Our survey already began long ago . . . / Ho, song of mi-i-ine" ("Zdravstvuite, dachniki, zdravstvuite, dachnitsy,/ S''emki u nas uzh davno nachalis . . . / Gei, pesn' moia-ia-ia"). Later, when the narrator is absent, disaster strikes: "That same evening mother told me what had happened without me, told me about her son. 'The disorders began . . . Kolya left for the school three days ago and not a thing has been heard . . .'" In the second fragment the mother tells of the shooting in which she and Kolya were caught: "'I see suddenly—something began knocking on the wall and the plaster flew in all directions.—And Kolya . . . Kolenka . . .' Here the mother's voice suddenly grew tender and warm, then it trembled, and she sobbed. Then she wiped her eyes and continued: 'And Kolenka embraced me, and I felt that he . . . was covering me . . . covering me with himself.'" In the third fragment Kolya returns safely, as he actually did from the Engineering School during the incident upon which the story is based (and from the gymnasium during the Petlyurite siege), and the family is reunited. It expresses the "joy that all of us are again together and alive . . . It's good at home! It's warm . . ."[93] Thus the story, by recalling earlier happy returns, arouses the hope that the sons' absence this time will also end with a joyful reunion.

A question that remains unanswered is what specific event of February

15, 1920, made it such a turning point in Bulgakov's life. While no certain response can be given, indications are that yet another imminent shift of power in Vladikavkaz—the approach of the Bolsheviks—played some role. The only document linked to Bulgakov and dated February 15 is the first issue of a newspaper, *Kavkaz,* which lists him, together with a number of popular Moscow and Petersburg writers, among its contributors.[94] It is the editor of this paper who, at the beginning of *Notes on the Cuff,* informs the hero of the approach of the Reds.[95] It was perhaps the idea of renewed fighting, during which he would be called upon once more to use his medical skills in the service of death, that led Bulgakov finally to reject medicine.[96]

In any case, he had every intention of escaping from Vladikavkaz together with other Whites. This proved impossible, however, because he came down with typhus, and the doctor warned Tasya: "If we retreat, he cannot go." By the time Bulgakov recovered, the Bolsheviks were already in power. It is to this somewhat later period that Tasya dates Bulgakov's rejection of his medical career: "In Vladikavkaz, after his typhus, he said, 'I'm finished with medicine.'"[97]

Bulgakov's spiritual exhaustion in the wake of the Civil War and his desperate need for peace and solitude are captured in a fictionalized portrait of him by Yury Slezkin, a then-popular writer who befriended him in Vladikavkaz: "He was tired, wanted to rest, to collect his thoughts after his long wanderings, after battle conditions . . . He wanted, finally, to sit down at his desk, leaf through his notebooks, gather his soul, which he had left in pieces, now here, now there—in the cold, hunger, unbearable pain of sufferings nobody needed."[98] Unfortunately, as so often in his life, Bulgakov was not granted the rest he longed for.

Approximately a year after he had decided to devote himself exclusively to literature, Bulgakov, by then the author of a few feuilletons and several plays that had enjoyed some success on the Vladikavkaz stage, wrote disconsolately to his cousin, Konstantin: "My life is a torment . . . You can't imagine how much sadness filled my soul because my play was showing in this God-forsaken hole, because I delayed for four years what I should have begun doing long ago: writing" (5:391). He added rather self-pityingly: "At night I sometimes reread my previously published stories (in newspapers! in newspapers!) and I think: where is the collection? Where is my name? Where are the lost years?" (5:393).

If Bulgakov thus sorely felt the inauspiciousness of his literary debut— occurring when he was already twenty-nine years old and in the remote

and alien surroundings of the Caucasus—Vladikavkaz nevertheless proved
not at all a bad place for a literary apprenticeship. Given the scarcity of
established writers, most of whom had fled the approaching Bolsheviks,
Bulgakov immediately gained a prominent position on the local literary
scene. Moreover, his first immature efforts, appearing as they did in the
ephemeral periodicals and theaters of a distant backwater, vanished virtually without a trace, thus allowing him a second beginning in Moscow with
some experience already behind him.

Vladikavkaz was in an appalling state after the Civil War. There was
widespread hunger and disease, marauding raids by indigenous Ingush and
Ossetian bands, homeless and starving orphans wandering the roads. The
Bolsheviks, however, immediately set up the hierarchical order for which
they were famous. A Revolutionary Committee was established, and, rather
incongruously, given the total devastation in the town, even the first grop-
ing steps toward organization of the arts were under way by the time
Bulgakov had recovered from typhus.[99]

Bulgakov's new friend, Yury Slezkin, had been appointed head of the so-
called Subdepartment of the Arts *(Podotdel iskusstv)*, a division of the People's Commissariat of Enlightenment, which had been established shortly
after the revolution to supervise both education and culture. Slezkin came
to Bulgakov when he was still bedridden and asked him to head the Literary Section (Lito).[100] Although this seems an impressive post for a newly-
hatched writer, there was in fact little in the way of literature to head and
virtually no paper on which to print any that might appear. Therefore,
Bulgakov's function consisted largely of organizing lectures and readings—
a better way in any case of reaching the largely illiterate masses who were
the main target of Bolshevik "enlightenment."

The first indication of Bulgakov's activities was a notice appearing on
April 9, 1920, in a local newspaper. Signed "Head of the Literary Section
M. Bulgakov," it invited "lecturers on the theory and history of literature"
to come to the Subdepartment of the Arts. A rather grandiloquent plea
was appended for "masters of poetry and prose" wishing to read "lecture
courses on the history and theory of literature, on new paths in creativity,
the theory of poetry, etc."[101] Among those most responsive to Bulgakov's
call for lecturers was, apparently, Bulgakov himself. One good reason was
the struggle with hunger. One suspects, however—given the importance of
the theme of enlightenment in his writings—that the idea of spreading culture among the masses was not, in principle at least, uncongenial to him.

His first appearance of which any record has been found took place on

May Day, 1920, when he delivered introductory remarks to a performance of Arthur Schnitzler's play on the fall of the Bastille, *The Green Parrot*.[102] In the ensuing months he gave numerous lectures on literature, music, and drama. An idea of the range of Bulgakov's activities can be culled from the words of the character Slezkin fashioned upon him: "I've been running around all day like a squirrel in a wheel . . . In the morning I headed Lito: I wrote a report about a network of literary studios and an appeal to the Ingush and Ossetians on the preservation of their ancient monuments . . . Then I dropped by . . . at the theater . . . and then I became in turn a historian of literature, a historian of the theater, a specialist on museum science and archaeology, a know-it-all in the area of revolutionary posters—we're getting ready for a week of the Red Army Soldier."[103] In connection with his multifarious duties, Bulgakov came into contact with numerous writers who passed through Vladikavkaz: the playwright and director Nikolai Evreinov, the poets Ryurik Ivnev and Osip Mandelshtam, the prose writers Boris Pilnyak and Aleksandr Serafimovich, among others.[104]

This cultural whirl was not without its risks, for if Bulgakov looked upon literature as a bloodless battleground, he did not have to wait long for his first skirmish. In Red Vladikavkaz, he was particularly vulnerable to attack because of his bourgeois past. Thus, the reviewer of the May Day celebration mentioned above commented insinuatingly on "the writer Bulgakov, who was also satisfied with his successfully delivered introductory remarks, where he managed to avoid ticklish discussions of 'politics.'"[105]

"Ticklish discussions" were not to be avoided for long, however, although the subject turned out not to be politics, but Russia's greatest poet, Alexander Pushkin. It might seem strange that Pushkin became the center of a heated polemic immediately after the Civil War in distant, ravaged Vladikavkaz, but the situation there actually reflected an ideological split on the question of culture at the highest levels of the Soviet hierarchy. The Commissar of Enlightenment himself, Anatoly Lunacharsky, believed that the working class must learn from the classics and absorb lessons from the great artists of the past (a position Lenin was soon to mandate), but there existed a strong countermovement in those early days. The proletarian arts organization, Proletcult, and the avant-garde Futurists, who had gained a powerful foothold within the arts establishment, advocated rejection of the past, the establishment of a new, qualitatively different revolutionary art; their call to dump the classics made the aristocratic Pushkin a particular target. The outstanding Futurist poet, Vladimir Mayakovsky, for example, in his poem of 1919, "It's Too Early to Rejoice" *("Radovat'sia rano"),* called for an attack on the old-guard "general" Pushkin: "And why/ not attack Pushkin/ and other/ generals of the classics?"[106]

The fervent young Futurists in Vladikavkaz were quick to respond to Mayakovsky's call. In *Notes on the Cuff,* Bulgakov describes how a callow local poet "wiped [Gogol and Dostoevsky] off the face of the earth" at one lecture (1:480) then at another subjected Pushkin to similar treatment. Bulgakov was challenged to defend the poet at a later debate, and several days later he did so. As reconstructed by one investigator who had access to contemporary newspaper accounts, Bulgakov's speech, entitled "Pushkin— Revolutionary of the Spirit," responded to the accusation that Pushkin was not a revolutionary, since he had not actively participated in the Decembrist revolt (the abortive aristocratic uprising of 1825).[107] Bulgakov's answer to this charge was characteristic, in that it distinguished between the "real" world of everyday phenomena and the spiritual sphere: "In the history of every nation there are periods when spiritual changes occur in the depths of the popular masses, which determine movement for entire centuries. And a considerable role in these complex processes of qualitative renewal belongs to art and literature. They become a spiritual catalyst, they help to ripen a new consciousness among millions of people and raise them to the performance of great exploits . . . Pushkin was such a revolutionary of the spirit of the Russian people."[108]

For his impudence in dubbing the aristocrat Pushkin a revolutionary, Bulgakov, along with another hapless defender of the poet, was roundly berated by a local practitioner of *ad hominem* sociological criticism: "The Russian bourgeoisie, unable to persuade the workers with the language of weapons, is compelled to try to conquer them with the weapons of language . . . These talks . . . reveal the 'counterrevolutionary nature' of these defenders of Pushkin's 'revolutionary nature.'"[109]

Bulgakov's theatrical work in Vladikavkaz was also early marked by conflict with the ever-vigilant critics. About a month before the controversial Pushkin dispute, at the end of May 1920, he was made head of the Theatrical Section of the Subdepartment of the Arts (Teo), his first professional association with the theater.[110] This position was an important one, because the theater, with its agitational potential and ability to reach a mass audience, was considered one of the most effective of the arts for furthering the goals of revolution. There was, however, a dearth of new revolutionary plays, and therefore, perhaps once again spurred on in part by the need to ward off hunger, Bulgakov himself stepped in to fill the gap. (Tasya remembers that playwriting was the only theatrical activity in Vladikavkaz that actually paid money. For Bulgakov's introductory remarks and her own work as an extra, they received only "lenten oil and cucumbers," and the Subdepartment did not pay Bulgakov in money either.)[111]

Bulgakov wrote five plays in Vladikavkaz, of which four were produced. The first was apparently a modest effort, a one-act comedy entitled *Self-Defense (Samooborona)*, performed on June 6 and 8, 1920. It had a topical theme: the formation by citizens of Vladikavkaz of self-defense detachments during the Civil War.[112] The author's sister later wrote him that she considered the play "weak," and he did not demur.[113]

Bulgakov's second theatrical work was more ambitious. A four-act drama entitled *The Turbin Brothers*, it premiered on October 21, 1920, and reportedly enjoyed great success, running a record four times. The play was a family drama, which unfolded against the background of the 1905 revolution.[114] Slezkin remembers that there were two brothers, "one an ether addict [*efiroman*] and the other a revolutionary."[115] The use of the name Turbin (belonging to Bulgakov's maternal grandmother and later to appear in *The White Guard* and *Days of the Turbins*), as well as the interweaving of family and revolutionary themes, indicate that this was both the most personal of Bulgakov's Vladikavkaz plays and the one most integrally connected with his other writings. Nevertheless, the author, as he wrote his cousin, found its stage success more bitter than sweet: "I thought: 'but my dream has come true, after all, . . . but in what distorted form . . . instead of the drama I had cherished about Alesha Turbin, a hastily done, immature thing'" (5:391).

The critic in the local newspaper agreed with Bulgakov's harsh aesthetic evaluation. More disquieting, however—especially after the controversy surrounding the Pushkin speech—was the accusation that its author had expressed antiproletarian sentiments: "In the first act, in the scenes at Alesha Turbin's, the author, through the lips of his *raisonneur*, speaks mockingly about 'the mob,' about 'upstarts,' about how art is incomprehensible to the crowd, about 'enraged Mitkas and Vankas.' We resolutely and sharply note that such phrases should never be used, not from behind any cunning masks."[116]

To compound this misdeed, a few days after the premiere of *The Turbin Brothers*, on October 26, Bulgakov participated in a second Pushkin evening, at which he again stood up for the poet.[117] Perhaps not coincidentally, these two events usher in what appears to be a particularly difficult period for the writer. Soon afterward he was fired as head of the Theatrical Section—the abbreviation *"bel."* (white) appearing in parentheses after his name on the report being particularly disturbing.[118] Then Bulgakov's situation deteriorated still further when a ban was imposed on literary evenings. As he writes in *Notes on the Cuff:* "It's over. It's all over! . . . They have banned the evenings . . . It is a frightful autumn. A slanting rain is lashing down. I can't figure out what we're going to eat. What are we going to *eat*?!" (1:486).

This question was far from rhetorical, for there is no record of any public appearances by Bulgakov or any productions of his plays between November 1920 and March 1921. The rejection, probably dating from this period, of what he considered his best play to date, *The Clay Bridegrooms (Glinianye zhenikhi),* a "three-act comedy-bouffe of the drawing room type," was yet one more blow. It was not staged, Bulgakov wrote his sister, "in spite of the fact that the commission, when listening to it, laughed through all three acts" (5:397). But then he hints that the genre was not what the times called for: "A drawing room [comedy]. Drawing room! You understand."

Although obviously discouraged, Bulgakov continued to write, declaring in a letter of February 1, 1921, to his cousin: "I clenched my teeth and work day and night" (5:392). He mentions two works in particular, one which he was in the process of writing, the other already finished. The first was clearly the most serious of Bulgakov's Vladikavkaz efforts, a novel that he described as "the only well-thought-out thing during this whole time" (5:393). He sensed, however, that, like other works for which he had any regard, it was out of step with the times: "But sadness once again: this is individual creation, after all, and now something entirely different goes."

The novel *The Ailment (Nedug),* a reworking of a story written while Bulgakov was still in Kiev, was apparently his first attempt to give novelistic form to his Civil War experiences.[119] He continued to work on it during his first period in Moscow but finally abandoned it in favor of the different conception embodied in *The White Guard.* While little is known about the work, Nadezhda revealed to Yanovskaya that a fragment of this lost novel does survive in the story "Morphine" (1927). In its finished form, the story, which takes place in 1917, mentions the political events of that year only in passing, although its hero was in Moscow during the October Revolution. Yanovskaya hypothesizes that the original novel focused upon precisely what the story omits, the revolution as seen through the eyes of a weak intellectual. The idea receives support from Yury Slezkin's diary of 1921–1922, in which he notes that Bulgakov "read his novel about some drug addict." [120]

The second work Bulgakov mentioned to his cousin was the play *The Paris Communards,* the first of his writings on a historical theme, written in commemoration of the fiftieth anniversary of the Paris Commune. Clearly less the product of "individual creation" than *The Ailment,* it apparently resulted in something of a turnabout in Bulgakov's fortunes. It was staged in mid-March 1921, after which the writer's position seems to have improved somewhat. [121] A few of his works were now published. They include a feuilleton, "The Week of Enlightenment"; a theater review; and an article on the actor S. P. Aksenov. [122] Another sign of a return to grace was his appointment in April to an administrative post as dean of the Theater Department of the newly formed Mountain People's Art Institute. [123]

The Paris Communards was followed by Bulgakov's final Vladikavkaz play, *Sons of the Mullah.* A revolutionary drama with an Ingush setting, it was written in only a few days, in collaboration with a native lawyer who provided the local color. The work was performed at the beginning of May 1921 and was a rousing success among the native peoples. [124]

In a letter to his sister Vera, the author wrote that his "creative work is sharply divided into two parts: the genuine and the forced [*vymuchennoe*]" (5:397). *Sons of the Mullah* is the most patent example of the "forced" variety, and Bulgakov on more than one occasion expressed his total abhorrence of the play. In his sketch "Bohemia," for example, he wrote: "I can say one thing: if there is ever a contest for the most senseless, untalented, and insolent play, ours will receive first prize" (2:467) [125] Elsewhere, writing of his total Vladikavkaz theatrical oeuvre, Bulgakov declared: "I lived in the far-off provinces and put on three plays on the local stage. Later, in Moscow in 1923, after having reread them, I hastily destroyed them. I hope that not a single copy remains anywhere." [126] By an odd twist of fate, *Sons of the Mullah* is the only one of Bulgakov's Vladikavkaz plays that survives.

While their artistic immaturity was undoubtedly one reason why Bulgakov later destroyed all his Vladikavkaz writings, he was, understandably, particularly pained at the memory of his "forced" work. Even there, however, as far as one can determine from what remains, he succeeded in not fundamentally betraying his convictions. The two literary works that survive, the feuilleton "The Week of Enlightenment" and the play *Sons of the*

Mullah, were certainly among his "forced" creations. (He described the former to his sister as a "totally idiotic thing" [5:397].) Both, however, manage to treat with some honesty the central Bulgakovian theme of enlightenment.

The title of the feuilleton alludes to the Subdepartment of the Arts' practice of organizing "Weeks of Enlightenment," during which free plays, concerts, and lectures were offered to Red Army soldiers and workers. (Bulgakov's play, *The Paris Communards,* was performed during the particular week that inspired the sketch.)[127] The satire of this rather feeble piece derives from the absurdity of this notion of "instant" enlightenment.

The story's narrator, a Red Army soldier named Sidorov, tells how the military commissar, upon discovering that Sidorov is illiterate, sends him to see *La Traviata.* The soldier interprets this as a dire punishment, but the commissar explains: "You're not being punished, it's good for you. They'll enlighten you there" (2:211). Sidorov and a friend dutifully attend the opera, and Bulgakov, applying the Tolstoyan technique of estrangement, gives a mildly amusing summary of *La Traviata* as seen through the soldier's uncomprehending eyes. When the performance is over, Sidorov expresses relief that the odious process of getting enlightened is at an end. His jubilation is short-lived, however, for the next day the commissar announces that he is sending him to other performances throughout the week. When asked if the whole company is going, the commissar answers indignantly: "The literate ones won't . . . It's only you, illiterate devils" (2:215).

Sidorov, after pondering his plight, decides that the only way out is to join the ranks of the literate by going to school. The story ends: "Well, I went to [the school] for a while, and what do you think? They really taught me! And now I'm not the devil's brother, because I'm literate!" (2:216). The story thus concludes with an ironic reversal. Sidorov's pride in his literacy—in marked contrast to his earlier despondency at being "force fed" culture—indicates that the Week of Enlightenment has, in spite of itself, done some good, for, in order to escape its false enlightenment, the soldier turns to genuine, basic educational work.

The theme of enlightenment of the masses is given fuller and more interesting treatment in *Sons of the Mullah.* Although the writer never heaped as much abuse upon any of his works as on this one—and it is indeed a crude and hastily written piece—even here he managed to place his individual stamp, to assert his genuine moral values. Because of the unfamiliarity of the work, which has not yet been published, I will describe it in more detail than its intrinsic worth merits.

Like *The Turbin Brothers, Sons of the Mullah* is a family drama played out against the background of revolution. Here also there are two brothers, one a revolutionary and the other not. As in "A Tribute of Delight," moreover, the values of home and of a reunited family are stressed, the revolutionary brother declaring upon coming home that "it is wonderful at home. And I am glad I have returned."[128]

The play takes place on the eve of revolution among the Ingush, one of the indigenous peoples of the Northern Caucasus. It opens with a mass scene, a feast in honor of Mullah Khassbot's son, Mahomet, an officer home on leave from the war. When asked how the war will end, Mahomet reveals his basic character trait, unquestioning submissiveness to authority: "Who knows. We don't interfere in that business. It is our business to fight. And so we perform our duty—we fight." A little later Khassbot's other son, the student Idris, unexpectedly arrives as well and soon hints that he has become a revolutionary. He informs his father that he is no longer a student, that "the time has come for me to teach others a few things." Lest the mullah think that he plans to be a teacher in the ordinary sense, he adds: "I am not the kind of teacher you are thinking of and I will not receive any salary for it. I would like only to teach our people how they should live in a new way."

As the play unfolds, one discovers that Idris's words about teaching are not a mere figure of speech. He actually does represent the revolutionary as teacher, who, by bringing enlightenment to his backward and superstitious fellow villagers, hopes to transform their lives. He does, of course, support political and economic revolution as well, and the play contains more than its share of overblown revolutionary clichés. Even in Idris's inflammatory speeches, however, the emphasis is on eliminating the abysmal ignorance of the people, the root cause of their poverty and slavery. Thus, at one point he says to his brother: "Have you seen our poor folk, who live worse than slaves? Our women, who are also mute slaves? Impenetrable darkness and ignorance everywhere."

It is the play's love intrigue, however, having nothing to do with revolution, that actually gives Idris his main opportunity to struggle with the old ways. His brother Mahomet and a girl named Aminat are in love, and Mahomet wants to arrange a marriage before his leave ends. He is faced, however, with the opposition of his tradition-bound father, Khassbott. In

Act Two the revolutionary son predictably expresses his disagreement with his father's position. He at first arouses Khassbot's ire, but in the end he manages to reach the mullah by reminding him of how badly the arranged marriage of his daughter has turned out. From this confrontation, Idris learns an important lesson for a teacher—the need for endless repetition: "But, after all, the words affected my father . . . Now I understand how one must act with them. Keep talking and talking about one and the same thing until you break through that gravestone of prejudices that is crushing them."

By the beginning of Act Three, when it has become clear that an arranged marriage is impossible, even the passive Mahomet is finally aroused to break with tradition. He thinks of abducting Aminat, and Idris encourages him: "I am disgusted by that word, abduction, when it is a question of a woman. She is not a thing. But since they have you by the throat with their ridiculous customs, struggle with them. That is what I would do. I would carry off the one I love . . . simply to show everyone that marriage is not a matter of buying and selling, and woman is not an inanimate block you can dispose of as you like."

At the play's climax the district chief, accompanied by police constables, comes to arrest Idris, who puts up an armed struggle. The mullah is mortified by the shame his son has brought down upon his house, but everyone else defends Idris: "He is not a thief and not a murderer . . . Do not touch him." Confronted with this "revolt," the district chief threatens to arrest the entire family, at which point Idris surrenders. While giving himself up, he addresses the constables. After seeing how upset the chief grows at his comments, Idris delivers a speech that clearly shows him as a revolutionary for whom words, not guns, are the main weapons: "Do you hear how afraid he is that I will tell you the truth? Do you hear? Honest to God, my words are more terrifying to him than my revolver. You are blind, benighted people, you do not see that I am being arrested for nothing, that I am a friend of yours, and he is the enemy of everyone. Why do you obey him?"

At this point, Idris's comrade Yusup arrives, a veritable deus ex machina, and announces that revolution has come to Russia. Those present promptly release Idris and arrest the district chief. The most zealous among them wants to kill the chief, but Idris opposes this. Here once again he acts as enlightener, preaching nonviolence and due process—not very popular notions among revolutionaries: "What are you doing? You want to commit murder out of irrational rage. I will not allow it. Anyone who touches him touches me. I have declared him arrested and will answer for him to the Revolutionary Authority." After this both Mahomet and Khassbot see the truth and accept the revolution in the name of freedom. The former, tearing off his epaulets, says to his brother: "I also want to be free like you." Then Idris says to his father: "Now do you see that I was right when I spoke about oppression and slavery?" Khassbot replies: "I see, I see now, but I really did not know that it would be this way."

The conclusion of the play shows that for Idris freedom is not merely an empty word. When one of the characters asks which of the mullah's two sons will now become the district chief, Idris replies: "Ali-khan, now there will not be any district chief at all." Ali-khan objects that they will still need some leader and that Idris should be the one. But Idris again demurs, insisting upon free elections. He is duly elected, and the play ends with a resounding cry for freedom: "Long live free Ingushetia."

Thus, in this crude revolutionary play, Bulgakov's hero-enlightener works an inner transformation in his people, bringing them truth, freedom, and justice. Although a less than minor example of the type, Idris, like the Pushkin of Bulgakov's speech, is a "revolutionary of the spirit" rather than of the gun. This type will receive its final and greatest embodiment in Yeshua in *The Master and Margarita*. However incomparable the heroes of Bulgakov's earliest and latest works are, both morally and artistically, there are nevertheless similarities. Yeshua, like Idris, is arrested by an authoritarian government, and his words too are feared more than the weapons of the active insurgent, Var-Ravvan. It is probably only a coincidence that, while Idris addresses the police constables, Yeshua at least contemplates speaking with the centurion Krysoboi (whose function is analogous to that of the police in the play). And Pilate is no more pleased at the idea of such a conversation than is the district chief, retorting to Yeshua: "I imagine . . . that you would cause the legate of the legion little joy if you took it into your head to talk to any of his officers or soldiers" (5:29).

In any case, Idris's teachings on freedom, truth, and nonviolence make him closer to Yeshua than to the real revolutionaries Bulgakov had encountered during the Civil War. Indeed, one reason the author might have so detested this play was that he had allowed himself to place some of his most cherished ideals in a cheap agitprop work.

It was inevitable that Bulgakov would leave Vladikavkaz as soon as a suitable occasion arose. From the very beginning he felt stranded in this remote and desolate town, far from both his family and the literary centers where he could gain recognition as a writer. Moreover, as time went on, it became harder and harder to eke out a living there, because the arts organizations were collapsing around him. Tasya recalled that by the time of their departure "the theater had closed, the actors had dispersed, the Subdepartment of the Arts had been disbanded."[129] Most important of all, however, it was becoming ever more dangerous to be identified as a White in Vladikavkaz. Tasya even asserted that "if we had stayed any longer, they would have shot us."[130]

Bulgakov actually had plans to leave Vladikavkaz from as early as the winter of 1921. On February 1, he wrote his cousin: "I'll leave Vladikavkaz in the spring or summer." At the same time, however, he pointed to his basic dilemma: "Where to?" (5:393). A letter written later that month outlines his options in somewhat more detail: "In Vlad.[ikavkaz] I've ended up in a situation of 'neither forward nor backwards.' My wanderings are far from over. In the spring I should go: either to Moscow (perhaps very soon) or to the Black Sea, or somewhere else" (5:394).

Bulgakov, in fact, found himself literally at a crossroads in his life. Should he go to Moscow and test his literary prowess in the center or to the Black Sea and, by implication, across the sea, into emigration? The former path obviously held some attraction, for it alone could lead to literary fame in his native country. He had already submitted three of his plays, *Self-Defense*, *The Turbin Brothers*, and *The Paris Communards*, to the Studio of Communist Drama in Moscow, headed by Meyerhold, and still had hopes that *Communards* would be produced.[131] In his letter to Konstantin, moreover, he inquired about private publishing companies in Moscow and asked him to send their addresses.

Nevertheless, the second alternative evidently exerted a greater pull on Bulgakov initially. In his correspondence of early 1921, there are various hints of a contemplated departure abroad and concern for the manuscripts he would leave behind. In an undated letter to Nadezhda, probably written in April 1921, he requested: "In case I go far away and for a long time, I ask you to do the following: some manuscripts of mine remain in Kiev . . . Write for these manuscripts, . . . and together with *Self-Defense* and *Turbins*—into the stove" (5:395). He added: "I am sending some clippings and programs . . . If I leave and we don't see one another again—take them as a keepsake of me" (5:396).

At the end of May, Bulgakov left Vladikavkaz for the Georgian capital of Tiflis, using the money he had acquired from the production of *Sons of the*

Mullah. He left by himself, and a letter to his sister written the same day suggests that he contemplated a prolonged, perhaps permanent, separation from his wife: "In case Tasya appears in Moscow, do not refuse to receive and advise her like one of the family during the first period, when she is getting her affairs in order" (5:398). After he was in Tiflis for a short time, however, he sent for Tasya, and they later departed together for the Black Sea port of Batum.

Tasya recalls that in Batum her husband mostly sat and wrote, and she thinks that he began *Notes on the Cuff* there. Their financial situation was desperate because newspapers did not accept any of his writings.[132] Worst of all, it seems, was Bulgakov's continued indecisiveness. "Where am I going? Where?" he wrote in *Notes on the Cuff* (1:489). Unable to resolve his inner conflict, what he did was to split himself in half, so to speak, by sending Tasya as an emissary to Moscow while he himself remained in Batum. The fact that he did not take the opposite course suggests that emigration still exerted the more powerful attraction. Indeed, Tasya recollected many years later that Bulgakov did try to leave: "'You know, maybe I'll manage to leave,' he said. He carried on negotiations with someone, wanted them to hide him in the hold or something. He told me to go to Moscow and wait for news from him . . . 'I'll send for you, I've always sent for you.' But I was sure we were parting forever."[133]

Nadezhda saw Tasya in Kiev soon afterward and, in a letter of August 24 to her husband, expressed pity for her sister-in-law and exasperation at Mikhail's vacillations: "[Tasya's] position is miserable. Misha has taken off, hurtled into space, no one knows where, he himself having no very good idea of what will happen next. For now he is sitting in Batum and has sent her to Kiev and Moscow on a reconnaissance—for their things and to test the ground, to find out whether one can live there."[134]

According to *Notes on the Cuff,* Bulgakov did at long last make one attempt to leave Russia on a ship bound for Turkey, but was not let on board. After this failure—unlikely to deter someone whose resolve is single-minded—Bulgakov finally decided to follow the other alternative and remain in Russia. He spent a few blissful days with his mother, at least partially satisfying his longing for home, expressed in "A Tribute of Delight" and *Sons of the Mullah.* As he wrote her a few months later from Moscow, where he had arrived in late September: "My most pleasant memory of the recent past is—guess what? How I slept on your sofa and drank tea with French rolls. I would give a lot to lie down again like that, if only for two days, after having drunk my fill of tea, and not think about anything" (5:405).

Bulgakov would not experience the charms of home again, however, for Varvara Mikhailovna died of typhus in February of the following year. Shortly before her death she had found out that her son Nikolai was safe in emigration, and the family would learn in March 1922 that Ivan was also residing abroad.[135] And so for Bulgakov the end of the old era and the breakup of the family coincided. Now he would have to make a new home for himself—in a new city in which he would live for the rest of his life: Moscow.

2

Looking Backward:
Early Autobiographical Fiction

Bulgakov arrived in Moscow "without money, without things, and without shelter," as his sister Nadezhda recalled.[1] Late 1921 was a terribly cold and hungry time in the capital, the situation further aggravated by a severe housing shortage and galloping inflation. Thus, in a letter to his mother in November, Bulgakov complained that the previous month he had earned only a million rubles, while a loaf of white bread cost 14,000 rubles (5:402, 403).

Faced with such daunting obstacles, the writer exhibited impressive energy in his struggle for existence and for a literary career. He managed, first of all, to get housing for himself and Tasya—a room in a communal apartment formerly occupied by his brother-in-law, Andrei Zemsky. He held on tenaciously to these miserable living quarters, fending off efforts by his fellow tenants—workers from a neighboring printing shop who formed the first workers' commune in Moscow—to evict him. He even wrote for help to Lenin's wife, Nadezhda Krupskaya, chairperson of the government organization of which Lito was a part, and, thanks to her favorable response, the Bulgakovs were officially registered in the house. Their apartment, No. 50 at 10 Bolshaya Sadovaya Street, together with its dreadful occupants, was later to figure prominently in Bulgakov's satiric stories, undergoing its final transformation as the diabolical apartment 50 in *The Master and Margarita*.[2]

Bulgakov also soon found work, and at an all-too-familiar institution: Lito, at which he was hired as secretary. As he proudly wrote his mother: "Having arrived in Moscow a month and a half ago with just the clothes on my back, I've gotten, it seems to me, the maximum I could get within such a period. I have a job. True, that's not the main thing by far. One must also know how to acquire money. And imagine, I've gotten the latter" (5:402).

As secretary of Lito, Bulgakov performed various clerical tasks. His literary activity, apparently, was of the most modest kind, consisting primarily of slogan writing. One of his first works written in Moscow, "The Muse of Vengeance," an article on the poet Nekrasov, was accepted by Lito's Bureau of Artistic Feuilletons but was never published.[3]

In his letter to his mother, Bulgakov expressed the fear that Lito would soon shut down, just when the harsh winter was about to set in, and the fear was soon realized. A new job, as chronicle writer for a newspaper, *Torgovo-promyshlennyi vestnik (The Trade and Industrial Herald)*, managed to keep hunger at bay for a short time, but it too ceased operation in mid-January 1922. Bulgakov was then completely without work, and by early February, as his diary attests, he and Tasya had reached a new low: "This is the blackest period of my life. My wife and I are starving."[4] Soon after, however, the situation improved, for he found work in two places at once: on a large newspaper, *Rabochii (The Worker)*, and, with the help of Andrei Zemsky's brother, Boris, as head of the publishing section of the Air Force's Scientific-Technical Committee. A month later he was working at yet a third job: as master of ceremonies at a small theater (5:413, 414).[5]

After this difficult beginning, Bulgakov gradually gained a more and more secure foothold in the world of the Soviet periodical press, and by 1923 his stories and feuilletons were being published with some regularity in a number of magazines and newspapers.[6] (His most important associations, with the newspapers *Nakanune* and *Gudok*, will be examined in detail later.) While these mostly topical writings helped Bulgakov earn his keep, at the same time he was leading a second, nocturnal literary existence, which transported him back from contemporary Soviet reality to the cataclysmic events of the recent past. This nighttime writing would eventually lead to the creation of his first novel, *The White Guard*, and play, *Days of the Turbins*, but during the first months in Moscow he was still laboring over literary works begun in Kiev and Vladikavkaz. Thus, in the letter to his mother of November 1921, he wrote: "I am writing *Notes of a Zemstvo Doctor* in snatches at night. It might turn out to be a substantial thing. I am polishing *The Ailment*. But there's no time, no time! *That is what is painful for me!*" (5:404).

Neither of these works came to immediate fruition. The story cycle appeared in print in revised form only several years later, in 1925 and 1926. And *The Ailment*, which, judging by his words, was close to completion in 1921 he abandoned entirely. The question of why Bulgakov set these early efforts aside cannot be answered with any certainty. Judging from the

works he proceeded to write, however, it appears that events of the immediate past had gained a more powerful hold on his imagination, that after
the many traumatic events of the Civil War, he needed, through his fictionalized self, to move backwards step by step, to "gather his soul, which he
had left in pieces here and there," to quote from Slezkin's fictionalized
portrait of Bulgakov. The autobiographical fiction of the twenties thus
follows a roughly reverse chronology. *Notes on the Cuff*, the first completed
work in this line, is based upon events of 1920 and 1921 during the
author's stay in Vladikavkaz, Batum, and his first months in Moscow. Then,
of the three Civil War stories that appeared in quick succession in 1922, the
first two, "Unusual Adventures of a Doctor" and "The Red Crown," concentrate on events of late 1919, after the hero had left his native Kiev for the
south, while the third, "On the Night of the Second," probes somewhat
further back, to February 1919, the time of Petlyura's withdrawal from
Kiev.

The early autobiographical works all employ fragmentary genres, such
as "notes" and "diaries," to approximate the breakdown both of the old
world and of the old self of their hero. These tentative probings, however,
allowed the author finally to perform an act of formal and thematic synthesis in his novel, *The White Guard*, set at a slightly earlier period, in
December 1918. Only after at least partially restoring—and redefining—
the autobiographical hero's moral universe in the novel did Bulgakov return to the still earlier period and more positive version of his persona
abandoned in the early 1920s: that of the idealistic doctor of *Notes of a
Young Doctor*.

The earliest autobiographical stories all follow a similar pattern. The
authorial persona, whose principles and temperament belong very much
to the old world, is placed within an alien and hostile environment created
by the Civil War and its aftermath. While the hero's traditional moral and
cultural values emerge as unquestionably superior to the violence and
nihilism surrounding him, he himself is weak and, powerless to fight for
his principles, takes fright and flees.[7]

Notes on the Cuff

Bulgakov almost certainly began *Notes on the Cuff* in the Caucasus in 1920
or 1921 and completed it by the end of 1922 in Moscow. The writer's first
major work, it remains a source of both fascination and bafflement. Bulgakov himself had some difficulty in defining its genre, commenting: "A

novella [*povest'*]? Why, no, it wasn't a novella, but, well, something or other on the order of memoirs."[8]

These recollections of the author's earliest literary experiences—Part One taking place in Vladikavkaz and Batum, Part Two in Moscow—are ostensibly a collection of brief jottings the narrator was forced to make on his cuff for lack of more conventional writing materials. It is a memoir of a highly unusual kind—fragmentary, sometimes to the point of incoherence, the autobiographical kernel transformed by the author's grotesque, hyperbolic imagination. The work as we know it, moreover, is even more fragmentary than Bulgakov intended, for he did not succeed in getting it published in full, and those parts that did not appear in print in 1922 and 1923 have not been found. To further complicate matters, the published sections came out in four separate periodicals, which at times give slightly different versions of the same material.[9]

Fitting for a work presumably written on a cuff, the memoir is marked by extreme compression, complex events broken down into short and simple syntactical and narrative units. Such terseness was characteristic of many writers of the early Soviet period, such as Isaac Babel, Mikhail Zoshchenko, and Evgeny Zamyatin, to mention three of the most talented. One reason was undoubtedly their common response to a chaotic era, when the leisurely pace of traditional literary prose seemed out of place.[10] At the same time, however, there were literary antecedents. Of special importance for Bulgakov, according to Nadezhda, were the popular comic-satiric writers of the teens associated with the magazine, *The Satyricon*. She says that he was certainly influenced by them and "had a high opinion of the talented *Satyricon* writers, A. Averchenko and T. [sic.] Teffi."[11] The most characteristic genres for the "Satyriconians" were the feuilleton and the very brief short story and play, commonly called miniatures. Mikhail Zoshchenko, another major satirist influenced by the *Satyricon* writers, commented on the work of Teffi: "Everything is short. Three seconds long. Everything is intense. It's impossible to get bored . . . It's all on three pages."[12] One paradoxical feature of the miniature, also noted by Zoshchenko, is its hyperbolization. The more concentrated the narrative becomes, the larger the few remaining characteristic details:

Poshlost' [petty vulgarity] is magnified a thousand times.
   Stupidity is magnified to the point where people often seem unreal, lifeless.
   However, two or three of the most characteristic traits are left—and

this is where all the mastery and talent are—outrageously exaggerated, they give life and movement to the characters.[13]

Zoshchenko also comments upon another essential feature of Teffi's humor: "And try to retell any, even her funniest story, and, truly, it will turn out not at all funny. It will be absurd, and perhaps tragic as well."[14]

In *Notes on the Cuff,* Bulgakov shows that he learned the lessons of the "Satyriconians" well. Much in evidence are their compression and hyperbolization, the presentation of a situation at once both deadly serious and absurd, narrated in a comic mode. Bulgakov's originality lies in his application of the miniature form to incomparably more frightening subject matter than that of the *Satyricon* writers. The additional literary influences of his favorite nineteenth-century writers, Gogol and Saltykov-Shchedrin, intensify the fantastic in his work, the coexistence of the comic and the nightmarish.

In keeping with its miniaturized form, *Notes on the Cuff* is a highly selective memoir, concentrating almost exclusively on the narrator's literary life. The dedication to Part One suggests that it is also, to some extent, a generalized comment on the fate of writers immediately following the Civil War: "To sailing, voyaging, and suffering Russian writers" (*"Plavaiushchim, puteshestvuiushchim i strazhdushchim pisateliam russkim"*).[15] This paraphrase from the Orthodox liturgy was bound to remind Bulgakov's Russian contemporaries of the fuller and even more doleful original: "For those who are sailing, voyaging, ailing, suffering, are imprisoned, and for their salvation, let us pray to the Lord. Lord, have mercy."[16]

The emphasis on travel in the epigraph is significant, for one of the "characteristic traits" of the miniaturized hero is his panic-stricken impulse to flee. After one "blank" chapter, of which only the title, "The Caucasus," is given (suggesting that the beginning of the work was excised), the narration opens abruptly at the moment when the Bolsheviks are about to take over Vladikavkaz. A "contributor to the defunct *Russian Word*" (*Iz* 1:665) reads a telegram and then quickly disappears. The terrified hero also longs to escape, but his head is hurting and he is feverish: the first signs of typhus.

If his illness prevents him from fleeing in the literal sense, however, the delirium he experiences brings *imagined* escape from the detested Caucasus to the primeval Russian forest, using literature (the works of Melnikov-Pechersky) as its vehicle: "Woods and mountains. But not these cursed Caucasus ones . . . Melnikov-Pechersky" (*Iz* 1:666). In a conversation with his landlady, a second dream of flight—abroad to Paris—joins the first. And finally he sinks into the fullest escape, total unconsciousness.

When the hero recovers, he is wrenched from the dark refuge of his delirium to the "sun" of the new world (*Iz* 1:670). Earlier, while he was still ill, Yury Slezkin tried to persuade him to join the Subdepartment of the Arts, where the two of them might fulfill their high calling: "We are art" (*Iz* 1:670). On the hero's first visit to the subdepartment, this grandiose view of art seems indeed to prevail, as he catches a glimpse of a writer (Slezkin?) as creator *ex nihilo*, "molding the subdepartment from chaos" (*Iz* 1:671). The two writers, however, hardly seem appropriate instruments of art's demiurgic power, for far from being godlike, they (true to the miniature of which they are a part) appear *smaller* than life. Thus, Slezkin's head, shaven after typhus, resembles that of the small boy's from Mark Twain, an "egg sprinkled with pepper" (*Iz* 1:668). And the narrator, with his repeated cry of "'Mama! Mama!!'" (*Iz* 1:669, 670),[17] also seems childlike, the impression of vulnerability reinforced by the aftereffects of his illness, which has left him "tottering and nauseous" (*Iz* 1:671).

Soon, indeed, they find whatever power they have acquired under fierce attack when poets of a new type arrive, ones who do not conceive of themselves as creators, like the narrator and Slezkin, but as annihilators of the ideological and aesthetic foe. This destructive function is supported by the work's imagery. Thus the first new writer to appear is compared to a torpedo boat: "He pierces into groups and they fall to pieces. The way a torpedo boat cuts through the water" (*Iz* 1:671). He is soon joined by a messy poetess, in whose verses a machine again replaces the human: "In my heart a dynamo machine beats/ Ta, ta, tam." Later arrivals are also described in nonhuman terms, alternating between the mechanistic and the bestial. One of them, like the persona in the poetess's verse, has a "dynamo machine in his heart" and another an "eagle face and an enormous revolver at his belt." And they are soon joined by "metallic" arrivals from Tiflis: a young man who is "all broken and unscrewed" and introduces himself as "a brawler in poetry" (*"deboshir v poezii"*) and another clad in a bronze collar: "In br-o-onze . . . I'm not joking!! In bronze, understand!" (*Iz* 1:673).

The hero, although eager to avoid crossing the combative young poets, comports himself quite admirably in his first conflict with them. When challenged to defend Pushkin, he overcomes his timidity, inspired by the great poet's verse: "...false wisdom flickers and decays/ Before the sun of the immortal mind..." (*Iz* 1:672). He carries through the poem's imagery of light and dark, expressing his determination to vanquish the foe: "I'll show them. I threatened the black night with my fist." And in the literary fisticuffs that ensue he does emerge the victor; he has his opponent flat on his back (*"na obeikh lopatkakh"*) and reads in the audience's eyes: "Pin him down! Pin him down!" (*"Dozhmi ego! Dozhmi!!"*).

The authorial persona's moment of triumph ends all too soon, however, for he does not long stand fast against the poets. Indeed, he rapidly returns not only to his former small dimensions, but shrinks further—a continuing process that can be traced in the imagery throughout Part One. Thus, in the face of press attacks after his Pushkin speech, the hero first becomes a tormented animal: "I am a stray dog in an attic. I sit, writhing. At night they'll ring. I am trembling" (*Iz* 1:673). Then, when attacked yet more virulently by the "brawler in poetry," he shrinks further, from animal to insect: "I'll perish like a worm." The insect imagery continues in the next chapter, which portrays the narrator and Slezkin (whom the "bronze collar" has just replaced as head of the Subdepartment), sitting on the latter's balcony on a starry evening. The grandeur of the heavens brings them no relief, however, because "in a few hours the stars will fade and the fiery sphere will blaze up above us. And again, like beetles on pins, we will be expiring." A bit later, another parallel is drawn between the writers and insects: "Have you seen flies on tangle-foot [fly paper]?" (*Iz* 1:674).

The chapter's title, "Boys in a Box," is an allusion to Slezkin's newborn son, lying in a dress box on the windowsill. The plural form, however, broadens the reference to include the writers, boxed in as they are in Vladikavkaz. The description of surrounding nature reinforces the sense of enclosure and implicitly returns to the theme of escape to the expanses beyond: "The mountains enclosed us . . . Far, far to the north are boundless plains. To the south are ravines, gaps, turbulent streams. Somewhere to the west is the sea. Above it shines the Golden Horn" (*Iz* 1:674). Later, when the writers go into Slezkin's room—termed, fittingly, a "cage"—the description shifts from their own plight to the bitter fate of Russian writers in general. The following chapter turns to some of these writers—among them Mandelshtam, Pilnyak, and Serafimovich—who, wandering from place to place like leaves caught up in a wind, pass through Vladikavkaz.

The occasion that brings about the hero's further diminishment is a second Pushkin evening. When a comical mishap turns it into a fiasco, he is again described in terms of derogatory animal imagery, as he scurries from the theater "like a rat" (*"krysinym khodom,"* Iz 1:678). And now, as he is belittled once again, his emotions, true to the logic of the miniature, become all the more hyperbolized. The culmination occurs the following day, when an article by the "brawler in poetry" appears with the menacing headline, "AGAIN PUSHKIN!" The hero now lets out a cry that violates the very conventions of the comic genre of which he is a part, pleading with God to kill off his tormentor: "Lord! Make the brawler die! People all around, you know, are sick with typhus. Then why can't he get sick? After all, this cretin will get me arrested!..."

The hero's wish is not fulfilled, of course—indeed, things grow still worse for him, since the literary evenings are now banned. The following brief but important chapter depicts the depths of his despair. Trudging home through puddles on a rainy fall night and sensing that he is being followed, he looks upon the world surrounding him as unspeakably ugly: the heavens have been replaced by a filthy foot binding (a cloth used instead of socks), and a mouse, also black, is in his heart. The enigmatic words he mumbles hint at the depths to which he has descended: "Alexander Pushkin. Lumen coeli. Sancta Rosa. And his threat like thunder" (*Iz* 1:679). The Latin words ("Light of the sky. Sacred rose") and those following are from Pushkin's poem, "In the world there lived a poor knight" (*"Zhil na svete rytsar' bednyi"*).[18]

The poem tells of a knight who, guided by his fervent love of the Virgin, goes to Palestine during the Crusades to rout the infidels. This image of the lone knight battling for his exalted ideal—close to Bulgakov's model of the writer as spiritual fighter—offers a striking contrast to the writer-hero of *Notes on the Cuff.* For him there is no longer any "light of the sky" to inspire him, only a foot binding above. And, unlike the poor knight, whose "threat like thunder/ Stunned the Mussulmen"[19] (to complete the Pushkin quote), Bulgakov's hero is now himself mortally threatened by the cultural "infidels" of his time and place, the young poets of Vladikavkaz.

Bulgakov's hero, who may be imagining he is being followed and wonders if he is going crazy, does not so much resemble the poor knight as he does another Pushkin hero, Evgeny of "The Bronze Horseman." For it is Evgeny who, after clenching his fist at the bronze equestrian monument to Peter the Great (recall how Bulgakov's hero earlier clenched his fist at the "metallic" poets of the new order), imagines on a nasty fall evening that he is being pursued—by Peter's statue, a symbol, among other things, of the power of the state over the individual. And the "threat" and "thunder" of the "poor knight" poem, alluded to by Bulgakov, also appear in the text of "The Bronze Horseman," where Peter is described as "the threatening tsar" (*"groznogo tsaria"*) and the gallop of his bronze horse is likened to the "crashing of thunder" (compare the acoustically similar lines of the two poems: *"I kak grom ego ugroza,"* *"Kak budto groma grokhytan'e"*).[20] Within the context in which the Pushkin quote is placed, finally, the "his" whose threat is so terrifying can be construed as Pushkin himself. Not only the belligerent young writers, after all, but the great poet as well have proved a menace to Bulgakov's hero, for his attempts to defend Pushkin and his subsequent failure to live up to the ideal of the writer he represents account for the narrator's present plight.

In the rest of Part One, Bulgakov's hero continues to follow Evgeny's path of fear and flight, both from his literary antagonists and from his unattainable literary ideal. In the brief chapter just discussed, the narrator is not yet entirely broken, for his vow, "I won't carry my heart and brain to the bazaar, even if I croak" (*Iz* 1:679), is an indication that his spirit, the special realm of the artist, is intact. Even this resolve, however, soon wavers for a reason given in the following brief but powerful chapter. It consists only of a title ("No Worse than Knut Hamsun"—a reference to the Norwegian writer's novel, *Hunger*) and the words "I am starving."[21] Faced with this eventuality, the hero finally succumbs, does in a sense sell his heart and mind, by writing *Sons of the Mullah*. In a chapter entitled "Run! Run!" (*"Bezhat'! Bezhat'!"*—compare with *"bezhat' pustilsia"* in "The Bronze Horseman"), the narrator describes how writing the play filled him with profound shame. He also feels joy, however, for the hundred thousand rubles he receives allow him to follow Evgeny's impulse and run: from Vladikavkaz to the port of Batum, and from there abroad to Paris.

Escape, however, proves as impossible for the hero as for Evgeny, and once he reaches Batum, he collapses "like a dead man" (*Iz* 1:681) on the bank of the Black Sea. He now descends yet farther down nature's scale and blends with the sea itself, his "tears as salty as the sea water." And when a final attempt at escape, on a ship bound for Constantinople, fails, he, again like Evgeny at the end of the Pushkin poem, appears totally broken: "One's store of strength has its limits. There isn't any more. I am hungry, I am broken! There's no blood in my brain. I am weak and easily frightened" (*Iz* 1:682).

Paradoxically, however, once the path to escape is closed and he has stopped running, the hero feels renewed energy. As he confronts life in Russia, a note of anticipation offsets the fear—perhaps because he, unlike Evgeny, has a home he can to return to, thus fulfilling one of the most deeply felt desires of the Bulgakovian persona: "[Going] home. By sea. Then by unheated freight train. If there isn't enough money—by foot. But home. My life is ruined. Home. To Moscow! To Moscow!!" (Iz 1:612).

Aside from the existence of a home, moreover—and more important in the long run—Bulgakov's hero differs from Evgeny in that he possesses an artistic gift. And now that he no longer seeks escape from the dangerous lot of writer in a tyrannical state, he follows the model of Pushkin himself— the spiritual fighter, going to practice his inherently subversive calling in the very center of power: Moscow.

The hero's change of direction is evident from the very beginning of Part Two. If Part One traces the diminishment of the artist and his panic-stricken flight, Part Two depicts a rehabilitation of sorts, as he faces and struggles against the adversities he encounters in Moscow.

To be sure, at first the capital seems even more frightening than Vladikavkaz, as the narrator arrives by train late one night and the pitch darkness and din create a terrifying atmosphere: "Bottomless darkness. Clang. Crash" (Iz 1:682). The stifling closeness of Vladikavkaz, however, is replaced by boundless space, as the title of the first chapter, "The Moscow Abyss," at once indicates. Everything here seems immense, awesome, suffused with a mysterious, demonic spirit, as the "unprecedented [nevidannaia] gray snake" of the crowd crawls, to the sound of "demonic voices," through the "inferno" (Iz 1:683, 684).[22] The eerie ambience, however, does not arouse in the hero the panic of Part One, but excitement and anticipation: "Again darkness. Again a ray. Darkness. Moscow! Moscow" (Iz 1:683).

The second chapter brings a sharp transition from nocturnal to diurnal Moscow. The city, however, proves no less vast and frightening by daylight, as the hero seeks, from all the rooms in all the apartments in the countless "enormous" six-story buildings of the city (Iz 1:685), the one room where the Moscow Lito is located. The house he comes upon, with its "dead" elevator, also inspires dread, as does the apartment, whose door is adorned by the alarming inscription "Khudo" (usually "bad," but here an acronym for "Artistic Department"). And when he finally finds the door with the tattered inscription "Lito," he stands awestruck, imagining the splendid quarters of the Moscow Lito, no doubt staffed by such luminaries as Gorky, Bryusov, and Bely. His expectations are dashed, however—and the images of immensity so far associated with Moscow reversed—when he opens the door and finds before him only a few ramshackle pieces of furniture and a couple of forlorn-looking writers. Indeed, alongside these misfits, the hero cuts quite an imposing figure. He is immediately made secretary of Lito, and when he makes some halting observations about the lack of supplies, one of the writers responds ecstatically: "A business-like guy . . . He'll straighten everything out for us!" (*Iz* 1:687).

The hero's sudden rise in stature is, of course, treated ironically, yet the basic shift from the diminishment of Part One to the aggrandizement of Part Two is significant, signaling a restoration of pride and self-confidence. Certain plot parallels between the two parts make this especially clear. Thus, while the attempt to "mold the subdepartment out of chaos" in Vladikavkaz was doomed to dismal failure, the hero in Part Two energetically carries out his demiurgic role, related in mock heroic tones: "To the . . . historian [of literature]: in Lito there were neither chairs nor tables nor ink nor light bulbs nor books nor writers nor readers. In short: there was nothing. And I. Yes, from out of the void I got an ancient mahogany office desk" (*Iz* 1:688). Most importantly, he gets Lito "switched on" *(vkliucheno)*, after which he concludes: "To my future biographer: I was the one who did all this" (*Iz* 1:689, 690).

Relative harmony reigns at the Moscow Lito, offering a sharp contrast to the literary wars in Vladikavkaz. This is perhaps because the Soviet Union is now in the comparatively tolerant period of the New Economic Policy (NEP), and the work, in any case, consisting primarily of slogan writing, has little to do with genuine artistic creation. The principal source of conflict, in fact, is not the literary world as such but the bureaucracy, and in this sense Part Two points more to Bulgakov's satiric prose of the twenties than to other early autobiographical works.

The eerie nature of the bureaucracy is revealed one day when the narrator arrives at work late and discovers Lito has entirely disappeared. He comments: "It had already seemed to me for a long time that everything around me was a mirage" (*Iz* 1:693). The phantasmagorical nature of the bureaucratized big city immediately evokes the image of Gogol, and the narrator sees on a door, in the form of a "fiery inscription, as in the cinema," the beginning of Gogol's story "The Nose." He feels he is going crazy and, inspired by Dostoevsky, another writer who depicts the madness inherent in modern urban life, contemplates visiting Razumikhin, Raskolnikov's friend in *Crime and Punishment*.[23] He decides instead to search for Lito in the "positively terrifying" building; and its "dark convolutions" and "niches," the clattering typewriters, flashing inscriptions, and sudden plunges back into darkness foreshadow the bureaucratic nightmare world of *The Diaboliad*. As in Part One, when the hero feels that he is going mad, he walks about in the miserable weather, trudging through puddles. This time, however, he refuses to be pulled under, and the following day he convinces himself that he is sane, that Lito must be somewhere, and that he will find it. And this he finally does, in "entrance 2, 1st floor, apt. 23, rm. 40" (*Iz* 1:694).

If in Part One the excesses of the hero's literary adversaries were mostly concentrated in the single person of the "brawler in poetry," in Part Two the evils of the bureaucracy are personified by a certain Mme. Kritskaya, who is holding up payment of the Lito staff.[24] The hero comes to hate her almost as much as he did the "brawler" and here once again wishes his enemy dead: "I am against capital punishment. But if they lead Mme. Kritskaya out before a firing squad, I will go and watch" (*Iz* 1:696). In contrast to his relations to the "brawler," however, the hero does not leave all to a longed-for deus ex machina but himself wages a fierce battle. And finally, although it takes twenty-two days, the staff does receive its salary.

The narrator's struggle against hunger is also more successful in Part Two. No longer can his situation be summed up with the words, "I am starving"; instead, a chapter entitled "How One Must Eat" describes how he *over*eats when he finally gets paid. And, whereas Part One points to the similarity between the narrator and Knut Hamsun, now the author of *Hunger* is berated: "You who sit hungry in an attic over a feuilleton, don't follow the example of the namby-pamby *(chistopliui)* Knut Hamsun. Go visit those who live in seven rooms and have dinner" (*Iz* 1:699).

If the hero thus succeeds in reversing in Moscow many of his failures of Vladikavkaz, he is nevertheless powerless to prevent Lito's demise, described in the final extant chapter. This unhappy ending, however, cannot in any way be construed as a personal failure, for the closing is part of a general cutback involving many organizations. Moreover, a comparison of the conclusions of Parts One and Two makes clear how much the hero has changed. Both parts end with ship imagery, but if in the first part the hero was not even allowed on board, he now becomes the captain, who does not abandon ship until the very end: "...Like a captain from his ship, I got off last . . . I extinguished the lamp with my own hand and left" (*Iz* 1:700). He then goes out into "terrible" snowy Moscow and gazes at the building where he has struggled so hard. Mme. Kritskaya and her cohorts may have triumphed, but this time he has no reason to be ashamed. He bravely faced every challenge as it arose, and the reader has little doubt that he is equal to the difficult struggle for existence.

Thus in Part Two of *Notes on the Cuff* Bulgakov was able to create a positive, if still gently ironic, image of self—probably inspired by his own energetic behavior during his first days in Moscow. The relatively minor, mock-heroic victories of his hero, however, were apparently insufficient to eradicate the author's sense of moral defeat engendered by real combat. To accomplish this, he still had to follow his weak autobiographical hero backward into the past.

Early Civil War Stories: The Hero as Deserter

In his fictional portrait of Bulgakov, Yury Slezkin commented that the writer's greatest desire was to write a novel. He added: "He would call it *The Deserter*, if it weren't for the reader's stupid manner of always seeing the author in the novel's hero."[25] Although it would be foolish to apply this insidious remark to Bulgakov uncritically, the fact remains that the central theme of his earliest Civil War stories—as, indeed, of Part One of *Notes on the Cuff*—is some form or other of desertion, whether literal escape or moral evasion.

Insofar as the heroes of the stories are fictional counterparts of the author himself (the "stupid manner" of Slezkin's reader being quite appropriate in this case), their depiction suggests that Bulgakov remained deeply troubled by his role in the Civil War. The characters, however, are not of mere psychological interest, for just as the hero of *Notes on the Cuff* is in some ways representative of the writers of his time, so do the shortcomings of the authorial personae of the Civil War stories reflect those of the larger stratum of which they are a part: the intelligentsia. In these stories, as in the later *The White Guard* and *Days of the Turbins*, Bulgakov thus gives fictional embodiment to one of the central oppositions of the time: the intelligentsia and the revolution.

"Unusual Adventures of a Doctor"

"Unusual Adventures of a Doctor," the first of Bulgakov's Civil War stories to appear in print,[26] is closely akin in form, style, and treatment of the hero to Part One of *Notes on the Cuff*. It too is composed of a series of mini-atures, strung together to form a memoir of sorts. Written in a similar elliptical style, its hero is once again diminished to fit the dimensions of the work. The first episodes take place in Kiev, but the bulk of the story re-counts the hero's experiences as doctor for the Whites in the Northern Caucasus. It is quite possible, indeed, that Bulgakov incorporated parts of the missing first chapter of *Notes on the Cuff* in "Unusual Adventures of a Doctor."

The portrayal of the hero of "Unusual Adventures" is, on the whole, even more ironic than in *Notes on the Cuff*, the narrative structure of the story serving to further distance the fictional character from the author. While in *Notes on the Cuff* the dividing line between Bulgakov and his first-person hero is all but invisible, the story's introduction explicitly dissociates narra-tor from hero: the latter is described as a friend, Doctor N, who might have perished during the war but might be "alive and well and living in Buenos Aires" (1:431). Doctor N's biography does in general outline coincide with Bulgakov's, but, in conformance with the miniature, it is a very simplified and one-sided portrayal, including some autobiographical traits but add-ing others whose function is to diminish the hero's stature.

Thus, in the framing introduction, where the narrator enumerates the contents of the suitcase Doctor N left behind, one finds amidst his largely banal belongings a medical book that was a part of Bulgakov's library. A second book, however, A. Amfiteatrov's novel *Maria Lusieva*, about the misadventures of a Russian prostitute, attests to the doctor's philistine literary tastes, far from the author's own.[27] And when in the memoir proper Doctor N describes himself, the sedentary side of Bulgakov's nature is emphasized to the exclusion of all else. While he shares the writer's attach-ment to the "green lamp and the books in my study" (1:432), he totally lacks his creator's attested love of adventure tales: "Ever since childhood I have hated Fenimore Cooper, Sherlock Holmes." In the ensuing "adven-tures," therefore, Doctor N emerges as the most *un*adventurous of heroes, Bulgakov rather disconcertingly turning some of his most traumatic Civil War experiences into miniaturized semicomic anecdotes. This is especially evident in the first brief chapters, set in Kiev, which depict incidents treated very differently in the writer's later works.

Thus, the rout of the hetman's forces by Petlyura, the principal subject matter of *The White Guard*, is here reduced to a single page-long chapter, related with semicomic irony. The hero's most striking trait is his solipsism, his total indifference as to which of the battling parties is "theirs" and which is "ours" (1:432). He soon runs away from pursuing Petlyura troops and, climbing a fence, encounters a vicious dog on the other side. Within the context of deadly military conflict, this creates a comic impression, as does the hero's undignified pose atop the fence. The doctor's way out is also absurd: he strikes the dog with a jar of "splendid German iodine," after which it "instantly turned red, let out a howl, and disappeared" (1:433). Once the doctor reaches home safely, his main concern is for his small private loss: "I dreadfully regret the iodine."

In the following chapter, based upon one of Bulgakov's most disturbing experiences during the Civil War—his mobilization by Petlyura's forces—self-demeaning irony again prevails. In contrast to later variants, the hero concentrates exclusively on his own misery. When he later escapes and runs home, he uses the same rodent imagery already familiar from *Notes on the Cuff:* "I am a doctor, I am preparing a dissertation, and at night I sat hiding like a rat in a strange courtyard!" (1:433). Similar diminishment is apparent when the narrative shifts to the Bolshevik occupation of Kiev, at which time Doctor N's main activity is one later associated only with such negative characters as the landlord in *The White Guard:* an unsuccessful struggle to preserve his private property (his gramophone) and his living space.

The doctor's remaining "adventures," described in the greatest detail, involve the Whites, who mobilize him and bear him off to the Caucasus to serve in a Cossack unit. In these episodes, Bulgakov, like Isaac Babel in his *Red Cavalry,* juxtaposes his educated, urban hero to the Cossacks, who embody the elemental violence unleashed by the revolution. Unlike Babel's protagonist, however, Doctor N is not attracted in the least to the wild "other." His feeling of repugnance, indeed, accounts for another of his literary antipathies—toward Mikhail Lermontov, who exalted the untamed Caucasus in prose and verse: "This Lermontov is disgusting. I never could stand him. Hadji. Uzun" (1:437).

It is not surprising, therefore, that once in the Caucasus the doctor's greatest desire is again to run away. Thus soon after his arrival he mentions the desertion of "medical assistant [*fel'dsher*] Golendryuk—a clever man" (1:438). At the end of the story the doctor, guided by the example of the "immortal Golendryuk" (1:442), also flees—for the third time in the course of the work. Thus the ironic portrait of the timorous intellectual, dragged willy-nilly from the comfort of his study into a detested world of danger and adventure, continues in Caucasus episodes. And yet the irony, so consistently applied in the Kiev section, wavers in the second part of the story. The main reason for this is that the distance so essential for irony is often missing here, in particular when abhorrence is expressed toward the unbridled violence of the Cossacks. For the "adventurous" world, to which Doctor N's sedentary nature was ironically contrasted in earlier episodes, turns out to be filled with moral abominations, and therefore the doctor's tamer values grow more positive in comparison.

The doctor's moral superiority is shown in his outrage at the Cossacks' burning of the villages (auls) of the Chechens, their poorly armed foe. Here the important Bulgakovian theme of guilt and retribution, already detectable in "Prospects for the Future," again appears: "I'll stake my life that all this will end badly. And it serves them right—don't burns *auls*. And it will end badly for me too" (1:438). Later, when the doctor comes upon the plundered body of a Chechen, its cruciform position foreshadows, perhaps, the Christian theme in Bulgakov's later work: "His arms were thrown out cross-like. His head was flung back. The rags of a Circassian coat" (1:439). Because of the genuine horrors surrounding him, Doctor N's fearfulness is portrayed at times with sympathy, even a heightened lyricism. The quiet pleasures of home, formerly treated ironically, gain in value, as the domestic lamp is juxtaposed to the frightening light of the bonfire crowned by the "lampshade" of the heavens: "Now a lamp under a shade, now the gigantic dark lampshade of night, and inside it the dancing flame of the bonfire. Now the quiet scraping of a pen, now the crackling of the fiery cornstalks . . . Sabres have begun to thunder, guttural voices have let out a howl, daggers have begun to gleam" (1:437).

The superiority of Doctor N's world of learning and moral boundaries is clearest near the end of the story, when a catastrophe occurs: the drunken engineer of the train in which he is traveling crashes headlong into another train and the cars are "crushed like matchboxes . . . Groans and howls" (1:441). Against the background of this calamity, the doctor is portrayed, however briefly, without irony. Using his medical training to treat the wounded, he emerges, indeed, as the only principle of order and healing in the midst of chaos and death.

After this the image of the deserter Golendryuk appears once again: "The shadow of *fel'dsher* Golendryuk arose before me... But where to, the devil take me! I am an intellectual [*intelligent*]" (1:441). Doctor N's selftaunting words imply that the moral code of the intellectual has prevented him from deserting thus far. It does not, however, bind him for much longer, and after one more catastrophe he decides to follow Golendryuk's example: "To be an intellectual does not necessarily mean to be an idiot... Enough!" (1:442). He then deserts, letting out a cry that recalls the hero of *Notes on the Cuff*: "The sea is ever closer! The sea! The sea!"

Because of the alternation of irony and sympathy with which the hero is portrayed in the Caucasus episodes, the reader is uncertain how to regard this final act. Should Doctor N be condemned for compromising the strict code of the intellectual? Or, on the contrary, has the code itself become irrelevant, given the dreadful chaos and destruction portrayed in the story? This unfocused image of Doctor N must be regarded as a flaw in the work, a result, no doubt, of the author's own unresolved ambivalence toward his hero. A related problem, moreover, is the inordinate degree of irony in the hero's portrayal throughout, especially in the first half of the story. On the surface his behavior does not, after all, warrant such contempt, for, although he does run away repeatedly, his escapes are justifiable, given the dire—and mostly abhorrent—alternatives.

The excessive irony could be attributed simply to a psychological aberration, stemming from the author's unreasonably high demands upon himself during the Civil War and consequent self-disillusionment. A less personal explanation can be found, however, if one regards Doctor N not merely as the authorial persona but as a representative of the intelligentsia as a whole. Then his fear and successive escapes, however justifiable when taken individually, become symptomatic of the intelligentsia's general powerlessness—in spite of its higher moral development—to deal with the barbarous forces unleashed by the Civil War. By not managing to struggle against atrocities, by running in fear instead, the story implies, the intellectual is abdicating his moral responsibility. Indeed, in later stories, the autobiographical heroes feel guilt for horrors that, although they were not directly to blame for, they did not do enough to prevent.

"The Red Crown"

Although "The Red Crown" appeared almost simultaneously with "Unusual Adventures,"[28] it nevertheless is a strikingly different work, both formally and in the portrayal of the autobiographical hero. Although it too is very terse, the miniature form of both *Notes on the Cuff* and "Unusual Adventures," with the concomitant diminishment of the hero, has been modified. Indeed, the story makes a reverse impression of magnification, with isolated fragments of a larger picture focused upon in order to extract an emotional and moral significance not evident to the naked eye.

"The Red Crown," like the works already discussed, is a kind of memoir, but this time the hero, who is mentally ill and in an insane asylum (hence the story's subtitle, *"Historia morbi"*), is treated with complete seriousness. The total absence of irony not only distinguishes it from the earlier published stories but also makes it virtually unique among Bulgakov's writings. At the same time, however, "The Red Crown" anticipates thematically some of Bulgakov's most important writings (especially *Flight* and *The Master and Margarita*); therefore, although aesthetically flawed, it has become the most analyzed of the Civil War stories.[29] When viewed in the context of the other early short fiction, moreover, the story reveals much about the inner workings of the autobiographical hero and represents a key step in his evolution.

The hero of "The Red Crown" may be regarded as the authorial persona as we have observed him so far *in extremis*. Thus, whereas the narrator of *Notes on the Cuff* feels on occasion that he is going mad and finds the daytime world illuminated by "the fiery sphere" (*Iz* 1:673) inimical, the hero of "The Red Crown" is literally insane, and his first words in the story are: "Most of all I hate the sun" (1:443). In addition, the fear that drives the personae of both *Notes on the Cuff* and "Unusual Adventures" reaches pathological proportions in "The Red Crown": "I fear people so much that in the evening, if I hear strange steps and voices in the corridor, I begin to scream out." If the narrator of "The Red Crown" thus represents the ultimate psychological collapse of the autobiographical hero, this does not prevent him from being far more sympathetic than other early personae, a character worthy not of mockery but of deep moral probings. A central reason for this involves the causes of his madness and fear, for, unlike the heroes already discussed, the persona in "The Red Crown" is not concerned primarily about himself. Rather, he loses his mind out of horror at atrocities committed against others. Moreover, although not directly responsible for the abominations he witnesses, he feels a searing guilt and thus reveals his high moral demands upon himself.

The story recounts two separate incidents. The first, the hanging of a worker from a street lamp in Berdyansk, is told sketchily: "I left in order not to see how they hang a man, but fear left together with me on trembling legs" (1:443). After the hanging, the hero is torn with guilt because he did not speak out to the general responsible for the atrocity. He wishes he could have another chance, imagining that he "now would boldly say: 'General, you are a beast! Don't you dare hang people'" (1:443–444). His torment reaches such proportions that he feels equal responsibility for the crime: "General, I agree that I was no less criminal than you, I am terribly responsible for the man dirtied with soot" (1:445). At the end of the story, he even expresses his willingness to take all responsibility upon himself, if only the general would experience, at least once, torments equal to his own.

The hero's lacerating sense of guilt seems at first disproportionate to his minor crime of omission. His speaking out, after all, would probably not have changed things except to make his own position more precarious. The source of his feelings becomes clear, however, if one recalls Bulgakov's conviction, expressed most explicitly so far in *Sons of the Mullah*, that words are the intellectual's most potent weapon. The significance of the hero's failure to employ this weapon in "The Red Crown" becomes evident if one compares the story to the play *Flight*, where a young orderly does speak out against his general in analogous circumstances. If in "The Red Crown" the hero wonders if "the dirty one, in soot, from the lamppost in Berdyansk" (1:448) comes to torment the general, in *Flight* something like this does in fact happen.[30]

The second incident in the story, closely related to the subject of the early "Tribute of Delight," has as its source Bulgakov's sense of responsibility for his brothers' disappearance during the Civil War. Here for the first time the author treats, however tentatively, some of the issues that become central in *The White Guard*, the subject shifting somewhat from the hero's personal courage to an examination of the very relevance of the traditional notion of martial valor in the context of the present conflict.

The question is first raised when the narrator's mother begs him to bring his younger brother, Kolya, back from battle. She justifies this request, entailing as it does desertion, by pointing to the insanity of the conflict itself: "You're intelligent and have understood for a long time that all this is madness" (1:444). The hero does promise to bring Kolya back, although at this stage he believes his mother is being "fainthearted [*malodushna*]," (1:445). After witnessing the hanging of the worker, however, he comes to agree with her that "everything is madness" and firmly vows to carry out her wish.

When he finds his brother and tells him that he must return with him, Kolya says that he must first go on a short maneuver, explaining: "I cannot leave the squadron" (1:445). The narrator agrees, thinking: "What can happen in one hour?" (1:446). He miscalculates, however, and Kolya returns mortally wounded. As he observes his brother riding back, the narrator feels as though he is watching a "strange masquerade," and his description contrasts the false appearance of military splendor with the horrible reality. Thus, although it looks as if Kolya has exchanged his gray military cap for a red one, that "he is going on parade" and is "proud in the saddle," the cap turns out to be a "crown" of blood, Kolya's parade-like pose is maintained by the horsemen supporting him on both sides, and, although "proud in the saddle, . . . he was blind and mute."

Afterward the apparition of Kolya in his red crown literally haunts his brother and drives him mad. When the vision appears, "he always says one and the same thing. Honor. Then: 'Brother, I cannot leave the squadron'" (1:447). The separately placed "honor" provides the key to the hero's unbearable feeling of guilt, for, although he understood that the war was madness, a vestigial respect for that martial virtue—dictating that his brother "cannot leave the squadron"—resulted in his death. Given the moral anarchy of the Civil War, honor thus proved not only meaningless but harmful. Moreover, it forced the hero to break his oath to his mother, to go against the values of the family, which emerge as the most genuine in the story.

While the contrasting values of home and war were treated with much ambivalence in "Unusual Adventures," in "The Red Crown" the former are unquestionably superior. This becomes clear in a dream the hero has but once, in which he is transported back to the family living room, with its old plush furniture and its various objects of beauty and culture: a portrait on the wall, flowers, a score of *Faust* on the piano. Here Kolya appears as he was before the war, a student in a chalk-smudged jacket. His bright eyes (which had become "two red stains" after his injury [1:446]) have been restored, their light eradicating all the consequences of that awful day: "The living room was light from the ray that stretched from his eyes, and the gnawing burden dissolved within me. That ominous day had never been" (1:447).

The dream, in which the very existence of the dreadful day of his brother's death is denied, bears much resemblance to the end of *The Master and Margarita*. There Pontius Pilate, united in a beam of light with Yeshua, is assured that the latter's execution (which Pilate had not done enough to prevent) never took place.[31] The hero of "The Red Crown," however, is not granted Pilate's absolution, for his blissful dream disappears, replaced by the awful apparition of his brother on horseback, "to intensify [his] hellish torment" (1:447). Because there is no forgiveness, the story ends on a note of unrelieved despair, with the hero trying unsuccessfully to end his life. And when he overhears the medical assistant's word, "hopeless," he thinks to himself: "It's true. I have no hope" (1:448).

If "The Red Crown" thus leaves its hero in despair, the treatment of the concept of honor in the story does hold out hope for the autobiographical personae of Bulgakov's works in general. For if the military principles of old—demanding that one must stand fast and not desert—have been invalidated by the madness of the Civil War (a possibility also raised at the end of "Unusual Adventures"), then the "deserter" hero stands a chance of being exonerated.

"On the Night of the Second"

"On the Night of the Second" is the last in the series of Civil War stories Bulgakov published in 1922.[32] Described in its subtitle as an excerpt "From the Novel *The Scarlet Stroke* [*Alyi makh*]," it is actually a fragment from the ending of an early variant of *The White Guard*.[33]

While in the earlier works the autobiographical hero was transported from home to an entirely alien environment, in this story—the first to take place entirely around Kiev—the cherished old world is nearby. Here one can discern the broad panorama of the novel, with the hero moving between the chaos and destruction brought on by the Civil War and the still intact, although threatened, old world of family and city. The work depicts the retreat of the Petlyurites from Kiev, already briefly treated in "Unusual Adventures." Here, however, as in "The Red Crown," the miniature form has been modified, and the character's motivation is explored more deeply.

The story begins abruptly by conjuring up, in the form of a *pan kurennyi* (a Cossack military commander), the violence of the Petlyurites. The commander, who "glittered with hoarfrost like a Christmas tree Santa [*elochnyi ded*]" (1:511), at first makes a festive impression in the blinding light of a street lamp. His association with domestic cheer and the sacred holiday only serves, however, to intensify the shock at his profane words: "[Fuck] God and your mother!!" (1:511). The blasphemy contained in the commander's standard oath soon is realized when, like a veritable demigod, he threatens God's heavens with the merry lightning and thunder of his shots: "The *pan kurennyi* waved his mauser, aimed it at the star Venus, hanging over Slobodka, and pulled the trigger. The slanting lightning ripped five times, five times thunder struck with deafening merriment from the hand of the *pan kurennyi*."

At this point the authorial persona appears and, especially in juxtaposition to the powerful commander, makes his usual comic-pathetic impression. His scholarly pursuits as "a future university lecturer [*privat-dotsent*] and qualified specialist" (1:511) sound incongruous within this chaotic milieu, and his name, Mikhail Bakaleinikov [*bakaleinik* = grocer], offers a comic variation of Mikhail Bulgakov. His first act, moreover—in stark contrast to the commander's bold challenge to the heavens—immediately demonstrates his weakness: he falls off the bridge into a snow bank beneath. Although Bulgakov vividly conveys his hero's pain and discomfort, the details given nevertheless underline the comedy inherent in the doctor's undignified plunge. Thus, the snow feels like "boiling water in his drawers" (1:511) and, when the doctor tries to stand, he "made a giant pirouette against any wish of his own, . . . and sat down right on the ice" (1:512). The episode concludes with the doctor's harsh self-assessment, addressed to the "trembling stars": "I'm a fool. I'm a pitiful bastard [*svoloch'*]."

The mocking portrait of Bakaleinikov is so far most akin to that of Doctor N in "Unusual Adventures," but he is a far more complex and sympathetic character. One may go even further, for, if Doctor N's is a miniature portrait, Bakaleinikov, in his conversation with the stars, has been magnified beyond his natural proportions. He and the *pan kurennyi*, in their interaction with the heavenly bodies, resemble large, generalized figures in a mystery play, the latter, with his blasphemy and threat to Venus, representing the forces of chaos and destruction, the hero standing for order and civilization.

Bakaleinikov, addressing the "magical sky" (1:512), is the first of Bulgakov's heroes to make anything like a political statement, although his utterances indicate that he is suffering from the same kind of moral crisis implicit in the early stories, stemming from the failure of his former ideals to effectively oppose the evil around him. This accounts for the paradoxicality of his words, for although a monarchist, he prays to God to send the Bolsheviks: "Lord. If you exist, make the Bolsheviks appear this minute in Slobodka . . . I am a monarchist by conviction. But at this given moment the Bolsheviks are needed here." The Bolsheviks for Bakaleinikov represent a force of retribution. Much as the authorial persona in *Notes on the Cuff* longs for some external being to kill off his enemies (the "brawler in poetry"; Madame Kritskaya), so does the hero here plead mentally with the Bolsheviks to execute the two Cossack leaders: "I am against capital punishment . . . but one must kill these two like mad dogs. They are scoundrels. Vile pogrom organizers and robbers." Bakaleinikov, however, goes one step further than his predecessors, for not only does he ask for the death of his enemies, but he also expresses his intention (although one does not believe him, of course) of killing them himself: "Yes, c-comrades. I'll shoot them myself!"

In his longing for escape, Bakaleinikov once again resembles the earlier heroes, but his motivations are treated more sympathetically. Thus, although he, like Doctor N, has a self-centered reason to escape—the desire to return home—the concept of home is no longer treated mockingly but, like much else in the story, is broadened and elevated. As in *The White Guard*, home exists within the framework of the city, Kiev, whose long history and spiritual values are symbolized by the illuminated cross-bearing statue of St. Vladimir. The physical and moral landscapes of the story are made to coincide, the chaos of the Petlyurite-occupied suburb counterpoised to the urban, domestic world of order and culture on the other side of the bridge. And here for the first time in Bulgakov's works, the theme of peace sounds clearly: "Here it is—the city—here! Vladimir's cross burns on the hills beyond the river . . . Home. Home. My God! Oh, peace! Oh, blessed rest!" (1:513).

Joined to Bakaleinikov's longing for home, moreover, is a second, more unselfish, force driving him to escape, which links him to the hero of "The Red Crown": he is tormented by the atrocities of the Petlyurites and his own powerlessness to prevent them. In his reaction to the horrors he witnesses he again goes one step further than the earlier heroes. Thus, when he is told that "a Yid is being flogged" (1:513) and spies the flogger's subhuman visage, "a broad-cheekboned something, vaguely reminiscent of a human face" (1:513–514), he instinctively cries out: "What in the world is this?!" (1:514). Bakaleinikov thus succeeds in raising his voice against evil, as the hero of "The Red Crown" does not. He comes close to violent protest as well, for if the howling were to last one more second, "he would have, with a light and easy heart, dug his nails into the mouth of the broad something and torn it up until it bled." Indeed, only the maelstrom of troops, which separates Bakaleinikov and the "something," prevent "irreparable harm to the future university lecturer."

If during this incident Bakaleinikov acts more decisively to oppose evil than any of the earlier heroes, during the main horror of the story he remains totally helpless. Once again the victim is a Jew, whom the *pan kurennyi* beats to death with a ramrod. During the murder, described in bloody detail, the doctor stands petrified, his "legs became cotton, they bent" (1:520), and afterward he breaks down, sobs, staggers drunkenly. He turns again to the heavens, and, in contrast to the heroes of earlier works, he finds consolation there. Whereas in *Notes on the Cuff* "the starry cloak" gives "no relief" (*Iz* 1:673), and in "Unusual Adventures" "the velvety dome with its diamond fragments" offers only a "turbid white bird of melancholy" (1:436), Bakaleinikov witnesses "a miracle in the sky" (1:521) at the very moment that the Jew dies: "The star Venus suddenly exploded in the frozen heights over Slobodka like a fiery snake, spattered fire, and struck deafeningly. The black distance, having long endured villainy, at last came to the rescue of the enfeebled man, pitiful in his feebleness. After the star, the distance gave a terrifying sound, it struck like thunder, heavily and long. And right then a second star burst, but lower, right above the roofs buried under the snow." What seem like bursting stars are actually rockets or flares sent up by the approaching Bolsheviks, historical and cosmic forces thus acting in concert to answer Bakaleinikov's earlier prayers.

At the sound of the explosions, the Cossacks run in an uncontrolled mob, and all that is most hateful disappears: "The *pan kurennyi* disappeared . . . Slobodka remained behind forever" (1:521). Once Bakaleinikov crosses to Kiev, "the beautiful city, the happy city," he (like Doctor N in "Unusual Adventures") runs off behind a white, columned church and disappears. When he arrives home to his wife and family at three in the morning, he is in a state of physical and emotional collapse and "bursts into sobs like a woman" (1:522). His final words reveal his total self-contempt: "[The Petlyurites are] bandits!... But I... I . . . am intellectual scum [*intelligentskaia mraz'*]!" (1:523).

These self-demeaning words notwithstanding, "On the Night of the Second" is the first of Bulgakov's Civil War works to conclude on a harmonious note. Although Bakaleinikov cannot forgive himself his weakness, he has acted more boldly than his predecessors and has been pitied by the heavens. He thus achieves what the haunted hero of "The Red Crown" cannot—reunion with his family—and is also granted the rest he so longed for: "In an hour the city slept. Doctor Bakaleinikov slept" (1:523). As a final sign of harmony returned, the cosmos itself is miraculously restored—although the reddish color of Venus and the crossbelt of the Milky Way are hints, perhaps, that the fighting and suffering are not over: "The sky was hanging—a velvet cloak with diamond fragments, Venus, glued together by a miracle, was again playing over Slobodka, slightly reddish, and the white crossbelt was lying—the silver, milky way."

Variations on a Theme: The Jew and the Prince

"The Raid"

"The Raid (In a Magic Lantern)," published at the end of 1923,[34] is Bulgakov's only Civil War story without obvious autobiographical roots. It is nevertheless clearly related, both stylistically and thematically, to other early works. By here generalizing his own experiences, by detaching the ethical issues from his own persona, Bulgakov is able to treat them with greater objectivity and balance and thereby comes one step closer to *The White Guard.*

As in "On the Night of the Second," the plot centers on the vicious beating of a Jew by Cossacks. This time, however, the story is told from the point of view of the Jew, Abram, and takes place not in Kiev but (perhaps in deference to its publication in *Gudok,* the railway workers' newspaper) at some undesignated point along the railroad line. The story, like "On the Night of the Second," begins on a snowy winter night, the interplay of dark and light creating a jumbled, nightmarish atmosphere, as if the component parts of the universe have come unglued.

Only gradually does the reader piece the fragments together to perceive the total picture: three sentries, Abram, Streltsov, and Shchukin (the third already dead at the story's beginning), are raided by Cossack forces. Because Abram does not immediately answer one of the horsemen's questions, he is beaten so ferociously that he goes deaf in one ear. The Cossacks then notice that Abram is a Jew and mutter threateningly: "A Yid! A Yid!" (1:460). Their attention, however, is deflected to the second sentry, Streltsov, who taunts them: "Ooh, you bandits. May your souls rot" (1:461). After this Streltsov replaces Abram as the main butt of the Cossacks' brutality, and they beat him until his face is a bloody pulp. Finally both sentries are shot and left for dead, although Abram has survived.

In "The Raid," patterns apparent in other early works can be discerned. As in "The Red Crown" and "On the Night of the Second," there is a triangular configuration: the general–the hanged worker–the narrator; the Cossack commander–the murdered Jew–Bakaleinikov; the Cossack–Abram–Streltsov. The recklessly brave Streltsov is, of course, very different from the timid authorial personae, as his martial sounding name (*strel-* is the root of such words as *shot, shooter, arrow*) at once indicates. Rather, by shouting out and deflecting the blows from the defenseless victim onto himself, he embodies the ideal of spontaneous valor that the earlier heroes are incapable of achieving—although Bakaleinikov, in his encounter with the bestial "something," approaches it. His generic tie to the autobiographical hero, moreover, is suggested by the unfinished "To a Secret Friend," written in 1929. There the narrator has a dream recalling events of "On the Night of the Second": the beating of a Jew by a Petlyurite. Unlike Bakaleinikov—and like Streltsov—the narrator's shout of protest in the dream is heard, and he perishes (4:551).

The center of "The Raid" is not, however, Streltsov, but the Jew, Abram. Here for the first time the survivor is not an autobiographical figure (although the presence of Bulgakov's initials, M. A. B., in Abram's name perhaps hints at a connection). This allows the author to treat the theme of survival more dispassionately than before, without the usual intermixture of lacerating self-reproach. Indeed, Abram is treated with total sympathy, although he, like the Bulgakovian personae, is terrified by the chaos and violence surrounding him. In general, Abram is no conventional hero; he does not, like the impetuous Streltsov, engage in thoughtless bravado but sensibly avoids needless pain. Thus, when the Cossack warns him not to shoot, he immediately drops his rifle, thinking: "It was useless to shoot" (1:459). And, after being struck once by his attacker for not revealing his regiment, he tells him when asked again, realizing "that the second blow will be still more terrible than the first" (1:460). Like the autobiographical heroes, he feels out of place amidst the unbridled elements, thinks longingly of the civilized pleasures of home, "the fire in the black stove, the unfinished watercolor on the wall—a winter day, home, tea, and warmth" (1:459). And, when he submits to seemingly certain death, his last thoughts are of this lost bliss: "There's no way that I'll see the watercolor again, or the fire" (1:462).

He never does see the home fire again, but when he comes to he spies another fire, however inferior, a "yellowish, low light" (*ogon'* = either fire or light) from a watchman's hut (1:462). He stares fixedly at this sign of life and, with overwhelming difficulty, follows it in spite of his nearly fatal wound. As he crawls Abram thinks "about why he hadn't gone out of his mind, about the amazing miracle, and about the yellow light..." All of these factors actually contribute to his survival: he is alive because he—unlike Streltsov, who "went wild" (*ostervenel'*) (1:461)—had kept his head, because he had been miraculously left for dead (compare to the "miracle in the sky" that saves Bakaleinikov in "On the Night of the Second"), and because the yellow light now holds promise of shelter and victory over death.

While the yellow "fire" is obviously tied to life, it is not an entirely positive symbol, for it is inextricably connected with the new version of Abram's life as pain. As he lies delirious in the watchman's hut, the light seems to be causing the unbearable pain in his head, its struggle with the "icy candle . . . in his heart" (1:463) one between life and death. Ever on the side of life, however, Abram longs to lie down on the "burning hot bricks" of the stove (1:464).

In the final episode, which occurs years later, Abram is in yet another shelter, this one typical of the collectivized Soviet period—the club of a workers' school *(rabfak)*. A bearded portrait on the wall (probably of Lenin) has replaced the unfinished watercolor of Abram's memories of home. Here once more fire plays a crucial role: "And an event occurred as joyous as it was supernatural: firewood had been brought to the club" (1:464). As at the beginning of "On the Night of the Second," there are associations with Christmas, for a "dried-out fir wreath" is hanging on the wall. (The story was published on December 25.) But here again the sacred imagery has been subverted in this poor substitute for home, the "supernatural" fire illuminating the wreath not divine, but diabolical: "The mouth of the stove belched forth deformed, fiery devils."

In imitation of the traditional domestic hearth, the stove draws the collective "family" of workers together, and they take turns telling stories. A certain Yak Gruzny describes his rather conventional bravery during the Civil War and is followed by Abram, who, compared to the powerful Yak, cuts a comic-pathetic figure, "small, rumpled, like a sparrow" (1:464), with a permanent "polite, confused smile" due to his deafness (1:465). He proceeds to describe his horrible ordeal, addressing the fire throughout, "as if the fire there sketched this picture for him." He relates his tale in the third person, and the others, who assume he is talking about someone else, are amazed when he informs them: "It happened to me."

In this story Bulgakov as author thus saves the little Jew, as his fictional personae could not in his other works—and as he himself, apparently, was unable to do in actual life. Moreover, he not only allows Abram to live, he reveals the tenacious strength behind his weak, pathetic appearance. Abram might not possess the physical courage of Yak or the instinctual valor of Streltsov, but he is able to struggle doggedly for life. Moreover, in his devotion to domestic values, he stands for the principles of order and civility necessary for a genuinely *human* life, his love for the watercolor hinting that he possesses the seeds of culture and enlightenment as well. It is significant that at the story's end he is studying at a *rabfak,* that his comrades address him as a "real professor" (1:464), and that after telling his tale he goes to the club library. Thus, by defending Abram, a man who thirsts for the simple pleasures of home, for culture and learning rather than combat, Bulgakov at the same time offers an indirect justification for his authorial personae, who embody similar principles.

"The Khan's Fire"

"The Khan's Fire," published in 1924,[35] seems to have even less connection with Bulgakov's autobiographical prose than "The Raid." Both in subject and style, the story stands apart from Bulgakov's other early works. Its setting, a magnificent estate outside Moscow modeled upon Arkhangelskoe, and its hero, the fierce-tempered former owner of the estate, Prince Tugai-Beg, are very different from the modest settings and heroes that inhabit the other early fiction.[36] Moreover, the work's polished, lapidary prose has little in common with the usual jagged, nervous style of the early Bulgakov. There is evidence, in fact, that the author consciously set out here to write a "well-made" story, so rare an entity in the years following the revolution. One of his colleagues at *Gudok* recalls a discussion among staff members about the weakness in plot construction of contemporary prose compared to the stories of O. Henry. Bulgakov reportedly said: "I'll write a story and tie the plot together in such a way that you won't untie it until you've read the last line."[37] Although he did not succeed in achieving O. Henry's level of plot virtuosity, "The Khan's Fire" remains one of his most fully realized stories. And, of course, it possesses a complexity and broad symbolic suggestiveness not to be found in the popular American writer.

The basic plot is actually quite simple. Prince Tugai-Beg, a former member of the high aristocracy who fled from Russia during the revolution, returns a few years later to his estate, now a museum, disguised as a foreign tourist. When the tour ends, the prince secretly remains behind and, after spending some time in his study, sets the house on fire and disappears into the darkness.

"The Khan's Fire," obviously, has no autobiographical basis. Curiously, however, the author occasionally signed his works "Tugai," suggesting that he felt an inner kinship with his hero. It is perhaps relevant that in his autobiographical remarks Bulgakov mentions his family's Tartar origin, his descent on his mother's side from the "Turbin hordes."[38] And the fact that the name *Tugai Beg* contains an amalgam of letters from *Turbin* and *Bulgakov* may not be coincidental. Close examination does indeed reveal some hidden ties between the prince and the authorial personae of other works, and this striking but rather enigmatic story is much clarified when placed within the context of Bulgakov's autobiographical prose. "The Khan's Fire," in turn, sheds some light on later works, especially *The White Guard* (which the author was working on simultaneously) and *The Master and Margarita*.

The story, for all its apparent uniqueness, represents a variation on the constant theme of Bulgakov's Civil War prose: revolution as loss of home. Here, however, the concept of home gains immensely in significance. If earlier the dwelling was usually sketchily portrayed, evoked through fleeting images of warmth, light, culture (the stove, the lamps, the score of *Faust*), the palace in "The Khan's Fire" is described in meticulous detail. One might even say that the estate, not its former master, is the main hero of the story. The house is no longer simply the dwelling place of an individual or family; it is also a repository of history. Time passes, entire eras disappear, but in the house the artifacts of the past are left behind, variegated and complex human tradition made visible and concrete.

The atmosphere of a vanished past is created at the very beginning in the description of a statue of the god Apollo, standing in front of the palace and disappearing at sunset into the shade. Against this elegiac background, the author proceeds, using the tourist excursion as a pretext, to describe with delicacy and grace the interior of the splendid baroque edifice. For example: "Six white columns with fretwork leaves at the top supported a gallery on which there once gleamed the trumpets of musicians. The columns ascended joyfully and chastely, the light gilt chairs stood decorously under the walls . . . Cupids wound and interlaced in garlands, a nude woman danced in the tender clouds" (2:387).

The palace is not, however, only an example of Western culture transplanted into Russia during its aristocratic eighteenth century, as the quote might suggest. The story's title, as well as the estate's name, "Khan's Head-

quarters" *(Khanskaia stavka),* points at once to the Tartar origin of its
former owners. This merging of West and East is later given vivid visual
embodiment in the palace's portrait gallery, where, in close proximity to a
large picture of the German Catherine the Great, "in ermine, with a dia-
dem on her fluffed white hair" (2:387), hangs a portrait of the legendary
founder of the Tugai clan, the "forefather [*rodonachal'nik*], sovereign of the
Small Horde, Khan Tugai, with slanting eyes, black and rapacious, in a
murmolka [a flat-topped fur or velvet hat] with colored stones, with the
semi-precious handle of a sabre" (2:388). The entire Tugai family, extending back five hundred years, is portrayed in the room: "For half a mil-
lenium the family [*rod*] of Tugai-Beg princes looked down from the walls,
a distinguished, spirited family, filled with the blood of princes, khans,
tsars. Dimmed by spots, the history of the family arose, now with spots of
martial glory, now of disgrace, love, hatred, vice, depravity..."

The mixed blood of the Tugai-Begs, the succession of splendid heights
and shameful depths in their past, make the family a virtual microcosm of
old Russia: straddling the border of Asia and Europe, combining refined
European culture and the brutal power associated with the Tartars. One
may go still further, for the family stands not only as an emblem of the
Russian past but of imperfect historical man as a whole. As such, the
Tugai-Begs are by no means idealized; rather, they exemplify that combination of dark and light, evil and good, that are inextricably interwoven in
human history, that combination which, according to the devil in *The
Master and Margarita,* is necessary for human life in general.[39]

At the time of the story, however, in the early 1920s, the history of the
Tugai-Begs is coming to an end. The last prince, childless, has been banished from the "Khan's Headquarters," and this site of centuries of private
family passions is now a public place, the common property of the new
Soviet man. The only living remnant of the old world is the former servant,
Iona, now working there as a watchman. The story opens with the arrival
of a tour group, which includes a bespectacled foreigner—the former
prince incognito. This fact, however, is revealed only later. Most prominent
at the beginning of the story is a group of cheerful, casually dressed young
people, accompanied by a strange man of about forty, one Semen Antonov:
"The man was entirely naked, if you don't count his short, pale coffee-col-
ored pants, which didn't reach his knees and were pulled in at the stomach
by a strap with the nameplate 'First School' [*real'noe uchilishche*], and also
a pince-nez glued together with purple sealing wax on his nose. A brown,
chronic rash covered the stooping back of the naked man, and his legs were

different, the right one was thicker than the left, and both his shins were sketched all over with knotty veins" (2:427)

If the naked Antonov is jarringly out of place in the splendid old palace, this is only symptomatic of his implacable ideological hostility to its aristocratic spirit. In the course of the tour, he constantly denounces both the former owners and their way of life, much to the consternation of Iona. Antonov, clearly an educated (or semieducated) man, would, it seems, like to strip history bare to match his own nakedness; by eliminating the Tugai-Begs, he implies, the new society will also eradicate the dark stains that mar the portraits of the past. Antonov's views are particularly significant because, judging from his nameplate, he is the teacher of the young people on the tour, a member of the new Soviet intelligentsia, whose ideas are being passed on to future generations. Yet the repulsiveness of his own naked body suggests that "stripping man bare" of history and tradition cannot remove the flaws from inherently imperfect humanity and create an ideal "new man" and new society. On the contrary, without the apparel of culture, mankind's defects appear all the more glaringly.

The tourists view various rooms of the palace, ending up in its most intimate spot, the prince's former bedroom: "In a niche of pink tulle there stood a carved double bed. It was as if just recently, that same night, two bodies had slept in it" (2:390). Here the contrast between the private room and its present public function is most evident and made explicit in Iona's thoughts: "Iona . . . felt pain, injury, and a twinge in his heart when the row of strangers' feet filed past over the rugs, when the strangers' eyes indifferently fumbled about the bed. Shame."

The excursion comes to an end and Iona discovers that the "foreigner," who now reveals his true identity, has remained behind. And so for the prince the dream of coming home, shared with so many of Bulgakov's early heroes, has come true. Yet the story's elegiac tone—not to mention political realities—indicates that the past cannot really be restored. Unlike the palace, which preserves the past intact, time does not spare mortal humanity. The prince has grown old, has changed so much that even his devoted former servant does not at first recognize him. In fact, Tugai-Beg himself has no illusions about a permanent return; he has come only for a moment in order to get some documents.

When he comes to understand more fully the extent of public invasion into his private life, however, the rage and ferocity inherent in his Tartar character burst out. When Iona tells him that a certain "Aleksandr Abramovich Ertus from a committee" (2:394) is going through the Tugai-Beg papers and is planning to open a library for peasants in the palace, the prince reacts: "I'll hang that Ertus there, on that linden, . . . the one by the gate." His rage, moreover, spreads to the other Soviet "intellectual" in the story, the naked Antonov, whom he pledges to hang alongside Ertus, although the historical situation makes his words ring hollow.

Tugai then tells Iona that he even came close to shooting Antonov during the tour, when he insulted the prince's mother, but controlled himself in time. Thus the fierce prince, so different from Bulgakov's autobiographical heroes in other respects, reveals that he too stood helpless before an outrage. He, however, cannot be suspected of being cowardly or weak—indeed, he had to restrain himself from shooting, for under the circumstances "it would have been weak and inept [*neudachno*], and I wouldn't have carried out any of the things I came to do" (2:395). Thus the former categories are reversed: by making rational restraint, not spontaneous opposition, a sign of strength, Bulgakov takes one more step toward justifying his autobiographical hero.

The final episode begins several hours later, near midnight, with the prince sitting alone in his study. In the deceptive candlelight it seems at first as though the past has been resurrected: the portrait of Alexander I "came alive and, bald, smiled softly from the wall," while the prince himself is in his old horse-guard helmet, and its "eagle soared triumphantly above the tarnished metal with a star" (2:396). But, to the implacable ticking of the clock, constant reminders of the shadowy, ghostly nature of this past are given. Tugai glimpses "a murky horse-guardsman with a shining helmet" who approaches him in the glass of a bookcase (2:397), but, when he realizes it is his own reflection, he furiously flings down the helmet and immediately grows old. Then he sees "grayish, flickering people arise and disappear in the bookcases," probably reflections of the photographs on the walls. Finally he approaches a photograph in which "frozen and thus immortalized, people with eagles on their heads" are grouped around an unprepossessing man resembling an army doctor—evidently the last tsar.

Tugai stares for a long time at his own likeness in the picture and says: "This cannot be . . . It is a dream" (2:397). He wonders if he is truly alive when all that gave his life meaning has been expropriated by others: "They walked and trampled through my living blood, amidst all that is alive, as if [walking] through something dead. Perhaps I really am dead? Am I a shadow? But, after all, I am living . . . I sense, feel everything. I clearly feel pain, but most of all rage" (2:398). This rage now takes control, and Tugai-Beg, using as his instrument the flames of the candelabra that have just created the ghostly vision of his lost life, burns down the palace where that life unfolded. Here the domestic flame, once the family and all it represents have been denied, is transformed from a symbol of life to an instrument of destruction and retribution. As the prince mumbles, after setting Ertus's manuscript and other papers aflame: "Nothing will return. Everything is over. There is no point in lying. Well then, we'll carry all this off with us, my dear Ertus" (2:399).

His final act takes place in the pink bedroom, which embodies most fully the perversion of the original significance of the house. In this former site of love, the prince, moved by the opposite emotion, ignites the bed and watches the room go up in flames. He then leaves the house, plunging into the darkness. Thus, by following the vengeful practice of his Tartar fore-bears and burning the palace to the ground, the prince preserves it as an integral part of his past, taking it away from the new collective world, which denies the values it embodies.

In numerous ways, Tugai-Beg foreshadows the diabolical Woland in *The Master and Margarita,* who also arrives at sunset disguised as a foreigner; conjures up at midnight, to candlelight, the ghosts of a past negated by the Soviet present; and leaves conflagration in his wake.[40] (The fact that "The Khan's Fire" was originally to be included in the *Diaboliad* collection suggests that Bulgakov intended some link between Tugai-Beg and the devil.)[41]

While there is no direct biographical tie between the author and the vengeful prince, Tugai-Beg serves as a *literary* alter ego of Bulgakov. His act of retribution against the enemy—of which the doctor-heroes of the auto-biographical prose can only dream and which Bulgakov could not, of course, carry out in real life—*could* be performed in the writer's fictional universe. It is there—not only in "The Khan's Fire" and *The Master and Margarita* but also in "No. 13. The Elpit-Workommune" and *The Fatal Eggs*—that Bulgakov commits literary arson, using all-consuming fires as instruments of retribution. This force of destruction becomes, moreover, a fundamental part of the writer's literary personality, a necessary comple-ment to the constructive values of the doctor-intellectuals of the early prose, who are usually powerless to oppose evil. These opposite but joined halves, indeed, take their final form in *The Master and Margarita,* where the "prince of darkness," retribution-dealing Woland, and the mild-mannered, bright ideal, Yeshua (who, doctor-like, cures Pilate's headache) stand side by side.

3

The White Guard

Although Bulgakov's first attempts to write a novel date from the very beginning of his literary career, he arrived at the conception for *The White Guard* only in 1922 and wrote the work in 1923–1924.[1] From what one can gather, the various stages in the composition of the novel follow, curiously, a backwards chronology similar to that of the early Civil War stories. Thus, according to a magazine notice of March 1923, the time and place of the action were to be those of "Unusual Adventures" and "The Red Crown": "Mikhail Bulgakov is completing a novel, *The White Guard,* embracing the period of struggle with the Whites in the south (1919–1920)."[2] By April, however, the first part of the novel, at least, took place at an earlier date and in Kiev; its title, "The Yellow Banner"—an allusion to the yellow and blue Petlyurite flag—indicated that its subject had shifted to Petlyura's takeover of Kiev at the end of 1918.[3] Even that title, however, fits not Part One of the completed novel but Part Two, which depicts Petlyura's forces, with their "bi-colored banner—a blue kerchief and a yellow kerchief on a staff" (1:277). Bulgakov apparently concluded his backward movement and wrote Part One, with its lyrical, nostalgic evocation of home and family, only in May 1923, after an assignment in Kiev for the newspaper *Nakanune,* the immediate result of which was the feuilleton "Kiev-Town," a retrospective look at the author's native city.[4]

This was Bulgakov's first trip to Kiev since his mother's death at the beginning of 1922, and seeing her grave for the first time, visiting Father Aleksandr Glagolev (the model for Father Aleksandr in the novel) in the small church where her funeral service had been held, might have been that "ineffaceable, immense stimulus" to writing the novel that Bulgakov claims his mother's death provided.[5] It may be significant, moreover (as

Yanovskaya suggests), that, while Varvara Mikhailovna died in February, in the novel her funeral occurs in May, the month Bulgakov was in Kiev. In any case, it was apparently after the visit to Kiev that *The White Guard* took its present form. By the end of August 1923 a first draft was completed, followed by approximately another six months of revision.

Initially the author conceived of *The White Guard* as a trilogy (the first part entitled *The Midnight Cross*) that was to carry the action forward to the final collapse of the White movement in the south of Russia.[6] As it turned out, however, even the first novel did not appear in full in the Soviet Union during the author's lifetime. After the publication of two installments in 1925 in *Rossiia*, the journal was closed down; the full *White Guard* came out only several years later in France. By then circumstances had forced Bulgakov to abandon his plan for a trilogy, and therefore he wrote a new, more "final" last chapter. It is this version that was printed in the first complete Soviet edition, over a quarter of a century after the author's death, and in subsequent editions.[7] Only in 1987 did proofs of the 1925 ending surface, although with the final pages missing.[8]

One would have thought that publication of the early proofs would provide a clearer conception of the original shape of the novel. In fact it marked the beginning of a heated controversy—and something of a textological mystery story—that has not as yet been fully resolved. Thus Yanovskaya asserted that the published proofs are actually the earlier of *two* sets, with the later set, now missing, much closer to the final version of the novel's ending.[9] And in 1991, while browsing in a used bookstore in Moscow, an engineer and book collector from Riga, Igor Vladimirov, made a phenomenal discovery: the typewritten text on the back side of newspaper clippings he was leafing through turned out to be the missing ending of the 1925 version of *The White Guard*.[10] Certain Bulgakov scholars, however, dispute that Vladimirov's finding is really a continuation of the 1925 proofs, considering it instead a fragment of a yet earlier draft.[11] Because of these unresolved textological problems, my analysis is based upon the 1929 version of the novel, despite the basically chronological approach of this study. I do, however, refer to the early versions when relevant to my discussion of the evolution of the novel and its hero.

Bulgakov's decision to structure *The White Guard* around the Turbin family was dictated as much, perhaps, by the exigencies of the novel genre as by thematic considerations. His earlier difficulty in writing a novel on the Civil War, his turning instead to shorter, more fragmentary genres, was far from an isolated phenomenon, for the destruction of the old order had dealt a serious blow to the novel form. A period when the old social fabric had disintegrated, when human contacts tended to be brief and discontinuous, was better captured by shorter genres, such as the poem, the short story, or at most the novella *(povest')*. Even early attempts at novels, such as Boris Pilnyak's celebrated *The Naked Year* (1922), tended to be heterogeneous montages whose very lack of unity captured the spirit of the times.[12]

Only at about the time when Bulgakov was writing *The White Guard,* when the cataclysmic events had already receded somewhat into the past and could be seen more dispassionately, was the novelistic form beginning to reassert itself.[13] Bulgakov himself, by returning to a period when the old social order had not yet entirely broken down (although its impending collapse is made amply clear), by centering upon the family with its shared traditional values, brings to his work something of the aura of an old-fashioned novel. This is enhanced by frequent allusions to nineteenth-century literature, by the fact that both the author and the family itself constantly interpret events in the light of the Russian classics, especially Pushkin, Tolstoy, and Dostoevsky. In particular, *The White Guard,* with its alternation of domestic and battle scenes, its combination of features of the family novel and the national, historical saga, has often been compared to *War and Peace*—indeed, Bulgakov himself, in his letter to the Soviet government of 1930, acknowledged Tolstoy's influence (5:447).[14]

It would be a mistake, however, to look upon the novel as merely a return to the realistic tradition of the nineteenth century. Rather, coexisting with its psychological realism, *The White Guard* adopts modernist techniques to reflect the growing chaos, the dissonance characteristic of both much modern art and modern life. Bulgakov's rather self-conscious—and not entirely successful—use of language betrays the influence of the "ornamental prose" so fashionable in early Soviet literature: the frequent use of alliteration and other sound instrumentation, of macaronic language—especially the intermixture of Russian and Ukrainian—the insertion of fragments of conversation, of interjections and sound effects.[15] The unity of narrative tone is also broken down by the frequent shifts from the serious to the ironical and even farcical, thus creating what one critic has termed the "double-voiced word" of the novel.[16] By subjecting some of his heroes' most cherished ideas to the weapon of mockery, the author, as he wrote in his 1930 letter to the Soviet government, attempts to rise above any partial truth, "to stand dispassionately above the Reds and the Whites" (5:447). In order to achieve a broader perspective, moreover, the traditional sequential plot—although by no means disappearing completely—is no longer the only organizing principle of the novel. It coexists with a musical structure (also characteristic, under Bely's influence, of many modernist works), with leitmotifs uniting seemingly disparate pieces of the narrative.[17]

Finally, a combination of nineteenth- and twentieth-century influences can be seen in the overall narrative strategy. Whereas both the use of scenic shifts and the interweaving of various plotlines to form a broad panorama recall *War and Peace,* Tolstoy's leisurely pace has been replaced in *The White Guard* by the speed and abrupt transitions more typical of the twentieth century. As we have already seen, this succinct style was characteristic of many writers of the early Soviet period and, under the probable influence of the *Satyricon* writers, is already apparent in Bulgakov's first stories.[18] One might, however, add another, extraliterary, influence: the cinema. Bulgakov, in an essay on Yury Slezkin, associates narrative rapidity with the movies: "Where do the pictures fly so fast? Where do they flash up and immediately die out, yielding their place to others? On the movie screen."[19] Evgeny Zamyatin, a friend of Bulgakov's and one of the most influential writers of the early twenties, considered such speed as essential a part of modern literature as of modern life: "The old, slow, creaking descriptions are a thing of the past; today the rule is brevity—but every word must be supercharged, high-voltage."[20] When writing of Bulgakov's *The Diaboliad,* Zamyatin notes specifically "the rapid, cinematic succession of scenes."[21]

Thus in *The White Guard* Bulgakov already displays one of his remarkable traits as a writer: his ability to synthesize the achievements of nineteenth-century realism and twentieth-century modernism. It must be stressed that this is not merely a case of derivative eclecticism, for in the form of his novel the author embodies his basic credo on the continuity of culture, illustrating the possibility of adopting the new without that categorical rejection of the old characteristic of so many writers of his time.

Topography

Aleksei Turbin, the autobiographical hero of *The White Guard,* as well as much of the novel's plot, is already familiar in general outline to readers of Bulgakov's early Civil War stories. Yet a comparison of the novel with these tentative efforts shows the impressive feat of reintegration and synthesis the author has achieved. No longer does one encounter the solipsistic hero facing alone the horrors of Civil War; by now he is surrounded by an environment at once dense and vast, within which he occupies a relatively small place and where his responsibility for the outcome of events is narrowly circumscribed. The Turbin milieu, as Sharratt has aptly put it, can be represented as a series of concentric circles,[22] although I would identify rather different circles from hers: those of family and friends; the Whites as a whole; the city; the surrounding Ukrainian countryside with Bolshevik Moscow beyond; nature; the cosmos; God. In addition to this synchronic spatial environment, the Turbins are also placed within the chronological context of history, carried along by the inexorable flow of time. For them as inhabitants of Kiev, the center of medieval Russian culture, history is ever present and ever relevant, interwoven into the texture of their everyday lives. In the style and imagery of the novel as well Bulgakov draws upon the Old Russian associations of the city, combining them with allusions to both the nineteenth century and the contemporary world to make his work a monument to the long evolution of Russian culture.

The White Guard, indeed, begins like a chronicle,[23] one of the most popular genres of ancient Rus. The narrator in this way immediately offers a panoramic perspective, both temporal and spatial, in which one year is singled out from the long chain of human history: "Great was the year and terrible the year of our Lord 1918, the second since the beginning of the revolution. The summer was abundant in sun and the winter in snow, and two stars stood especially high in the sky: the shepherd's star—evening Venus—and red, trembling Mars" (1:179). The ascendant stars foreordain coming events, pointing to the forces that are to dominate: love and, especially, war. (One recalls the "reddish Venus," incorporating both forces, in "On the Night of the Second"). In general, the cosmos in *The White Guard,* in keeping with the archaic quality of its opening, plays a distinctly premodern, prescientific role, foretelling and participating in human affairs. The Promethean, hubristic quality of so much early Soviet literature is almost declaratively absent here, humanity instead clearly subordinate to and dependent upon the heavens. Moreover, as the novel's second epigraph, taken from Revelation, at once indicates, the Christian God also continues to reign, and divine justice will ultimately prevail: "And the dead were judged out of those things that were written in the books, according to their works" (Rev., XX, 12).

Once the narrative turns to the earth, however, this divine justice is nowhere in evidence. Indeed, at the very beginning, at the funeral of the Turbins' mother, the youngest son, seventeen-year-old Nikolka, complains to God of *in*justice, asking a question repeated in various ways in the course of the novel: "Why such an injury? Such an injustice?" (1:180). He receives no answer, of course, and the narrator's comment actually raises more questions at this point than it answers: "Nikolka himself did not yet know that whatever might happen is always as it must be, and only for the best."

The mother's death is but a foreshadowing of future misfortunes, the first step in the disintegration of the family and the society of which it is a part. Further intimations of woe are soon given by the family priest, Father Aleksandr. Predicting yet "more trials," he quotes a passage from Revelation—this one not comforting like the epigraph: "The third angel poured his cup into the rivers and springs; and it became blood" (1:182). The sense of apocalyptic doom this quote evokes does in fact pervade the novelistic world as a whole, where all parties to the conflict—the Petlyurites, the Whites, the Bolsheviks—are infiltrated by diabolical forerunners of the Apocalypse.[24]

When one descends from the transcendent world entirely to earth, one finds the topography in *The White Guard* similar to that of "On the Night of the Second." The world is again divided into two inimical spheres: the city, where the novel's educated, cultivated heroes dwell; and the unstructured, threatening open spaces beyond, inhabited by the peasant supporters of Petlyura. The urban locale, although obviously Kiev, is never named but is referred to throughout simply as the City (capitalized) in order to underline its general significance as a center of human civilization and culture.[25] Within the City the moral nucleus is, characteristically for Bulgakov, the home, this time the Turbin apartment at 13 Aleksei Slope (*Alekseevskii spusk*).

Consistent with the earlier works, the dwelling place is depicted here as a refuge from the cold, threatening world outside, "hot, cozy, the cream-colored shades drawn" (1:184–185). The guardian spirit of the household, the beautiful, redheaded sister, Elena, preserves the atmosphere of order and refinement created by the deceased mother, setting the table with a white starched tablecloth and fine china, "in spite of the cannons and all this languor, alarm, and nonsense" (1:186). Even the "two blue hydrangeas and two sombre, sultry roses" that grace the winter table are not mere signs of frivolity but "affirm the beauty and stability of life, in spite of the fact that a treacherous foe was at the approaches of the city."

Home in *The White Guard,* as in "The Khan's Fire," is not simply a place of shelter and comfort, however; more important, and more durably as it turns out, it is a repository of family, cultural, and historical tradition. Thus the stove—its warmth and light already providing a central symbol of home in "The Raid"—summons up the entire past of the Turbin family: "Many years before [the mother's] death, the tile stove . . . had warmed and reared little Elenka, the older Aleksei, and the completely tiny Nikolka" (1:180). The stove, moreover, bears witness not only to the Turbins' distant past but also, in the form of various notes jotted upon it, to their activities and attitudes over the past year: their politics ("Beat Petlyura!" [1:183]), their culture ("Lenochka, I got hold of a ticket for Aida" [1:184]), and, through a number of untranslatable puns, their insouciant gaiety at the worst of times.

Again as in "The Khan's Fire," Bulgakov contrasts people and their passing fashions, which time ultimately destroys, to genuine artifacts of culture preserved in the house, which are no less than immortal: "Such sleeves disappeared, time flashed by like a spark, their professor father died, everyone grew up, but the clock remained as before . . . But the clock, fortunately, is entirely immortal; immortal too are the Saardam Shipwright and the Dutch tile, life-giving and hot at the most distressing of times, like a wise cliff" (1:180). The most intangible and therefore most indestructible vessel of culture is music, which fills the Turbin house. Especially singled out (foreshadowing *The Master and Margarita*) is the Gounod opera *Faust:* "All the same, when the Turbins . . . are gone from this world, the keys will again begin to sound, motley Valentine will come out before the footlights, . . . because Faust, like the Saardam Shipwright, is entirely immortal" (1:199).

As for the historical past, its traces in the Turbin household—appropriately for this royalist family—are overwhelmingly monarchist in form. The oft-mentioned *Saardam Shipwright,* first of all, is a children's book on Peter the Great.[26] In addition, images of royal personages appear on the Turbin rugs: Tsar Alexei Mikhailovich "with a falcon on his hand," "Louis XIV, luxuriating on the shore of a silk lake in the garden of paradise" (1:181). Perhaps the most potent source of historical (as well as literary) tradition, however—one also with monarchist underpinnings—is contained in the Turbin bookcases, "smelling of mysterious old chocolate, with Natasha Rostova, the Captain's Daughter." The two works concretely alluded to here, *War and Peace* and *The Captain's Daughter,* are, significantly, historical novels, in which tsars—Alexander I and Catherine the Great, respectively—play prominent roles. Both works take place at times of national crisis and conclude with harmony and order restored—the monarch secure on the throne and family happiness achieved by the heroes.

The monarchism of the Turbins, who long for the life of the "chocolate books," is founded upon this interdependence of the social macrocosm and microcosm, whereby the nuclear family and the family of state, headed by the tsar, are two inseparable parts of the same hierarchical, harmonious whole. They, however, cannot expect the same happy ending as the heroes of the Pushkin and Tolstoy novels, because the tsar, the *pater* (or *mater*) *familias* of the former world, is dead, and the entire old order is thereby threatened. Thus, whereas in *The Captain's Daughter* Catherine the Great succeeds finally in suppressing the Pugachev uprising, in *The White Guard* no tsar remains to crush the analogous Petlyura revolt theatening the Turbins and Russia as they know it. This implicit patriarchal view of Russia, founded upon the notion that national harmony is attainable only within traditional hierarchical structures, elucidates the words of the Turbin friend, Myshlaevsky (quoted from Dmitry Merezhkovsky's play, *Paul I*): "In Rus only one thing is possible: the Orthodox church and autocratic rule!" (1:213).

Monarchs also peer out at the reader of *The White Guard* from other locales where old world principles still reign, although—reflecting Bulgakov's attempt at impartiality—the motives of others are not always as pure as are the Turbins'. Thus, in the apartment of their landlord, Vasily Lisovich (nicknamed Vasilisa), "an engineer and coward, bourgeois and unsympathetic," there is a "floor lamp depicting an Egyptian princess [*tsarevna*]" (1:201) and an "equestrian-copper Alexander II" (1:203). The mercenary Vasilisa, however, far from sharing the Turbins' idealism, cherishes the images of the tsars most as they appear on the money he has stashed away: the "fifteen 'Catherines,' nine 'Peters,' and ten 'Nikolai I's'" (1:203).

Another variation of monarchism, this time congruent with the Turbins', appears at the gymnasium, which is used as a gathering point for the hetman's forces. In its entrance hall there hangs an immense equestrian portrait of Alexander I leading his artillery at Borodino—the site of the Russians' victory over Napoleon, celebrated in *War and Peace*. The hetman's unseasoned troops—many recent graduates of the school—identify with the past martial glory of Russia and sing a song based upon the famous Lermontov poem: "It is not in vain that all Russia remembers/ About the day of Borodino!" (1:257). And Myshlaevsky stirs them up still more by pointing to the image of the tsar: "Didn't you see the Emperor Alexander the Blessed, or what?"[27]

Finally, the external topography of the City, its parks and monuments, is also imbued with the monarchical spirit. This is especially apparent in Aleksei's lyrical dream of the City near the beginning of the novel, in which the splendid Royal Garden *(Tsarskii sad)*, like the artifacts in the Turbin house, is called "eternal" (1:218). And, of course, the most important City landmark, the statue of the cross-bearing St. Vladimir, rising high over the Dnieper River, is yet another monument to royalty. A culmination of that entire Russian autocratic and Orthodox culture so valued by the Turbins, the monument to the Kievan prince who first Christianized Russia serves as a leitmotif throughout the novel; it becomes, indeed, as much a symbol of Kiev as the monument to Peter the Great is of St. Petersburg in Pushkin's "The Bronze Horseman" and Bely's *St. Petersburg*.[28]

If *The White Guard* thus intones a hymn to traditional monarchist Russia, the strains of this music, as must already be apparent, are distinctly funereal. The Turbin house itself, it is said at the very beginning, will collapse, and its precious contents will be destroyed: "The walls will fall, the alarmed falcon will fly off from the white gauntlet, the fire will go out in the bronze lamp, and the Captain's Daughter will be burnt in the stove. Mother said to the children: 'Live.' But they will have to suffer and die" (1:181).

The gymnasium, whose system of education was such an integral part of the old order, is, in fact, already defunct, "a dead, four-tiered ship, which had once carried tens of thousands of lives into the open sea" (1:253). The identification of the young troops with Alexander I's Borodino artillery therefore appears tragically naive. One indication of the hopelessness of their cause involves yet other images of monarchs—the moribund, draped portraits of the last tsars in the school auditorium, which "looked like deathly, pale stains" (1:257). Later Aleksei, looking at the deadness all around him, calls Alexander to their aid: "Will you, Alexander, will you really save the perishing house with your Borodino regiments? Come alive, lead them down from the canvas! They would beat Petlyura" (1:264). The obvious futility of this request points to the inevitable end of the old monarchical society as a whole and of its heart, the City, in the face of the uprising of the surrounding countryside.

While there is no question of where the author's sympathy lies in the struggle between country and city, he nevertheless describes the genuine grievances of the Ukrainian masses with a certain Olympian balance: "Oh, a great deal had accumulated in these hearts. The blows of the lieutenants' riding crops on their faces, and the running shrapnel fire in unruly villages, backs flogged with the ramrods of the hetman's Cossacks [*serdiuki*]" (1:230). It is understandable why the masses view the City and its culture very differently from the educated classes, for the entire course of Russian history, begun by that same St. Vladimir whose monument crowns the City, has brought them little but oppression. Thus, for the "outcast" who skulks about the statue on a cold, snowy night, the illuminated cross, seen from afar, is invisible. He sees only a "cast iron black Vladimir," which "is standing on a frightfully heavy pedestal" (1:266). The monument, like Pushkin's "Bronze Horseman," thus becomes a multivalent symbol: although the rulers they memorialize raised their country to a higher level of development, the needs and dreams of the little man were largely sacrificed in the process. Petlyura's revolt is fueled by these very same dreams, of an "enchanted, imagined Ukraine, without masters [*pany*]" (1:231) and with no place for the City's high culture. Amidst the chaos and devastation wrought by the Petlyurites in the City, therefore, the golden inscription gracing one monument of culture, the museum, appears bitterly incongruous: "For the blessed enlightenment of the Russian people" (1:304).

Standing in irreconcilable opposition to the City and all it represents, popular revolt is associated throughout with the elemental, untamed forces of nature—most consistently with the snowstorm: "A certain rough peasant fury . . . ran through the snowstorm and the cold in torn bast shoes, with hay in its uncovered, tangled hair, and howled. In its hands it carried a great cudgel, without which no undertaking could get by in ancient Rus" (1:237). The snowstorm as symbol of elemental revolt has a long pedigree in Russian literature—which Bulgakov acknowledges in the first epigraph of the novel, from *The Captain's Daughter*, where the blizzard is linked to the Pugachev rebellion. Later, in the iconography of early Soviet literature—beginning with Aleksandr Blok's renowned poem, "The Twelve" (1918)—blizzards and other types of storms commonly serve as symbols of spontaneous revolt.[29] But if Bulgakov adopts a familar image, it is to express his own, quite uncommon, view—one equally far from the Slavophile and Dostoevskian idealization of Russian peasants as "God-bearers," as Myshlaevsky ironically calls them (1:192), and from the tendency of his own time to glorify popular uprising. Indeed, in direct opposition to Blok, who, at the end of "The Twelve" has his recklessly destructive Red Army soldiers led by no less than Jesus Christ, Bulgakov links his Petlyurites to the devil.

Carrying through the apocalyptic imagery of the novel, the narrator reports rumors that the imprisoned Petlyura occupied cell 666—the number of the beast in Revelation (1:228). Later, in the immense mass scene marking the triumph of the Petlyurites—the religious procession from St. Sophia Cathedral followed by the parade of Petlyura's troops—diabolical and apocalyptic imagery abounds, contrasting ironically with the Christian setting and occasion. The shrill, cacophonous "yapping" of the church bells, for example, sound "as if Satan, the devil himself in a cassock, was raising a rumpus" (1:384), while blind beggars sing a "terrible, heart-rending" song: "'Oh, when the end of the age ends,/ And then the Last Judgment approaches...'" (1:384–385). In his description of Petlyura's parade, Bulgakov utilizes a folkloristic negative simile in the style of the most famous work of Old Russian literature, "The Lay of Igor's Campaign,"[30] whose reptilian image once again recalls the devil and the beast of the Apocalypse: "That is not a gray storm cloud with a snake's belly spreading out through the city, . . .—those are the countless forces of Petlyura going on parade to the square of old Sophia" (1:386).

While reversing Blok's Christian interpretation of popular revolt, Bulgakov also denies a fundamental tenet of the "revolutionary romanticism" of his time: that the peasant masses are an ineluctable historical force. The Scythians, for example—a highly influential literary grouping that included, among others, Blok, Bely, and Pilnyak—looked upon the revolution as a triumph of the countryside over the city, of old Russian peasant ways over the westernized, urban life first brought to Russia by Peter the Great.[31] In *The White Guard,* on the contrary, the peasants' fury, "the great cudgel," is a constant of the Russian character, having little to do with the concrete historical situation and no lasting influence on history. Because the revolt contains no constructive, civilizing element, even its leader, Petlyura, is no more than a myth: "There was no such Simon at all in the world . . . Simply a myth, begotten in Ukraine in the fog of the terrible year 1918" (1:229). All that attests to his existence is death and destruction: "And only the corpse was evidence that Peturra was not a myth" (1:422). Ultimately even these purely negative signs will disappear, like the snow in springtime: "The snow will simply melt, the green Ukrainian grass will rise up, will crisscross the earth... . . . and no traces of blood will remain."

The spontaneous revolt, like some natural disaster, exists outside history, sometimes disrupting it, but unable finally to change its course. There is, however, another revolutionary force that operates within the confines of history and the city—the Bolsheviks. The real struggle lying ahead will take place between the proponents of two different ideas of the city: the Whites, supporters of the traditional past, and the Reds, with their vision of the mechanized, rationalized urban culture of the future. Only intimations of this struggle, however, appear in *The White Guard*, and they will be discussed later. The deepest conflict in the novel is not between the Whites and some external enemy force at all but within the ranks of the Whites themselves.

War and the Family

The Turbin family serves in some ways as a microcosm of the old world facing extinction. Like that world, it is being threatened not only from without but from within, most concretely by Elena's husband, Sergei Ivanovich Talberg, a dashing officer serving on the hetman's general staff. From the beginning of the marriage, Talberg, with his "two-layered eyes," has had a baleful effect upon the Turbins; it was as if "a kind of crack had formed in the vase of the Turbins' life and the good water left it imperceptibly. The vessel is dry" (1:194). And now that the Turbin world is under mortal attack this crack becomes a yawning gap, for Talberg, having found out that the Germans are leaving Kiev, plans to escape with them and leave his wife behind.

By thus abandoning the home, Talberg deals a serious blow to the values of the civilized world as the Turbins understand them. This takes visible form in the transformation of the bedroom—especially the lamp, so pregnant an image in Bulgakov—as Talberg prepares to depart: "...In half an hour everything in the room with the falcon was ravaged . . . And then... then it was repulsive in the room, as in any room filled with the chaos of packing and, still worse, when a shade is pulled off a lamp. Never. Never pull a shade off a lamp! A lampshade is sacred. Never run away from danger, scurrying like a rat into the unknown. Doze by the lampshade, read—let the blizzard howl—wait until they come to you" (1:196).

Here Bulgakov approaches the important theme of flight, so central in his early stories, but with a key difference. Whereas in *Notes on the Cuff* it is the autobiographical hero who longs to escape abroad, and in "Unusual Adventures" he apparently succeeds (and Bulgakov's own attempted flight, like Talberg's, entailed leaving his wife behind), in *The White Guard* the act of desertion is detached from the authorial persona and attributed to the negative Talberg. His act, moreover, is only symptomatic of larger events—the mass flight that has brought the privileged strata of Moscow and St. Petersburg to Kiev and will soon carry them out of the country, joined by the Ukrainian hetman, the entire high command of his army, and most of the staff officers. By running off covertly, moreover, the hetman's retinue commits an act of treachery, leaving his fighting men (who include the Turbins and their friends) to the mercy of Petlyura's far more numerous and better equipped forces.

The Turbin brothers, Aleksei and Nikolka, are in some ways typical of the two generations who remain to fight: the officers—experienced soldiers, tempered in the World War—and the untried cadets, who make up the bulk of their troops. This normative function is one reason why Aleksei Turbin is so different in important respects from earlier authorial personae. Thus, unlike his predecessors, he took part in the war, in "difficult marches, service, and misfortune" (1:179). He is intensely involved in unfolding events and is so distressed by the Bolshevik revolution that he has "grown older and gloomy since October 25, 1917" (1:184). Furthermore, far from avoiding mobilization, he announces that, if not taken on as a doctor, he will enlist as a private. In general, Aleksei emerges as a champion of the White cause, even declaring naively that, had troops been gathered in time in the City, they could have not only defeated Petlyura but "swatted Trotsky in Moscow like a fly" (1:209).

Because of his fervent allegiance to the old world, Aleksei is particularly upset by the defection of Talberg, attributing his behavior to a lack of "the slightest idea of honor" (1:217). He sees this as symptomatic of a general moral failure among the upper echelons of the Whites, for Talberg "is an officer of the Russian military academy. That is the best that should have been for Russia." Aleksei's profound disgust, however, is directed not only at Talberg but also at himself. For although the role of deserter has been transferred to his brother-in-law, Aleksei remains, like the earlier heroes, a weak intellectual. He already manifested this weakness at the time of Talberg's departure, and in a characteristically Bulgakovian way: by not speaking out. Indeed, he actually kisses his brother-in-law goodbye. Therefore that night Aleksei severely excoriates himself, virtually equating his own moral failure with Talberg's: "[He] is a scoundrel, but I really am a rag" (1:217). (Note the syntactic parallel with Bakaleinikov's words in "On the

Night of the Second": "[The Petlyurites] are bandits!... But I... I... am intellectual scum" (1:523).

Aleksei's further thoughts upon honor are therefore relevant to himself as well as to Talberg. He opens a copy of Dostoevsky's *The Devils* and comes upon the sentence: "For a Russian man honor is only a superfluous burden..." (1:217). He then falls asleep and dreams of a short man in checked pants (an allusion to the devil who haunts Ivan in *The Brothers Karamazov*), who declares: "Holy Russia is a wooden country, impoverished, and... dangerous, and for a Russian man honor is only a superfluous burden." Thus not only the Petlyurites but also the Whites are infested by devils, spawned by Aleksei's weakness and Talberg's selfishness, adding to the work's apocalyptic ambience.

The theme of honor introduced here is central to the novel as a whole, and most particularly to the development of the authorial persona. Aleksei's "burden of honor" is actually twofold, for he is beset not only by his personal weakness but also, like the hero of "The Red Crown," by the obsolete concept of honor he holds in common with many of the Whites. The latter is apparent in an early episode, when, during a funeral procession for some young officers, Aleksei hears a voice behind him casting a slur on the Whites' honor. He turns around but cannot single out the culprit and therefore attacks a chance victim, a newsboy. He then skulks away, "feeling shame and absurd nonsense" (1:251), the traditional notion of defending one's honor having proven inapplicable in this mass conflict against a faceless foe. Another more central episode occurs on the eve of battle, when Aleksei's "superfluous burden" makes him so nervous and erratic that he is literally regarded as superfluous by Colonel Malyshev, the commander of his division. Malyshev, looking at Aleksei "sullenly" (*"khmuro,"* 1:261), orders him to report for duty only at two o'clock the next afternoon, not at seven in the morning with the troops.

Aleksei's "burden" of honor thus results from flaws both in his conceptions and his character, and the novel traces the theme along these separate, although obviously related, lines. It first presents alternative examples of genuinely admirable martial behavior, then applies to the autobiographical hero this new notion of honor and personal valor. In the process two themes already familiar from the early works emerge as central: domestic versus military values and flight.

The process of undercutting the traditional concept of honor begins early, with the artistically flawed but thematically important "prophetic dream" (1:229) Aleksei has immediately after the visitation of the Dosto-evskian devil. In the dream he is transported to a special military heaven where he encounters two men, Colonel Nai-Turs (who actually dies later in the novel) and Sergeant-Major Zhilin (who perished under Dr. Turbin's care during the World War). Their knightly garb and their eyes, "pure, bottomless, illuminated from within" (1:233), conform to Aleksei's chivalric views of military glory, yet Nai-Turs's words, pronounced in his guttural accent, imply that the traditional concept of glorious death is but a dangerous plaything: "Dying is not playing at death" (*"Umigat'—ne v pomigushki ig'at'"*). The dream goes on to shake Aleksei's conviction that the Whites have exclusive claim to honor, for he discovers that a place in heaven has been reserved for the Bolsheviks. Zhilin, quoting God Himself, explains: "'Well, they don't believe,' says He, 'what can you do . . . One believes, another doesn't . . . all of you, Zhilin, who are slain on the field of battle are the same to me'" (1:236). Stripped of its ideological trappings, war is reduced to mutual carnage, and all those sacrificed in battle, regardless of their convictions, are granted a place in heaven.

After Aleksei's notion of honor is thus undermined, Bulgakov depicts two other characters as models of genuinely honorable behavior: the Colonels Malyshev and Nai-Turs. On the surface the two are very different. The well-fed and clean-shaven Malyshev, who strikes Aleksei as "probably a careerist," although "not stupid" (1:246), hardly conforms to the conventional image of the valiant hero, while Nai-Turs, with his war wound and "mournful eyes" (1:295), has the aura of martyrdom hanging over him from the very beginning. As different as the officers are, however, their motivations turn out to be essentially similar.

Malyshev's most salient feature is that he does not "play at death"; he is totally free from the false romanticism of the young men under his command. Thus, when on the day of battle he receives secret information about the treachery from above, Malyshev immediately orders his troops to disband. He is confronted by cries of indignation from the cadets—his assistant, Studzinsky, even calling for his arrest—but the colonel gains control and rebukes Studzinsky, whose hotheadedness, a traditional martial virtue, is treated as a weakness. Of central importance, Malyshev is moved not by some abstract notion of honor but by a fatherly feeling for his troops, whom he addresses as his children (although they are not much younger than he): "Listen, my children! . . . I . . . take everything upon my own conscience and take responsibility for everything. Everything!!... I am sending you home" (1:274). Here family values are applied to the military unit. Since those same values were violated by the hetman's government when it abandoned the troops, the tie binding the White movement as a whole has been severed, and Malyshev manifests his genuine honor (as if belatedly heeding the request of the mother in "The Red Crown") by sending his men home and saving their lives.

Nai-Turs also is motivated most of all by a paternal concern for his troops. Indeed, he even mounts an armed attack on a fellow White officer for refusing to issue his men felt boots. If Nai had known in advance of the betrayal by his superiors, he undoubtedly would have behaved in much the same way as Malyshev, but he senses that something is amiss only when already in battle. As soon as he does, however—although fearless as ever—he orders a retreat. And when his cadets are wounded and the hetman's troops are nowhere to be found, he gives his men "a strange command, never before heard by them" (1:301): to run.

If Malyshev's unconventional honor was highlighted by his conflict with Studzinsky, Nai-Turs finds his foil in the seventeen-year-old Corporal Nikolka Turbin, who, after the desertion of his superiors, finds himself commander of his unit. Having led his men to an "entirely deathly crossroads" (1:308), Nikolka is dumbfounded to see Nai's cadets running past. His first time in battle and eager to show that he "can be a hero" (1:310), he orders his own men to stay put and reproaches Nai-Turs: "Colonel! . . . your cadets are running in panic!" When Nai orders Nikolka's men also to run home, the command, so far from Nikolka's notion of military valor, almost drives him mad. The colonel, however, goes on to display his extraordinary bravery by staying behind and manning the machine gun—an act motivated not by some abstract concept of honor but by his desire to protect particular human beings. On the other hand, he regards Nikolka's refusal to run as mere bravado and yells, "Get lost, you stupid kid [*malyi*]!" (1:312). And when mortally wounded, he declares: "To the devil with playing the hero" (1:313).

Thus the two models of honorable military conduct are guided first and foremost by the familial ideal of personal responsibility. If in "The Red Crown" the ethics of war prove inferior to the values of the family, in *The White Guard* family principles actually define military honor. Since their superiors have violated these principles, the only remaining concern of Malyshev and Nai-Turs is for the safety of those in their charge, and the only proper behavior for the troops is not to "play the hero" but to run away. Bulgakov thus presents two forms of flight in *The White Guard*. There is, on the one hand, the self-serving treachery of Talberg and other staff officers, which violates the family ethic and is therefore unforgivable. But there is also the simple drive for survival when fighting has become pointless. This is viewed not only as justifiable but as the best course. If one looks backward, finally, this distinction offers some justification for the authorial personae of the early prose, since their "desertions" fall largely into the second category.

Against this background, Bulgakov returns to Aleksei Turbin, who, significantly, does not manifest his weakness by running away like previous autobiographical heroes but by lingering too long. Aleksei, who oversleeps and is unaware of the debacle, finds Malyshev at headquarters (formerly Madame Anjou's dress shop). The colonel, only now realizing that he forgot to warn the doctor of the changed situation, gives the already familiar order—to run—and hastily departs himself. Aleksei, however, intellectual that he is, lingers, in thrall to his "sluggish, crumpled thoughts" (1:307). Only after much time has passed does he dash out, and even then he does not go directly home but is drawn irresistibly toward the center of the struggle, the museum. His failure to run is again presented not as a brave act but as passive submission to a mysterious force: "There really is a force that sometimes makes one look down from a precipice in the mountains... . . . And in this way he was drawn toward the museum" (1:345). When Aleksei steps onto Vladimir Street, he immediately senses danger, and Malyshev's voice distinctly whispers within him: "Run." But he again hesitates, allowing the Petlyurites to spy and pursue him.

Up to this point Aleksei's behavior on the streets of Kiev follows in general outline that of Doctor N of "Unusual Adventures," who also looks for his unit on Vladimir Street and, when Petlyurites pursue him, takes to his heels. After this, however, the differences illustrate the great change that has taken place in the portrayal of the hero. If in the early story the hero's escape is treated mockingly, in *The White Guard* the instinct for flight has become a positive phenomenon—one that transforms Aleksei from intellectual "rag" to "wise wolf": "It is enough to pursue a person with shots and he turns into a wise wolf; in place of the mind, very weak and truly unnecessary in difficult circumstances, there arises wise animal instinct" (1:347). This instinct, moreover, rids Aleksei of his fear, which "jumped right out through his whole body and through his legs into the ground. But rage returned through his legs like ice water and, while on the run, came out of his mouth like boiling water." This rage in turn leads Aleksei to perform an act of which his predecessors could only dream: he shoots at the enemy. Thus flight ceases to be a sign of cowardice; on the contrary, it serves to reverse Aleksei's former weakness and allows him to resist the dreaded Petlyurites, who threaten his life and that of the entire City.

If Aleksei's flight thus gives him strength by awakening animal instinct in the abstract intellectual, the mechanism involved at the same time serves to strip bare, in the Tolstoyan manner, the very notion of military valor. Far from being founded upon the lofty ideals of the Turbins, bravery is reduced here to the most basic, universal instinct for self-preservation, having little to do with genuine honor. The latter, exemplified, as we have seen, by Nai-Turs and Malyshev, involves more—the familial impulse to protect others and, if necessary, to risk oneself in the process. Another instance of such behavior now occurs, as a woman rescues the wounded Aleksei. Later it is she who informs Aleksei that he killed one of his pursuers and has joined the ranks of the brave: "They jumped out, and you began to shoot, and the first one crashed down... Well, perhaps you wounded him... you're brave... I thought I would faint... . . . You're probably a captain?" (1:353).

The woman who rescues Aleksei, Yuliya Reiss, is the first of the feminine saviors in Bulgakov's works,[32] to be joined by Elena Turbina later in *The White Guard* and by Margarita in *The Master and Margarita*. Like Margarita, Yuliya's savior-like quality is combined with a demonic aura, the positive and negative poles associated with fire embodied in her: her hair "ashy, it seems, pierced through with fire, or perhaps golden, and her brows coal-like and her black eyes . . . You couldn't make out what was in her eyes. Fright, it seems, alarm, and perhaps vice as well . . . Yes, vice. When she sits like that and a wave of heat passes over her, she seems marvelous, attractive. A savior" (1:353–354).

Yuliya not only saves Aleksei but bestows upon him the gift of human intimacy. As he lies in a high fever, he kisses her on the lips and later pulls her down until she is lying alongside him, and "through his sick fever, he felt the living and bright warmth of her body" (1:355). One at last understands why Venus as well as Mars is in the ascendant during the "terrible year" 1918: sensual love is a saving miracle against the background of universal destruction. It also explains why, in Aleksei's "prophetic dream," the soldiers were admitted into heaven together with their women and Aleksei had a fleeting vision of one we now recognize as Yuliya: "Someone's eyes, black, black, and birthmarks on the lustreless right cheek, dully glowed in the darkness of sleep" (1:234). Sexual love counters the horrors of war and therefore, although traditionally considered sinful, its bearers are granted a place in heaven.

Aleksei's rescue is termed a "miracle" (1:348), and it recalls the previous miracles in Bulgakov's works, which led to the survival of Abram in "The Raid" and of Bakaleinikov in "On the Night of the Second." Earlier in *The White Guard* Nikolka also thought of his escape after Nai-Turs was killed as a miracle: "Now this really is a miracle of the Lord God . . . Notre Dame de Paris. Victor Hugo" (1:314). In Aleksei's case, the miracle Yuliya performs is in fact only the first in a series required to snatch him from death, to reverse, or at least delay, the historically inevitable destruction of the Turbins.

The first minor miracle is linked to the comic-pathetic figure of Lariosik Surzhansky, the Turbins' Zhitomir cousin, who appears unexpectedly at the very moment of Aleksei's return. When the hapless but generous Lariosik gives Elena his entire thick bundle of badly needed money, Nikolka thinks: "What a character . . . A miraculous apparition" (1:332). A second miracle is performed by a doctor, who, "persistent and very able" (1:339), serves as the embodiment of civilization, the very antipode of the terrifying Petlyurites, who are haunting Aleksei in his delirium. Soon after the doctor's "miracle-working injection . . . the gray figures [of the Petlyurites] ceased their outrageous behavior" (1:340).[33]

The human "miracles" performed by Lariosik and the doctor, however, are insufficient to save Aleksei, who has contracted typhus. Therefore Elena, shortly before Christmas, seeks divine help. If in "On the Night of the Second" and "The Raid" Bulgakov introduces Christmas imagery to underline the perversion of traditional values, in *The White Guard* the holiday's manifold associations have direct relevance: "From year to year, for as long as the Turbins could remember, the [icon] lamps were lit in their home on the twenty-fourth of December, at twilight, and in the evening the green fir branches were lit with flickering, warm lights" (1:410). Here one has the ever-repeating "immortal" event within the stream of passing time; light in darkness; the miracle of life (the fir branches) at a dead season. Especially important is the fact that Christmas is a family holiday, not only *for* the family, but also in honor *of* the holy family.[34]

Elena, therefore, seeking to save her brother, turns to the Mother of God: she lights a candle before an icon of the Virgin and begs that the Turbins be not entirely destroyed. Like Nikolka at the novel's beginning, she seeks some justification for their suffering, which she considers excessive: "You are sending too much grief at once, mother-intercessor. Thus, in one year you are finishing a family. What for?... You took our mother from us, I don't have a husband and I won't have one, I understand that . . . And now you are taking away the eldest. What for?... . . . Mother-intercessor, can it really be that you will show no pity?... Perhaps we are bad people, but why punish us so?" (1:411).

Elena entreats the Virgin to intercede with her son, "the Lord God, to send a miracle" (1:411). She prays passionately for hours, until "the one Elena had beckoned through the intercession of the dark-skinned Virgin arrived entirely soundlessly. He appeared alongside a toppled sepulchre, entirely resurrected, gracious and barefoot." Elena, in a rush of self-sacrifice, agrees to give up her husband if only her brother be saved. After she sees the Mother of God's lips unseal on the icon and her eyes become "extraordinary" *(nevidannye)* (1:412), Elena sinks to the floor. When she comes to, she finds out that Aleksei, like Christ in her vision, is resurrected and will survive.

And so Aleksei, almost destroyed in battle, is ultimately saved by the family. And while still in a delirium, he comes to understand that only domestic values, in the broadest sense, are worth fighting for, "to preserve human rest and the hearth. Because of that [man] wages war, and under no circumstances should he wage war for anything else" (1:340).

Illusions and Eternal Truths

It has become commonplace to say that *The White Guard* not only recounts the military collapse of the Whites but also exposes the illusions under which even its best members operate. Although only partially true, this assertion is worth exploring further. The most interesting analysis of the ideological breakdown of the Turbin world is given by Altshuler, who shows that the major episodes in Part Three serve as a rebuttal to numerous Turbin beliefs expressed earlier.[35]

The Turbins' cousin, Lariosik, first of all, serves as a diminished, comic double of Aleksei, parodying some of the doctor's actions and most cherished beliefs. Lariosik's arrival at the very same moment the wounded Aleksei returns home is the first hint of a tie, reinforced when he changes into Aleksei's clothes while the latter lies dying. Moreover (as Altshuler does not mention), Lariosik's adventures on the way to the City offer a comic variation of Aleksei's near death. During his eleven-day train ride, Lariosik too is almost killed by Petlyurites, but he is saved not by a beautiful woman but by his bird: "And you know what? the bird saved me. I'm not an officer, I said, I'm a scientific bird breeder, and I show the bird..." (1:332). Most important, the Turbins' elevated view of home sounds ridiculous when Lariosik waxes lyrical over the "cream-colored shades" behind which "our wounded souls seek rest" (1:359). As Myshlaevsky responds: "Well, you know, as far as rest is concerned, I don't know how things are in Zhitomir, but here in the City I don't think you're going to find it..."[36]

Other major episodes in Part Three also reveal the Turbins' delusions. Thus Altshuler regards the mass religious procession and Petlyurite parade discussed above as a response to Aleksei's dream of the City as center of elite civilization. The sight of these countless masses finally brings home to members of the Turbin circle the dimensions of the opposition, disabusing them of their belief in their own might fostered by their leaders and expressed with special fervor by Aleksei. Now Nikolka thinks to himself: "Ekh... ekh... here's fifteen thousand for you... Why in the world did they lie to us" (1:389).

The following episode, which recounts Nikolka's trip to the morgue in search of Nai-Turs's corpse, is a response to the Turbins' beautiful vision of military glory. Altshuler sees here a denial of the vision of military heaven contained in Aleksei's early dream: if Nai-Turs in the dream has "pure, bottomless" eyes (1:233), in the morgue his "open, glassy eyes" stare "senselessly" at Nikolka, his repulsive face is "touched by barely perceptible green," his body is bloodstained (1:406). It is likely, however, that Bulgakov intended not a simple negation of the dream vision but a contrast between heavenly justice, which will ultimately prevail, and the absence of such justice on earth. The morgue scene is actually a more exact refutation of Nikolka's earlier imaginings of a beautiful military death: "'Who are they burying, my dears?' 'Junior Officer Turbin...' 'Oh, what a handsome lad...' And music. It's pleasant, you know, to die in battle" (1:309).

Finally, at the last gathering of the Turbins and their friends as they await the Bolsheviks' entry into the City, things seem no different from the beginning, but already certain objects that defined their way of life have disappeared: the "somber, sultry roses"; the beloved family china, broken by the hapless Lariosik on his first day at the Turbins'; the shoulder insignia, which have "floated off somewhere and dissolved in the snowstorm outside the windows" (1:418). The "immortal" stove remains, of course, but its inscriptions have been wiped off, except for one indicating the family's attachment to timeless culture: "...Len... I've gotten hold of a ticket for Aid..." (1:422).[37]

The Turbins' delusions and the collapse of their world are amply revealed at the end of *The White Guard,* but the family is by no means on the point of surrendering to its inevitable fate. Even at the last moment a spirited tsarist march sounds in their apartment: "The piano beneath Nikolka's fingers spewed forth the desperate march, 'The Double-Headed Eagle,' and laughter could be heard" (1:420). Although one may regard this as merely an instance of tragic irony, pointing to the continued blindness of the Whites, that would certainly be too simplistic. For whatever mistaken notions the Turbins might still entertain, the old world to which they remain devoted did not consist only of delusions but also of values worth defending, even in a lost cause. In the novel, as we have seen, the distinction is repeatedly drawn between the transitory—mere fashion, which inevitably changes and disappears—and the eternal: the Saardam Shipwright, the Royal Garden, Faust. Although their concrete, material forms can obviously be destroyed, the latter are "immortal" because they embody a higher ideal. Bulgakov here repeats an idea expressed more explicitly by Aleksandr Blok in his essay, "The Intelligentsia and Revolution": "Don't worry. Is it possible that even a grain of something genuinely valuable can disappear? . . . A palace that can be destroyed is not a palace. A kremlin wiped off the face of the earth is not a kremlin. A tsar who himself falls from his throne is not a tsar. We have kremlins in our heart, tsars in our head. Eternal forms, revealed to us, can be removed only together with our heart and our head."[38]

It is Nikolka Turbin who, although the youngest (or perhaps *because* he is the youngest), represents the genuine ideals of the old world in their purest form. It is he who believes that "not a single person should break his word of honor, because it would be impossible to live in the world" (1:321). After the death of Nai-Turs, moreover, it is he who becomes the spiritual successor of the heroic colonel (the relationship hinted at through a similarity of names: *Nai-Turs–Nikolai Turbin*). Thus, Nikolka, together with Nai's sister Irina, goes to the morgue and finds his corpse. He lays Nai out in his coffin, placing his St. George's ribbon on his chest "with his own hand." And afterward Nai's sonless mother symbolically adopts the motherless Nikolka, calling him "my son" (1:407).[39] Later, as Nikolka leaves the morgue, his "conscience . . . entirely calm" (a state extremely rare in Bulgakov's works), he is deemed worthy to see beyond the murk and storms that cloak the heavens throughout the novel to the transcendent world beyond, "the stars in crosses and the Milky Way."[40] Near the end of the novel the deathlike aura surrounding Nai is explicitly transferred to Nikolka. Elena dreams that he will die, will (to borrow Blok's words) give up his ideals only "together with his heart and head": "He had a guitar in his hands, but his entire neck was bloody, and on his forehead was a yellow wreath with icons" (1:427).[41]

Aleksei's position at the novel's conclusion is much more difficult to define. Moreover, our task of tracing the evolution of the authorial persona in Bulgakov's early fiction has been much complicated by the publication of the early drafts, in which Aleksei differs markedly from the more familiar hero of the end of the final version. In the 1925 proofs, Aleksei retains many of the traits of the weak intellectual to the end, when he is still described as "a soft man, entirely too soft" (1:529). The final version, in contrast, presents a "resurrected Turbin" who has "changed dramatically" (1:413). Softness is no longer his dominant characteristic, as the stern expression on his face indicates: "Two folds had apparently stuck to his face forever, at the corners of his mouth; the color of his skin was waxy, his eyes had sunk in shadows, and had become forever unsmiling and gloomy." He appears rid of his illusions, for his thoughts are no longer "sluggish" but "harsh, clear, joyless."

The development of Aleksei into a stronger figure by the final version is probably attributable in part, as Chudakova suggests, to the influence of the Aleksei of *Days of the Turbins,* created between the two versions of the novel's ending.[42] The 1929 version, however, was probably influenced not only by the heroic, although far from autobiographical, protagonist of the play but also (as we shall see in the next chapter) by other variants of the authorial persona created between the redactions of the novel's conclusion: the heroes of "I Killed" and *Notes of a Young Doctor.* This would conform to the gradual strengthening of the autobiographical hero traced in this study.

One should not ignore, however, the less radical change that Aleksei has already undergone by the end of the extant 1925 version. This is apparent from one symbolic act (retained in the final version) that reverses his kiss of Talberg at the novel's beginning. When Elena receives a letter stating that her husband is about to remarry in emigration, Aleksei mutters: "What a pleasure it would be to land him one in the mug." Elena asks to whom he is referring and Aleksei replies, burning with shame: "To myself, . . . for having kissed him that time" (1:420). He then proceeds to tear up Talberg's portrait.

The question of Aleksei's precise ideological position at the end of the novel—in both the early and late versions—remains unanswered, however. His readiness to reject the negative aspects of the White movement represented by Talberg seems to imply that he, in contrast to his brother, has grown disillusioned and is about to abandon his former course. Something else, however, is suggested by a closer examination of the novel's inner structure, in particular the relationship between Aleksei and an important character who has not yet been introduced: Mikhail Semenovich Shpolyansky, a dandified modernist poet from St. Petersburg who serves in the hetman's armored car division.

The poet represents yet another form of flight in the novel, one ultimately more damaging to the White cause than Talberg's treachery: defection to the Bolsheviks. On the eve of Petlyura's entry into the City, Shpolyansky performs an act of sabotage, plugging up the carburetor jets of three of the hetman's armored cars. He then escapes and is apparently killed, but later we catch a glimpse of him in the company of the Bolsheviks. The motivation for Shpolyansky's treachery is not easy to pinpoint. The poet does not desert out of fear, like the mass of staff officers in the novel; indeed, it is said that he is "famous throughout the division for his exceptional bravery" (1:294). Nor, it appears, is ideological conviction the reason. One motive he gives is simply boredom: "They're all scoundrels . . . But besides that Petlyura is a pogrom organizer. That's not the most important thing, however. I've become bored because I haven't thrown any bombs lately" (1:289). The boredom of the elegantly dressed Shpolyansky is emphasized by his striking resemblance to Evgeny Onegin, Pushkin's egoistic dandy whose constant pursuit of self-gratification also leads to boredom. And just as Onegin's cold egoism is responsible for the pointless killing of the poet Lensky, so do Shpolyansky's actions cause a death, of the "ruddy enthusiast Strashkevich" (1:389), commander of the only operative armored car, left to face the Petlyurites alone.

Shpolyansky is a particularly intriguing character because he is largely modeled upon a major literary figure, the famous formalist critic, Viktor Shklovsky, and thus introduces a note of literary polemic to the novel.[43] As readers of Shklovsky's memoirs, A Sentimental Journey (1923), are aware, he like Shpolyansky came to Kiev from St. Petersburg in late 1918, joined the hetman's armored division, and, after having plugged up the carburetors of the hetman's armored cars, went over to the Red Army. Some of Shpolyansky's literary activities, moreover, coincide with Shklovsky's. Thus, Shpolyansky is a critic as well as a poet, the author of a "scholarly work, 'The Intuitive in Gogol'" (1:126). He reads his work at the literary club, "Dust," its Russian name, *Prakh*, formed from the first letters of *"poety-rezhissery-artisty-khudozhniki"* ("poets-directors-actors-artists," 1:288, 220); Shklovsky read at an analogous club, its name, *Khlam* (Rubbish), derived from the initials of "Painters, literary men, actors, musicians *(Khudozhniki, literatory, aktyory, musykanty)*."[44] In addition, Shpolyansky heads the poetic group, the "Magnetic Triolet" (1:288), a transparent reference to Elsa Triolet, the object of Shklovsky's unrequited love, celebrated in his epistolary work, *Zoo*, published in 1923, shortly before *The White Guard*.

While Shklovsky was by no means a dandy in the sartorial sense, like Shpolyansky and Onegin, Bulgakov imparted to his fictional counterpart the *spiritual* dandyism he apparently detected in many modernist artists—especially his old enemies, the Futurists, with whom Shpolyansky is identified and with whom Shklovsky was closely allied.[45] Taking the form of an obsession with *aesthetic* fashion, such dandyism leads to the abandonment of absolute moral and artistic standards. This ethos has already led Shpolyansky and his circle to forsake traditional morality in favor of the decadence so modish in the early twentieth century, and now, sensing another shift, the poet lightheartedly severs his modernist artistic ties to join the vanguard of history. This easy rejection of former loyalties in the name of the new could only be regarded by Bulgakov as a degeneration of genuine culture, which is, as we have seen, "immortal."[46] This attitude is, of course, the very antithesis of all the Turbins stand for.

Aleksei never actually meets Shpolyansky in the novel; in fact, he learns of the poet's existence only near its conclusion. Nevertheless, certain plot correspondences—especially in the final version—make of the two virtual negative doubles. Thus in the course of the novel both are given up for dead and are then "resurrected," having in the process undergone a transformation. Before his "death," Shpolyansky's relations with two characters—the syphilitic poet, Rusakov, and Yuliya Reiss—are shown in the greatest detail. It is these very people who enter Aleksei's life *after* he is wounded. If, moreover, the influence of the decadent Shpolyansky on the two is pernicious, Aleksei, who offers a more positive model of the intellectual, brings wholesome moral values into their lives.

Aleksei's relations with Rusakov begin only at the very end of the novel, when the poet comes to him to be treated for syphilis. Rusakov, author of "God-struggling" (*bogoborcheskie*) poems, contracted his disease and became a cocaine addict under Shpolyansky's influence. He provides a good example of the degeneration of the modern intellectual, as described by Blok: "There are fewer and fewer intellectual [*intelligentnye*] people who are saved by the positive principles of science, social activity, art . . . Another, higher principle is needed. Since this does not exist, it is replaced by all kinds of rebellion and rowdiness, beginning with the vulgar 'struggle against God' by the decadents and ending with imperceptible and open self-destruction—through debauchery, drunkenness, suicide of all kinds."[47]

When we first encounter him, Rusakov in fact already regrets his rebellion, having found his "higher principle" in a return to God. In a prayer he confesses his sinfulness and cries out: "Replenish my strength, save me from cocaine, save me from weakness of spirit, and save me from Mikhail Semenovich Shpolyansky!..." (1:291–292). Aleksei is, apparently, the answer to his prayers, signaling yet another "miracle" in the novel. Although the reader has been aware all along that Aleksei is a venereologist, this is the first time he is actually shown practicing medicine. (The episode appears in almost identical form in the 1925 proofs: 1:539–542.) It is as though he needed first to be "resurrected" before being deemed worthy to cure others. It is in his aim of curing Rusakov's syphilis that Aleksei emerges as the opposite of Shpolyansky, for while Shpolyansky (to quote Rusakov's high-flown words) "inclines women to debauchery and young men to vice" (1:416), Aleksei insists upon abstinence: "Cocaine is forbidden. Drinking is forbidden. Women too..." (1:415).

It is from Rusakov that Aleksei first hears of Shpolyansky. The poet's former "struggle against God" now replaced by a rather crazed religious exaltation, he places Shpolyansky—and the Bolsheviks as a whole—within an apocalyptic framework. He calls the poet the "evil genius of my life, the forerunner of the Antichrist" (1:415) and terms Moscow "the city of the devil" and Trotsky the Antichrist himself. What we are told of Shpolyansky's relations with Yuliya Reiss supports the sinister image of the poet, for decadent passion and discord dominate. When Shpolyansky spends the night at her place shortly before carrying out his plans and sips her "aromatic cognac," she is "tormented . . . and crushed by the kisses of the passionate Onegin" (1:292). While joined in physical passion, there is apparently no spiritual bond between the two, for Yuliya expresses total incomprehension of Shpolyansky's schemes: "I am very sorry that I have never understood and cannot understand your plans."

Aleksei enters Yuliya's world the day after Shpolyansky leaves her to join the Bolsheviks. Now it is he who drinks her cognac, and she brings him an exotic robe—"long, with a sweet, bygone aroma, Japanese, with strange bouquets" (1:351)—which had surely been worn before by Shpolyansky. Aleksei, like Shpolyansky, kisses Yuliya passionately, and he sleeps with her on this first night. These similarities, however, only underline the reversal of moral ambience: while Yuliya expressed disapproval of Shpolyansky's actions, she praises Aleksei for his bravery. And in their physical intimacy, there is no "torment," only the life-giving solace provided by human closeness.

Later, when Aleksei returns to see Yuliya after his recovery, he continues to feel irresistible physical attraction toward her and again embraces and kisses her. He immediately places his emotions within a family context, however, by giving her his mother's bracelet, and from the bracelet "her arm became still more attractive, and all of Reiss seemed still more beautiful..." (1:417). The one discordant note sounds when Aleksei notices a portrait of a man on Yuliya's table, whom she claims to be her cousin and identifies as Shpolyansky. Aleksei remembers the name from Rusakov and is shaken: "Something trembled in Turbin, and he looked for a long time at the black side whiskers and black eyes... An unpleasant, gnawing thought lingered longer than the others as he studied the forehead and lips of the chairman of the 'Magnetic Triolet.' But it was unclear... The forerunner . . . What is disturbing? What is gnawing [at him]?"

Here a hint remains of a conflict, at once personal and political, that was no doubt to develop between Aleksei and Shpolyansky in the following volumes of the trilogy. In the political confrontation, as history has proven, the "Bolshevik" Shpolyansky was bound to vanquish Aleksei, who has thrown in his lot with the old world. Even the name of Yuliya's street, Malo-Provalnaya (instead of the actual Kievan Malo-Podvalnaya), leaves no doubt that her world is doomed to destruction. Its root, *proval,* signifying *collapse, failure, disappearance,* recurs in the rescue scene: Yuliya "half disappeared [*provalilas'*] into . . . a wall" and Aleksei "disappeared [*provalilsia*] behind her" (1:348). Once he is in her apartment, moreover, he understands that all the things there already belong to the past: "God, what ancient things [*kakaia starina*]!... . . . There was peace, and now the peace is killed. The years will not return" (1:352).

Although from a purely pragmatic point of view Aleksei errs when he replaces Shpolyansky in "the strange and quiet little house" (1:417), his action is justified by his view of history. While Shpolyansky regards the Bolsheviks as "a third historical force and possibly the only right one" (1:293), for the Turbins history is not an impersonal, mechanistic clash of "forces" among which one may choose with impunity. As the entire course of the novel has shown, it is a continuum stretching back to the beginning of civilization, of which they are an integral part. They could not abandon the past and all its "immortal" essences without betraying the very core of their own being.

This old world, although corrupted by the likes of Shpolyansky (Rusakov's syphilis, Yuliya's sinfulness), with its "stains," to borrow a term from "The Khan's Fire," is also a place of lasting beauty, tradition, and spirituality that will outlive passing political and artistic fashion. Therefore even if loyalty to the world of Malo-Provalnaya Street (on which Nai-Turs's family, with whom Nikolka casts his lot, also lives) involves the Turbins in a *historical* lost cause, at the same time it shows them to be *morally* superior to such worshippers of the new as Shpolyansky. This remains true even if (as others have noted) the Turbins' truth is partial—if they do not, like Rusakov and the author himself at the novel's end, rise above the historical moment to catch a glimpse of eternity.[48]

While Aleksei has no connection with the literary world, it is tempting to regard his confrontation with Shpolyansky as a foreshadowing of Bulgakov's own literary struggle with such modernist writers as Shpolyansky's prototype, Viktor Shklovsky. For it is to the defense of precisely the same "immortal" values that Bulgakov himself is committed in *The White Guard* and other of his best works. He thus stands opposed to those avant-garde writers who were ready to throw over old humanistic ideals, first for *fin de siècle* decadence and then for the new mechanistic world and the new man, "without noble wormholes," as Rusakov describes Shpolyansky (1:289).

It is important to note, however, that in the 1925 proofs the moral rightness of Aleksei's attachment to Yuliya is not yet apparent. Their relations are much less serene and in fact are marked by a melodramatic mix of jealousy and lies, largely centering on the figure of Shpolyansky. On one visit, Aleksei, enraged when Yuliya rejects his proposal, grabs her by the throat and asks whose portrait formerly stood on the table. Another time he actually draws a revolver and demands that she tell him of her relations with the poet. In the early draft of the very end of the novel, Aleksei has a "prophetic dream"—a "heavy, sick, jealous dream"—about the affair of

Yuliya and Shpolyansky, in which we learn of Shpolyansky's affiliation with the Cheka. When Aleksei bursts in on the couple and tries in vain to shoot them, Shpolyansky's "faceless face [*bezlikoe litso*] becomes menacing and dangerous . . . and one senses menacing support behind him . . . Turbin already feels that the extraordinary commission [*chrezvychainaia komissia* = Cheka] has come for his soul . . . They're coming! The Chekists are coming!"[49]

As depicted in the 1925 proofs, Aleksei's involvement with Yuliya has blinded him to some higher truth, for, while walking home one night, he ignores the message of the stars: "The sky hung hard, immense, and stars were impressed upon it, red, five-pointed. Most immense of all and most alive of all was Mars. But the doctor did not look at the stars. He walked and mumbled: 'I don't want trials. Enough. Only this room'" (1:544). In his disregard of the heavens Aleksei contrasts with Nikolka, who, when he runs into his brother after a visit to Irina Nai, is "studying the stars" (1:537).

It may be that at this time Bulgakov wanted to distinguish between the two images of the past to which Aleksei and Nikolka bind their destiny—that he regarded Yuliya's old world as a receptacle of dubious, transitory values while the high moral principles of the Nai-Turses were placed among the eternal essences. One detects here faint traces of the conception of two of the Vladikavkaz dramas *(The Turbin Brothers, Sons of the Mullah),* with their contrast of two brothers, one an active struggler for his cause, the other passive. One also recalls the distinction made in an even earlier work, "Prospects for the Future," between those who are "intrepidly performing their duty" and "those who skulk in the rear cities of the south, under the bitter delusion that the cause of the country's salvation will get by without them."[50] At the same time, in his desire for an end to his "trials," in his distance from the stars, the Aleksei of this early redaction foreshadows the Master, who is granted peace but is unworthy of the light.

In any case, by the final version—indicative of a positive shift in attitude toward the Aleksei/Yuliya relationship—it is the similarities between the Turbin brothers that are stressed. This is apparent from Aleksei's words when the brothers meet by chance after their respective trysts: "Evidently, brother, Peturra has flung the two of us onto Malo-Provalnaya Street. Eh? Well, what can you do, we'll keep on visiting here. And who knows what will come of it, eh?" (1:418).

The White Guard concludes on the same fateful "night of the second"—the date of the Petlyurites' retreat from Kiev—already depicted in the earlier stories. In the early draft, Aleksei is mobilized by the Petlyurites, and his experiences precisely echo those of Bakaleinikov in "On the Night of the Second."[51] By the final version of the novel, however, Aleksei is entirely spared the traumatic experiences of his predecessors, an indication of how far the authorial persona had evolved by then. The episode of the murder of a Jew by a Cossack officer does, to be sure, still appear in the novel; indeed, it is transcribed almost verbatim from the early draft. This time, however, there is no guilt-ridden authorial persona present, for Aleksei has not been conscripted and is at home asleep, not implicated in any way in the atrocities. Because of the evolution of the autobiographical hero—in *Days of the Turbins, Notes of a Young Doctor,* and "I Killed"—the later Aleksei is no longer the same weak creature as the early heroes and for this reason is spared their harrowing ordeal. His profound dread of the Petlyurites, to be sure, is still apparent in his final dream, in which they shoot at him outside Yuliya's house: "His feet stuck to the sidewalk on Malo-Provalnaya and Turbin was perishing in the dream" (1:423). The episode concludes on a positive note, however, for Aleksei wakes up, and, after the comforting thought that the Petlyurites "will never be here again" (1:423)—his final thought in the novel—he falls back asleep.

The Bolsheviks' place in the moral landscape of the novel is not nearly as clear-cut as that of the Petlyurites. On the contrary, the image of the Bolsheviks is contradictory, alternating between the extremes of heaven and hell. Thus, while Rusakov describes Trotsky as the Antichrist, in Aleksei's dream the Bolsheviks are admitted into heaven. And counterposed to the diabolical Shpolyansky is the positive image of the "light man" (1:392), who stands above the milling Petlyurite crowd in Khmelnitsky Square and attempts to bring order to the chaotic throng. Even Myshlaevsky admires the deftness with which the orator and his comrades (including Shpolyansky!) escape from the enraged mob: "Well, I'll tell you one thing, Karas, the Bolsheviks are fine fellows [*molodtsy*]" (1:397).

In the final vision of the Bolsheviks, as they prepare to occupy the City, the hellish and heavenly are fused. On the one hand, the armored train *Proletariat* stands like a veritable beast of the Apocalypse, its weapon aimed directly at the most potent symbol of the old world, the cross of St. Vladimir:

> The multifaceted hulk of the locomotive showed black, from its belly there tumbled out a fiery square, spreading out on the tracks, and from the side it seemed that the womb of the locomotive was packed full of red-hot coals. It rasped quietly and maliciously, something trickled

through the side walls, its blunt snout was silent and squinted at the forests along the Dnieper. From the last platform a very broad barrel in a sealed muzzle aimed at the black and dark blue heights, to about twelve versts away, and directly at the midnight cross (1:424).

This hellish apparition, however, is soon replaced by a positive figure: a sentry, who, very cold and tired, stares fixedly at the five-pointed "reddish, living star" Mars (1:424). Occasionally dozing off, he sees the sky "all red, glittering, and all dressed in Marses in their living glitter." This seemingly infernal vision of strife, in which the red star of the Communists merges with the red Mars, fills the sentry's soul with happiness. It is immediately joined by intimations of heaven, as the same Zhilin from Aleksei's dream appears to the dozing man. The sentry wakes up and the red star on his chest, "small and also five-pointed" (1:426), now echoes the reddish Venus (combining love and strife) in heaven.

One must turn to the Apocalypse to make sense of this seemingly paradoxical jumble of images, for there bloody conflict both destroys the old world and conforms to the higher purposes of heaven. It is in this sense that "whatever might happen is always as it must be, and only for the best," as the narrator comments at the beginning of the novel. This does not mean, of course—as some Soviet critics have asserted—that Bulgakov is equating the coming Communist era with the "new heaven and new earth" (1:426) of Revelation.[52] There is, on the contrary, no indication that justice is imminent. In the ensuing battles the idealistic Nikolka will sacrifice his life while all signs point to the continued good fortune of the various dishonorable Talbergs and Shpolyanskys. Of those in the Turbin circle, only Elena's suitor and probable new husband, the opportunistic Shervinsky, can expect to thrive, as the song he sings in Elena's dream implies: "Live, we shall live!!" (1:427).

Rusakov, who has the final apocalyptic vision in the novel, envisages the Last Judgment still far in the future, beyond the rivers of blood that still await humanity. Only after millenia have passed will all be "judged according to their works" and will those whose names do not appear in the book of life perish. This long perspective, indeed, finally assuages Rusakov's torment, rids him of fear, and gives him peace: "Illnesses and suffering seemed to him unimportant, not essential . . . He saw the blue, bottomless haze of centuries, the corridor of millenia. And he did not experience fear, but wise submission and awe. His soul grew peaceful . . ." (1:426).

The final segment of the novel, describing a splendid starlit night, conforms to Rusakov's vision, for even at present, although God and His ways are not visible, the star-covered curtain of heaven hints at His presence beyond. The entire universe is like a church, with a vespers service taking place "in the immeasurable heights, behind the dark blue cloak at the holy gates" (1:427–428). At present, to be sure, Vladimir's "midnight cross," which "was rising from the sinful and bloodied and snowy earth into the black, murky heights," looks like a "menacing, sharp sword" (1:428). But if one takes the long view, the narrator concludes, fear—which has so long haunted Bulgakov's heroes—disappears, the sword "is not frightening. Everything will pass. Suffering, torments, blood, hunger, and pestilence. The sword will disappear, while the stars will remain even when the shadows of our bodies and deeds are gone from earth . . . So why is it that we do not wish to turn our gaze toward them? Why?"

In this conclusion to *The White Guard,* the narrator turns his eyes to the nocturnal heavens, as the authorial personae often did in the early works. As in *Notes on the Cuff* and "Unusual Adventures," the starlit sky here offers no immediate relief, and yet, because of the immensely broadened perspectives of the novel, the narrator finds consolation, a justification for the apparently needless suffering and unpunished outrages with which the novel abounds. The heavens, which existed before humanity and which will outlive it, become an emblem of eternity, a place where higher justice will finally prevail, beyond historical time and the bounds of the "sinful earth."

More Versions of the Autobiographical Hero

From Intellectual to Fighter: *Days of the Turbins*

White Guard: The Play

Even after Bulgakov completed *The White Guard,* the Turbins did not cease to fill his thoughts and dreams. The experience of Maksudov, the autobiographical hero of *Notes of a Dead Man (A Theatrical Novel),* was apparently close to the author's own. Maksudov describes how, some time after the publication of his novel, he was awakened one night by a snowstorm and there arose before him the people and setting about which he had written: "And again the same people, and again the distant city, and the side of a piano, and shots, and again someone flung down on the snow. These people were born in dreams, they came out from the dreams and settled down in my cell in a most permanent way. It was clear that I couldn't part from them just like that. But what could I do with them?" (4:434).

Maksudov's and Bulgakov's solutions were identical: they found a home for these people in another literary work, one written in the "three-dimensional" genre of drama. Bulgakov began working on his play on January 19, 1925, several months before *The White Guard* was even published.[1] Well after this date, on April 25, apparently by pure coincidence, he received a note from V. I. Vershilov, a director at the Moscow Art Theater, who had read the recently published first part of *The White Guard* and wanted Bulgakov to turn it into a play.[2]

The Moscow Art Theater was at a critical point in its history. The pioneer of a quarter of a century earlier had, in the context of the bold experimentation of Meyerhold and others, acquired the reputation of being hopelessly old-fashioned, both in its theatrical aesthetics and its repertoire.[3] It was therefore searching intensively for suitable Soviet plays and, owing to the scarcity of such, was turning to writers of narrative prose to adapt their works for the stage.[4] *The White Guard*, with its psychologically persuasive characters and lively dialogue, must have struck the theater as promising dramatic material, despite the novel's essentially lyrical construction.

The first version of the play, also entitled *The White Guard*, was completed in September 1925.[5] It was immensely long, although Bulgakov had already simplified the plot and eliminated certain characters:[6] gone entirely was the Shpolyansky subplot—and with it Aleksei's involvement with Yuliya Reiss and Rusakov—as well as most of the Petlyurite episodes. Nevertheless, much from the novel remains, including its mystical coloration and ideological ambiguity. The authorial persona, Aleksei Turbin, retains many of the traits of the character in the novel; he is a doctor, sensitive and high-strung, who acts as spokesman for the Whites and on occasion as *raisonneur* for the author.

At the same time, the new Aleksei has grown rather stronger, as a comparison of several key details indicates. Thus he does not repeat the act of kissing Talberg goodbye, which so tormented him in the novel—indeed, he does not say goodbye to his brother-in-law at all. And now the division commander, Malyshev, does not order him to report for duty in the afternoon, but at 8:00 A.M., only an hour after the troops. Most important, the doctor's role on the day of battle has changed fundamentally. He no longer plays the inept intellectual who pointlessly lingers too long. Now he remains and is wounded because of his determination to save Nikolka—thus displaying the familial devotion that is among the highest ethical ideals for Bulgakov. And although Aleksei does still witness Petlyurite atrocities, including the murder of a Jew, this now occurs only in a dream, and therefore there is no question of personal guilt.[7] The fact that he wakes up screaming and wishes in vain to help the Jew shows only his heightened moral sensitivity, a concern for others also demonstrated by his search for Nikolka.

If in this first version of the play Aleksei is thus already stronger than his predecessors, he remains a dramatically weak character whose primary function is lyrical. Even his main deed—the search for Nikolka—is soon overshadowed by Nai-Turs's far more heroic act of sacrificing his life to save the cadets.[8] The problem is further compounded because Aleksei's convictions are more than a little ideologically suspect. This is especially evident in the final act, when the Turbins and their friends hold a mock meeting to decide what to do in the face of the Bolsheviks' impending arrival.

In the play, here and in subsequent versions, the Bolsheviks' entry into Kiev has shifted from its actual historical date, February 2, to January 19, the eve of the Epiphany. The reason is elucidated by the 1925 proofs of the novel, which begin on Epiphany eve and end on February 2. The play, observing the laws of dramatic economy, simply telescopes the two episodes. Bulgakov explained to a friend why he retained the Epiphany setting, even though it entailed historical inaccuracy: "It was important to use a Christmas tree in the last act."[9] In the 1925 proofs the tree is clearly associated with Aleksei's "death" and "resurrection." If on Christmas Eve the formalin used to treat the dying Aleksei killed the first tree, "the second, and last will not perish today, on Epiphany eve. It will be, it is, and here he, Turbin, got up yesterday . . . And his wound is healing marvelously. Supernaturally" (1:525). The play thus counterpoises the tree, linked to the eternal mystery of death and resurrection, to the destructive transformations of the Bolsheviks.[10]

The notion of eternal forms in the midst of change is also central in the discussion in the final act. Nikolka and Studzinsky advocate going abroad to fight for the Whites, but Myshlaevsky and Aleksei decide to remain in Russia. Aleksei bases his decision not on ideological grounds but on the belief that, whatever changes might occur, something eternally Russian will survive. This view was also held by the Russian émigré "Change of Landmarks" movement (smenovekhovstvo),[11] and Myshlaevsky's remark, "I'm for the Bolsheviks, only I'm against the Communists" (p. 105), strengthens the connection. While seemingly just a comical indication of his political illiteracy, his words echo a characterization of "Change of Landmarks" in an article published just when Bulgakov was working on this first version of the play (and which contains a critique of *The Fatal Eggs*, making it very likely that he read it): "'Change of Landmarks' has tossed out the slogan: long live Soviet Russia—down with Communism! . . . *Such is the slogan of all fellow travellers, in all fields.* Long live the Bolsheviks, as the regenerators of great Russia, down with the commune, as international utopia!"[12]

Bulgakov himself and other less than fully committed writers were frequently accused of sympathy for "Change of Landmarks"—a charge made more plausible because of his connection with the group's newspaper, *Nakanune*. Whether or not this was the case,[13] the writer apparently considered such views—not an instant conversion to Communism—as psychologically the most plausible motivation for his heroes' decision to remain in Russia. For the ideological guardians of the mid-twenties, however, the characters would have to welcome the Bolsheviks more unambiguously.

If the first Aleksei Turbin of the play thus proved not only dramatically ineffective but ideologically unacceptable, the problem was compounded by the fact that the truly heroic characters, Malyshev and Nai-Turs (already combined in the revision of the first redaction) are but episodic figures who appear only in the battle scenes and play no role in the larger action. This double dilemma surely accounts at least in part for the radical change made in the second version of the play, one that remains intact in the final redaction: the merging of Aleksei Turbin, Malyshev, and Nai-Turs. The change, according to Bulgakov's second wife, was suggested by Stanislavsky, the codirector of the theater, but apparently the author did not put up much resistance. He "hesitated," she recalls, and "was sorry to part with Nai-Turs, but he understood that Stanislavsky was right."[14]

One would think that Bulgakov would have felt sorrier to part with the old Aleksei, since in the new version all that remains of his authorial persona is the name; the sensitive, contemplative doctor has been totally transformed into a masterful, fearless colonel. Yet (although a degree of coercion was most likely involved) there is a certain inner logic to this most extreme metamorphosis of the persona. For if the earlier doctor heroes were tormented by their weakness, racked by guilt and an irrational sense of responsibility for the atrocities they witnessed but could not prevent, in the colonel Bulgakov creates a strong character who actually *is* responsible for others, who can and does save lives. After gradually strengthening the authorial persona, Bulgakov here replaces him entirely by one who possesses all he lacks. In this sense, the transformation of Aleksei Turbin may not be simply the result of external pressure but of deep inner impulses.

In any case, the ramifications of the change for the play as a whole are many and profound. Indeed, the entire tone changes, as Aleksei becomes an exemplar, quiet, commanding, sober. Thus, in that touchstone episode, the farewell scene with Talberg, Aleksei no longer experiences any of the inhibitions of his former self but enters into open conflict with his brother-in-law. Even a duel is intimated, and only the entrance of Elena cuts short the exchange. In general, Aleksei has become a rather abstract, idealized figure, lacking the concrete particularity not only of his former self but of his other component parts, Malyshev and Nai-Turs. What the play has gained in dramatic economy, therefore, it loses in liveliness and psychological-moral complexity. This was perhaps one reason for another fundamental structural change: the arrival of the Turbins' hapless cousin, Lariosik, in the first instead of the fourth act. This increases the comic, parodic ambience surrounding the Turbins from the very beginning.

Because of the comic diminishment of the Turbin milieu, the heroic Aleksei now stands somewhat apart from his family circle. He has grown sober and cautious and no longer gets drunk in the banquet scene but warns the others not to drink too much. While he expresses some of the same sentiments Doctor Turbin did before, the colonel is more terse, far-sighted, and gloomy. He senses impending disaster and even has a presentiment of the grave: "on the parade ground . . . it was snowing, fog in the distance, and, you know, it seemed to me I saw a coffin".[15] And when all sing the tsarist anthem at the end of the scene, he does not join them as previously, but warns them: "Gentlemen, what are you doing! You mustn't" (Milne, p. 45).

The most important structural change accompanying Aleksei's transformation is his death in the middle of the play. Like Malyshev previously, he dismisses the troops in the gymnasium when he hears of the hetman's treachery. He himself, however, refuses to leave until the support troops arrive. When they do, he orders them to run, while he, like Nai-Turs, stands fast and dies in order to save his men. A remark Nikolka made earlier hints that, aside from the safety of his troops, a second motive led Aleksei to remain: "I know why you're sitting [here]. I know. You—the commander—are waiting for death because of the disgrace" (Milne, p. 74). While it is unlikely that Aleksei commits suicide, as some have suggested,[16] it appears that by confronting death he seeks to reverse the "disgrace" of his superiors, who in fleeing violated the moral code of their class. By defending his men to the last, Aleksei alone (except for Nikolka, who remains by his side as he earlier did with Nai-Turs) unbendingly follows his principles, although they result in his death. He—like Streltsov in "The Raid," Nai in the novel, and Yeshua in *The Master and Margarita*—achieves the highest level of heroism not by killing others but through self-sacrifice.

Because of Aleksei's early death, the functions the authorial persona formerly filled in the later acts of the play and in the earlier fictions are transferred to other characters. Thus, it is Nikolka, only slightly hurt in the first redaction, who is now seriously wounded, and it is Myshlaevsky alone who at the end advocates remaining in Russia. The constant theme of the early prose, guilt for the death of another, is transferred to Studzinsky, who, after Elena reproaches Aleksei's friends for his death, attempts to shoot himself. Finally, the two central themes of love and loyalty are developed through the unlikely character of Elena's admirer, Shervinsky, a much more important figure here than in the novel.[17]

In the novel Shervinsky is the only morally ambiguous friend of the Turbins, an inveterate liar who, with his highly developed instinct for survival, resembles most the detestable Talberg. In the play, however, he proves his superiority to Elena's husband by refusing to leave with the hetman when told he could not take her with him. He then calls Colonel Turbin and warns him of the hetman's flight, explaining: "I'm informing you because I feel sorry for our officers . . . Save the division." When he hangs up, he declares (uttering the same words as Nikolka in the novel after burying Nai-Turs): "And my conscience is clear and calm." Although Shervinsky later goes back to his irresponsible, mendacious ways, his practice here of the familial virtues of loyalty and personal responsibility outweighs his flaws. Therefore it is now he who is given the symbolic act performed by Aleksei in the novel of tearing up Talberg's portrait, after which he repeats: "And my conscience is clear and calm" (Milne, p. 93).

In general outline the final act follows the same course as in the first version, except, of course, for the absence of Aleksei. Here once again Studzinsky and Nikolka advocate going abroad, while Myshlaevsky alone defends the idea of remaining in Russia. As yet no one expresses active support for the Bolsheviks. Indeed, the play's finale (almost identical with that of the first version) emphasizes, through music and lighting as well as dialogue, the noninvolvement of the Whites in the new world. Thus, when they hear a cannon salute announcing the arrival of the Bolsheviks, the Turbins and their friends sit down to play cards. And when Nikolka begins to sing the Communist "International" ("Arise"), Myshlaevsky makes it clear that, although he has left the White Army, he is not about to join the Bolsheviks: "Arise! I've only just settled down comfortably and again arise! No, I won't arise any more, dear comrades" (Milne, p. 103). Nikolka then repeats the cadet song he sang at the play's beginning, substituting a valedictory "Farewell, citizens" (Milne, p. 104) for the initial "Hello, vacationers," and distant music, signaling the arrival of the Bolsheviks, "blends strangely with Nikolka's guitar."

At the conclusion Lariosik declares, in his usual rapturous way: "You know—this evening is a great prologue to a new historical play..." (Milne,

p. 104). Once again, however, Myshlaevsky prevents the play from rising to a rhetorical pro-Bolshevik crescendo, declaring: "But no, for some it's a prologue, but for me it's an epilogue. Comrade viewers, it's the end of the White Guard. Nonparty member, Captain Second Class Myshlaevsky, is leaving the stage." The lights then go out. Only Nikolka remains illuminated, but after singing two more lines, he too "is extinguished and disappears." The ending makes it clear that none of the White Guard are about to take an active part in the new world. On the contrary, the blackout conveys in forceful theatrical language Myshlaevsky's assertion that he—and with him the entire White movement—will disappear, will "leave the stage" of history.

The second version of the play went into rehearsal on January 24, 1926. It aroused high hopes, with Stanislavsky himself—at first skeptical about the undertaking—declaring that the production was "on the right path," that the work done so far was "correct, successful, and necessary."[18] At the same time, however, this was a period of collective revisions that forced upon Bulgakov many painful compromises.[19] He did resist Stanislavsky's demands for a change of title—from *The White Guard* to *Before the End*—and for the removal of the scene of Petlyurite brutality.[20] He was unable, however, to stand fast against the Main Repertory Committee (*Glavrepertkom*, the rather euphemistic name of the censorship board), among whose members were V. Blyum and A. Orlinsky, two vigilant critics who were to be among Bulgakov's most active persecutors. Blyum condemned the play as "an out and out apologia for the White Guards," while Orlinsky demanded that the Whites be shown more negatively and endorsed the suggestion of the play's director, Ilya Sudakov, that Nikolka, as the youngest, reject the White cause and become the "embodiment of a turn to the Bolsheviks."[21] The theater acquiesced to these revisions as well as to a change of title to *Days of the Turbins*, but it still took the intervention of the Commissar of Enlightenment himself, Anatoly Lunacharsky—and, it seems, someone yet higher up in government, perhaps Stalin himself—for the play finally to win approval.[22] Moreover, a few more changes were still required: the episode of the Petlyurites' murder of a Jew was removed, and at the end the Communist "International" gradually grew louder rather than softer.[23]

Once the play received approval (for performance only at the Moscow Art Theater), the polemics only intensified. Even before the scheduled opening on October 5, public discussions were held at which the work was violently attacked—not only by the likes of Orlinsky and Blyum but also by such outstanding cultural figures as Lunacharsky (in spite of his support for the production) and the great Futurist poet, Vladimir Mayakovsky.[24] Nevertheless the play was allowed to open, although its author was not invited to attend the premiere.

Days of the Turbins

While *Days of the Turbins* remains one of the best Soviet plays, the final alterations made under coercion seriously mar the work. Thus the last-minute elimination of the episode depicting the killing of the Jew much diminishes the sense of raw horror the Petlyurite atrocities produced in Bulgakov's works. In keeping with Orlinsky's directive, moreover, the aura of nobility surrounding the Whites is lessened in a number of small ways. Shervinsky's high-minded motives for warning Colonel Turbin are toned down, and in the gymnasium scene the division is shown in a more negative light. This serves to isolate the heroic commander from his petty, squabbling troops, much as he is set apart from his family and friends in the first act.[25] Of greater importance from an ideological point of view (and less justifiable, both aesthetically and psychologically) is Colonel Turbin's recognition shortly before his death of the utter hopelessness of the White cause: "I tell you: it's the end of the White movement in Ukraine . . . The people are not with us. They are against us. That means it's over!"[26] In the first and second versions, Myshlaevsky already came to essentially the same conclusion by the end of the play, but the recognition of the bankruptcy of the Whites' cause by their most noble and valiant representative halfway through the work fundamentally alters the ideological tone.

In the last act, the characters' attitude toward coming events has also been much realigned. Now Studzinsky is the only one who advocates remaining with the Whites, for, following Orlinsky's directive, Nikolka has changed sides. There are, however, hints in the text that Bulgakov resisted Nikolka's facile shift to the Bolsheviks. The younger Turbin, so loquacious in earlier versions, is now muted because he has been more seriously wounded than previously and has been left a cripple (pp. 114, 119). This creates the impression that not only Aleksei but Nikolka as well—the very best representatives of the old world—have disappeared as active participants in the future. The main roles at the end are left to lesser figures: the rather colorless Studzinsky and the highly engaging, but more limited, Myshlaevsky.

Myshlaevsky's attitude toward the Bolsheviks in the final play becomes, predictably, much more positive. It is not enough for him simply to announce his unwillingness to fight on either side; he now expresses a readiness to join the Bolsheviks: "Let them [the Bolsheviks] mobilize me! At least I'll know that I'll be serving in the Russian army. The people are not with us. The people are against us. Aleshka was right!" (p. 117).[27] And now his "Change of Landmarks" remark from the play's first version—"I am for the Bolsheviks, only I'm against the Communists"—is restored and expanded. When Lariosik informs him that Bolshevism and Communism are the same thing, Myshlaevsky retorts: "Well then, I'm also for the Communists" (p. 116).

The play's earlier subtle and theatrically effective ending suffered most from the interference of the censors. Even here, however, through the use of musical motifs, Bulgakov preserved in the midst of the general jubilation at least a hint of the former sense of foreboding and uncertainty. Nikolka now repeats a military song he sang in the first act, a musical setting of Pushkin's "The Lay of Wise Oleg," which retells a medieval legend about a soothsayer's prophecy of Prince Oleg's death and its later fulfillment. Earlier the song hinted at the misfortunes awaiting the Turbins, and its repetition near the conclusion points to the trials they have endured and, perhaps, to those that still lie ahead. Nikolka then begins the song's rousing refrain: "So, band, play the victory louder/ We have vanquished, the enemy is running, running, running" (p. 121). Instead of singing the final couplet, however—"So for the tsar, the homeland, and the faith,/ We roar out a friendly: 'Hurrah! Hurrah! Hurrah!'"[28] (which even in the first act only the impulsive Lariosik sang aloud and only up to the word "tsar")— Myshlaevsky substitutes: "So for the Council of People's Commissars..." Then all but Studzinsky burst out with a triple "Hurrah!" Bulgakov, however, does not end the musical sequence on this major accord but has Nikolka repeat the disquieting Pushkin lines, leaving in the text a small hint of future ill fortune: "From the dark forest there came/ To meet him the inspired soothsayer..."[29]

Only the most attentive reading, however, reveals this echo of a previous conception, which is now all but drowned out by the booming Bolshevik cannon salute and the crescendoing sound of the "International." This time no card games or cadet songs distract the Turbins, and at the sound of the Communist anthem Myshlaevsky does not refuse to "arise" as before. He declares momentously: "Gentlemen, do you hear? The Reds are coming" (p. 122), and all run to the window.

The play concludes with Nikolka and Studzinsky mouthing the dialogue formerly given to Lariosik and Myshlaevsky, thereby robbing it of its wry irony and humor. Nikolka utters his only positive statement about the Bolshevik future in a rhetorical style more characteristic of the flowery Lariosik: "Gentlemen, this evening is a great prologue to a new historical play" (p. 122). Bulgakov thus formally fulfills Orlinsky's demand that Nikolka turn to the Bolsheviks at the end. Yet by making him a cripple, the author robs the act of its symbolic implications, the link between the strength and enthusiasm of youth and the Communists. Moreover, he still gives the last word to the unrepentant White, Studzinsky, although within the context of universal conversion to the Reds his course seems all the more doomed: "For some a prologue, and for some an epilogue."

Days of the Turbins immediately enjoyed immense success with the public and made Bulgakov a famous writer. Predictably, however, the play was greeted by a veritable howl of abuse from the critics—some of it of the most scurrilous kind. Particularly vicious were the author's *Glavrepertkom* enemies, Orlinsky even coining the strange word, "Bulgakovism" *(Bulgakovshchina)*.[30] Bulgakov himself recalled in his 1930 letter to the Soviet government how critics branded Aleksei Turbin a "son of a bitch" and called the author "'a literary janitor,' picking up the leavings after 'a dozen guests have vomited all over'" (5:444). There was, however, one viewer whose opinion outweighed all the rest and who liked the play very much: Joseph Stalin.[31]

The Intellectual as Fighter: *Notes of a Young Doctor* and "I Killed"

Notes of a Young Doctor

In August 1925, at the very time Bulgakov was working on the first version of *Days of the Turbins,* his story "The Steel Throat" appeared in the magazine *Krasnaia panorama (Red Panorama)*. Subtitled "Story of a Young Doctor," it was followed that year and the next by several closely related works, published in the doctors' journal *Meditsinskii rabotnik (The Medical Worker)*.[32] Footnotes to several of the stories indicate that a collection entitled *Notes of a Young Doctor* was planned, but it never appeared. Only in the 1960s were these attractive, vivid works unearthed from the obscure periodicals in which they lay buried, thus revealing another facet of the author's many-sided talent.[33]

The idea of writing about his life as a *zemstvo* doctor dates back, as we have seen, to 1919, and by autumn of that year Bulgakov had already written *Notes of a Zemstvo Doctor*.[34] The deceptively artless style of the published stories has led some to assert that they are essentially identical with the first variant.[35] Although the plot kernels (based upon autobiographical material) can, in all probability, be traced back to the early sketches, on the whole this assertion is unconvincing, and other investigators have assumed that the story cycle in its final form was written shortly before publication.[36] For one thing, the apparent simplicity and relaxed tone of *Notes of a Young Doctor* are actually not characteristic of Bulgakov's earliest works, with their artistic self-consciousness and extreme intensity. *Notes of a Young Doctor*, moreover, differs fundamentally from the earliest autobiographical stories in its use of the first-person narrator. While *Notes on the Cuff* and "Unusual Adventures of a Doctor" reproduce the narrator's diary, his impressions in the thick of events, now he is writing well after the fact, looking back at his younger self with a mellowness and affectionate irony that only time bestows. Occasionally he mentions the time lapse explicitly, as in "Towel with a Rooster," where he comments on the futile attempts of his younger self to look older than his twenty-three years: "As I understand now, after the passage of many years, all of that turned out very badly" (1:73–74). While this may be a later interpolation, emphasis upon the hero's extreme youth and inexperience throughout the narratives suggest that the stories were written much later.

Both in imagery and in the depiction of the protagonist, to be sure, *Notes of a Young Doctor* does have ties to the earlier works. Thus the opposition of city and country, with storms and chaotic darkness linked to the uncivilized countryside and its peasant inhabitants, is again apparent (although placed in an ostensibly nonrevolutionary context).[37] Here once more the hero finds refuge in his dwelling place, the cold and darkness without contrasted to images of warmth and light (both physical and intellectual) associated with the doctor's residence: the stove ("The snowstorm began to drone somewhere in the flues . . . A blessing on fire, warming the medical staff out in the sticks!" ["Egyptian Darkness," 1:115]); the green desk lamp in the doctor's study ("In a few minutes I was at the green lamp . . . My pale face was reflected in the pitch-black glass [of the window]," ["Towel with a Rooster," 1:82]); the lantern at the hospital entrance ("We rode for a long, long time until the small but ever so joyous, eternally dear lantern twinkled at the hospital gate" ["The Missing Eye," 1:127]).

As in *The White Guard* especially, the positive connotations of light in *Notes of a Young Doctor* are best exemplified by the city: "Where are the electric lamps of Moscow? People? The sky? Outside the windows there is nothing! Darkness..." ("Egyptian Darkness," 1:112). The city's lights and glitter, moreover, are not mere external show but are the outward sign of its function as center of enlightenment—most important the locale of the university, whose splendid clinic stands as the young doctor's ideal: "In the dreams that were born to the light of the lamp with the green shade, there arose a huge university city, and in it a clinic, and in the clinic—an immense hall, a tile floor, glittering faucets, white sterile sheets, an assistant with a pointed, very wise, graying beard..." ("Egyptian Darkness," 1:117).

As for the young doctor himself, he is akin in numerous ways to the early, timid authorial personae. He too is fearful and filled with self-pity when he first comes to the unstructured, chaotic countryside: "I confess that in a burst of faintheartedness I whispered a curse upon medicine and upon the application I had submitted five years before to the rector of the university" ("Towel with a Rooster," 1:71). This "faintheartedness" (*malodushie*, a word the hero repeatedly applies to himself, together with the related adverb, *malodushno*) stems primarily from a sense of inadequacy to his mission: the struggle against death and disease.[38] Having arrived directly from medical school with no clinical experience, the doctor conjures up on his first night the terrible diseases he will be called upon to treat and works himself into a virtual panic. Rather humorously, he is particularly frightened by the idea of a hernia and "faintheartedly leafed through a pharmaceutical guide" in search of a treatment. Fear's "demonic voice," however, continues to taunt him until he "surrendered and almost burst out crying" ("Towel with a Rooster," 1:76).

The young doctor also shares the early heroes' urge to flee: "I very much wanted to run away there [to the district town] from my station. They had electricity there, four doctors, one could consult with them, in any case it wouldn't be so terrifying" ("The Steel Throat," 1:92). The important difference between the young doctor and the heroes of Bulgakov's earlier works is that, inspired by the high principles of his medical calling, he overcomes his urge to flee: "But there was no possibility of running away, and at times I myself understood that this was faintheartedness. After all, it was precisely for this reason that I had studied at medical school..." (1:92). If his ability to surmount his "faintheartedness" distinguishes the young doctor from the earliest heroes, it allies him with Aleksei Turbin of *The White Guard*.

Indeed, the psychological process leading to the doctor's conquest of fear is akin to Aleksei's experience when pursued by the Petlyurites: "superfluous" reason drops away and a second personality emerges, reversing the workings of his conscious mind.[39] This occurs on the doctor's very first night at his post, when a young girl whose legs were mutilated by a flax-braking machine is brought to him ("Towel with a Rooster"). Although his reason tells him "there is nothing more to be done here" (1:79), the doctor, "not recognizing his own voice," nevertheless calls for camphor. His assistants protest that it is pointless to try to save the girl, and the doctor himself prays that she might die as quickly as possible, but then: "Everything grew light in my brain." This light, having little to do with his conscious, terrified mind, guides the doctor, and, without help from people or books, he performs the operation brilliantly: "Only my common sense, urged on by the unusual nature of the situation, worked for me. With a circular motion and adroitly, I slashed the thigh with an extremely sharp knife, like an experienced butcher, and the skin parted without giving a single drop of blood" (1:80). After the amputation, the doctor's assistant tries to persuade him not to touch the second leg, and the doctor himself hopes only that the girl will wait to die until he leaves the operating room. Nevertheless, "prodded by an unknown force" (1:81), he sets the second leg in a cast "with inspiration," and by a miracle the patient survives.

The emergence of a double personality when facing a dangerous operation is even more apparent in "The Steel Throat," where the doctor, confronted with a critical case of diphtheria, decides to perform a tracheotomy. The passage deserves to be quoted at length:

> "Here's what," I said, amazed at my own calmness, "this is how things are. It's late. The little girl is dying. And nothing will help her except for one thing: an operation."
>
> And I myself wondered in horror why I said it, but I could not help but say it. "And if they agree?" the thought flashed through my mind . . .
>
> "I don't agree!" the mother said sharply . . .
>
> "Well, as you like," I added hollowly and thought: "Well, that's it! I'm relieved. I said it, suggested it . . . They refused, and I'm saved." But I had only just thought this when another someone uttered for me in a stranger's voice: "What, have you lost your mind? What do you mean, you don't agree? You are destroying your little girl. Agree." . . .
>
> "No!" screamed the mother once more.

Within myself I thought this: "What am I doing? After all, I will slaughter the girl." But I said something else:

"Well, come on, come on, agree! Agree! After all, her nails are already turning blue." (1:95–96)

The mother finally agrees and the doctor, who has never even seen a tracheotomy, proceeds. His fear does not disappear during the operation, and when it at first seems that he has failed, he is filled with remorse and fright: "I wanted to ask someone's forgiveness, to confess to my frivolity for having enrolled in medical school . . . I already wanted to throw everything over and burst out crying" (1:98). He does ultimately succeed, however, through a combination of talent and luck. And so the doctor once again transcends himself at a moment of crisis, a new self arising involuntarily and supplanting the ordinary, timorous conscious personality.

It is fitting that when his new self takes over the doctor, like Aleksei Turbin in *The White Guard,* is said to behave "like a wolf" ("Towel with a Rooster," 1:80). In *Notes of a Young Doctor,* however, it is not simply animal instinct at work but a synthesis of the hero's moral nature, his innate gifts, and his knowledge. This combination of character, talent, and knowledge is shown most clearly in "Baptism by Rotation," where the doctor must perform a dangerous delivery for which he feels woefully unprepared. He runs back to his office to check a textbook but can make no sense of it. The midwife then briefly describes the procedures followed by the previous doctor, an experienced surgeon, and this teaches him more than all his textbooks. Of equal importance, he draws from his own innate gifts and moral strength, from "the sense of measure, without which a doctor is good for nothing . . . I should be calm and cautious and at the same time boundlessly decisive, fearless [*netrusliv*]" (1:89). Guided by his inner resources, the doctor successfully delivers the baby alive. The narrator is not suggesting here that book learning is superfluous; indeed, when he looks again at the textbook after the operation, "an interesting thing occurred: all the previously dark spots became entirely comprehensible, as if flooded with light, and here, to the light of a lamp, at night, out in the sticks, I understood what real knowledge means" (1:91). He concludes: "One can acquire a lot of experience in the country, . . . only one must read, read, a little more... read..."

The doctor's confrontations with death do not always end successfully, and when he fails his sense of guilt and self-reproach rivals that in the early stories. Thus he thinks, after the delivery of a stillborn baby whose arm he broke: "I felt defeated, broken, crushed by cruel fate . . . Take away my diploma, I am unworthy of it, dear colleagues, send me to Sakhalin" ("The Missing Eye," 1:126). Like the hero of *Notes on the Cuff,* he uses demeaning animal imagery, comparing himself to a "pitiful dog, a hound, homeless and incompetent" (1:127). In contrast to the heroes of the early prose, however, the doctor quickly quells such feelings. The sight of the "eternally dear lantern" outside the hospital makes him abandon his fruitless self-laceration and recall his positive achievement: "The arm is nonsense. You broke it when the infant was already dead. You mustn't think of the arm, but of the fact that the mother is alive."

In general, this process of overcoming setbacks, of not succumbing to despair and self-doubt, recurs often in the stories. The narrator tells how "every day my work in the God-forsaken sticks [*v zabytoi glushi*] brought me amazing cases, insidious [*kaverznye*] things, forcing me to exhaust my brain, to be at a loss hundreds of times, and once more to find my presence of mind and once more to take wing in the struggle" ("The Starry Rash," 1:138). Through this constant confrontation with disease and his own fears the doctor gradually grows stronger.

He encounters one more obstacle, however, which proves more intractable than his fears and than disease itself: the woeful ignorance of the peasants. This provides the central theme for two stories, "Egyptian Darkness" and "The Starry Rash." "Egyptian Darkness" opens on a dark, stormy night on which the medical staff is celebrating the doctor's birthday. They tell anecdotes showing the abysmal ignorance and superstition of the peasants, and the darkness without comes to be identified with their patients' inner benightedness. After his guests leave, the doctor vows to fight against this blackness: "I will struggle against the Egyptian darkness for precisely as long as fate keeps me here in the sticks" (1:117). That very same evening he has a chance to test his words on a miller who has contracted malaria. Although the miller seems to the doctor a reasonable man, "truly a ray of light in the darkness" (1:119), subsequent events prove him wrong, for the patient almost kills himself by swallowing all his quinine at once. Yet in spite of his disappointment, the doctor vows to continue his struggle: "The Egyptian darkness spread out like a shroud... and I appear to be in it... with something like a sword, or perhaps a stethoscope. I am walking... I am struggling... Out in the sticks" (1:121). The sardonic concluding words of the story—"A dream is a nice thing!..." ("*Son—khoroshaia shtuka!...*")—reminds the reader that reality does not live up to this vision. Nevertheless, the ideal, however distorted in actuality, continues to guide the doctor, who, in spite of his *malodushie*, becomes a genuine hero.

"The Starry Rash" shows how the treatment of one disease—syphilis—is a battle against both the physical and spiritual maladies of illness and ignorance. The doctor finds, indeed, that the main problem is not so much the disease itself as the peasants' unwillingness to understand its gravity, that "what was terrifying there about syphilis is that it was not terrifying" (1:144). Therefore he engages in an all-out struggle, and, in spite of many reverses, his resolve does not waver. In the process he himself changes: "I grew more mature [*vozmuzhal*], became focused, at times gloomy."

The degree of his determination is revealed one day when a young woman with three little children comes to him. She, typically, is dubious when he says they are suffering from a "dangerous, terrible illness" (1:145), but he frightens her into remaining in the clinic. On the wake of this victory, the doctor tells his assistant that he plans to get permission to open an inpatient syphilis ward. The assistant is incredulous, but the hero repeats doggedly: "I will get it." Indeed, a month later he achieves his goal. However ill-equipped the clinic might be, the "syringe lay . . . proudly" there (1:146). Furthermore, although still "mentally dying of fright" each time he has to give the difficult injections, the doctor's "soul was much calmer."

That the struggle is not over is apparent when the woman with the children insists upon leaving before completing the treatment. The doctor calls her a fool, adding: "You look at Vanka! What, do you want to destroy him? Well, I won't let you do it!" (1:146). The woman agrees to stay another ten days, and the narrator does not regret having called her a fool: "What is swearing in comparison to the starry rash!" His abrasive bedside manner here (typical of his relations with his patients) is justified, for he is thereby fulfilling the intellectual's duty to speak out, so regularly abrogated in the early works. Although his words result in only partial success (the extra ten days are insufficient), he is sure that nobody could have done more, and therefore his "conscience was calm." These words—almost identical to Nikolka's in *The White Guard* after burying Nai-Turs and Shervinsky's in *Days of the Turbins* after warning Aleksei of the hetman's desertion—indicate that the authorial persona himself has at last achieved the eradication of that guilt with which previous fictional embodiments have been plagued.

The positive image of self and of the intellectual in general in *Notes of a Young Doctor* is conveyed symbolically in "The Blizzard,"[40] where the doctor and his driver are caught in a raging snowstorm while returning home from a medical emergency. The hero, as so often, is at first treated ironically as he succumbs to self-pity and hypochondria: "Then I began feeling sorry for myself: how hard my life is. People are sleeping now, their stoves are heated up . . . A blizzard is bearing me like a leaf. Well, and so I'll come home and, for all I know, I'll again be taken away somewhere . . . And so I'll catch pneumonia and I myself will drop dead here" (1:107–108). He then falls asleep and when he wakes up discovers that they have lost their way in the storm. Once again the doctor is filled with self-pity and fear but he overcomes his terror, much as he does in his medical practice. Reproaching himself for his "fainteartedness" (1:108) and warning the driver that "we mustn't give in to our despondency" (1:109), he takes over the reins and leads them out onto a road in about fifteen minutes.

Their troubles are not over, however, for they are soon pursued by wolves, and at first the timorous side of the doctor's character again comes to the fore. As the beasts approach the sleigh—a tiny island of humanity in the boundless sea of wild nature—he fearfully pictures an announcement of their death in some obscure corner of the newspaper. But then his other self emerges and, taking out his revolver, he says "in a voice, but not [his] own": "I'm going to shoot now" (1:110). After he shoots, the doctor is once more filled with "mortal terror" when what feels like an immense, sinewy body falls on his chest. It turns out, however, to be only a heavy sheepskin. The wolves are nowhere to be seen and the doctor spies instead "a most enchanting eye, which I would have recognized from out of a thousand . . .—the lantern of my hospital was twinkling." The doctor's successful struggle against the wild forces of nature is thus rewarded with the light of home and the hospital. The pattern here is similar to that in *The White Guard* when Aleksei escapes from the Petlyurites. Both men are at first terrified when threatened by death, but then a second self takes over and shoots at the pursuers. And both are granted shelter.

Earlier, when the doctor found himself stranded in a howling snowstorm, he felt "angry with Leo Tolstoy" (1:108), a hint of a polemical stance toward Tolstoy's novella, *Master and Man,* which also depicts a man and his driver lost in a snowstorm. Tolstoy's work shows how the indigent, downtrodden driver, by calmly submitting both to raging nature and to death—and thereby to God's will—proves wiser than his wealthy passenger. The latter, terrified at sacrificing his worldly goods, tries in vain to escape death. Only at the end, when he gives up his fruitless efforts and lies on top of his dying driver—thus saving another's life by sacrificing his own—does he achieve a joyful epiphany, yielding to the purposes of God and nature. In "The Blizzard," in contrast, the doctor saves the driver (and himself) not by submitting to the elements and to death but by actively struggling against them. Indeed, this struggle against death and treacherous nature is emblematic of the lofty mission of the doctor in general. Nature, in *Notes of a Young Doctor* and in much of Bulgakov's early fiction, is, in contrast to Tolstoy's story, something that must be transcended if one is to become a full-fledged human being. Therefore the person who stands both morally and cognitively above the perilous elemental world, who is willing to struggle against chaotic darkness and death, is the ideal. For this reason, as the story's conclusion indicates, the doctor will willingly go out again into the blizzard in order to continue his struggle. At first, to be sure, he repeats the driver's words: "Ply me with gold . . . but I wouldn't [go out] any more . . ." (1:111). But the blizzard itself retorts: "You'll go... you'll go-o-o..."

"The Missing Eye" sums up the young doctor's many achievements and few failures during his year at the country hospital. Most emphasized are the changes that have taken place in him. When he looks at his face in the mirror, he observes the marks that the terrifying and complicated cases of the past year have left: "My eyes became sterner and more restless, and my mouth more confident and manly, the crease at the bridge of my nose will remain my whole life, as will my memories" (1:127). The stern visage of the matured doctor recalls that of the "resurrected" Aleksei Turbin in the final version of the conclusion of *The White Guard*, written after the story: "The folds had apparently adhered forever to his face, at the corners of his mouth, . . . his eyes had sunk in shadows and had become forever unsmiling and gloomy" (1:413). This suggests that the portrait of the young doctor, while influenced by the Aleksei of *The White Guard*, at the same time contributed to the stronger image of the hero as he appears in the final redaction of the last chapter.

As the young doctor recalls his accomplishments of the past year, he feels entirely purged of the fear that he, in common with earlier autobiographical heroes, had at first experienced: "I . . . lay in bed and, while falling asleep, I thought how enormous my experience now was. What do I have to be afraid of? Nothing . . . My hand is courageous, it does not tremble . . . How I trembled formerly from a knock at the door, how I mentally cowered in fear... But now..." (1:131). The story ends, it is true, on a gently ironic note, as the hero encounters a mysterious case of a disappearing and reappearing eye that he is incapable of diagnosing. Chastened by this experience, he regrets his former overconfidence: "Never, even when falling asleep, will I proudly mumble that nothing can surprise me" (1:133). The struggle is far from over and the main weapon continues to be knowledge: "It means that one must humbly study." This cautionary ending, however, like the light self-irony that marks the cycle as a whole, by no means casts doubt upon either the loftiness of the doctor's mission or upon his worthiness to pursue it. On the contrary, the fact that the young doctor is still far from his goal makes the ideal yet higher and his efforts to reach it all the more heroic.

One small but significant indication of the authorial persona's changed image (since the early Civil War stories) is the hero's shift in attitude toward those adventure tales that Bulgakov himself was fond of as a boy. In "Unusual Adventures," we recall, Doctor N reveals his timorous nature by expressing his hatred of Fenimore Cooper and Sherlock Holmes. The young doctor, on the contrary, declares "how as a child I craved for Cooper's *The Pathfinder*" ("The Missing Eye," 1:125) and later compares himself to Sherlock Holmes: "I have seen all kinds of stumpers [*kaverzy*] . . . I figure them out as Sherlock Holmes does his mysterious documents. . ." (1:131).

The young doctor does, to be sure, share certain traits with Doctor N and other early heroes. He too likes nothing better than to pore over the books in his warm study to the light of a green lamp. And, as we have seen, he is also filled with fear and self-doubt. At the critical moment, however, a bolder self comes to the fore, and he is transformed into a valiant fighter. Indeed, his struggle is often presented in military terms: the doctor's daily effort to save lives is a "battle" ("The Blizzard," 1:101) in which, armed with stethoscope instead of sword and accompanied by his medical legions ("The Egyptian Darkness," 1:121), he is usually a "conqueror" ("Baptism by Rotation," 1:91) but is occasionally "vanquished" ("The Missing Eye," 1:126). The difficulty of this combat is overwhelming, and sometimes the hero is discouraged: "They can bring me whatever insidious or complicated case they like, most often a surgical one, and I must face it, with my unshaven face, and conquer it. And if you don't conquer it, go ahead and suffer" ("The Missing Eye," 1:126). In spite of the difficulty, however, the hero does not give up and is usually victorious.

In *The Notes of a Young Doctor*, Bulgakov thus succeeds in reconstructing that childhood ideal of self as adventurous, chivalrous, and strong that was destroyed during the trials of the Civil War. He thereby creates a positive image of the intellectual, strikingly at variance with his earliest portrayals of the type. The restoration, as we have seen, was a gradual one, with an important breakthrough achieved in the depiction of Aleksei Turbin in *The White Guard*. At the end of the novel, even of the first version, Aleksei is deemed worthy of resuming his medical calling. And in his role as physician in *Notes of a Young Doctor*, the autobiographical hero finally becomes the valiant fighter that his predecessors were incapable of becoming in actual battle.

"I Killed"

After the restoration of self in *Notes of a Young Doctor*, Bulgakov once more confronted his persona with the bestial Petlyurites in the minor but thematically significant story, "I Killed," published in 1926.[41] A comparison of this, Bulgakov's last Civil War story, with his first, "Unusual Adventures of a Doctor," demonstrates how radically the depiction of the autobiographical hero has changed. Here as there, the story is placed within a narrative frame and the hero, now named Doctor Yashvin, is introduced as the narrator's friend. But while details describing Doctor N in "Unusual Adventures" emphasize his banal nature, Doctor Yashvin emerges as a gifted and intriguing individual. While a very good doctor, "bold, lucky" (2:648), the narrator informs us, he is by no means typical of his profession. He loves to go to the theater and speaks about it "with great taste and knowledge"; he dresses foppishly (particularly striking are his "patent leather shoes and yellow spats"), but this does not create an unpleasant impression. Most important, Yashvin is a splendid storyteller, and the narrator concludes: "You are a very decent [*ochen' neplokhoi*] doctor, but nevertheless you've set out on the wrong path, and a writer is the only thing you must be." What one has here, of course, is a thinly disguised and quite flattering portrait of the author himself, whose love of the theater, dandified clothes, and gift for storytelling are well attested.[42] For the first time in Bulgakov's Civil War prose, moreover, there is explicit mention of the hero's creative gifts, an indication, perhaps, of the shift to a new persona— the writer—soon to occur in Bulgakov's serious work.

The story opens late in the evening of February 1, 1926, with several doctors, including Yashvin, gathered in the narrator's room. At midnight, Yashvin tears the old date from the wall calendar and stares at the "two," as if seeing before him "a mysterious picture, accessible to him alone, somewhere beyond the wall of my room and perhaps far beyond nocturnal Moscow, in the menacing smoke of the February frost" (2:648). The topic being discussed, it happens, coincides with Yashvin's thoughts. The narrator is denying that doctors are responsible for the deaths of their patients and declares that he has never met a doctor who is a killer. Yashvin retorts that he himself is such a doctor, that he killed a patient quite intentionally, and on precisely that night seven years before in his native Kiev.

He then recounts the events of February 1–2, 1919—one night before the "night of the second" so familiar from Bulgakov's other Civil War works. On that day, when he returns home from work, he is mobilized by two of Petlyura's men, who take him to a house where a certain Colonel Leshchenko is quartered. They leave him alone in a glaringly lit empty room, and his "attention . . . is riveted by ginger and red stains in the corner, alongside a machine gun, where an expensive tapestry hung in shreds" (2:653). He recognizes the red smears as blood and his heart contracts. The presence of the ruined tapestry in this chilling still life provides yet one more example of Bulgakov's vision of the interconnectedness of all the values of civilization, the link between an assault upon human life and the attainments of high culture. Another tapestry, "with shepherdesses," disappears as the colonel throws open the door and enters the room.

Even before his appearance, the colonel's voice gives some idea of his character, as he is heard screaming from the other room "A Yid?!" (2:653). Once he enters and learns that Yashvin is not a Jew, he snarls that the doctor is "no better than a Yid" and threatens him with a court martial: "You'll be shot for sabotage!" Then the doctor directly witnesses Leshchenko's violent behavior, as he strikes a trembling, ragged deserter in the face with his pistol. The soldier "began to choke on his own blood, fell on his knees. A stream of tears began to pour from his eyes..."

The principal episode occurs after the regiment moves to another house. While treating frostbitten soldiers, the doctor frequently hears screams from downstairs and understands that someone is being beaten with ramrods. He is later called to see the colonel, who has been stabbed with a penknife, and thinks: "Someone couldn't stand his tortures and threw himself on him and wounded him" (2:655). At this point a distraught woman tears into the room and cries out: "Why did you execute my husband?" (2:656). She then turns to the doctor and accuses him of betraying the high calling of the intellectual: "What a scoundrel you are... You studied at the university, and [you're] with this rabble... . . . He bashes and bashes a person in the face. Until he goes crazy... And you treat his wound?..." Yashvin is stung by her reproaches and tries to justify himself, but she has by now turned back to the colonel and spat in his face. For this Leshchenko orders that she be flogged twenty-five times with a ramrod. The woman's boldness now infects Yashvin, who fulfills the duty of the intellectual by speaking out: "[Beat] a woman?" Leshchenko glances malevolently at him and says in his half-Russian, half-Ukrainian: "Now I see what kind of bird they gave me instead of a doctor" (2:657). Yashvin then shoots the colonel. The doctor describes the death with clinical exactitude: "I had apparently driven one of the bullets into his mouth, because I recall that he swayed on the stool and blood ran out of his mouth, then at once stains grew on his chest and his stomach, then his eyes grew dim and turned from black to milky, then he crashed down on the floor."

Thus Yashvin, like Aleksei Turbin, kills. His motivation, however, is morally superior, for if Aleksei shoots out of the instinct for self-preservation, Yashvin is reacting primarily to Leshchenko's threatened violence against another, a woman. By performing this act, he represents the final step in the evolution of the Civil War persona: if the hero of *Notes on the Cuff* prays that his opponents be killed off by others, if Bakaleinikov in "On the Night of the Second" only imagines shooting the Petlyurite beasts, and if Aleksei Turbin shoots at random and is uncertain whether he has actually killed, Yashvin succeeds in murdering the perpetrator of evil. This act exerts a decisive influence on the portrayal of Aleksei Turbin in the final version of the last chapter of *The White Guard*, for only there does he, like Yashvin, declare himself a murderer (1:413). Moreover, after Yashvin's brave act the later Aleksei is spared altogether the ordeal suffered by so many autobiographical heroes: facing Petlyurite atrocities and the inability to oppose them.

After committing the murder, Yashvin manages to save his own life, but only through luck. He would certainly have been caught had he not escaped through a window and, like the heroes of "Unusual Adventures" and "On the Night of the Second," found a hiding place, a chink between two contiguous walls. Repeating a favorite image, Bulgakov places a single star over Yashvin's head, which he believes is Mars. Like Venus in "On the Night of the Second" and Mars in *The White Guard*, the planet seems to explode as the first shell goes off, betokening the arrival of the Bolsheviks (one day earlier than in actuality). When it finally grows quiet, Yashvin leaves his hiding place and finds everything deserted, "as though neither Colonel Leshchenko nor the cavalry regiment had ever existed" (2:657). He walks to the city and then goes home.

In conclusion, the story returns to the narrative frame, and the narrator asks Yashvin whether the colonel died or was only wounded. To this Yashvin replies, "smiling his rather strange smile: 'Oh, rest assured. I killed him. Trust my surgical experience'" (2:657). Thus, Yashvin does not try to justify his behavior, in contrast even to the later Aleksei ("I'm a murderer. No, I shot him in battle"); on the contrary, he emphasizes the premeditation of the killing. Judging by the strangeness of his smile, the episode has left its mark upon him, but he is able to recall it coolly and even with some pride, for he faced the terrible chaos underlying life's usual civility and, rather than simply running in fear like his predecessors or shooting wildly like Aleksei Turbin, he opposed the horror on its own terms. By murdering, he overcame the inhibitions that previously left Bulgakov's heroes powerless against the elemental forces of evil they encountered.

In this portrayal, Bulgakov thus fully embodies the rather unsettling notion that the constructive ideas of the intellectual—the healing powers of the doctor, in the specific case of his authorial personae—are insufficient, that a touch of the wrathful, destructive Tugai-Beg is essential if one is to oppose evil effectively. And after Yashvin commits his "just" murder, thus annulling the impotence of the authorial personae that so long obsessed Bulgakov, the autobiographical Civil War hero (with the exception of the changed Aleksei in the final version of *The White Guard*'s conclusion) disappears entirely from the narrative prose.

Return of the Weak Intellectual: "Morphine" and *Flight*

"Morphine"

The story "Morphine" somewhat complicates the line of development traced thus far. Published, like most of *Notes of a Young Doctor,* in the magazine *Meditsinskii rabotnik* (although a year later than the last of the other stories, at the end of 1927),[43] it stands apart from the rest. In "Morphine," the hero of the cycle, now named Bomgard, plays a relatively minor role; the story is primarily devoted to the diary of his medical-school friend, Polyakov. As Yanovskaya has discovered, this diary can be traced to a much earlier time, to Bulgakov's first attempt at a Civil War novel, *The Ailment*, abandoned soon after his arrival in Moscow.[44] Thus "Morphine" has the odd distinction of containing *two* authorial personae deriving from different stages in Bulgakov's literary development. (A hint of the relations of both to the author appears in their surnames, which contain letters from Bulgakov's own: *Bomgard, Polyakov.*)[45]

Bomgard has since been transferred from his remote post to the nearby district town, which, by comparison, is "civilization, Babylon, Nevsky Prospect" (1:148). He now reads James Fenimore Cooper "with strange interest" and, from the vantage point of his relatively soft life in town, recalls his former work as a series of daring feats worthy of Cooper's heroes: "I had forgotten my battle post, where I alone, without any support, had struggled against illness, getting out of the most extraordinary situations through my own strength, like a Fenimore Cooper hero" (1:149). Once more he thinks of how his experiences have made a brave man of him: "I became a courageous person... I am not afraid..." (1:150). That very night, Bomgard receives an urgent letter from Polyakov, who has replaced him in his former district. His friend writes enigmatically that he has contracted a pernicious disease and pleads with him to come and try to save him. Before Bomgard can go, however, he finds out that Polyakov has shot himself and has been brought to the town hospital. As he lies dying, Polyakov hands Bomgard his diary, which the remainder of the story reproduces.

As Polyakov's story unfolds, he emerges as different from Bomgard in the most fundamental ways. If the latter looks upon life in the country as immensely difficult, a heroic battle against disease and ignorance, Polyakov regards it as an escape, thus reviving an old Bulgakovian theme. His wife, an opera singer, has just left him, and he greets his new post as a refuge from his private woes. Polyakov is thus motivated by the need to save himself, not others, and this ultimately destroys him. The external conditions he faces are actually more favorable than those that confronted Bomgard. Having arrived in the country with some experience in a military hospital, he loses his fear more quickly, finds the work "not as terrifying as I thought earlier" (1:157). Most important, he forms a close relationship with a genuinely good woman, the midwife Anna K., whom he comes to recognize as "the only true and real person for me," who "should be my wife" (1:163). Nevertheless, he is incapable of overcoming his preoccupation with his private problems, and when morphine offers him further escape, he does not resist.

At first Polyakov attributes the effects of morphine to his own courage (thus introducing a variation on an old theme): "For half a month now I haven't returned once in thought to the woman who deceived me . . . I'm very proud of this. 1 am a man" (1:159). Later, however, he acknowledges the real source: "All the same, thanks to morphine for that" (1:163). The drug also makes him oblivious to the momentous political events of 1917. Polyakov is actually in Moscow, undergoing treatment, at the time of the October Revolution. Precisely at this point it is said that "about twenty pages have been torn out of the notebook" (1:166), and Yanovskaya hypothesizes that a large segment of the original novel, where the revolutionary theme was to play an important role, has here been omitted.[46] All that remains in the story is another instance of morphine-induced "courage": "Thanks to morphine for making me brave. No shooting is terrifying for me. And what, in general, can frighten a person who thinks about only one thing—about the marvelous, divine crystals" (1:166–167). Once Polyakov returns to the country, morphine brings him total escape from events in Moscow: "Dishevelled, turbulent Moscow is far, far away . . . Burn, light, in my lamp, burn quietly, I want to rest after my Moscow adventures, I want to forget them. And I forgot" (1:169–170).

After this (in contrast to Bomgard, who becomes ever stronger during his stay in the country) Polyakov's personality rapidly degenerates. He begins to have hallucinations (of a witch on a broom!) and cannot force himself to return to Moscow for a cure, in spite of Anna's urging. Anna, although worthy of being one of Bulgakov's feminine saviors, is not only incapable of rescuing the weak Polyakov but is dragged down by him. As he acknowledges: "I've done her in . . . Yes, there is a great sin on my conscience" (1:174). The "sin" of ruining Anna's life contrasts to Bomgard's calm conscience in "The Starry Rash" after saving lives. In a final effort to rid himself of his addiction, Polyakov writes to Bomgard but then suddenly changes his mind, deciding it would be "shameful to prolong my life by even another minute" (1:175). At this point the diary ends, the doctor having achieved his final escape through suicide.

In the brief conclusion, Bomgard notes that he is publishing Polyakov's notes "in full, without any changes whatsoever" (1:175–176). It is tempting to consider this a hint that Bulgakov himself has reproduced a fragment of his earlier work with minor or no changes.[47] While this is impossible to prove conclusively, given the absence of early manuscripts, the story's diary form, its fragmentary, elliptical style, and its weak, solipsistic hero all liken it to Bulgakov's earliest serious prose.

At the end Bomgard asks whether these notes, written so many years before, are still necessary, and whether he has the right to print them. To both questions he responds emphatically in the affirmative. This leads one to ask in turn why, after the passage of so many years, after the author's gradual and painstaking molding of an attractive and admirable persona, he found it so necessary to return to an earlier and sorrier version of self. The reason may be that the creation of ever more positive versions of self in Bulgakov's fiction involved ever greater suppression of the negative traits reflected (albeit in exaggerated form) in the earliest stories. In "Morphine" the writer, however haltingly, begins to redress this imbalance: with his authorial "I" still firmly anchored to the strong, courageous frame narrator, Bomgard, he is making his first tentative approach, as if from the outside, to his early hero.

Bulgakov's earlier explorations of the nature of courage, especially in *The White Guard* and *Notes of a Young Doctor,* allow him now to depict his weak hero with greater equanimity. Courage in those works often appears independently of the hero's will, tied to a second, unconscious self, that arises in moments of crisis. Polyakov is someone who simply lacks this second self, whose illness, indeed, makes his weakness as involuntary as the strength of other personae. Therefore, although not absolved of responsibility, he evokes not only censure but sympathy. Polyakov compares his terrible torments to pallid textbook descriptions: "No, I who have come down with this awful illness warn doctors to be more compassionate toward their patients. It is not a 'depressed state' [*tosklivoe sostoianie*], but slow death that takes possession of the morphine addict" (1:165–166). He turns to Bomgard, indeed, precisely because his friend is "healthy, strong, but soft" (1:174), and therefore may offer the sympathy *("uchastlivost'")* other doctors have withheld.

Softness and sympathy are not traits one readily associates with early Bulgakov. In "Morphine," however, after having already created a positive model of self and explored the inner mechanisms governing courage, he is able to treat with greater understanding the weaknesses he had so excoriated earlier. The oddity of "Morphine" is that the positive and negative poles of Bulgakov's own personality are divided between its two heroes. This proved a necessary transitional step, however. For only after Bomgard could sympathize with his alter ego, Polyakov, was Bulgakov able to broaden the range of his compassion in *Flight* and—still more important—create a balanced image of the autobiographical hero in the late prose.[48]

In certain ways, indeed, the later authorial personae—Maksudov of *Notes of a Dead Man* and the Master—bear some resemblance to Polyakov. While the latter has beautiful hallucinations under the influence of morphine, the writers are transported by their artistic gifts to a superior imagined sphere. Their solitary creation, like Polyakov's drug addiction, is not permissible in their society, and once they emerge from isolation, they face opposition for which their fragile nervous structures and impractical artistic temperaments make them singularly unfit. Therefore Maksudov, like Polyakov, commits suicide, whereas the Master, also like him, suffers from a nervous disorder and dies at the end. There is, of course, a crucial difference, for while Polyakov retreats from difficult reality into sterile, drug-induced fantasies, the writers create entire alternative worlds, more real in the deepest sense than the mendacious quotidian life surrounding them. By evoking these worlds with words, moreover, Maksudov and the Master, like Streltsov of "The Raid" and Krapilin of *Flight*, "forget themselves" and speak out in the fullest way. Their deaths, therefore, are not simply a sign of weakness but also a form of self-sacrifice reserved for the bravest heroes of the early prose.

Flight

Bulgakov wrote the first version of *Flight* in 1926–1927, concurrently with "Morphine." A play in "eight dreams," it depicts in surreal, comic-grotesque style the defeat of the Whites in the south of Russia and their subsequent life in exile in Constantinople and Paris. One of Bulgakov's most vivid and striking works, the play was accepted for production at the Moscow Art Theater, but despite the support of influential people, including Maksim Gorky, it was banned in 1928 by the *Glavrepertkom*. Several attempts to produce the work in the 1930s failed, and the play was performed for the first time in the Soviet Union only in 1957.[49]

Flight is not autobiographical, but it provides a transition from the early Civil War fiction to the later novels and therefore deserves to be examined here, if only briefly. In some ways, as many critics have noted, the play is an outgrowth of *Days of the Turbins*, although both the style and the cast of characters are quite different. Thus, whereas *The White Guard* and *Days of the Turbins* foresee the destruction of the traditional home and family by the anarchic forces of Civil War, in *Flight* these have indeed disappeared, replaced by a random collection of people, a veritable "Noah's Ark,"[50] fleeing ever farther down the map of Russia, to end up finally in emigration. These include a young Petersburg lady, Serafima Korzukhina, in search of her husband, a government official with ties to the Whites; Sergei Golubkov, a Petersburg intellectual, who falls in love with Serafima; and the semichivalrous, semicomic Major-General Grigory Charnota and his "camp wife" Lyuska. At the moral center of the play is the White general, Roman Valerianovich Khludov, dread perpetrator of innumerable and unspeakable Civil War atrocities[51]—a theme that links *Flight* to many of Bulgakov's early Civil War stories.

The original title of *Flight* was *Serafima's Knight*,[52] and the chivalric configuration of knight–dragon–captive maiden (suggested by an icon of St. George slaying a dragon hanging in the train station that serves as Khludov's headquarters, p. 423) is still detectable in the plot. Thus, Khludov arrests and plans to execute Serafima for renouncing him as a "beast, a jackal" (p. 430). Subsequently the general sarcastically dubs Golubkov, who undertakes her rescue, a "knight" ("*rytsar*," p. 443). Then, when Golubkov proves unequal to this role, Serafima is saved by Charnota, who bears her off on a ship named "The Knight" *(Vitiaz')*. This chivalric schema, however, with its diametric opposition of good and evil, does not do justice to the morally nuanced characterizations in *Flight*—perhaps one reason Bulgakov changed the title.

In the play, in contrast to earlier works, even the beastly military commander, Khludov, is treated with compassion. The reason is that he, like Polyakov in "Morphine," is ill: "He is sick with something, this man, completely sick, from head to foot . . . He arouses fear. He is sick—Roman Valerianovich" (p. 423). In the course of the play Khludov goes entirely mad and (fulfilling the wish of the hero of "The Red Crown") is haunted by the apparition of his last victim, the orderly, Krapilin, whom he ordered hanged for speaking out against his outrages. Bulgakov's compassion toward this perpetrator of war crimes becomes clear when one compares analogous episodes in *Flight* and "I Killed." The latter's hero, Yashvin, kills the Petlyurite commander after he orders the beating of a woman, while Golubkov in *Flight* threatens to kill Khludov for *his* mistreatment of Serafima. Golubkov, however, cannot kill, because he realizes that Khludov is mentally ill: "No, I have understood everything! You are crazy!" (p. 442). Khludov therefore arouses pity: "No, I cannot shoot you, I find you pitiful, and frightening, and loathsome! You have killed!" (p. 443).

Golubkov's refusal to kill, to be sure, is attributable in part to his weak, indecisive nature, but by the final "dream" a spirit of reconciliation touches even Khludov's former victims. Thus the general begs the ghost of Krapilin, who for months has tormented him unspeakably, to lighten his spiritual burden: "Well, relieve my soul, nod! Nod at least once, eloquent orderly Krapilin... So! (He cries out quietly.) He nodded! It's decided!" (p. 466). Pity for Khludov also moves Serafima, who, having witnessed his madness and self-torment, says: "I have come to feel sorry for you, Roman Valeri-anovich" (p. 466). Then, when he reminds her of her earlier harsh words, she promises reconciliation: "All that has passed. We will forget. And don't you remember."[53] Krapilin's and Serafima's attitude to Khludov faintly pre-figures Yeshua's final pardon of Pilate, after many centuries of suffering and remorse, in *The Master and Margarita*. (Serafima's "angelic" name, per-haps, hints that a Christian theme is already present.) It is surely no coinci-dence that Pilate too is ill (with a migraine), that he calls himself a "fero-cious monster" (5:21) and at his first appearance demonstrates his cruelty by ordering Yeshua whipped for having called him a "good man."

The spirit of compassion evident in the portrayal of Khludov also figures in the characterization of Golubkov, who, although not strictly speaking an autobiographical personage, has much in common with the early authorial personae. (Wright notes that the letters of his name are almost identical to Bulgakov's.)[54] Thus he exhibits a similar solipsism, joining the Whites not out of political conviction but simply because "there is hunger in Peters-burg and I can't work there" (p. 434). In the midst of his wanderings, he nostalgically recalls his "lamp on Karavannaya Street, the books..." (p. 413), and numerous times he is disparagingly called an intellectual *(intelligent)*.[55] In the course of the play, Golubkov, indeed, acts even more reprehensibly than the weak heroes of the early fiction: he does not merely fail to speak out against the general's atrocities, but, under threat of torture, actually signs a statement accusing Serafima of being a Communist. This weakness, however, does not arouse the bitter irony typically directed at earlier he-roes. Serafima only wonders when she reads his statement against her: "Has he fallen ill or something?" (p. 436).[56] And later Golubkov, who does everything within his rather limited powers to right his momentary wrong, is rewarded by reunion with his beloved. In his behavior, indeed, he, like Khludov, prefigures Pilate, who, fearing for his own welfare, also condemns one to whom he feels strongly attracted—Yeshua. Pilate later tries to make up his lapse as well, and finally—although almost two millennia later—is rejoined with Yeshua.

A fundamental reason why Golubkov and Khludov are ultimately forgiven is that they are unable to control their shameful behavior. They succumb, like Polyakov in "Morphine," to an "illness" they cannot conquer—paralyzing fear of pain in one instance and madness in the other. It is significant, indeed, that the only major character who is *not* forgiven is Serafima's husband, Korzukhin, a more extreme version of Talberg from *The White Guard* and *Days of the Turbins,* in that his despicable deeds spring not from mental breakdown but from rational self-interest. Thus he not only denies Serafima in the Crimea, where, as Khludov's remark makes clear, admission of the relationship would have meant his death: "And if she . . . is really his wife, I'll hang Korzukhin!" (p. 430).[57] Even when safe in Paris and very well off, he refuses to send money to his destitute wife. Significantly, Golubkov brands Korzukhin—not the murderer Khludov— "the most loathsome, the most heartless [*bezdushnyi*] person I have ever seen" (p. 460) and adds: "And you will suffer retribution! It is not far off." Retribution of a sort, indeed, occurs right away, when Charnota wins a fortune from him at cards, money he intends to share with Golubkov and Serafima.

With the exception of Korzukhin, all the major characters of the play, although flawed, are treated with considerable sympathy. They are all imperfect human beings who at times behave admirably, at others not.[58] Thus, although Charnota acts valiantly in war and carries out the chivalrous rescue of Serafima, once a civilian in Constantinople he almost ruins the same Serafima and his lover, Lyuska, by gambling away their paltry capital on a cockroach race. As for Lyuska, she remains steadfastly by Charnota's side in battle, but when starvation threatens in Constantinople, she abandons him and becomes the mistress of the detestable Korzukhin. Even the heroic orderly, Krapilin, whose unconsidered outburst costs him his life, shows weakness when his everyday consciousness returns and he asks for mercy: "Your excellency, have pity on Krapilin! I forgot myself!" (p. 432). It is precisely this loss of nerve that results in his execution, as shown by Khludov's response: "No! A bad soldier! You started well, but ended like a pig!" He then orders Krapilin hanged. Finally, the brave and virtuous Serafima suffers a lapse when she lets Golubkov go off to Paris, possibly to his death: "You know, it was madness to let him go then! I cannot forgive myself for that!" (p. 466). Serafima's remorse echoes faintly the searing guilt of the hero of "The Red Crown" for letting his brother go to his death. It also foreshadows Margarita's regret at having left the Master alone when her presence might have prevented his disappearance and possible death.

Thus, all the characters in *Flight*, even the most positive, are fallible human beings, yet none except Korzukhin suffer unqualified condemnation—not even the monstrous Khludov and the weak intellectual Golubkov, types so unsparingly treated in early works. Compassion, however, is not synonymous with absolution, and there remains a moral reckoning at the end. Khludov in particular must perform a final act of contrition—a return to Russia—before achieving redemption. He decides upon this path even though he faces certain death at the hands of his compatriots:

> Serafima: Madman, has it occurred to you that they will execute you immediately!
>
> Khludov: In an instant, in a flash! . . . And my burden is dissolving. (p. 467.)[59]

Charnota, on the other hand, who is not guilty of atrocities and who has fully demonstrated his bravery, chooses to stay in the "cockroach race" of emigration. As he says: "I didn't run away from death, but I won't go out of my way to find death among the Bolsheviks either" (p. 469). As for Golubkov and Serafima, their flight all along was motivated by the personal, not the political, and it is fitting that they return to Petersburg for purely personal reasons. As Serafima says: "Where, why did we run? . . . I want to go to Karavannaya again... I want to see the snow" (p. 470). She and Golubkov now regard the horrors of Civil War and emigration as a bad dream (or the "eight dreams" of the play's subtitle) from which they are about to awaken, safe at home once more:

> Golubkov: We will wake up. We will forget the dreams, we will live at home.
>
> Serafima: At home... At home... [Going] home... Home... The end... (p. 470.)[60]

Here, as in *The White Guard* and the early redactions of *Days of the Turbins*, home is the true reality, infused as it is with the immortal essences of life, whereas the violent eruption of history the heroes have just experienced was but a transitory, although horrifying, apparition.

The words of Golubkov and Serafima at the end of the first version of *Flight* strikingly echo those of the hero of *Notes on the Cuff* at the conclusion of Part One. The latter, whom the Civil War also carried far from home, cries in despair when his path to emigration is blocked: "I have no blood in my brain" (1:490)—a cry Golubkov, after the tribulations of exile, repeats: "There is no more blood in my brain..." (p. 469). And when the earlier hero resigns himself to remaining in Russia, he repeatedly utters the word "home," as do Golubkov and Serafima when they decide to return to St. Petersburg. If Bulgakov's last Civil War work has thus taken us back to the first, the parallels only underline crucial differences. For at the end of Part One of *Notes on the Cuff* the narrator has reached rock bottom, and his decision to return home is a sign of defeat; whereas for Golubkov returning to Russia is a joy, a return to real life after long suffering and deprivation. More generally, Golubkov, despite his weakness, does not at the end share the burden of guilt and shame of other early heroes. He has benefited from Bulgakov's own long journey back to the core of his Civil War experience in earlier works, from which he emerged with greater tolerance for human frailties.

Flight, indeed, marks the end of that backward journey in Bulgakov's serious writing. From now on he will move in two other directions: forward to the contemporary Soviet world and outward, beyond the self, to the broader expanse of history. These new directions bring with them a new hero, the writer (Maksudov, the Master; Molière, Pushkin), who fights not with bullets (or stethoscopes) but with words. Here we return to Bulgakov's notion of the "revolutionary of the spirit"—a role, one must add, that the later heroes do not fulfill unimpeachably. They, like the early personae, have failures of courage, make painful compromises; Bulgakov, however, now looks upon such shortcomings with greater equanimity, and his heroes, whatever their flaws, are ultimately redeemed by their creative achievements. Of central importance here is the ethos of sympathy and noncondemnation of "Morphine" and *Flight,* which receives its fullest embodiment in *The Master and Margarita* in the beliefs of Yeshua—the model for all "revolutionaries of the spirit." As *Flight* already demonstrates, most people do not have the strength to face death in the burning sun, like Yeshua. Yet despite their failings, they remain, in Yeshua's words, "good people," and blame is tempered with forgiveness.

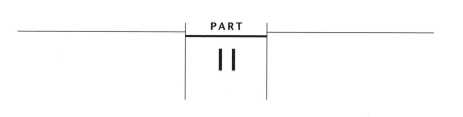

PART

II

Satire—Comedy—Fantasy

The Soviet Human Comedy: Satirical Feuilletons and Stories

Bulgakov's short satirical works of the 1920s, with their vivid vignettes of urban and provincial life, present in the aggregate a veritable *comédie humaine* of the New Economic Policy (NEP) period. Although very different in genre and mood from the serious works, they offer a complementary perspective and give variations within a civil setting of the moral concerns that the turmoil of war awoke in the author.

Bulgakov began to write feuilletons in Vladikavkaz, of which only two, "In The Café" (dating from the White period) and "A Week of Enlightenment," have thus far been unearthed. After moving to Moscow, he published his satire in many periodicals, but most regularly in two very different newspapers, *Nakanune (On the Eve)* and *Gudok (The Whistle)*. The former was an institution peculiar to the early 1920s: a periodical published abroad (in Berlin) but distributed daily both within and outside the Soviet Union and numbering among its contributors Soviets and émigrés alike. An organ of the "Change of Landmarks" movement, its *Literary Supplement* was edited by the well-known writer Aleksei Tolstoy, who was to return to Russia in 1924.[1] (Among those who returned with him was the famous feuilletonist Vasilievsky-Ne-Bukva, whose young wife, Lyubov Evgenievna, met Bulgakov in early 1924 at a reception celebrating the émigrés' return and married him several months later.)[2]

As Emily Mindlin, secretary of the Moscow editorial board of *Nakanune*, recalls, Bulgakov's pieces for the newspaper met with considerable success; indeed he and his then friend Valentin Kataev became among its most popular writers.[3] If *Nakanune* thus offered Bulgakov a measure of recognition, it did not provide sufficient income to support himself and his wife. This explains why he joined the staff of *Gudok*, the organ of the railroad workers' union. Aron Erlikh, a *Gudok* staff member who in the hungry days of 1921 had worked with Bulgakov at Moscow Lito, recalls how one evening in early 1923, after a splendid dinner in a luxurious NEP-period restaurant, he ran into Bulgakov on the street, dressed in a strange, shaggy fur coat and looking listless. When Erlikh found out that his former colleague had no steady income, he arranged a job for him as a corrector for *Gudok*.[4]

Gudok, whose main goals were to indoctrinate and to air issues of concern to its working-class readership, was a very different kind of newspaper from *Nakanune.* Its feuilletons were mostly based upon material sent in by its so-called worker-correspondents *(rabkory),* and being a corrector meant turning these semiliterate correspondences into something fit to print. This work Bulgakov detested, as he declares in "To a Secret Friend": "All my life I did no more revolting work . . . It was a torrent of hopeless gray boredom, uninterrupted and inexorable" (4:557). To be sure, he was soon promoted from corrector to feuilleton writer, but, given the nature of the newspaper, this was to prove only slightly more fulfilling. For one thing, the subject matter was alien to Bulgakov, whose creative energies were stirred most by what touched him personally. While the *Nakanune* pieces grew out of his own experiences and observations in Moscow, his work for *Gudok* was drawn almost entirely from the life of the provincial working class, about which he had no personal knowledge and evinced little interest.

Moreover, the stylistic limitations imposed by the newspaper, whose mass audience could be expected to understand only the simplest language and most unsophisticated humor, allowed none of the irony and complexity so typical of the writer. Thus at the First All-Union Congress of *Gudok Rabkory,* held in January 1925, the well-known *Pravda* feuilletonist, L. S. Sosnovsky, complained that in most feuilletons "one encounters such subtle humor and such expressions, that . . . they can be entirely misunderstood by current readers." And one of the instructions at the close of the congress was: "To carry forth further work in simplifying the language, making the newspaper still more popular and easily grasped by the mass reader."[5] In "To a Secret Friend" Bulgakov bemoans the effect of such demands: "My taste fell sharply. Hackneyed expressions, worn out similes began to pop up more and more often in my writings. In every feuilleton one had to make people laugh, and this led to crudities . . . Your hair would stand on end, my friend, from the feuilletons I composed there" (4:561).

Bulgakov's low regard for his *Gudok* pieces has understandably led some of his best critics to minimize their importance.[6] It is, however, a question worth exploring further. A number of other *Gudok* feuilletonists, after all, who would later make major contributions to Russian literature—Ilf and Petrov (not yet collaborators), Valentin Kataev, Yury Olesha—looked back fondly at their *Gudok* days and regarded working there as excellent training. Bulgakov, it is true, stood rather apart from the rest; he was somewhat older than the others and his demonstratively dandified dress and refined manners, emphasizing his sympathy with the prerevolutionary world, were considered pretentiously out of place by the ragtag, bohemian *Gudok* staff.[7] And whereas most of the writers plunged eagerly into the avant-garde artistic world and rejected the old in the names of Mayakovsky, Meyerhold, and Tatlin, Bulgakov was already a settled family man, "with principles"[8] and with more traditional aesthetic tastes. Finally, most of the *Gudok* writers were to the left of Bulgakov politically and found less belittling than he the humble task of rewriting and creating feuilletons from workers' correspondences.

These differences notwithstanding, Bulgakov's later writings betray the *Gudok* training he had in common with his former colleagues. Thus he, like Ilf and Petrov and to a lesser degree the early Kataev, draws from a seemingly boundless comic store; his ability to string together a series of loosely connected, almost self-sufficient episodes, one funnier than the next, was very likely enhanced by his considerable practice as a feuilletonist. Moreover, *The Master and Margarita,* in spite of its complexity, succeeds, like Ilf and Petrov's rollicking works (and unlike much of Bulgakov's early serious writings, with their forays into ornamental prose and other modernist stylistic devices), as an entertainment, attracting and satisfying a broad spectrum of readers who are able to ignore the novel's philosophical and aesthetic intricacies.[9]

The genre of the feuilleton is a vague and capacious one, "created historically and not . . . as the result of analysis," as Shklovsky puts it.[10] Under its rubric the most various material comes together, from literary and political articles to personalized reportage to short stories and even novels. The single trait that unites these subcategories, as one early Soviet investigator remarked, is their publication in newspapers as supplementary material, providing the reader with interesting additional information or light reading.[11]

Historically the "feuilleton-as-article" predates the "feuilleton-as-story." As practiced by such mid-nineteenth century Russian writers as Dosto-

evsky, Goncharov, and Nekrasov, feuilletons took the form of correspon-
dence-chronicles of varied content, which could include theater and music
reviews, portraits of various human types, and aspects of the passing scene.
What differentiated them from other newspaper material was the distinc-
tive and individualized authorial voice. As L. F. Ershov has noted: "A feuilleton often took the form of a witty authorial monologue, interrupted by
digressions from the basic theme, with a free and easy interweaving of
narrative and colloquial intonations."[12]

It is to this subcategory that Bulgakov's *Nakanune* feuilletons for the
most part belong. They are loosely structured correspondences that include descriptions of the transformations taking place in Moscow, character sketches, and accounts of particular events. All the feuilletons are unified primarily by the narrative voice, sometimes ironic, sometimes directly
commenting and interpreting.[13] Organized as they are around a city, Bulgakov's *Nakanune* pieces are generically close to Dostoevsky's *Petersburg
Chronicle,* although their lighter, more humorous-satiric tone indicates
additional influences, perhaps of Vlas Doroshevich (the most popular
feuilletonist of the turn of the century).[14] The structure of the feuilletons
betrays modern influences as well, with the associative transitions of the
photomontage and the cinema often replacing the chronological flow of
earlier works in the genre.[15]

If Bulgakov's feuilletons in *Nakanune* belong primarily to the correspondence type, then the *Gudok* sketches approach the short story. This "belle-
lettristic" type traces its origin to a later period in the development of the
Russian feuilleton—the works of the *Satyricon* writers, whose influence
upon Bulgakov has already been discussed.[16] Although the *Gudok* pieces are
generally based upon fact, provided by the *rabkory* and typically quoted
in the epigraph, documentary accuracy is less important than drawing a
sharp and amusing satiric point. Therefore the characters and anecdotes
are highly generalized and fictionalized, and there is on the whole more
plot inventiveness than in the *Nakanune* writings. The hyperbolic is more
in evidence than is mirror-like realism, exaggeration of necessity replacing
subtlety in order to bring the moral home to the unsophisticated *Gudok*
readers. While the *Nakanune* correspondences tend to be wide-ranging,
with the narrator playing a central role as commentator and organizer, the
Gudok works usually concentrate upon a single phenomenon. They are
scenic rather than panoramic (to adopt Percy Lubbock's distinction),[17] the
narrator becoming all but invisible except occasionally in the frame. In-

deed, this tendency is carried so far that the feuilletons often consist almost entirely of dialogue, taking the form of miniature plays.[18]

Both types of feuilleton structures left a mark on Bulgakov's later prose. The panoramic vision of the *Nakanune* pieces, the depiction of a wide range of discrete occurrences united by the urban landscape and the narrative voice, is apparent in both *The White Guard* and *The Master and Margarita*. The scenic perspective of the *Gudok* feuilletons, on the other hand, their anecdotal structure and use of hyperbole, sometimes to the point of grotesquerie, continues to dominate in individual satiric episodes, both in *Notes of a Dead Man* and in *The Master and Margarita*.

Nakanune

The *Nakanune* feuilletons are unique among Bulgakov's works for their generally bright and optimistic picture of Soviet life.[19] They are a reflection of the early NEP period (1922–1924), when, after the destruction wrought by the Civil War, life was reasserting itself. A prototype is the article "Trade Renaissance," written in January 1922 and sent by the author to his sister in Kiev in the hope (vain, as it turned out) of having it published in a Kiev newspaper. In this vividly written but rather primitively structured work, the author recounts the commercial resurrection of Moscow. The reawakening city is portrayed, typically for Bulgakov, in terms of light and dark: "In the depths of the rundown premises light bulbs began to burn and to their light life began to stir" (2:216). Accompanying the light is movement: "On Kuznetsky a crush of pedestrians seethes on the frozen sidewalks all day, the cabbies ride in a single file, and the automobiles fly, honking their horns" (2:217).

In spite of its lively, personalized tone, its occasionally figurative language, and snatches of dialogue, "Trade Renaissance" remains a piece of reportage whose primary purpose is to convey factual information on a particular subject. In contrast, the *Nakanune* feuilletons are far broader, presenting varied panoramas of Moscow of the early twenties. They depict the present day but also include remnants of the past and hints of the future; they convey the city's immense variety and many contradictions, its healthy vigor and its vices. The principle of organization is sometimes chronological, sometimes based on spatial contiguity or thematic association, all united by the describing and commenting authorial voice.

One of the most interesting is the first feuilleton, "Red-Stoned Moscow"[20] (the usual epithet, "white-stoned Moscow," reversed to denote the Communist city). The work offers a panoramic view of Moscow on one summer day in 1922, but with images alluding to past and future providing a chronological subtext. Thus the work opens at a site left over from the old world of "orthodoxy and autocracy": the immense Church of Christ the Savior (later to be blown up by the Communists, only to be rebuilt in the post-Soviet period). Behind the church stands an empty pedestal, which until recently supported a monument to Alexander III, "a massive chest of drawers on which there is nothing, and nothing, apparently, is anticipated."[21] From out of this scene from the vanished Russian past emerge two figures—one, with a "hump" of rations on his back, connected with hungry times also fast disappearing; the other characteristic of the more prosperous present: "Well dressed. White starch, striped trousers . . . A Red specialist [*spets*]" (A1:259). The latter is humpless because he can shop at the gigantic Eliseev store, which is groaning with food: "Black caviar gleams in jars. Smoked salmon [*sigi*]. Pyramids of apples, oranges" (A1:260). To be sure, there is much deceptive in this vision of plenty, foreshadowing the illusory nature of the material "good life" in *The Master and Margarita*. Thus the salesman does not cut "from the piece . . . which was fresher, but from one alongside, where it was more suspect" (A1:259–260). And of the two bills the specialist gets in change one is counterfeit.

Once back out on the street, we observe the full spectrum of NEP-time types, old and new, from nouveaux riches NEPmen to drivers of horse-drawn cabs, who are "the same as they were in 1822 and the same as they will be in 2022" (A1:260). The bewildering mixture is shown in various ways: in the "motley masquerade" of clothing, in the strange amalgam of street signs, where mysterious new Soviet acronyms ("Tsupvoz. Tsustran. Mosselprom.") coexist with the traditional "Old Rykovsky Tavern." Suddenly, however, one famous poster injects a dark note, offering a peek at the grimmer side of the Soviet present, which the urban "masquerade" covers up:

In the motley jumble of words, letters on a black background, a white figure—a skeleton—stretches its hands to the sky. Help! H-u-n-g-e-r. In a crown of thorns, in a frame of matted hair, the face of a little girl covered with deathly shadows and eyes burnt out in the torment of hunger. In photographs, bloated children, the skeletons of adults, their skin taut, loll on the ground. You stare intently. You i-ma-gine—and the day grows gray right before your eyes. However, those who have eaten all the time do not understand. The nouveaux riches run past, without a backward glance... (A1:261–262).

Although the negative aspects of NEP, its glaring dissonances, are thus by no means glossed over, the general tone of "Red-Stoned Moscow" is optimistic, imbued with a feeling of recovery. And if the beginning offers a tableau from the vanished past, the end indicates that the Bolsheviks' hold on the future is firm, sanctioned even by the heavens (an idea also present in some of the Civil War works). Thus an unregenerate *spets* prays to God to send rain and hail the following day, a "red holiday." It is, however, ideally clear, leading one peasant woman to say: "In heaven, it seems, they're for the Bolsheviks" (A1:262).

The contradictory yet dynamic mixture of positive and negative in "Red-Stoned Moscow" is characteristic of the *Nakanune* feuilletons. On the one hand, they contain a virtual rogues' gallery of negative types of the NEP period, while on the other, they point to bright, hopeful aspects of the new society. As for the satiric types, especially prominent are the NEP-men, "strong, toothy, malicious, with stone hearts" ("Forty Times Forty," A1:298). They instantaneously earn phenomenal sums ("Capital in a Pad") and spend them just as fast on champagne and caviar in their gaudy restaurants, in the company of their fur- and diamond-clad lady friends ("Capital in a Pad," "Forty Times Forty").

Money madness is at the root of two other popular targets of satire of the time, embezzlement ("The Cup of Life," "Belobrysov's Book") and black marketeering ("Under the Glass Sky"). The selfishness of the old bourgeoisie, trying to hold on to the remnants of its privilege, is exposed ("Moscow Scenes"), as are the drunkenness and brutality of the working class ("Moonshine Lake"). To the large sins of greed and dissipation, moreover, are joined numerous smaller breaches of good manners, ranging from shoving on trolleys ("Red-Stoned Moscow") to the swearing of coachmen ("Capital in a Pad") to eating sunflower seeds and spitting out the shells ("Capital in a Pad"). Indeed, these minor violations of order are of great significance, for they are signs of an unregenerate humanity that, unless changed, will undermine all social and economic transformations. As Bulgakov explains in the case of sunflower seeds: "They have to be banned. Otherwise we will build a high-speed electric train, and the Dunkas will spit shells into the mechanism, and the train will stop—everything will go to the devil" (A1:289).

It should be emphasized that the *Nakanune* satire, however sharp it occasionally becomes, rarely goes beyond the limits of the allowable during the NEP period. Almost all of its targets fit into two permissible categories of the time: "relics of the past" and the "grimaces of NEP" (the latter actually a variant of the former, a flaring-up of bourgeois decadence and greed, which accompanied a partial return to capitalism). In practice, to be sure, the distinction between holdovers of the past and products of the new is not always clear, as the best-known of Bulgakov's stories published in *Nakanune,* "The Adventures of Chichikov,"[22] illustrates. The work is a literary conceit recounting the return of Chichikov, the rapscallion hero of Gogol's *Dead Souls,* to the Moscow of 1922. When he arrives, Chichikov finds that nothing has changed, that his old cronies are everywhere: "Wherever you spit one of your own is sitting" (A1:265). Here, although the vices of the present are viewed as throwbacks to the bourgeois past, the story paints an unusually dark picture of NEP, creating the impression that the Soviet Union is no improvement over imperial Russia—indeed, is even worse, since the old vices seem only to have mushroomed with the breakdown of former restraints.

Such an unrelievedly dark view of Soviet Moscow is, however, atypical of Bulgakov's *Nakanune* works. Most frequently the negative is offset by bright, positive features, one of the most important of which is construction.[23] Thus in "Capital in a Pad" renovation is deemed no less than a god *("bog Remont")* who has settled down in the Moscow of 1922. The narrator enumerates various signs of the god's presence, then declares, only half ironically: "This season they were renovating, plastering, gluing. Next season, I believe, they will be building . . . Perhaps it is the fantasy of a Muscovite true believer... But in my opinion, say what you like, I see—a Renaissance" (A1:277). Other references to construction are marked by similar heightened intonations. In *"Chanson d'été"* the narrator implores: "Build, build, build! . . . In construction is our salvation, our way out, our success" (A1:350). And in "Moscow of the Twenties" he asserts: *"We must finish building Moscow."* The feuilleton concludes: "Moscow! I see you in skyscrapers!" (A1:417).

A second aspect of the new Communist government that is depicted approvingly is its role as imposer of order (an image of the Bolsheviks congruent with that of some of the Civil War prose). Thus, in "Capital in a Pad," after describing the grotesque incongruities of Moscow in 1923, the narrator offers the new Communist organization as a solution: "Amidst the Dunkas and the illiterates a new organizational skeleton, penetrating all corners of existence, is being born" (A1:290). Rather unnervingly, Bulgakov shows—approvingly—that punitive force is an essential component of this new organization. One sees this especially in "Capital in a Pad," where the narrator gives several instances of how through police action "order . . . is born from chaos" (A1:286). He tells of a black-bearded man fined twenty million for smoking under a "No Smoking" sign. When he refuses to pay, something "supernatural" occurs, similar to the appearance of the diabolical force of vengeance (Koroviev) in *The Master and Margarita*: "Behind the back of the young man, without any signal on his part (Bolshevik tricks!), a policeman was woven out of air. This was a positively Hoffmannesque something... simply the embodiment of reproach in a gray topcoat, with a revolver and whistle. The black beard paid with supernatural, also Hoffmannesque, speed" (A1:287–288). The policeman, later referred to as a "guardian angel," also chases away sellers of sunflower seeds, and is again described as "an embodiment in gray, but this time not of reproach, but of rage" (A1:289). The narrator comments: "Citizens, this is holy rage. I welcome it." At the end of the feuilleton, after witnessing the benign influence a traffic policeman has on usually obstreperous cabbies, the narrator concludes: "Give us our foothold in order and we will move the globe" (A1:290). This new order is shown in other feuilletons as well, as punishment is exacted both for minor infractions ("Travel Notes," "Chanson d'été") and more serious illegalities ("The Cup of Life," "Moscow Scenes," "Belobrysov's Book").

In the Civil War stories, as we have seen, the autobiographical hero at times dreams of taking the punitive function upon himself, and in *Nakanune* this also occurs. Thus, at the end of "The Adventures of Chichikov," the narrator imagines himself punishing Chichikov severely: "A stone around his neck and into an ice hole" (A1:274). Similarly, at the end of "Moonshine Lake," the narrator envisions the draconian campaign he would wage against drunkenness: "Unlimited authority. On my orders haul people in immediately. A court examination within 24 hours, and no substitution of fines. I will rout all the Sidorovnas and Makeiches" (A1:346). That Bulgakov regarded his satiric writings themselves as a means of delivering punitive justice against social evils is suggested by the title he chose for a journal he and Kataev considered starting—*The Inspector General* (*Revizor*—the Gogolian force of justice and retribution).[24] The view of satire as a means of punishment is, of course, a commonplace, one expressed in the description of E. T. A. Hoffmann that Bulgakov applied to himself. What characterizes these early works, however, and distinguishes them from Bulgakov's better-known prose is that the weapon is used for the most part in support of government policies.

Only one suggestive fragment, from the feuilleton "Forty Times Forty," hints that, for all Bulgakov's approval of the Bolsheviks' harsh justice, he felt an underlying uneasiness about the new authoritarian order. The excerpt offers two views of the Bolshoi Theater. In the first it is fulfilling its new Soviet function as setting for a Party congress. While impressive, with its fiery inscription and red flags in brackets, the theater is also gloomy. The area around it is barricaded by armed and helmeted figures, the description of whom faintly prefigures that of the repressive Roman units policing Jerusalem in *The Master and Margarita* (the same word for horsemen—*vsadniki*—with its apocalyptic connotations is used in both cases): "Chains of unyielding figures . . . in helmets stretch out, carrying rifles with fixed bayonets. Horsemen in black helmets are sitting on their steeds [*na koniakh*] in the side streets" (A1:300).

In contrast, when the Bolshoi resumes its function as opera theater, it returns to what it always was, a friendly, animated place, filled with well-dressed people: "At the favorite hour of the theatrical muse, at seven thirty, there is no glittering star, there are no flags, no long chain of sentries by the public garden. The hulk of the Bolshoi stands as it has for tens of years. Dimmish yellow spots of light between the columns. Welcoming theatrical lights" (A1:300). Inside the theater people are dressed up as they used to be, the women with their coiffed hair, the men in their patent leather shoes. And the theater too "glitters gold and red in the light, and seems just as festively decked out [*nariadnym*] as before."

The juxtaposition of the "old" and "new" Bolshoi Theater, with implicit preference for the former, is, indeed, typical of the *Nakanune* feuilletons. It is such loyalty to the best of the old, also apparent in his Civil War works—and consonant with the ideology of the "Change of Landmarks" newspaper for which he is writing—that limits the degree of Bulgakov's support for the new Communist order, despite the enthusiasm expressed for Bolshevik construction and authoritarianism. In general, although the author describes sympathetically the speed and glitter of the modern city, support for radical transformation of society and of humanity itself, envisioned by the Communists and enthusiastically proclaimed by many of their supporters in the arts, is noticeably absent. On the contrary, the positive harbingers of the future more often than not point to a reestablishment of the old.

A couple of small examples are recounted in "Capital in a Pad." Thus the title character of "Supernatural Boy" amazes everyone on the street because he is not hawking his wares like all boys in recent years, not stealing, smoking, swearing, begging. Rather, he is doing what in the past all ordinary boys did: strolling to school. The second startling apparition is a man who, amidst all the "questionable jackets, threadbare service jackets," turns up dressed in tails. This intriguing phenomenon leads the narrator to ask: "What must the tails signify? Are they a museum piece in Moscow, amidst the service jackets of 1923, or does the tails wearer present a certain living signal: 'Have a taste. In half a year we will all be dressed in tails'" (A1:284).

One must add that in general the feuilletons distinguish between what is truly valuable in the past and mere empty form—what has become pointless, even pernicious, in the present day. Thus in matters of art the narrator at first rejects equally the old and the new: an antiquated production of the opera *The Huguenots* and Meyerhold's famous "biomechanical" production of *The Magnificent Cuckold* ("Capital in a Pad"). Finally, however, he opts for art with roots in tradition, finding the unpretentious skill of the circus clown and operetta performer infinitely preferable to new-fangled biomechanics: "Biomechanics!! The helplessness of these blue biomechanics . . . And this, please note, two steps away from the Nikitin Circus, where the clown Lazarenko drives one mad with his stupendous *salso*" (A1:285).

This distinction between the "eternal" essences of the past and that which deserves to disappear is also—and most significantly—present in the treatment of the central Bulgakovian theme of home and family.[25] This is apparent in two stories that take family as their subject, "Psalm" and "Moscow Scenes." The former, which, for all its slightness, is one of Bulgakov's most affecting works, depicts how the shattered nuclear family gropingly attempts to reestablish itself. Its three characters—the narrator, his neighbor, Vera Ivanovna, and her four-year-old son, Slavka—are all victims of domestic breakdown. The narrator is completely alone, while Vera Ivanovna is waiting, apparently in vain, for the return of her husband, who left for St. Petersburg seven months before.

The story begins with Slavka's visit to the narrator. In their conversation (the story is written almost entirely in dialogue) certain motifs appear that underline the loneliness and desolation of the characters. The first is a poem Slavka recites (reconstructed here from his halting, lisping performance):

> "I'll buy myself shoes to go with my tailcoat,
> And nights I'll sing a psalm...
> And I'll get myself a dog...
> It's all right... We'll live somehow." (A1:359)

The second motif has to do with the narrator's problems with buttons, introduced when Slavka repeats the observation his mother made while sewing on his (the narrator's) buttons—that he is lonely.

The domestic image of Vera Ivanovna sewing is soon reinforced when she appears in person, her hands wet from performing another household task, hanging up laundry. After her brief appearance, the narrator's relations to Slavka become imperceptibly more paternal, and he tells the child a cautionary tale about a boy who is punished when naughty, but rewarded—with a bicycle—once he mends his ways. Vera Ivanovna then returns to take her child off to bed, leaving the narrator alone with his thoughts. Variations of motifs already introduced reappear: the poem ("Nights I'll sing a psalm. We'll live somehow. Yes, I am alone" [A1:361]); buttons ("The most tormenting thing in life is buttons"); his neighbor's family situation ("He will not come . . . He's been gone for seven months, and three times I accidentally saw her cry" [A1:361–362]). In the narrator's ruminations on Vera Ivanovna's husband, physical attraction for the mother and fatherly concern for the son combine: "But the only thing is he's lost a lot by abandoning those white, warm hands. That's his business, but I don't understand how in the world he could forget Slavka..." (A1:362).

When Vera Ivanovna returns, she and the narrator gradually grow closer, drawn together both by his buttons ("It's impossible to live. All around are buttons, buttons, buttons..."[A1:362]) and her tears ("You will cry and I feel dreary... dreary..."). Once a bond is formed, earlier images of solitude and desolation—buttons, the shoes, tailcoat, and psalm of the poem—are negated, replaced by the narrator's fatherly decision to buy Slavka a bicycle. In this new context the poem's final line, now repeated, sounds less plaintive, more hopeful: "There are no buttons. I'll buy Slavka a bicycle. I will not buy myself shoes and a tailcoat, I will not sing a psalm at night. It's all right, we'll live somehow."

The movement toward creation of a family in "Psalm" is in marked contrast to its collapse in "Moscow Scenes." This satiric piece centers upon a member of the old bourgeoisie, a barrister, who, in his desperate attempt to hold on to his spacious apartment, actually wrecks it, desecrating the domestic space so revered by Bulgakov. Thus, in order to deceive the inspectors, he constructs "something like a clay coffin in the dining room" and makes "enormous holes in all the walls, through which he pushed thick black pipes" (A1:308). He conceals the library and study with all kinds of rubbish so that even the narrator, who knows the apartment very well, smashes himself and rips his clothing. Not only is the home wrecked, however, so is genuine family spirit, for the barrister takes in a couple of cousins not out of love or concern but solely to preserve his living space. Once the barrister is fined despite all his efforts, the family abandons any semblance of harmony and dissolves in a flood of mutual recriminations. At the end the disconsolate barrister raises his eyes to a portrait of Karl Marx (hung to deceive the inspectors), but the founder of Communism, understandably, shows no sympathy.

If the conclusion of "Moscow Scenes" seems to imply the triumph of the Marxist collective ideal over the selfish individualism of the hero, other treatments of the housing question disabuse one of that notion. In fact collectivism comes off even worse than attempts to preserve the bourgeois past, and precisely because, far from liquidating man's pernicious behavior, the new living arrangements only serve to cultivate it. Here, as in "The Adventures of Chichikov," the distinction between "relics of the old" and offsprings of the new is blurred, for the chaos and bestiality the Bolsheviks are reputedly eliminating flourish in the communal apartment, that microcosm of the collective world. Therefore these pieces, which contain the most biting satire in the *Nakanune* feuilletons, also present implicitly the most trenchant critique of the new order as a whole, significantly offsetting the overall optimistic tone of other works.

The most vivid depiction of communal living is "Moonshine Lake," set in the infamous "apartment No. 50," Bulgakov's residence during his first years in Moscow. The story begins, ironically, on Easter eve, when an extremely rare "blessed silence" at first reigns along the "cursed corridor" (A1:341). The calm lasts only an instant, however, interrupted by a sound that violates not only domestic laws, but also the laws of nature: a rooster crows, although it is not dawn, but ten in the evening. The narrator goes out into the corridor and witnesses a hair-raising scene: a drunken stranger is pulling handfuls of feathers out of the tail of a live rooster.

This is only one appalling example of the widespread brutality practiced by the apartment's residents (mostly child and wife beating), its cause drunkenness. What is striking is that these horrors on the "housing front" are structurally analogous—although obviously of a different order—to the war atrocities the hero of the Civil War prose witnesses. Here again the persona is a lone intellectual among the simple people, and within this very different setting he once more observes the wanton violence of the masses, this time his neighbors. Once again, moreover, the narrator longs for the death of one who most fully personifies this evil: "In the blessed silence the burning thought was born within me that my dream had come true and Grandma Pavlovna, who traded in cigarettes, had died. I decided this because the screams of her tortured son, Shurka, were not coming from her room" (A1:341). The narrator is powerless, like the Civil War personae, to change things fundamentally, all the more so because he himself is threatened: "If someone doesn't like it here, let him go where educated people live" (A1:342). Like Aleksei Turbin, he even disparagingly refers to himself as a "rag": "I announce publicly: if I were a man and not a rag, I would of course have tossed Ivan Sidorych out of my room. But I am afraid of him. He is the strongest person on the board after the chairman" (A1:343).

The similar position of the hero in "Moonshine Lake" to those in the Civil War stories suggests broader parallels between the authorial personae in *Nakanune* and the serious autobiographical fiction. One does in fact find in the satirical pieces an evolution of the hero from weaker to stronger analogous to that in the Civil War works. Indeed, it is a hypothesis worth entertaining that the development of the *Nakanune* hero (reflecting the author's own successes in coping with "Moscow of the twenties")[26] influenced the image of the authorial persona of the serious prose, superimposing a later, stronger vision of self upon the initially weak autobiographical figure. Thus, at the beginning of "Forty Times Forty," the narrator describes himself during his earliest days in Moscow in decidedly unheroic terms: "I declare categorically that I am not a hero . . . I'm an ordinary person—born to crawl—and, crawling about Moscow, I almost died of hunger" (A1:296). In his struggle against death, however, impressive strength arises within him: "I developed unheard of, monstrous energy. I did not perish, in spite of the fact that blows rained down upon me" (A1:297).

Heroic traits indeed develop, especially during his battle on the housing front: "My body became thin and wiry, my heart iron, my eyes sharp-sighted. I was tempered."

In "Moonshine Lake," his underlying helplessness notwithstanding, the narrator does behave admirably, interceding for the tormented victims as he generally does not in the Civil War works. He repeatedly tries to prevent Pavlovna from beating Shurka and tears a wife away from her drunken mate, with the words: "Don't you dare beat her!!" (A1:345). Of greatest importance, however, is the fact that the hero's principal field of battle has shifted from the real world to the realm of literature, where he is striving, undaunted, to achieve his most heroic feat: completion of his novel. In pursuance of this goal, an occasional tactical retreat, as before the dreaded Ivan Sidorych, is justified, for a confrontation might endanger the final artistic victory.

Indeed, in a curious reversal of the serious autobiographical prose, it is not the hero but his wife who displays weakness and even contemplates escape in morphine: "But you'll never finishing writing the novel. Never. Life is hopeless. I'll take morphine" (A1:345). In contrast, the narrator becomes filled with steely determination: "At these words I felt that I had become iron. I answered, and my voice was filled with metal: 'You will not take morphine, because I will not let you do it. And I will finish writing the novel and, rest assured, it will be a novel that will make heaven grow hot.'" In conclusion, in this same rush of strength the hero imagines himself leading a raid on all the moonshine establishments and thus drying up Moscow.

This, of course, is an unrealizable daydream, and in the final *Nakanune* feuilleton, "Moscow of the Twenties," the narrator admits his defeat on the housing front. He does so with equanimity, however, because his failure does not reflect upon his considerable strength of character: "Citizens, I am a remarkable person, I'll say this without false modesty. I got a work book in three days, stood in line only three times, six hours each, and not six months each, like all kinds of bunglers. I started five new jobs, in a word, I overcame everything, but, excuse me, I couldn't manage an apartment" (A1:414).

He goes on to offer two solutions to the housing crisis in keeping with the positive values of the *Nakanune* feuilletons as a whole: harsh punish-ment and construction. Yet the problem is so deep-rooted that a sim-ple intensification of the two fundamental functions of the Bolsheviks in the feuilletons seems insufficient. This is apparent in the image of Vasily Ivanovich, the drunken house manager, who in "Moscow of the Twenties" becomes a generalized symbol of all that is most intolerable in the new Soviet world: "I swear by all I hold sacred, every time I sit down to write about Moscow the cursed image of Vasily Ivanovich stands before me in the corner. A nightmare in a jacket and striped drawers has hidden the sun from me! I lean my forehead against a stone wall, and Vasily Ivanovich is above me, like the lid of a coffin" (A1:410). The narrator adds: "In a word, he is unthinkable in human society."

Just as no miracles of construction will take place as long as the Dunkas wreck the works with their sunflower seed shells, so is the "sun" of a harmonious future hidden by the crudity and cruelty of all the Vasily Ivanoviches. Fundamental changes are essential in human manners and morals, without which social and economic transformations are meaningless or even harmful. To effect these changes physical punishment is insufficient; moral castigation, for which literature is the best agent, is also necessary.

The Elpit House

Bulgakov's most interesting housing story, "No. 13. The Elpit-Workommune House," was published not in *Nakanune* but in *Krasnyi zhurnal dlia vsekh (Red Magazine for Everyone)* in late 1922.[27] The house of the title—already familiar from "Moonshine Lake" and "Moscow of the Twenties,"—is a fictionalized version of the Pigit House (named after its former owner), the formerly luxurious apartment building converted into a workers' commune, where Bulgakov and his wife lived in the early 1920s.[28] Predating both "The Khan's Fire" and *The White Guard*, "No. 13" is Bulgakov's first work in which a house acquires broad symbolic significance, both as a receptacle of history and as a microcosm of a particular social order.

From the very beginning the story juxtaposes the house's past and present, first through its strange-sounding name, Elpit-Workommune, *(El'pit-rabkommuna)* then through a description of the way things used to be before the revolution, when the building was simply the "chic Elpit House" (A2:368). As in "The Khan's Fire," the spirit of the house's past is first conveyed through a sculpture, of a "stone girl by the fountain" in the courtyard, who, "green-faced, mute, naked, . . . looked languidly all summer long into the round, bottomless mirror" (A2:368). The former dwellers are also described, a veritable cross section of the rich and powerful of tsarist Russia: a general who received Rasputin himself as a guest; the chinchilla-swathed mistress of a man so highly placed that he did not even have a surname; various bankers, industrialists, artists, doctors. Bulgakov does not idealize this old world; in a few brief paragraphs he recreates not only its glamour but also its immorality. He describes the spies languishing in the shadows as Rasputin caroused; the clever bank director with "the eyes of a criminal"; the factory owner, who indulged in "Roman orgies" ("afinskie nochi") (A2:369).

Not surprisingly, given the wealth of its inhabitants, the house was a model of comfort, shown, typically for Bulgakov, through images of light and warmth. Even when "the demon, pretending to be a blizzard," raged outside, "the gray accordions of the pipes in all seventy-five apartments filled with warmth, as if by magic. On the landings lamps burned in the brackets" (A2:369). When the Elpit house becomes a workers' commune, however, all of this vanishes. "Incredible folk" ("nevidannyi liud") settle into all the apartments, and the outer demonic gloom and chaos penetrate the house: "Primuses hissed snake-like, and day and night biting fumes floated along the staircases. The lamps disappeared from all the brackets, and every evening gloom descended. Shadows with bundles stumbled in it [the gloom] and cried out plaintively: 'Manya, hey, Ma-a-nya! Where in the world are you? The devil take you!'" (A2:370).

All that saves the house from destruction is the single person remaining from its past, "the most brilliant of all Moscow managers" (A2:368), Boris Samoilovich Khristi. Hired by the new workers' board, which understands that "without Khristi the house wouldn't stand a month" (A2:370), the manager does his job splendidly, maintaining some semblance of order among the unruly tenants and keeping the house heated against impossible odds. Khristi does all this, to be sure, not out of a belief in the new system but from loyalty to his old employer. Elpit is convinced that the house will be his again and promises the manager his just reward once the time comes: "Boris Samoilovich, save the house for me until all of this ends and I will know how to show you my thanks!"

The workers' commune is thus governed by an incongruous combination of old and new: "A monstrous combination: on the one hand, the noisy, calloused board, on the other—a 'custodian' [smotritel']!" (A2:370). The social structure of the house, indeed, serves as a microcosm of NEP itself, with Khristi a "spets" (specialist) called in, despite his suspect background, to pull the workers' commune out of its crisis. As in NEP generally, moreover, the alliance is an uneasy one, the commune very far from fulfilling the familial ideal of a genuine community. Guided by mutual antagonism rather than unselfish concern for others, the entire system is lubricated by greed and dishonesty: Khristi has to pay bribes to get heating fuel; Egor Nilushkin, the "sanitary supervisor" (*sanitarnyi nabliudaiushchii*, A2:371), accepts "tribute" from those committing violations (A2:372); the board itself has pilfered "the lion's share of Elpit's carpets" (A2:370). Khristi, moreover, convinced that the old world will return, has some bundles stashed away in a storeroom on the fifth floor—together, fatefully, with thirty cans of gasoline belonging to Elpit.

Even more striking than parallels with NEP, however, is the religious parody contained in the story.[29] The first hint of its presence is the house manager's name, Khristi, so close to that of Christ (*Khristos* in Russian). And there are similarities between the two. Like Christ, Khristi is a savior of sorts, for he delivers the Elpit house from destruction. Moreover, he, like Jesus, is regarded as a miracle worker: "But it was a miracle: Elpit-workommune was heated" (A2:370). "And at the mere mention of Khristi's name, the light magically began to burn" (A2:371). Khristi, however, far from being a Christ-like savior of souls, is concerned only with property, that material universe whose god is not in heaven, but in another part of Moscow: the former owner, Elpit.

Elpit's name suggests that he too is intended as a parody of divinity: the first syllables, *Adolf Elpit*, are identical to those of *Adonai Elohenu,* the *Lord our God* in Hebrew. Since the Bolshevik takeover, he is "without any signs of life" (A2:370) (thus resembling more Jesus after the crucifixion than God the Father). In spite of his apparently moribund state, however, he repeatedly commands Khristi to believe: "'Believe me!' Khristi believed" (A2:370). "Do you believe me? . . . Believe me" (A2:372). And Khristi's belief that the kingdom of the god-Elpit will return is what motivates his action.

Because of their materialistic values, however, the "divinity" of Khristi and Elpit is actually indistinguishable from the diabolical (perhaps also hinted at by Elpit's first name, Adolf, the first syllable of which is the Russian word for hell). Thus it is Khristi's materialism, his pride and haughtiness, so contrary to Christian humility, that is emphasized. Before the revolution he was "the swarthy possessor of the safe, trader in living wares" (A2:368), and after Rasputin's visit he "became . . . still more enigmatic, still more haughty. Sparks of steely pride appeared in his black eyes and the rent was cruelly raised" (A2:369). Because of this sinister aura, Khristi's magic seems more fiendish than divine, and when one tenant, Annushka, calls him a "cross-eyed devil" (A2:373), her words ring true.

Annushka herself, the "scourge of the house" (A2:373), is, to be sure, as unholy a creature as Khristi. Indeed, it is she who lets loose the forces of hell by disobeying the rules and lighting a fire in her little stove. In the description of the fire one again finds an ambiguous blending of the heavenly and hellish. At first, in its struggle against "the demonic snowstorm," the fire makes Annushka's room into a "paradise" (A2:373). The "little fiery prince" dancing in the stove, however, soon shows his fiendish nature, when "the glass [of the windows] was bloodied by snake-like trembling" (A2:374).

The subsequent spread of the fire is not, significantly, the fault of Annushka alone. Its cause is the combined forces of the greed of the old and the ignorance of the new, for it might have been controlled if not for Elpit's gasoline, stored in a neighboring room. These cans transform the blaze from a "little prince" to a "fiery king" (A2:374). And this absolute monarch of destruction turns the house into "hell. Pure hell" (A2:375). Here once again, after the desecration of the values of home, the domestic flame changes from a force of life to one of death, wreaking vengeance upon those who have shattered the house's harmony. In this case, however, the retribution is shockingly violent, with one after another of the tenants falling to a horribly bloody death—the hero's longing for retribution in other fictions realized here in an unnervingly graphic way. Thus, whereas the narrator in "Moonshine Lake" only wishes "Grandma Pavlovna" dead, in "No. 13" the same Pavlovna jumps to her death and becomes a "bloody pancake" [*lepeshka*] on the street (A2:374). And many others share her fate.

The main actors of the story—Khristi, Elpit, and Annushka—do not die. Khristi, however, resembles a martyr in Christ's image (or anti-image) as he stands by a tree trunk in the reflected light and heat of the conflagration, his chest bare, looking "as if he himself were burning in the fire, but was mute and could not cry out anything . . . Tears slowly crawled down his bluish cheeks" (A2:375). Elpit asks him to come with him, but the former manager refuses, and Elpit leaves alone and is "drowned among the shadows." Khristi then sees in the sky a hellish apparition, a "hot orange beast," as if set free at the destruction of the house. Whether he will later follow Elpit into the shadows (into Hades, the land of shades?) or, now that his former god has been unmasked, be resurrected to a new life is a question the story leaves unanswered.

The case of Annushka is clearer. She also observes the apocalyptic "belly of the beast" suspended in the sky, her own demonic nature revealed in "her face [which] was like a witch's from the soot and tears" (A2:375). The catastrophe, however, works a positive change in her, for it allows a beam of light to penetrate her soul: "And Annushka Pyliaeva was so worn out from suffering, so exhausted from the black thought of 'woe,' from that fiery belly-reflection triumphantly spilling all over the sky... . . . that a dull calm came over her and, most important, for the first time in her life a light dawned [*prosvetlelo*] in her head" (A2:376). Now she at last understands her own "darkness": "We are dark [*temnye*] people. Dark people. We have to be taught, fools that we are..." (A2:376). After this realization, she walks away, no longer looking at the beast; and the beast itself gradually fades until no trace is left. The story ends: "And no sign remained in the sky that the famous No. 13 Elpit-Workommune house had burned down."

Thus "No. 13" gives both a more penetrating and more pessimistic view of NEP-time Moscow than the *Nakanune* stories. Social transformation cannot be achieved by a simple change of name from "Elpit" to "Workommune." On the contrary, the disintegration of the old only gives venality and ignorance broader reign, unchecked by former social constraints. True betterment can be achieved only if there is an inner spiritual change in the "dark" people—the Vasily Ivanoviches, Dunkas, and Annushkas. This can be accomplished, as Annushka realizes at the end, only through education in the broadest sense—what Russians call *enlightenment (prosveshchenie).*

Gudok

The notion of enlightenment proves useful when approaching the tricky task of analyzing the *Gudok* feuilletons. This large mass of modest comic sketches, written on assignment to address specific abuses, does not easily lend itself to broad generalization. It is tempting to dismiss the feuilletons as hackwork, yet when one examines them in the aggregate, one is struck by certain repeated themes and images, which form a coherent pattern congruent with the writer's overall vision.

The reports of the *Gudok rabkory,* upon which the feuilletons are mostly based, gave Bulgakov a broader view of Soviet reality than he himself could gain in Moscow, and the sketches he wrote for the newspaper create a considerably more negative impression than do the *Nakanune* pieces. The vision of Soviet society they present, in fact, provides a transition from the general optimism of the *Nakanune* feuilletons—their enthusiasm for Communist authority and construction—to the very different view in later works, especially *The Master and Margarita,* where both the coercive force of the state and the edifices upon which it stands are justly undermined by the devils. A central reason for the shift has to do with the Bolsheviks' approach to enlightenment, broadly defined, which includes improvement in manners and morals as well as education proper. Connected with this is the question, already touched upon in "No. 13" and other housing stories, of whether social and economic reforms alone can make people better.

One slight feuilleton that takes the latter as its theme is "Concerning Wife Beating." The piece begins with a quote from a letter, which places the blame for most wife beating on poverty. The solution, the correspondent concludes, lies not in punishment but in bettering the husband's material lot. The body of the feuilleton reduces this apparently sensible idea to absurdity by telling how one husband's ever more violent attacks on his wife result in his successive promotions: "After he broke his wife's arm he was promoted from tenth to twelfth [rank]. Then he bit off her ear—to the sixteenth. Then he knocked out her eye with a boot twenty fourth rank . . . But there is no higher rank on the scale. One asks, what if he spills out her guts, what next?" (A2:271). The feuilleton concludes: "Wives are not beaten because of deprivation. They are beaten because of benightedness [or darkness = *temnota*], savagery, and alcoholism." Here, as in "No. 13," the root cause of the problem is the "darkness" of the people. The fundamental solution, therefore, is enlightenment—an idea already present in Bulgakov's earliest Vladikavkaz writings, the feuilleton "A Week of Enlightenment," and the play *Sons of the Mullah.*

Bulgakov's belief in the power of enlightenment does not in itself contradict the Communist position. On the contrary, education was a central part of the Bolshevik program, Lenin himself frequently employing imagery similar to Bulgakov's (actually commonplaces derived from the philosophical enlightenment), speaking of bringing "light" to the "darkness" of the Russian people.[30] Bulgakov, however, through repetition of certain character types and plot configurations, exposes the superficiality and wrongheadedness of the official approach.

One of the most common satiric types is in fact the ignorant teacher or lecturer.[31] A rather lighthearted example is the incompetent professor in

"The Electric Lecture," whose description of the perpetuum mobile indicates his level of learning: "The law of the eternal perpetuum [was] discovered by the famous steam scientist One-Step in the 18th century before the Birth of Christ while glancing at a teapot on a perfectly ordinary range in England, in the city of London..." (A2:61). After more such gibberish even the professor's rather passive students hound him from the classroom.

If this instructor is banished, however, many of his ilk turn up in other feuilletons. Most of them, strictly speaking, are engaged in the dissemination of propaganda rather than in education proper, but the two were not clearly distinguished either in Bolshevik theory or practice.[32] In a number of pieces the lecturer conceals his ignorance by using long, often foreign, words, which, far from enlightening the worker-peasant audience, only further befuddle.[33] In "They Wants to Show their Education..." *("Oni khochut' svoiu obrazovannost' pokazat...")*, for example, a worker, after listening to an impenetrable speech filled with such foreign words as *"prostratsiia"* (prostration), *"interventsiia"* (intervention), *"difamatsiia"* (defamation), *"amorfnyi"* (amorphous), (A2:213), cries out: "You have drunken all my blood!" (A2:214). There follow other emphatic protests, after which the speaker, like the professor in "The Electric Lecture," flees "like a hunted wolf" (A2:215).

Elsewhere the instructors are not so easily vanquished. On the contrary, they conquer through verbal intimidation or worse. Thus, in "World Champion," the lecturer responds to his audience's questions with a stream of abuse. After he stuns his audience to silence, someone cries out: "Bravo, encore . . . You laid them all flat on their backs. You're world champion!" (A2:316). In "Linkage with a Skull" *("Smychkoi po cherepu")* the violence actually shifts to the physical. Grandpa Omelko, after listening to an unfathomable lecture devoted to furthering the Bolshevik goal of "linkage [*smychka*] of city and country," complains that he didn't understand a thing. The offended speaker accuses Omelko of being a *kulak* (a rich peasant) and has a local official, Ignat, drag him from the hut. Ignat, declaring "I'll prove to you what kind of element you are" (A2:245), hits Omelko on the head "with something so heavy that it seemed to grandpa as if the midday sun had grown dim and stars had come out in the sky." The narrator comments: "With this the linkage with Grandpa Omelko ended. However, not quite. After the linkage grandpa grew deaf in one ear" (A2:246). And so if the ignorant instructors cannot bring about genuine learning, they create its semblance by means of intimidation and even outright violence.

An underlying reason for the failure to educate, the feuilletons imply, is the attempt to bring about instant enlightenment, a notion already mocked in "A Week of Enlightenment." This accounts for the absence of that genuine mastery Bulgakov so admired, whether in a clown ("Capital in a Pad"), a scientist (*The Fatal Eggs* and *Heart of a Dog*), or a writer *(The Master and Margarita)*. Such mastery entails not only the superficial acquisition of knowledge or skills but a change in the inner man. This neglect of what might be called the spiritual component by modern "enlighteners" is shown in certain recurrent plot patterns in the feuilletons.

Thus, the quite lighthearted humor of some feuilletons is based upon the incongruities and chaos resulting from an improper differentiation of the spiritual and material. "The Libraiter" *("Biblifetchik")*, for example, tells of a librarian who also serves as waiter in the buffet. Here the spiritual and material sustenance offered by his two jobs becomes hopelessly entangled. When someone asks for a book by Bukharin, the libraiter gets his terminology confused: "Absolutely fresh, just got it in. Gerasim Ivanovich! One order of Bukharin!" (A2:147). The customers also get mixed up, the readers crying out, "We read to your health!" and the drinkers ordering "two copies of Martovskoe [Beer]." Similar confusion arises in "Deviltry" *("Chertovshchina")*, which describes the bewildering variety of activities—some for the betterment of the soul and others for material improvement—scheduled at the same time by the Kuznetsk *mestkom* (local trade union committee). These range from the film *The Daughter of Montezuma* to a lecture on pork cutlets to a concert of Chopin polonaises to a Pioneer chorus booming out a march. The result of this indiscriminate mixture is, of course, total chaos.

"Main-Polit-Divine Service" *("Glav-polit-bogosluzhenie")*, verbally one of the most inventive feuilletons, describes the cacophony that results when a group of believers are given quarters alongside a school teaching political literacy, with its atheistic, materialistic underpinnings. At the beginning the drunken deacon recalls how the night before, during vespers, he saw the words "Religion is the opium of the people" written in fiery letters. He expresses fear of being converted to Communism and ending up in hell: "'And he, the deacon... he's in hell... in fiery Hygiene [*gigiena*].' 'In Gehenna,' the reverend father corrected him" (A2:108). A maddening counterpoint then begins between church and school, all the more unsettling because the ideological hostility is expressed in similar lexicon and rhymes:

"Labor will be the lord [*vladyka*] of the world!!"—was carried through the open windows of the neighboring premises.

"Ooh," the deacon sighed, drew back the curtain, and roared: "Bless me, Lord [*vladyka*]!"

"The proletariat has nothing to lose but its chains [*krome ego okov*]."

"Always, now and forever and through the ages [*voveki vekov*]," the reverend father joined in. (A2:109)

Here one sees how the contiguity of two antipathetic world views results in mutual pollution and debasement. The drunken deacon spews Marxist clichés, the political educators borrow ecclesiastical terms, and the outcome is total chaos and moral confusion.

Another common plot motif suggesting the dubious nature of Communist enlightenment is the disasters that befall both buildings and people in some way connected to culture. Striking here is the repeated use of military imagery. Although the Civil War has ended, false attempts at enlightenment, it is implied, serve only to perpetuate the violence in another form.

In some cases, such as "Stairway to Paradise," disaster occurs because of the simple negligence of those in charge. The piece describes the vain attempts of workers to get up the icy steps of an edifice of culture, a library. One worker, Balchugov, compares the feat to a military campaign: "I was wounded twice... A knapsack on my back, a rifle in my hands, boots on my feet, and here with Gogol, with Gogol—and not manage it..." (A2:32). The steps, however, prove more treacherous than combat, for the hapless Balchugov flies down the stairs and hits a bolt, which "landed right in his teeth" (A2:33). The bloodied worker, cursing "the librarian and the board of the club too," picks up the scattered pages of *Taras Bulba* and goes home.

Ice also defeats culture—again in the form of a library—in "Fire Chief Pozharov."[34] The chief, like Khristi in "No. 13," is more concerned about buildings than their inhabitants and therefore wages an indefatigable war against all stoves, killing off workers "like bedbugs" (A1:385).[35] He fails to close the club only because the *mestkom* "waged a battle against the destroyer of our way of life [*byt*] for seven meetings, no worse than Perekop." He does, however, win "on the library front" (A1:386), where he "entirely destroyed the stove idea, which is why Comrade Bukharin was covered with ice, together with his ABCs and Leo Tolstoy, and attendance at the library was ended now and forever." The narrator concludes: "Amen. Amen. Get enlightened where you like!"

In two feuilletons people involved in the struggle for enlightenment come to sad ends. Most important here is the purely external nature of government support, the lack of genuine commitment from paper-shuffling officials. In the first work, "How Buzygin Crashed," the hero is a railroad worker who wishes to open a club at his station. At first he is praised highly as a "hero of cultural work" (A2:25), but when renovations do not take place because the soulless bureaucracy provides no help, he is censured and takes to drink. In desperation, he decides to whitewash the ceiling himself, but falls and is killed. Thus the lack of support Buzygin experiences all along is literally realized in the plot, his lone fall dashing his cultural aspirations and his own person simultaneously.

In "How He Went Crazy" a frustrated attempt to repair another "house of enlightenment," a school, results in the madness of the school's director. In order to get the repairs done, the director corresponds endlessly with a certain official, but to no avail. Eventually his health fails and he has hallucinations, one of them of Peter the Great with his fist raised. Unlike Pushkin's Evgeny in "The Bronze Horseman," however, the director does not run in fear from this symbol of state power but grabs a knife and pursues the tsar. This act of insubordination results in his confinement in a hospital and, at the end of the story, in Chekhov's Ward No. Six.

Perhaps the most graphic instance of the collapse of enlightenment occurs in "How a School Disappeared into the Nether Regions" ("Kak shkola provalilas' v preispodniuiu"). The feuilleton, a skaz narrated by one Makar Devushkin (the name of the timid hero of Dostoevsky's Poor People apparently given to this garrulous railroad worker for the sake of comic incongruity), tells of a dacha that is to be converted into an elementary school. The project is promising—there is even an outhouse for ninety people—but the well needs repair. The school director goes through the usual bureaucratic maze and this time workers actually appear—real specialists, who get the job done in two minutes. They decide, however, to leave a few trifles until spring, thus demonstrating their lack of true commitment to their work. This leads to disaster, for when the ground begins to thaw, everything slides into the well, and within a few days the entire school disappears. All that remains is "an outhouse for ninety people and a sign on the gate: 'Primary School'" (A2:112). Devushkin concludes: "And so enlightenment came to an end among us."

The juxtaposition of the outhouse and the sign "Primary School" can serve as an emblem for enlightenment in Bulgakov's *Gudok* feuilletons. Without a sound foundation in knowledge and training, and especially without a change in the inner man, the edifice of enlightenment collapses. Whatever the deceptive sign might promise, all that remains is the outhouse, that monument to the most primitive in humanity.

The persistence of gross old habits beneath the cover of an enlightened new world is in fact a frequent theme in the feuilletons, one they share with the *Nakanune* housing stories. One example is "Work Reaches 60 Proof" *("Rabota dostigaet 30 gradusov"),* which tells of how Party members miss a cell meeting on Easter day because they have gotten drunk and are beating their wives. At the next meeting the *mestkom* secretary actually defends the workers, criticizing them only for mauling their wives in public: "A woman likes to be beaten at home. And don't beat her on the face, because the next day your woman walks around the whole station with black and blue marks and everybody knows. Beat her in various hidden spots!" (A2:255). The single righteous member is left only one recourse: to inform *Gudok*.

Another instance of the persistence of old violence beneath an enlightened surface is recounted in "Wall Against Wall" *("Stenka na stenku"),* which tells of a traditional fist fight that takes place in a village on a saint's day. Even the *fel'dsher* (medic) Talalykin, dressed for the holiday in distinctly bourgeois garb, succumbs to his primitive instincts, so contrary to his function as healer: this "servant of medicine ran to maim his patients" (A2:153). Like a human *matreshka* (stack doll), moreover, Talalykin's hypocrisy turns out to be multilayered. He not only conceals a brawler's heart beneath his bourgeois shirt front, but once the holiday is over both are covered by a de rigueur Bolshevik leather jacket: he is a candidate for membership in the Communist Party. Talalykin's black eye, however, betrays him, and he is refused admission.

While Talalykin is exposed, another feuilleton, "Sounds of an Unearthly Polka," suggests that his ilk—the hidden philistines and ruffians—are legion. The piece, depicting a ball at a provincial station, can serve as a microcosm of the seedy underside of early Soviet society. Its very locale, at the Lgov People's House *(L'govskii nardom),* suggests the deceptiveness woven into this life, for while the People's House is intended for the enlightenment of the common people, the station's name (*lgat'* = to lie) hints at falsity.[36] This deceptiveness is apparent at once in the ironic contrast between the "heavenly" words of the title song and the infernal atmosphere at the ball. While one dancer repeats the song's words, "dear angel," while "flying with [his partner] to heaven" (A2:170), the epithet applied to him, "possessed" *(osatanevshii)*, points to the diabolical. The young ladies, moreover, are "green," one of the guests "resembles a drowned man," and one sentence sums up the diabolical atmosphere: "An evil spirit [*nechistaia sila*] was rushing about in the hall as at a witches' sabbath." The scene then shifts from the dance floor to the buffet, where the one apparent attempt to further enlightenment—sale of "a mysterious pink liquid—to benefit the library" (A2:171)—proves a sham, for the liquid is moonshine. The men drink so much that they feel the house collapsing around them: "A storm was raging in the hall. The ceilings and floors were caving in. The old walls were rocking." This drunken vision contains an inner truth, for the "house" of Soviet enlightenment is being undermined by the old philistinism still thriving within its walls.

In *Nakanune* Bulgakov expresses much sympathy for the new organizational "skeleton" the Soviets were putting in place. In *Gudok,* however, no such enthusiasm can be detected. Because of the falsity of Soviet enlightenment, its ineffectiveness in bringing about inner changes, the structure that holds it together is not an organic skeleton but an external, deadening mechanism dominated by the bureaucracy. Bureaucracy, to be sure, was a prominent feature of Russian life during the tsarist period as well, satirized by Bulgakov's favorite writers, Gogol and Saltykov-Shchedrin, among many others. One of the Bolsheviks' initial goals in fact was to dismantle the tsarist bureaucracy. As shown in the *Gudok* feuilletons, however, they only expanded it into new areas, making greater and greater incursions into people's private lives.

A rather slight but typical example is "The Round Seal," which depicts a worker's wife engaged in what used to be an entirely private activity: buying groceries. Now, however, she is prevented from making her purchases at the "railroad car store" *(vagon-lavka)* because she does not have the required seal in her ration book. She runs first to the *mestkom,* where she is told "we have the seal, but we don't have the right" (A2:196). Another official then tells her he has the right, but not the seal. In desperation she runs back to the train, but by now it has left. Such instances of "round seals" and other bureaucratic impediments to the natural flow of life are legion in the *Gudok* pieces, as are the feuilleton's mechanical repetitions and its closed geometric form—the vicious circle.

Perhaps the most disturbing activity of the bureaucracy is its penetration into as private an aspect of the workers' lives as love and marriage. One of several examples is "How Buton Got Married," the epigraph of which states that a certain railway board is issuing food coupons only to married men, and therefore bachelors will apparently be forced to marry. The narrator relates the sad story of a certain confirmed bachelor, Buton-Netselovannyi (Buton-Unkissed). Buton at first valiantly resists the government's demand that he marry, but can find no way out of his dilemma: "I either have to lose my life to hunger or my precious freedom?!" (A2:241). He therefore submits to the inevitable, although not without hysterics. When a courier arrives and asks why Buton is howling, the official, typically, conceals the dreadful reality behind a false front: "He's gone mad from joy. A change of life in an official house [v kazennom dome]." Thus the incursion of the "official house" into the private realm of home and family both limits freedom and substitutes falsity and deceit for genuine human relations.

It is important to reiterate that Bulgakov's satire, however sharp it sometimes becomes, does not in general go beyond the bounds of the permissible during the early Soviet period. Lenin himself declared that "our worst enemy is the bureaucrat," and Mayakovsky—whose political convictions could not differ more from Bulgakov's—exposed remnants of old vices beneath a Sovietized surface, asserting that "philistinism [obyvatel'shchina] is more terrifying than Wrangel."[37] Harsh satire, moreover, was in keeping with Gudok policy, as indicated by an article of 1925: "Gudok in the future should mercilessly castigate rust-eaten administrators, red tape mongers, bureaucrats [chinovniki], law breakers, and do it more than up to now, and more strongly . . . We will reveal our ulcers, our shortcomings, and openly talk about them in order to uproot and get rid of them more quickly and easily."[38]

Some of Bulgakov's individual feuilletons, in fact, are not easily distinguishable from those of fellow Gudok writers, with similarities to Kataev especially striking.[39] Once all this is said, however, his pieces in the aggregate do make a more negative impression than those of his colleagues, partly due to an almost total absence of positive models and partly to a higher instance of violence, blood, and destruction. The latter stems not only from the old brutality (wife beating, brawling, etc.); malfunctioning of the new, as we have seen, also results in blood, serious injury, and even madness and death. Moreover, the numerous cases of collapsing edifices add to a sense of instability. Bulgakov's Gudok feuilletons, indeed, like the

Nakanune housing stories, leave the overall impression that the new system is not overcoming the senseless violence of the Civil War period but is perpetuating it. Whether the instrument be the Petlyurite bludgeon of "The Raid" or the heavy object of "Linkage with a Skull," the result is the same: the little man is beaten so badly he is left permanently damaged.[40]

Another feature of Bulgakov's feuilletons that creates a more negative impression than do those of his *Gudok* colleagues is the greater use of satiric grotesque, often bordering on—although seldom crossing over to—the supernatural. The senseless rigidity of the new life, its deceptiveness and falsity, are sometimes portrayed as so extreme that they border on the uncanny. This accounts for such titles as "The Dead Are Walking," "When the Dead Arise from their Coffins," "The Skull Hunters," "Adventures of a Dead Man."

The last-named feuilleton is one of a few where events reach such a pass that the "real" supernatural is required to intercede. It tells of a doctor who advises a dying patient to go to Moscow for an x-ray. The patient agrees, his ruminations on the potential benefits of the x-ray adding a characteristically grotesque note: "I'll be dying and I'll take a look at the snapshot—it'll be a comfort. Then my widow will hang the snapshot in the living room, will entertain the guests. 'And here,' she'll say, 'is a snapshot of my late railroad worker, may he rest in peace.' And it'll be pleasant for the guests" (A2:97). Unfortunately, the usual bureaucratic vicious circle denies the patient even this small comfort and he dies without his x-ray. Higher justice prevails, however, for, like Akaky Akakievich in Gogol's "The Overcoat," the dead man—now a skeleton—comes back to haunt one who earlier treated him so callously. As a supernatural being he at last gets the better of the terrified station director, who hastily sends him and his coffin on their way to Moscow for the x-ray.

In "The Invisible Boots" *("Sapogi-nevidimki")*—one of the more complex and interesting of the *Gudok* pieces—the "supernatural," as often in Bulgakov, is linked to a dream. In the "delightful dream" (A2:90) of the Kiev railroad worker, Petr Khikin, a sorcerer appears, who bestows upon him an item all but unattainable by ordinary means: a marvelous pair of boots. The only problem is that the boots are invisible, and when Khikin goes home and shows them to his wife (already dubbed "a witch"), she howls: "You're barefoot as an insect, you miserable alcoholic" (A2:91). When the children join in and turn his home into a "hell [*ad kromeshnyi*]," Khikin escapes to Kiev's main street, Kreshchatik. Things are no better there, however, for the well-dressed crowd hoots that he has "drunken away his boots" and threatens to beat him. Khikin's cry that the boots are invisible convinces no one, and his only means of escaping arrest is waking up. Real life, however, proves no better than his dream. There too his wish at first seems to come true when he sees boots for sale at the cooperative. These "real" boots, however, prove as insubstantial as the dream variety, for they are made of cardboard and disintegrate as soon as it starts to rain.

The relationship between dream and reality in "The Invisible Boots" can be interpreted in two quite different ways. On one level there is simple parallelism, the boots equally unreal whether Khikin is asleep or awake. There is a second, deeper point, however, for while the worker is victim in both cases, the reasons are quite the opposite. In his dream he is persecuted as a believer in a supernatural, "invisible" reality, which (at least in the dream context) actually exists but which the hellish "real" world denies. In his waking life, on the contrary, he, like everyone else, places his trust in the solidity of the material world and is deceived. Thus this slight feuilleton illustrates the plight of the Bulgakovian hero: belief in the spiritual world brings persecution, while trust in the material ends up in nothingness.

Another feuilleton featuring dream fantasy, "The Conductor and the Member of the Imperial Family," also has thematic links to Bulgakov's more serious works. It tells how a railway line issues incongruous instructions—on how to greet the royal family. One stunned conductor, Khvostikov, goes home and dreams of the emperor getting off a train. His encounter here with the autocrat cannot be reduced to a simple contrast between a righteous proletarian and a representative of the oppressive old order, for however cruel and tyrannical the emperor may be, the worker hardly comes off better. He turns out, indeed, to be a variant of that despised Bulgakovian type, the turncoat, a "former loyal subject and now comrade" (A2:223). That he is also a coward becomes clear when the emperor asks him if he is a Communist sympathizer:

> "I am a little," answered Khvostikov, "the tiniest bit [*samuiu malost*']..."
>
> "Ah, a tiny bit. But tell me, dear Khvostikov, whose portrait is that you have on your chest?"
>
> "It's... To a certain extent it's Comrade Kamenev," Khvostikov answered and covered Kamenev with his palm. (A2:223)

It is only after this pusillanimous behavior that the emperor—in this narrow sense behaving like Khludov after Krapilin's recantation in *Flight*—orders Khvostikov hanged. When asked the reason, the emperor recites a litany of Soviet "crimes," consisting of overblown rhetoric (all quotes from "The International") and new collective institutions, often the butt of *Gudok* satire: "For the trade union, for 'arise, you, branded by curses,' for the mutual aid fund, for 'we will tear asunder the whole world of violence,' for the portrait, for 'to the foundation,' and then... for other such things" (A2:224).

The emperor here, like Tugai-Beg in "The Khan's Fire" (another visitor to the Soviet Union from the Russian past), acts as a force of retribution against the new collective society that has destroyed the world of which he was so powerful a representative. Like Tugai-Beg, he is morally tainted, yet there is a certain justice in his vengeance against the mendacious and artifical new social structure personified by Khvostikov. In this sense, the emperor, although only a character in a feuilleton, contains within himself seeds of the devil Woland, prince of darkness and dealer in cruel justice.

Aside from dreams, another common locus for what may be termed the fake supernatural is the crooked schemes of those popular literary types of the 1920s, swindlers and embezzlers. A particularly intriguing example, given the later appearance of both a talking animal and a magic show in *The Master and Margarita*, is "The Talking Dog."[41] The feuilleton tells of a performer who puts on a show at a remote station. While his advertisements tout him as the "well-known cowboy and fakir JOHN PIERCE"—and also as a "white magician" (*"belyi mag,"* A2:72)—in the flesh he "turns out to be a puny man in flesh-colored tights with sequins" (A2:73). His star attraction, moreover, proclaimed as a "CLAIRVOYANT TALKING DOG, or MIRACLE OF THE 20TH CENTURY" (A2:72), is actually "a most unprepossessing looking dog of the mongrel breed" (A2:74). The dog does "talk," however, amazing not only the ignorant peasants but also the "cultural worker," the club chairman. The latter, indeed, is so impressed that he persuades Pierce to sell him the dog, whose verbal skills, predictably, disappear together with the magician. The feuilleton ends with a visiting official dismissing the chairman, who, "instead of doing cultural work, arranges a cheap show [*balagan*] at the club" (A2:75).

"The Talking Dog," in contrast to *The Master and Margarita*, does not involve the "real" supernatural. John Pierce, moreover, is not even a very active deceiver and swindler: his poster actually states that ventriloquism will be practiced (A2:72), and it is not he who initiates the sale of the animal. Here, typically for the *Gudok* feuilletons, the supernatural emanates from the "darkness" of the characters—the superstitiousness and gullibility not only of the simple peasants but of the cultural worker himself. Such sham supernatural serves only to hyperbolize the unreal quality inherent in Soviet life of the twenties—a life which, as Gorky wrote, "shimmers, changes, joining fantastically the red with the black and the white . . . where truth and untruth dance an extremely tangled and somber dance."[42]

Thus a hardly sanguine vision of Soviet society emerges from the *Gudok* feuilletons. In contrast to the sympathy for Bolshevik discipline and construction expressed in many of the *Nakanune* pieces, in *Gudok* fundamental reservations are most apparent. At the heart of the matter is the Communists' misguided approach to enlightenment, their failure to genuinely instruct, to modify people's inner essence. Because of this, their much-vaunted new organization is purely external, a deadening, rigid bureaucracy beneath which the "darkness" of the old world continues. This philistine underside of Soviet life is linked in one feuilleton, "Sounds of an Unearthly Polka," to the diabolical, and in numerous other pieces the incongruities, deceit, and ignorance interwoven into the fabric of the new society cast an uncanny light on everyday life.

The vision of Soviet society implicit in the *Gudok* feuilletons and discernible only after considerable efforts at generalization prefigures in numerous ways the more explicitly and consistently developed picture of contemporary life in *The Master and Margarita*. Thus there too the question of enlightenment is central. The novel's initial episode shows the antispiritual nature of Soviet enlightenment, with the literary editor Berlioz "teaching" the ignorant young poet Ivan Bezdomny that the entire transcendent world of Christ and the devils does not exist.

The ramifications of this false enlightenment are, moreover, similar to those in the *Gudok* feuilletons, although modified, given the different milieu and later time period portrayed. Here once again a coercive and unfair bureaucracy dominates, represented primarily by an organization *devoted* to enlightenment, MASSOLIT. In MASSOLIT the function of the various "round seals" in the feuilletons, required to carry out the most fundamental tasks, is fulfilled by the membership card. This document—an arbitrary and external sign replacing inner truth—once again lends a quality of meaninglessness to life, allowing untalented hacks to be labeled writers while the truly creative person, the Master, is denied the title. The distorted concept of the writer in a bureaucratized literature is remarked upon ironically by one of the devils: "A writer is not defined at all by his identification card, but by what he writes! How do you know what conceptions are milling around in my head?" (5:343).

Beneath the bureaucratic front of MASSOLIT, the old philistine vices continue to flourish. In this higher stratum of society, to be sure, the "People's House" of "Sounds of an Unearthly Polka" has been replaced by the chic restaurant at Griboedov's, where the motley collection of writers dance to the sounds of a jazz band. The restaurant, however, like the station in the feuilleton, is described as "hell" (5:61), and again a "heavenly" refrain—the popular song "Hallelujah" (5:60)—is ironically counterpointed to the diabolical atmosphere. In *The Master and Margarita,* moreover, the sham supernatural so common in *Gudok* again appears, although it has taken on a more sinister coloration during the Stalinist period, with hints of secret arrests. The mysterious disappearance of tenants from "cursed apartment no. 50," for example, is attributed to "sorcery" (5:75), and a bribe crawls by a "miracle" into the briefcase of the house chairman (5:98).

Of far greater significance, however, is the fundamental shift in the treatment of the supernatural in *The Master and Margarita,* where there exists not only the sham variety but the real thing. One reason for the appearance of the genuine supernatural is Bulgakov's changed view of authority. In the *Gudok* pieces the various vices and malfunctions of the system are typically—although by no means always—corrected by some higher level of state authority. Already in *Gudok* the agents of justice are more peripheral than in *Nakanune,* usually arriving from the outside at the very end and differing fundamentally from the concrete, almost always negative, authority figures within the microworld of the feuilletons proper. They appear, indeed, as virtual dei ex machina, rather like the inspector general in Gogol's comedy. By the time *The Master and Margarita* was written, this process has been carried to the logical extreme. The whole system has been so contaminated that neither the police nor any other branch of government can serve as instruments of righteous punishment. The only remaining source of retribution comes from outside human society altogether: from the devils.

A still more fundamental reason for the appearance of the genuine supernatural in *The Master and Margarita* is the change in the very concept of enlightenment. In *Gudok,* as in other early works, such as *Notes of a Young Doctor,* lack of enlightenment is largely equated with age-old ignorance and can therefore be mostly righted through cognitive education and training. This view at least partially coincides with that of the Bolsheviks, although Bulgakov exposes the Communists' inattention to the inner man, without which all the rest is mere sham. In *The Master and Margarita*, while learning in the narrow sense continues to be a positive value (see the contrast between the erudite Master and the ignorant Bezdomny), far greater emphasis is placed on spiritual enlightenment—the meaning of spiritual, moreover, altered radically since the early works. For at the center is no longer the inner "darkness" of the simple people but the total denial of a transcendent spiritual sphere by the Soviet elite, represented most fully by the highly educated Berlioz.

This accounts for an almost total reversal in the treatment of the supernatural. For while the feuilletons almost always brand as superstition the belief in some inexplicable power, it is the *denial* of some higher force that signals the limitations of enlightenment in *The Master and Margarita*. Because of this, certain superficially similar episodes in the feuilletons and the novel actually have very different points. Thus, whereas the magic show in "The Talking Dog" exposes the ignorance of the "cultural worker," who too readily believes in the supernatural phenomenon, the show in *The Master and Margarita* reveals the excessive skepticism of the supposedly "enlightened" viewers, whose materialist beliefs prevent them from acknowledging the *genuine* supernatural. And, whereas Khikin's "invisible" boots are meant primarily to illustrate a current problem—shoddy consumer goods—the analogous disappearance of clothing after the magic show in *The Master and Margarita* does not reflect the quality of the goods but the quality of the people themselves, who value too much the purely material side of life.

The shift in Bulgakov's treatment of enlightenment has both external and internal sources. The novel, first of all, depicts a later period than the feuilletons, when holdovers from the past, so bemoaned during NEP, were no longer treated as a central problem. The ills of society upon which Bulgakov focuses, especially within the relatively well-educated stratum he depicts, stem not from age-old ignorance but from the central dogmas of the new world: materialism, rationalism, atheism. A change, moreover, has taken place not only in society but in Bulgakov himself. It already began, indeed, in works written concurrently with the *Gudok* pieces—his novellas, *The Fatal Eggs* and *Heart of a Dog*—where, as we shall see in the next chapter, scientific enlightenment uncontrolled by spiritual values provides the central theme.

The Roads Not Taken:
The Satirical Novellas

The Diaboliad

The idea for *The Diaboliad* reportedly came to Bulgakov on a winter evening in 1923, when he ran into his old Lito associate Aron Erlikh. (This is the same encounter that led to Bulgakov's association with *Gudok.*) According to Erlikh, Bulgakov's recollections of their misadventures in the arts bureaucracy stirred his literary imagination: "'Do you recall our Lito?' he suddenly burst out laughing. 'Now there's one more theme—I'm just itching to get at it!'"[1] Elsewhere Erlikh quotes Bulgakov at greater length: "I'll write about a certain establishment in a huge building . . . about the department continually moving from one floor to another, about old-timers driven crazy by their own muddles . . . Well, of course, about receiving matches instead of money and so on . . . Deviltry, a diavoliada!"[2]

The incident with the matches did, apparently, provide the plot kernel for *The Diaboliad*,[3] which Bulgakov began some time before August 1923 and published in the almanac *Nedra (The Depths)* in early 1924. The novella reappeared in 1925 as the title story of the only significant separate volume of Bulgakov's works to come out in his lifetime. Confiscated almost as soon as it appeared, the book was reprinted in 1926, but thereafter the stories contained in it were not republished in the Soviet Union until the late 1980s.[4]

The theme of *The Diaboliad*—devilish goings-on within the Moscow bureaucracy—already figured in a work inspired more directly by the Moscow Lito, *Notes on the Cuff*, Part Two.[5] In the earlier piece Bulgakov made direct reference to Gogol and Dostoevsky, and in *The Diaboliad* the presence of his great predecessors is yet more apparent. For now the uncanniness and madness inherent in the modern, bureaucratized city are no longer refracted through the perceptions of an autobiographical narrator but of a favorite Gogolian and Dostoevskian hero—the government clerk. The particular kind of madness portrayed, moreover, has clear antecedents in the writings of Bulgakov's forerunners. The early Soviet bureaucratic sphere he depicts, with its endless replication of function, with the post defining the person and loss of individual identity a constant threat, is, like the official worlds of Gogol and Dostoevsky *(The Nose, Notes of a Madman, The Double)*, a fertile breeding ground for the multiplication of personality.[6]

V. Pereverzev was the first to note *The Diaboliad*'s tie to the Russian classics.[7] At the same time, he was struck by the novella's contemporaneity, as was Evgeny Zamyatin. In a brief but penetrating review, Zamyatin calls *The Diaboliad* "the only modern piece in *Nedra*" and notes in particular its formal ties to the cinema, its "rapid change of scenes, as in the movies," its "flat, two-dimensional" quality.[8] His comments on O. Henry in another article are also applicable to *The Diaboliad:* "In the cinema, the most important thing is motion, motion at any cost. And in O. Henry's stories the most important thing is dynamics, motion; hence his faults and his virtues."[9]

The title of the last chapter of *The Diaboliad*, "A Chase Movie" *("Parfosnoe kino"),* indicates that Bulgakov was consciously borrowing from the cinema. Indeed, the entire work is constructed like an early chase film, with the hero now pursuing, now being pursued, but the motion never flagging. The protagonist may also well owe something to a common silent film type, best exemplified by Chaplin's tramp: the little man, who is ever being put upon by his rigid society but who at the same time acts as an anarchic force, setting society itself on its ear.[10]

This influence of Western cinema is symptomatic of the cultural ambience in the early Soviet period, when readers, tired of the gray realism of much Russian fiction, were turning in vast numbers to foreign works for exciting plots and light entertainment.[11] Popular demand, indeed, resulted in such a flood of fantastic, adventure, and detective works by the mid-twenties that, as one scholar puts it, "only the lazy did not write [such works] . . . between 1924 and 1927."[12] And it was precisely the call for exciting plots that figured importantly in *Nedra*'s decision to publish *The Diaboliad*.[13]

The writer perhaps most associated with this turn to the West is Lev

Lunts, theoretician for the Serapion Brothers, a well-known grouping of talented young Petrograd writers. Chudakova suggests the influence of one of Lunts's stories on *The Diaboliad,* "Outgoing Paper No. 37" (1922).[14] The Lunts work takes the form of the diary of an office manager, who believes that the only way to achieve the Bolshevik aim of transforming society is to transform people. The hero succeeds in transforming himself into what he considers "higher material": paper.[15] He thinks in triumph: "All people are equal, in other words, all people are papers. Humanity's ideal is achieved."[16] His lofty thoughts are interrupted, however, when the man on duty picks him up from the floor and comments: "The paper is soft. It'll do." At this point the notes break off (the manager having come to an ignominious end as toilet paper?).

Chudakova points to an analogous incident in *The Diaboliad:* a bureaucrat turns into a white rooster, on which the word "outgoing" is written. While the detail may have come from Lunts, however, this only underscores the differences between the two writers—helps, indeed, to pinpoint the specific quality of Bulgakov's satire. Lunts, in his famous manifesto, "Why We Are Serapion Brothers," rejects the traditional demand on Russian writers to portray real life. He insists that a literary work should "live its own special life . . . Not be a copy from nature, but live on an equal footing with nature."[17] And his story is not rooted in quotidian reality but is instead a schematic combination of pathological psychology and pure fantasy. Bulgakov, in contrast, creates a concrete social-moral milieu in his work. His originality lies, indeed—as Zamyatin observed of *The Diaboliad* and later critics were to note often—in his creation of "fantasy rooted in everyday life."[18]

In *The Diaboliad,* moreover—typically for Bulgakov's early works—the fantastic does not even exist objectively. No otherworldly diabolical figures appear, as they do in a number of other works of the early 1920s.[19] At first, as in the *Gudok* feuilletons, what seems supernatural arises from the senselessness, verging on the uncanny, woven into the fabric of everyday life. And later the "fantastic" originates in the deranged psyche of the poor hero, driven mad by his absurd surroundings.[20]

Bulgakov's diabolical tale begins on September 20, 1921, around the time the author himself first arrived in Moscow.[21] The initial setting is the Main Central Base for Match Materials, known better by one of those unwieldy Soviet acronyms, often the butt of satire: *Glavtsentrbazspimat,* or more familiarly, *Spimat.* Typical of early NEP, traces of the office's former bourgeois function, as the Alpine Rose Restaurant—for example, the "immense, abandoned organ"(2:16) gracing the lobby—at once add a note of incongruity to the entire narrative.[22]

The hero is head clerk *(deloproizvoditel')* Korotkov, a "tender, quiet blond" (2:7). Although Korotkov is far from autobiographical, the writer has endowed him with certain of his own experiences and character traits. During his first days in Moscow Bulgakov, like Korotkov, tried to overcome the deprivations of the Civil War by finding a bureaucratic niche as secretary of Lito. There he immersed himself in office work, in one month handling "more than fifty different papers and letters, on which he left notations in accordance with all the rules of clerical work [*deloproizvodstvo*]."[23] Korotkov, to be sure, presents in extreme form Bulgakov's quest for bureaucratic security, for he regards the post he has held for an "entire eleven months" as an eternal refuge: he "entirely expunged from his soul the thought that the so-called vicissitudes of fate existed, and in its place inculcated the belief that he—Korotkov—would work at the base to the end of his life on the earthly sphere" (2:7). The clerk, although more removed from the author than are the Civil War heroes, is thus, as his name suggests (*korotkii* = short; *krotkii* = meek), yet another emanation of the timid part of Bulgakov's personality.[24] Like the Civil War personae he above all wants peace, although he seeks it not in a lamplit study but in an uncongenial bureaucratic setting. His shelter, like theirs, moreover, proves inadequate—becomes, indeed, a new battlefield, and one on which he is doomed to meet his end.

The falseness of Korotkov's sense of security at *Spimat* becomes apparent at once, when in place of his salary he receives "the products of production," matches (2:9). The matches, moreover, are defective: the first one goes out after giving off a green flame (the first sign of the diabolical), while the second shoots out *two* flames, one of which lands in Korotkov's eye. The cautious civil servant bandages the eye, after which he "began to look like someone wounded in battle" (2:10)—the first instance of war imagery in the novella. When he finally falls asleep near dawn, he has a terrifying and prophetic dream of a living billiard ball on legs in a green meadow. And there is the diabolical smell of sulphur.

As a consequence of these devilish goings-on, Korotkov arrives at work very late the following day and is therefore unaware of the identity of the extraordinary-looking stranger he meets in the corridor:

This stranger was so short that he came up only to the tall Korotkov's waist. The lack of height was compensated for by the extreme breadth of the stranger's shoulders. His square torso sat on crooked legs, the left one lame. But most notable of all was his head. It was an exact gigantic model of an egg, grafted on the neck horizontally and with the pointed end forward. It was also bald like an egg, and so shiny that electric lights burned, undimmed, on the stranger's crown. The stranger's tiny face was shaven to the point of blueness, and little green eyes, like pinheads, sat in deep hollows (2:11).

The stranger's lameness and green eyes, which "blazed up with yellowish sparks" (2:12) (recalling the green flame of the previous evening) immediately suggest the diabolical, but the "shortsighted Korotkov" does not heed the ominous signs. When the stranger blocks his way, the clerk does what he "should not under any account have done" (2:11): he unwittingly violates bureaucratic protocol by taking offense. Only when the angry stranger calls him "undeveloped" (2:12) and declares that he "will establish order" does the horrified Korotkov realize that he has insulted the new manager.

Ensuing events militate against Korotkov's efforts to right this bad first impression. Acting upon what he interprets as the manager's order—that "all typists . . . be issued soldiers' long underwear [kal'sony]" (2:13)—he discovers only the following day that he misread the new chief's surname, Kal'soner, as kal'sony. This new misstep brings catastrophe: Korotkov is dismissed, charged with "neglect of his duties" and "appearing at work in unsightly form, his face beaten, apparently in a brawl" (2:14). Thus, owing to a malfunction of the system (being paid in defective matches), the meek hero is perceived as a brawler, the victim taken for aggressor. Oddly, however, in the course of the narrative this initially false impression becomes self-fulfilling, for in his efforts to right the injustice against him, Korotkov grows ever more assertive. The process begins immediately, when, informed of his dismissal, he declares that Kalsoner "has no right" (2:15). He then pursues the chief, beginning the chase that ends only with the novella itself.

If the hero at once becomes a bit more forceful, however, both the imagery and unfolding events point to his continuing vulnerability. His voice, which sounds "like an Alpine goblet crushed by a heel" (2:14), is contrasted throughout to Kalsoner's siren-like roar. And his "feminine" weakness is underscored through physiological humor akin to that of the silent slapstick film: when he tries to approach Kalsoner, he finds himself "in the embraces" of the guard, Panteleimon (2:15), who "lightly pressed him to himself like a beloved woman" (2:16). Later, when he jumps on a trolley in pursuit of Kalsoner, he bumps himself, is buffeted by backpacks, and falls as he gets off.

These signs of physical vulnerability only foreshadow the assault on Korotkov's psyche once he follows Kalsoner into the terrifying *Tsentrosnab* (Central Supply Office) building. Opening door after door of this immense beehive, reminiscent of the Lito building in *Notes on the Cuff*, he is confronted alternately with scenes of absurdity (a middle-aged woman weighing an evil-smelling fish) and loss of individual identity (six identical typists). Both are combined in the "diabolical trick" (2:17) played upon him when he catches up with Kalsoner: "This was Kalsoner, but Kalsoner with a long Assyrian-corrugated beard coming down to his chest" and a "tender tenor" voice (2:18). A perfectly rational explanation for this "trick" appears in the story's subtitle: "A Tale about How Twins Destroyed a Head Clerk." Korotkov, however, not privy to this information, is staggered by the inexplicable change.

After this a second instance of doubling occurs, one that touches the hero yet more closely. There appears a diabolical-looking figure, a "lustrine old man in dark blue glasses" (2:19), who insists upon addressing Korotkov as Kolobkov. The hero then discovers, to his horror, that his documents have been pilfered, most likely by the same Kolobkov. Thus, his double, Kolobkov, has succeeded in doubly undermining Korotkov's sense of self, appropriating both his physical appearance and his paper identity. The clerk's attempts to restore his good name have resulted in the loss of his name altogether, his identification with the petty thief and seducer, Kolobkov (which continues throughout the novella), further besmirching his reputation.

That night Korotkov lies in bed and stares "as if enchanted" (2:22) at a portrait of Cromwell on the wall. Stirred, perhaps, by the image of the deposer of the British crown—a forerunner of the revolutionaries who destroyed the Russian monarchy[25]—Korotkov wages a symbolic attack on one who has just usurped *his own* rightful place. He throws the matches down and tramples on them, destroying his persecutor in his imagination: "'There! There! There!' howled Korotkov and with a crunch crushed the devilish boxes, dimly imagining that he was crushing Kalsoner's head."

The head clerk's rowdiness suddenly ceases, however, for the recollection of Kalsoner's "egg-shaped head" (2:22) and inexplicable doubling fills him with terror: "The doubled face, now overgrown with a beard, now suddenly clean-shaven, floated out from time to time from the corners, its green eyes glittering." One wonders if the double egg-shaped form of Korotkov's tormenters does not have a sexual subtext. In Bulgakov's next novella, *The Fatal Eggs*, puns on "eggs" (the Russian colloquial equivalent of "balls") are plentiful, and testes play a crucial role in *Heart of a Dog*. The brothers' surname, moreover, so close to the word for underpants (a secretary calls them "bald drawers" [*"podshtanniki lysye"*], 2:12), and their extremely short height—only up to Korotkov's waist—add to the impression of male genitalia on legs. The conflict between Korotkov, the meek, "feminine," old-style functionary, and Kalsoner, the assertive, powerful Soviet administrator, can, indeed, be couched in sexual terms. For if Korotkov considered himself wed to his job forever, the virile Soviet usurpers have won over his "bride."

In any case, thoughts of the Kalsoners lead to a series of changes in Korotkov that strikingly prefigure those in the three heroes of *The Master and Margarita* when they confront dark forces. First, Korotkov's fear, which "crawled through the black windows into the room" (2:22), foreshadows that of the Master, who, terrified, felt that "the autumnal darkness would break the window panes" (5:43). Then, like Ivanushka in the mental hospital, Korotkov feels "that his brain wants to crack from tension" and he "quietly burst out crying." Finally, after he drinks wine, half of his head hurts like Pilate's, his "left temple began to hurt tormentingly" (2:23). Korotkov's brain, like Ivanushka's, does indeed "crack" on that dreadful night, resulting in the most important instance of doubling in the tale— within the hero himself. While his old timid self does not disappear, a second, rowdy Korotkov, already prefigured earlier that day, becomes ever more dominant. The hero's brain, moreover, cracks in another sense, for he loses his grip on reality. From now on his hallucinations will blend confusingly with the world of ordinary, or at least explicable, phenomena.

Korotkov's psyche receives a further jolt the following day, when he finds the bearded Kalsoner sitting in his (Korotkov's) office, his "lacquered bald spot over the green broadcloth" (2:24) recalling the billiard ball nightmare. This is yet another instance of doubling, for the second Kalsoner has appropriated not only Korotkov's job but also his mild manners and high-pitched voice. After this and more alternating appearances of the brothers,

Korotkov's reason collapses altogether. He grows unruly and chases a Kalsoner to the lobby, where his coat gets caught on the organ handle and he falls.

At this point hallucinations begin, although the dividing line between Korotkov's demented perceptions and absurd reality is unclear. The organ (a player instrument, turned on when he fell?) spews out a tune about the Napoleonic war, and, just before Napoleon appears in the song, the first Kalsoner shows up, "vindictive and menacing [*groznyi*]" (2:27). The juxtaposition of Napoleon and Kalsoner (recalling the earlier parallel with Cromwell) links past usurpation and foreign invasion to the present *spiritually* alien usurpers of power in Russia.

Korotkov, however, refuses to surrender to these latter-day Napoleons. Crying out "I'll have it out with him" (2:27), he heads for the Claims Bureau, located in yet another nightmarish modern colossus. Not surprisingly, he cannot find the right room and ends up in an enormous hall, where he encounters a statue-like man dressed in Polish historical costume. The man identifies himself as a journalist and asks Korotkov for feuilletons and sketches (the only remnant of a literary theme in the story). He explains that his name—Jan Sobieski (that of a seventeenth-century Polish king)—is only a coincidence, and that he is about to change it to Sotsvossky.[26] Thus, with Moscow in the hands of the neo-Cromwells and Napoleons, the royal Sobieski is about to disappear behind a new socialist identity. In any case Kalsoner has taken his royal trappings, the "excellent Louis Quatorze satin furniture" (2:29).

Sobieski may be only a hallucination, for when Korotkov—still vainly searching for the Claims Bureau—returns to the room, it is empty except for a lifeless statue of the Polish king. Given the fine distinction in the story between social and psychological pathology, however, it is also possible that during Korotkov's ten-minute absence the room's occupants have in reality vanished. One recalls the hero of *Notes on the Cuff*, who, arriving one morning to find Lito gone, thinks "that everything around me was a mirage" (I1:693). He wonders if he is going crazy, but the "mirage" proves to be a product not of mental but of social insanity.

After this bewildering encounter, Korotkov walks downstairs and comes upon the bearded Kalsoner, whose actions and voice mirror his own: "Simultaneously their gazes crossed, and both, in their thin voices, began howling in fear and pain. Korotkov began to retreat upstairs backwards, Kalsoner backed downstairs, full of inescapable horror" (2:30). Kalsoner falls down and flies back up (at least in Korotkov's deranged imagination) as a black cat. This incident offers Korotkov a diabolical explanation for all the weird happenings: "I understand everything. Cats!" (2:31).

The climax of the novella occurs the following day, when Korotkov returns to the Claims Bureau. There he becomes enmeshed in ever more frenetic bureaucratic deviltry, which results first in the total denial of his identity and then in his physical annihilation. His troubles begin when the typist he approaches mistakes him for Kolobkov and whispers, "Why are you silent, tempter? . . . Kiss me" (2:32). She is soon joined by the lustrine old man, who accuses Korotkov of mass seductions of innocent young office workers. Thus, after the genitalia-like Kalsoners displace the "feminine" Korotkov from *Spimat,* the bureaucracy tries to force upon him an identity more in keeping with the "manly" new officialdom. He resists, however, crying out plaintively for a return of his true self: "She [the typist] will give herself to me, and I can't stand that. I don't want to! Return my documents. My sacred name. Restore it!" (2:34).

Kolobkov's function here and elsewhere in the novella in some ways echoes that of the double in Dostoevsky's novella of that name. Korotkov's "other," like the Dostoevskian double, is endowed with "all the petty baseness and mean skills . . . [the protagonist] associated with 'success'" (to borrow Fanger's formulation).[27] In Bulgakov as in Dostoevsky, moreover, the ethical opposition between the doubles is not as clear-cut as the protagonist would have it, for Kolobkov, like the "younger" Golyadkin in Joseph Frank's reading, sometimes "mirrors the suppressed wishes" of the ostensibly pure hero.[28] This can be seen in Korotkov's reaction to the directive that sets the plot in motion, by how he "exclaimed rapturously and trembled voluptuously when he imagined Lidochka in soldiers' long underwear" (2:13).

In any case, after this mistaken identity the whole office dissolves in unbridled phantasmagoria: the lustrine old man flies through the air, an official crawls out of a desk drawer, typists dance to a foxtrot played by the typewriters. When Korotkov can stand it no longer, he bangs his head against a desk and the lustrine old man decides to send him down to Dyrkin (*dyrka* = hole). As the hero rides the elevator to the "terrifying Dyrkin" (2:36), his reflection in the mirror produces "two Korotkovs," a visual concomitant of his psychological split. Only one, of course, gets off: "The first and main one forgot the second in the elevator mirror." That this "main" Korotkov has retained his newfound assertiveness is apparent from his "Satanic laugh" and reply when a fat man threatens to arrest him: "It is impossible to arrest me . . . because no one knows who I am." He adds that he is perhaps a Hohenzollern, thus continuing the royalty/usurper imagery.

The aggressive side of Korotkov's personality emerges still more fully in Dyrkin's office, although at first he is intimidated by the official, whose mechanical movements and rigid utterances exemplify the inhumanity of the bureaucracy. His combativeness returns only after Dyrkin, himself beaten and thus "humbled" by his superior, complains to Korotkov: "That's what I get for my zeal . . . Maybe you came for the same reason? Well... Beat Dyrkin . . . Maybe it'll hurt your hand? Then take the candelabra" (2:38). Korotkov, understanding nothing, does as Dyrkin says and the bloodied bureaucrat runs from the room. Hallucinations resume, as Kalsoner jumps out of a cuckoo clock, turns into the white "outgoing" rooster mentioned earlier, and flits out the door. Dyrkin then returns, howling "catch him, the bandit," and Korotkov flees.

In this final chase, Korotkov's combativeness develops apace. The formerly meek functionary, indeed, is transformed into a dangerous outlaw, and all because of his unattainable goal of keeping both his bureaucratic job and his identity. Once he is outside, pandemonium breaks loose and bullets start to fly. Korotkov's voice no longer squeaks but snarls "like a blacksmith's bellows" (2:39). His final struggle is described entirely in military terms, underlining the change he has undergone. He runs into an immense eleven-story building and tells the elevator operator: "We're attacking... Kalsoner... and he's taking the offensive" (2:40). He goes up to a billiard room on the top floor, from which he "surveys his position with an eagle eye" and gives a "battle cry: 'forward!'" From the room, whose "green squares with shiny white balls" recall the early prophetic dream, Korotkov aims balls at the heads of his pursuers. A machine gun, however, soon chases him out onto the roof, where, beneath an "emaciated sun" (2:41), he is fast overtaken by his enemies.

At first Korotkov's timid self comes to the fore, and he cries out weakly: "It's over, . . . over. The battle is lost" (2:42). But then his defiant side triumphs: "The valor of death poured into his soul." He climbs onto a parapet, straightens up, and cries: "Better death than disgrace!" Lured by the "sun's abyss," he gives a "piercing victory cry" and flies upward. The novella's conclusion reproduces Korotkov's sensation as he falls, first head up, then down, past the multistoried building: "He saw unclearly, very unclearly, something gray with black holes, as from an explosion, flying upward past him. Then he saw very clearly the gray thing falling downward, and he himself climbed upward toward the narrow chink of the lane, which turned out to be above him. Then the bloody sun burst with a noise in his head and he no longer saw anything at all."

And so Korotkov ends a victim of cruel forces, which refused to recognize his true identity and usurped his rightful place. As an official to the core, he is on the one hand a victim of his own delusions, done in by the same bureaucracy to which he so fervently joined his destiny. On the other hand, however, by choosing death over disgrace, the timid clerk performs a feat of which none of the authorial personae of the Civil War works (except for the only remotely autobiographical Aleksei of *Days of the Turbins*) are capable. For this reason, the sun, which tormented so many Bulgakovian heroes, bursts and disappears for him. Indeed, with his upward leap toward the sun, Korotkov prefigures the Master, who, also tormented and driven mad by the establishment, dies and literally flies away from the earth.

The question upon which one must conclude is why Korotkov's heroic transformation has gone largely unnoticed, why, on the contrary, he has on the whole been treated very deprecatingly by commentators.[29] There are a couple of reasons. The first is that he really is not very sympathetic—he is not only flatly portrayed (flat characters can be sympathetic) but is given no inner life beyond his attachment to his job. Described as "overcautious," "shortsighted," with a "stupid smile," when Korotkov loses his identity, he seems not to be losing much. The second impediment to interpretation is the nature of the fantasy in *The Diaboliad,* which toward the end grows so unbridled that the underlying psychological-moral thread is all but lost in the confusion.

Therefore, one must conclude that *The Diaboliad* is in balance an artistic failure, but it is a fascinating one, which presents some of Bulgakov's fundamental themes and motifs for the first time. Korotkov, indeed, has within himself the seeds of two heroes of *The Master and Margarita*, Ivan Bezdomny and the Master. Like Ivan, he is an establishment figure, who tries to right the wrongs perpetrated by diabolical forces but is driven mad and splits in two. And just as the Master's search for truth leads to his persecution, mental breakdown, and death, Korotkov's efforts to establish the truth about himself, although hardly comparable to the Master's artistic and historical seekings, nevertheless result in essentially the same personal catastrophe.

In *The Diaboliad,* finally, Bulgakov attempts to widen the scope of his satire, to broaden both the autobiographical focus of *Notes on the Cuff* and the narrowly topical subject matter of his journalistic writings. By following his scurrying hero about from one monstrous building to another, he succeeds in creating a broad and generalized panorama of hellish bureaucratic Moscow, although not without becoming enmeshed in an overly intricate and confused plot. Only in *The Master and Margarita,* indeed, where the peregrinations of the devils and their victims take the reader to an ever- widening array of satirically rendered locales, does a *Diaboliad*-like structure—embedded within the yet broader panorama of the novel as a whole—receive completely satisfying formal embodiment.

The Fatal Eggs

P. N. Zaitsev, editor of *Nedra,* recalls how in early September 1924 he informed Bulgakov that for ideological reasons he could not publish *The White Guard.* Seeing the writer's disappointment, he asked him to submit some other work, and Bulgakov answered: "I have a novella that's almost ready . . . a fantastic novella." A week later he brought in *The Fatal Eggs.*[30] In fact all of this must have occurred somewhat earlier, and Bulgakov must have been more dilatory than Zaitsev remembers, because by September 4 the editor had already sent a letter prodding him to finish the novella.[31] According to its printed version, Bulgakov did complete the work in October. It was published in *Nedra* in February 1925 and reappeared later that year in the *Diaboliad* collection.[32]

Even before its publication, Bulgakov held numerous readings of *The Fatal Eggs* for Moscow literati, among whom it aroused considerable excitement—a feeling that was to grow once the work appeared in print. It was, indeed, the first of Bulgakov's writings to attract widespread attention[33]—much more so than *The White Guard,* whose first installment appeared at about the same time. Published reviews, to be sure, were at best mixed,[34] with some proletarian critics, later to become the nemeses of Bulgakov and other insufficiently conformist writers, attacking the work. M. Lirov, for example, asked indignantly: "What is to be done with the allegory *The Fatal Eggs,* which, judging by its far from academic subject, seems to be intended exclusively for the White Guard press? How did it turn up on the pages of the Soviet *Nedra?*"[35] On the other hand, the *Novyi mir* critic gave the novella a glowing review. Judging it "the central piece of the *Nedra* collection," an "entertaining, fantastic story, saturated with contemporaneity, wit, with abundant small vignettes from everyday life," he granted its author a "unique place in our current literature."[36] Grossman-Roshchin took the middle ground, finding *The Fatal Eggs* ideologically "unreliable," but "in its own way brilliantly conceived and well executed."[37]

If the judgments of critics varied, the verdicts of writers and editors that have come down to us are almost uniformly enthusiastic, with such diverse figures as Andrei Bely and Maksim Gorky, the old-fashioned realist V. V. Veresaev, and the Serapion "young Turk" M. L. Slonimsky joined in their praise.[38] They all singled out Bulgakov's ability, already noted by Zamyatin in his review of *The Diaboliad*, to join "the real and the fantastic."[39] For Gorky, for example, the story performed the proper function of fantasy in the "quite fantastic" NEP period, showing "the unreal, semi-fantastic, the devilishly Russian in all its fullness."[40]

That the Serapions should like the novella is not surprising, for, as the *Novyi mir* critic noted, *The Fatal Eggs* eschewed the boring plotlessness they found such a defect in Russian literature: "We sin both against the entertaining and against the fantastic, usually dividing things into 'adventure' works and 'realistic' [*bytovye*] ones. 'Adventure' works are interesting and empty. 'Realistic' ones are profound and boring. All types of literature are good, except boring ones—that is a great truth."[41] Another way in which Bulgakov conforms to Serapion precepts is by turning once more— and more obviously than in *The Diaboliad*—to the West. Here his model was one of the most popular writers in the Soviet Union at the time, H. G. Wells, whose novel, *Food of the Gods*, serves in some respects as a proto-type.[42] Numerous specific parallels can and have been traced, but most important is the very fact that Bulgakov adopted the genre of science fiction, so fashionable in the Soviet Union of the twenties. Its appeal to him and other Soviet writers is best defined in Zamyatin's 1922 essay on Wells: "But imagine a country where the only fertile soil is asphalt, where nothing grows but dense forests of factory chimneys, where the animal herds are of a single breed, automobiles, and the only fragrance in the spring is that of gasoline. This place of stone, asphalt, iron, gasoline, and machines is the present-day, twentieth-century London, and, naturally, it was bound to produce its own iron, automobile goblins, and its own, mechanical, chemical fairy tales. Such urban tales exist: they are told by Herbert George Wells. They are his fantastic novels."[43]

The heroes of such "urban fairy tales," Zamyatin observes, rely not on magic carpets or fairy godmothers but on science to perform their feats. He adds: "This may seem paradoxical at first—exact science and fairy tale, precision and fantasy. But it is so, and must be so. For a myth is always, openly or implicitly, connected with religion, and the religion of the modern city is precise science."[44] *The Fatal Eggs* is just such a modern fairy tale, in which technological perils replace the enchantments of the forest and science replaces religion. Indeed, Zamyatin's description of a typical Wells novel would just as well fit *The Fatal Eggs* (if one substituted biological for physics and mathematics terminology): "This is what reveals itself as we enter those fantastic edifices, Wells's fairy tales. We find there, side by side, mathematics and myths, physics and fantasy, blueprints and miracles, parody and prophecy, fairy tales and socialism".[45]

Persikov and the Red Ray

The Fatal Eggs, unlike most science fiction, takes place not in the distant future or past but in 1928, just four years after it was written. Its hero, Vladimir Ipatievich Persikov, is a fifty-eight-year-old professor and director of the Moscow Zoological Institute. Numerous prototypes have been suggested for the scientist—among them a relative of the author's second wife, the zoologist father of a friend, and the renowned physiologist Pavlov[46]—and it is likely that Bulgakov drew from one or more of them. At the same time, Persikov has autobiographical roots, and ones much deeper than Korotkov's in *The Diaboliad.* For if the writer's contact with the bureaucratic world of his first novella was brief and superficial, he was long and deeply involved in science.[47] Persikov, moreover, shares essential traits with the doctor-heroes of the Civil War works: their solitude and solipsism. Totally engrossed in his research, he regards the revolution as an extraneous disturbance, impeding his work and personal comfort. Even when peace returns he manages to ignore all but his scientific experiments: "Professor Persikov didn't read newspapers, didn't go to the theater" (2:46).

A crucial difference between Persikov and the authorial personae—and Bulgakov himself—is that the professor, already an eminent scientist before the revolution, was not entirely deprived of home and profession, and by 1928 his life has returned to its prerevolutionary norm. Familiar motifs link the world that Persikov has regained to that the autobiographical heroes have lost: the green lamp in his study, the cream-colored walls of his institute, recalling the Turbins' cream-colored shades. In tracing the fate of Persikov, Bulgakov is thus exploring the scientific "road not taken." That he sometimes rued the direction his own life had taken instead is revealed in a diary entry of late 1923: "At moments of ill health and loneliness . . . I bitterly regret that I abandoned medicine and condemned myself to a false [*nevernyi*] existence. But, God is my witness, it was love of literature alone that was the reason for this."[48] By probing the moral assumptions of the scientist in *The Fatal Eggs*, Bulgakov was, perhaps, trying to overcome such lingering regrets.

The hero of *The Fatal Eggs* does indeed emerge as a morally ambivalent figure,[49] whose brilliance in science coexists with total ineptitude in worldly matters. This is reflected in people's contradictory reactions to him: "Everyone spoke to Persikov either with respect and terror or with an affectionate grin, as to a little, although large child" (2:79). Both the professional and public sides of the professor's character, in fact, arouse mixed feelings. Although his naiveté and indifference to everyday life lend him a semicomical, even lovable, air—as stereotypical absent-minded professor, unable even to put on his galoshes correctly—they prove a terrible flaw in a scientist of his magnitude, contributing to his downfall and the novella's final catastrophe. And although professionally he embodies to the highest degree the mastery Bulgakov so admires—possesses, indeed, "the eye of a genius" (2:53)—he sacrifices all human emotions to his obsessive pursuit of his calling.

Important here is the absence of family, so central to Bulgakov's other early works. Persikov's wife abandoned him in 1913, having left the note: "Your frogs arouse in me an unbearable shudder of revulsion" (2:46). All that remains of a home life is his housekeeper, who, in keeping with the professor's infantilism, watches over him like a nanny. At one point someone comments that "a frog can't take the place of a wife" (2:86), but this is essentially what has happened to Persikov, who values his animals above human beings. (He mourned the loss of a valuable toad during the Civil War more deeply than of his "irreplaceable watchman Vlas" [2:47].) Even his attachment to animals, moreover, is based purely on utility, and at science's command he cruelly sacrifices them. Thus, one frog, "crucified" by Persikov and his assistant, Ivanov (2:49), thinks reproachfully: "You are bastards [*svolochi*], that's what" (2:50).

Such words as "crucify" and "sacrifice" are used advisedly, for if science has replaced religion in the modern world, Persikov serves as its "divinity" (2:81). His first name and patronymic (*Vladimir* = *power* + *world*; *Ipatievich*, from the Greek *hypatos* = *supreme*) and the name of the watchman,

Pankrat (from the Greek *Pankrates* = *all-powerful*), suggest his godlike omnipotence in the laboratory, coexisting incongruously with the comic public persona associated with his surname (*persik* = peach). Like many an obsessed scientist in the literary tradition, moreover, Persikov's "divinity" is tinged with the diabolical, his laboratory called a "hell."[50] His divine-demonic power comes especially into play in his great discovery of the red ray, which "breathed a spirit of life" into the amoebae at which it is directed (2:53), thus endowing Persikov with godlike power. The amoebae, and later tadpoles, multiply at such an unheard-of rate and grow to such enormous size that Ivanov cries exultantly: "Professor Persikov, you have discovered the ray of life!" (2:56).

This exultation, however, reveals the scientists' moral limitations. Accustomed to defining life in purely material terms, they ignore the increased viciousness that accompanies the amoebae's growth: "The newborn creatures pounced ferociously, tore one another to bits and devoured one another. Among the newborn there lay the corpses of those who had perished in the struggle for existence. The best and the strongest conquered. And these best were terrifying" (2:54). When the experiment is repeated on frogs, they too grow "so malicious and voracious that half of them were immediately gobbled up by the other half" (2:55). They soon crawl out of the box and occupy the whole institute; only poison controls the infestation. Here increased physical prowess is not accompanied by analogous moral development; on the contrary, when natural evolution is accelerated, the Darwinian struggle for existence runs amok and brute force reigns.

Ever since the appearance of *The Fatal Eggs*, critics have commonly interpreted Professor Persikov's "revolutionary" experiments with the red ray as an Aesopian allusion to the radical social experiments of the Red Bolsheviks.[51] Although a link between the scientific and social levels of the novella certainly exists, a strict allegorical reading is too simplistic to accommodate the rich, complex portrayal of Soviet society in the novella. What, indeed, is most striking is the absence of the schematism generally associated with futuristic allegorical works—and how unsocialist the Moscow of 1928 in fact appears. The noise, lights, rushing cars, and teeming crowds make the city almost indistinguishable from other large modern metropolises such as New York or London: "It [Moscow] shone, lights danced, died down, and flashed up. On Theater Square the white headlights of buses and the green lights of trolleys revolved; above the former

Miur and Meriliz, over the added tenth story, an electrical, multi-colored woman was jumping, throwing out multi-colored words letter by letter: 'workers' credit.' In the public garden opposite the Bolshoi Theater, where at night a multi-colored fountain gushed, a crowd was pushing and buzzing" (2:73).

This is a strikingly modern, machine-driven world, the only remnant of an older spiritual tradition being the cupola of the Cathedral of Christ the Savior, blazing in the sun like a "helmet of Christ" the morning after Persikov's discovery (2:53). At the same time, however, various distinguishing signs of Bolshevism are fast fading: the word "comrade" has virtually disappeared from the vocabulary (A3:81),[52] and Civil War garb is entirely extinct, replaced by suit jackets even among the proletariat (2:81). Bulgakov is not imagining a socialist utopia here but the Moscow of the near future from the vantage point of the mixed system of NEP. His vision has clear ties to the *Nakanune* feuilletons, as he pictures how the construction and return of plenty, portrayed so vividly in the journalistic pieces, will evolve in a few years. Thus the housing crisis, the bane of his early Soviet existence, is at an end. And if a single tailcoat astonishingly appeared in one *Nakanune* feuilleton, in *The Fatal Eggs* the entire audience at Persikov's lecture is dressed in evening clothes.

In the *Nakanune* pieces, Bulgakov's depiction of NEP, although far from uncritical, is filled with the optimism of a recovery period, and *The Fatal Eggs* shares that mood. This was noted in the favorable *Novyi mir* review: "Some author or other of a utopian r-r-revolutionary novel could hardly arouse in his readers the same sense of a powerful, joyous country, a true New World." And even a more negative critic praises the "beauty" of the contrasts of old and new, the "running, rush, quickness, dynamism of our marvelous days."[53] The contemporary reader associated this glittering, speeding world not only—and not even primarily—with the new Bolshevik order but also with America. As the second critic observed: "Moscow has begun to live American style [*zazhila po-amerikanski*]. Moscow has become entirely Americanized [*"obamerikanilas'"*]."[54] Within the text, moreover, there are numerous links between this new world and America. Persikov's housing problem, for example, has been solved by the efforts of a "united American-Russian company" (2:48). And Persikov himself succumbs to the American lure, agreeing to see an impudent journalist because "all the same, there is something American in this scoundrel" (2:72).

Bulgakov, as we have seen, depicts this Americanized society with considerable élan, but there are implicit reservations. This is a place, after all, where artificial lights replace the natural, where the increased speed and growth brought about by technology have also increased the level of ruthlessness. This process, typical of modern, technological (not only socialist) societies, is analogous to the effect of the red ray on the amoebae, and specific parallels are drawn between society and Persikov's laboratory.[55] Similarities are especially apparent in the professor's relations with voracious journalists, which, like his own laboratory experiments, involve colored rays and magnification. Thus, when Persikov is out one evening, he is accosted by a reporter and blinded by a "violet ray" (2:62), evidently from a camera. The next day he sees himself, magnified, "on the roof, on a white screen, covering himself with his fists from the violet ray" (2:65). Such importunate journalists (who also figure in Wells's *Food of the Gods*) are, like the speed, crowds, and artificial lights of Moscow, a feature of the modern world as a whole, not only, or even primarily, of socialist society— yet another indication that Bulgakov's Moscow cannot be reduced to a schematic vision of the Communist future.

One must beware, however, of going to the opposite extreme and regarding the city as merely a generalized modern metropolis. The society of the novella reflects precisely the hybrid system of NEP, in which specific features both of the West and of Bolshevism play roles. The most salient feature of the latter—and one that does make the parallels between Persikov's laboratory and society more exact—is central control. For if the social Darwinism underlying laissez-faire capitalism is based upon an analogy with unfettered *natural* evolution, under socialism the laboratory model, with its central controlling and manipulating intelligence, is more pertinent.[56] From the beginning of *The Fatal Eggs* socialist control is indeed exercised, primarily by the GPU (the secret police). Thus, when the journalist Bronsky, "staff member of the Moscow magazines *Red Flame, Red Pepper, Red Journal, Red Projector,* and the Moscow newspaper *Red Evening Moscow*" (2:57), comes to see Persikov, the scientist at first summarily orders him thrown out, but when he learns that Bronsky also works for *Red Raven,* a publication of the GPU, he agrees to see him. This submission to state coercion is the first step in the professor's surrender of his scientific autonomy, which leads ineluctably to the final disaster.

One must add, however, that relations between the professor and the GPU are not, on the whole, adversarial. Later, indeed, Persikov himself calls in the secret police after a suspicious character offers him five thousand rubles to pass his discovery on to a foreign government. Then certain parallels between the scientist and the agents emerge, reinforcing the analogy between laboratory and social control. Thus the agents are also a blend of the heavenly and hellish: the first "was reminiscent of an angel in patent-leather boots. The second, shortish, [was] terribly gloomy" (2:68); the third, like Persikov, has extraordinary vision, "amazingly piercing [koliuchie] eyes" (2:69). The agents are also incredibly knowledgeable, coming up with the visitor's identity from a mere glimpse of a galosh he left behind. Then, when Persikov requests that the pesky reporters be shot, much as he killed off the tadpoles once they had gotten out of hand, one agent responds: "Of course that would be good . . . however, such a project is already being worked out [nazrevaet] at the Council of Labor and Defense" (A3:68–69).[57]

In some of Bulgakov's early works, the hero and/or narrator welcome the Bolsheviks as instruments of order, and Persikov, with his rage for control, regards the GPU in this light. His tragedy stems from the fact that he becomes a victim of his belief in control, for in the course of the novella the secret police not only try (and fail) to control forces inimical to him, but they and the government as a whole manipulate the man of genius himself. And so while Persikov is in one sense a "divinity" to his science-worshipping society, at the same time he is but a means to its end: just as he "crucified" his frog in a *scientific* experiment, so in the end he himself is "crucified" (2:114) in the state's larger *social* experiment. This power of the state is, to be sure, muted at the beginning, hidden beneath the glitter and dynamism of modern urban society. It becomes clear only after the eruption of a national crisis: the chicken plague.

The Chicken Plague and Rokk's Eggs

The chicken plague brings us to another locale, rural Russia, where the triumph of science and disappearance of traditional beliefs are not as total as in Moscow. Place names have been changed, to be sure, to eliminate Christian associations, and Drozdova, widow of the local archpriest who "died in '26 from anti-religious woes" (2:63), is now head of a thriving chicken cooperative. Local reaction to the chicken disease, however, shows that the uprooting of religion and superstition is far from complete. Thus Drozdova's neighbor attributes the illness to bewitchment, while the priest asserts that the chickens died because "the Lord has become angry with us"

(2:65). Within this provincial setting, indeed, the limitations of scientific control are most apparent, for it has succeeded neither in conquering nature (the chicken disease) nor in replacing traditional beliefs.[58] As in the *Gudok* feuilletons, beneath all the name changes the entire old world of religion and superstition is still alive.

The helplessness of science before the forces of nature becomes ever more evident as the chicken plague spreads throughout the country. At the same time, the disease acquires other levels of meaning, ranging from the frivolous to the very grave. Clearly of the first category are the scabrous associations evoked by the resulting egg shortage (*eggs* in colloquial Russian = *balls, testicles*).[59] For example, performers at a night club sing: "Oh, mama, what will I do without eggs?" (2:76). And a feuilleton addressing Charles Evans Hughes, American Secretary of State, ends: "Don't hanker after our eggs, Mr. Hughes—you have your own!" (2:78).

As the reference to Hughes indicates, however, even such seemingly lighthearted wordplay at times indicates another, nonsexual order of impotence in the USSR. It forms a part, indeed, of a complex web of topical political allusions in the novella. Thus it is significant that the plague comes to a halt precisely at the borders of the Soviet Union. As the narrator comments: "Whether the climate there was different or the defensive-cordoning [*zagraditel'nye-kordonnye*] measures taken by neighboring governments played a role, the fact is that the plague went no farther" (2:78). Such military-sounding terminology suggests a reference to the *cordon sanitaire* the Western powers placed around the Soviet Union to prevent the spread of the "contagion" of revolution.[60] One recalls that in the satirical allegory "The Crimson Island" (2:411–426), written shortly before *The Fatal Eggs,* the revolution itself is termed a plague, and a quarantine is enforced by the nervous imperialist powers. In "The Crimson Island," the plague is declared over six years after the revolution, at which time the French and British, together with White exiles, invade the island. And in *The Fatal Eggs* (written in the seventh year after the Revolution), the plague itself arouses fear of intervention. A voice from a loudspeaker calls out: "New attempts at intervention! . . . in connection with the chicken plague!" (2:75). A newsboy cries: "Poland is preparing for a nightmarish war!" (2:76).

Bulgakov envisions intervention and Polish invasion because of the political situation in 1923, shortly before he wrote *The Fatal Eggs* (that is, the six years after the revolution referred to in "The Crimson Island"). The fear began with French occupation of the Ruhr early that year and the concomitant threat of invasion of the Soviet Union by France's Eastern ally, Poland. It was exacerbated a few months later when the fiercely anti-Bolshevik Lord Curzon came to power in England and presented the Soviets with a very stiff ultimatum.[61] Bulgakov, in his diary entry of May 24, 1923, writes: "There is the smell of a break or even of war in the air . . . It's awful that both Poland and Rumania have begun stirring . . . In general we are on the eve of events."[62] In one of his *Nakanune* feuilletons, "Benefit Performance for Lord Curzon,"[63] he describes a mass demonstration against the Curzon ultimatum. Another source reports that Chicherin, the principal orator, gave as a reason for the crisis Lenin's illness, which convinced the Bolsheviks' enemies that "Soviet power is deprived of its firmness and can be overthrown by pressure from without." He concluded: "We firmly await our enemy at our threshold."[64] Thus on the political level the chicken plague emerges as a rather amorphous symbol, associated both with the revolutionary contagion with which the Soviet Union was threatening the outside world and with the weakness of Soviet Russia itself in 1923–1924, when the death of the powerful leader "emasculated" the country and invited foreign invasion.

In addition to this complex of political referents, the chicken disease also alludes to the country's already chronic agricultural problems, in particular to a serious drought threatening the harvest during the summer of 1924, the very time the novella was being written.[65] Indeed, the two measures taken in *The Fatal Eggs* to fight the chicken plague echo reactions by the Soviet government to both the agricultural and international crises of 1923–1924. In July 1924, an "emergency commission for combating the consequences of the deficient harvest" was set up,[66] whereas in the novella one has the "emergency commission for combating the chicken plague" (2:75). Bulgakov's Dobrokur (*dobro* = *voluntary; kuritsa* = *chicken*), moreover, also has a real-life prototype: Dobrokhim (*khim* = *chemistry*), formed in 1924 to find practical applications for chemistry, especially to defense.[67] The creation of organizations such as Dobrokhim reflected the increasing demand on scientists to redirect their research toward solving political-social problems. As Trotsky wrote in 1923: "All of us very much need a new orientation on the part of scientists: the adjustment of their attention, their interests, and their efforts to the tasks and demands of the new social structure." [68]

Persikov, who is made a member of both the emergency commission and Dobrokur, thus follows the path laid down by Trotsky, with obligations to the state eroding his intellectual autonomy. The real turning point, however, occurs with the arrival of the novella's second protagonist, Aleksandr Semenovich Rokk, director of the Red Ray Soviet Farm *(sovkhoz)*, who wants to put the red ray to immediate practical use to accelerate chicken breeding. Persikov at first vociferously opposes him and defends his scientific integrity, but after a telephone call from a powerful personage, he surrenders, declaring: "I wash my hands" (2:82). Thus, like Pilate in *The Master and Margarita*, Persikov experiences a failure of courage and yields to pressure from above.

If Persikov resembles Pilate at this crucial moment, Rokk's position is structurally analogous to Yeshua's, in that he forces upon his interlocutor the difficult choice between cowardly expediency and courageous principle. It hardly needs stating, however, that the *sovkhoz* chairman, in pressuring Persikov to act *against* his best impulses, functions as Christ's diametrical opposite—but one indication of Rokk's link to Jesus's diabolical antipode. An ominous, superhuman aura, indeed, precedes him into Persikov's study, when Pankrat portentously announces: "Rokk [*rok* = destiny] has arrived" (2:81). In his plan to "resurrect" the chickens, moreover (2:84), Rokk—to a far greater degree than Persikov—sacrilegiously usurps God's function. For whereas the scientist expresses strong reservations about applying the red ray to real life, Rokk has no qualms: "By God, it will come off, . . . Your ray is so famous you could even grow elephants, not just chicks."

Later, on the *sovkhoz*, Rokk's association with the diabolical becomes more explicit. Various natural disturbances occur after he subjects the eggs to the red ray, leading the maid, Dunya, to remark: "And do you know, Aleksandr Semenovich, . . . the peasants in Kontsovka said you're the anti-Christ. They say your eggs are devilish. It's a sin to hatch them with a machine. They wanted to kill you" (2:93). Rokk dismisses this as mere superstition, but (in contrast to the feuilletons) the beliefs of the benighted peasants have some foundation, for Rokk's experiments do produce giant beasts (anacondas and ostriches, from eggs mistakenly sent to the *sovkhoz*), which wreak untold destruction. That all this takes place near the village of Kontsovka (*konets* = end) adds to the apocalyptic coloration.[69]

To cull the full political message encoded in *The Fatal Eggs*, it is important to define more exactly who Rokk is. To regard him simply as a typical Communist proves too undifferentiated, as do many of one's first responses to this complex tale. A partial answer is offered as soon as he enters

Persikov's study. The professor is struck by Rokk's revolutionary garb, his leather jacket and "immense mauser pistol" (2:81), which make him look "strangely old-fashioned" in the Moscow of 1928. The narrator adds: "In 1919 this man would have fit in perfectly, he would have been tolerated in 1924, at its beginning, but in 1928 he was strange." Of special importance here is the precise date, "in 1924, at its beginning," for just at that time two events occurred—both noted in Bulgakov's diary—that might have led the writer when working on *The Fatal Eggs* the following summer to predict a significant shift in the Communist Party. The first was the death of Lenin on January 22. Yet more significant for *The Fatal Eggs* was an early sign of Trotsky's fall from power. On January 8, the writer quoted a newspaper bulletin announcing Trotsky's supposed illness and his "leave with full freedom from all duties for a period of no less than two months." He commented: "And so on January 8, 1924 they chucked Trotsky out. God only knows what will happen to Russia."[70]

Bulgakov attributed such significance to the announcement because of the bitter struggle then taking place within the Communist Party, which pitted the ruling triumvirate (Kamenev, Zinoviev, and Stalin) against Trotsky and other so-called deviationists. One issue dividing the two camps concerned NEP itself. While Trotsky criticized the policy as a retreat from revolutionary socialist principles, to be replaced as soon as possible by greater central control of the economy, the ruling coalition advocated the more popular line of continuing NEP.[71] Bulgakov, having observed the weakening position of the more doctrinaire branch of the Party but a few months before writing *The Fatal Eggs*, therefore describes the future Moscow with a flourishing NEP and with zealous revolutionaries virtually extinct—although evidently capable of a comeback at a time of crisis.

A comparison with *The White Guard*, moreover, offers further evidence of Rokk's link with Trotsky. The details of Rokk's biography, first of all, coincide in some ways with those of the diabolical Shpolyansky, Trotsky's most prominent follower in the novel.[72] Thus Rokk too was an artist before the revolution, although on a much more modest scale than Shpolyansky, suggesting a parodic relationship: he was a flutist "in the famous concert ensemble of Maestro Petukhov [Rooster], which every evening filled with harmonious sounds the lobby of the cozy Enchanted Dreams [*Volshebnye grezy*] Cinema in the city of Ekaterinoslav" (2:92). Revolution created a sharp break in Rokk's life, as in Shpolyansky's, for he replaced his flute with a "destructive mauser" and began wandering the country. Radically transformed himself, he set about transforming the nation, both through "enlightening" its populace (as editor of an enormous newspaper in Turkestan) and altering its physical characteristics as a member of a commission on irrigation works.

At the end of *The Fatal Eggs* Rokk's image is also congruent to that of Trotsky himself in *The White Guard* (the tie perhaps hinted at by Rokk's name, which is embedded in Trotsky's). In the novel, the poet Rusakov envisions Satan-Trotsky's legions coming from the "kingdom of the anti-Christ, Moscow" and invading Kiev (1:415), wheras in *The Fatal Eggs,* the diabolical snakes that hatch from "Rokk's eggs" (an alternative translation of the title) threaten Moscow itself. A number of Rokk's convictions and proclivities, moreover, coincide—in travestied form, of course—with Trotsky's.

There is, first of all, his belief in the power of science and technology to conquer nature. In *Literature and Revolution* (published in the summer of 1924), Trotsky imagines a future in which nature is entirely in man's control: "Through the machine, man in Socialist society will command nature in its entirety . . . He will change the course of rivers, and he will lay down rules for the oceans."[73] He also envisages physiological transformations, not in chickens, to be sure, but in people: "Even purely physiologic life will become subject to collective experiments. The human species, the coagulated *homo sapiens,* will once more enter into a state of radical transformation, and, in his own hands, will become an object of the most complicated methods of artificial selection and psycho-physical training."[74]

Rokk also parodies Trotsky's devotion to high art, his belief that in socialist society masterpieces of the past will elevate the ignorant proletariat: "What the worker will take from Shakespeare, Goethe, Pushkin, or Dostoievsky, will be a more complex idea of human personality, of its passions and feelings, a deeper and profounder understanding of its psychic forces and of the role of the subconscious, etc. In the final analysis, the worker will become richer."[75] Rokk tests this belief in the civilizing effects of art on a product of revolutionary change when he tries to charm one of the gigantic snakes hatched from his "fatal eggs" with music from *Evgeny Onegin.* The monster, however, proves impervious to classical culture, and when Rokk's wife cries out to warn the *sovkhoz* director, it chokes her to death—the first of an untold number of ghastly fatalities that result from the ill-conceived experiment.

Rokk, finally, shares Trotsky's connection not only with high culture but also with the newest, most technological of art forms, the cinema. Enthusiasm for motion pictures was widespread among political and artistic radicals of the time, Lenin himself having dubbed film "the most important of all the arts."[76] Trotsky, however, stated the case with particular force. In his article, "Vodka, the Church, and the Cinema," he looked to film, with its "spectacular images," to replace both tavern and church in Russian life; he even proposed to "make up for the separation of the church from the socialist state by the fusion of the socialist state and the cinema."[77]

Early in *The Fatal Eggs,* as we have seen, magnified images, created by artificial rays and projected on Moscow buildings, play a prominent role in the new society. In Rokk's case, to be sure, revolutionary transformation entailed *severing* his tie to the movies, abandoning the "dusty starry satin" of the Enchanted Dreams Cinema for the "open sea of war and revolution" (2:92). The narrator adds with obvious irony: "It turned out that this man was positively great, and of course it was not for him to sit in the lobby of Dreams." Rokk, however, does not so much reject the movie "dream" world as transfer it from the stuffy little theater out into the great world.[78] For now he is again involved in the cinematic activity of creating giant beings by means of an artificial ray—a task, moreover, that involves usurpation of the divine-religious function, as do motion pictures in Trotsky's view.

The cinematic motif, intertwined with religious imagery, is in fact carried through when Rokk escapes from the *sovkhoz* and tells his story to two GPU agents. They go to the greenhouse where the experiment is set up and find there a "strange cinematic light" illuminating a huge number of giant snakes and three experimental boxes resembling three "immense cameras" (2:101). Although armed with a splendid French electric revolver, the agents are destroyed by the snakes. The cinematic "enchanted dreams" thus turn into a nightmare, the blasphemous attempt at creation resulting in terrible destruction.

Rokk, then, is not simply a generalized Communist but is associated specifically with Trotsky and others who advocated a return to the accelerated revolutionary processes of the Civil War period. This does not, of course, imply identification of Trotsky and Rokk. There is in fact little external likeness between the brilliant comaker of the Russian Revolution and the provincial, semieducated *sovkhoz* director. Rather, Rokk demonstrates the untold havoc that Trotsky's grandiose ideas—his belief in the transforming powers of science and art—could wreak in the hands of his lesser followers. Thus the cause of the catastrophe in *The Fatal Eggs* is not the violence of the benighted simple people, as elsewhere in Bulgakov, but the abstract "dreams" of a minor deputy of Soviet power.

The End and Beyond

The snake incursion, like the chicken plague, contains a complex of sociopolitical referents, both foreign and domestic. The foreign origin of the eggs, first of all, and the exotic nature of the beasts that hatch suggest a link with threat from abroad. Bulgakov's diary in 1923 and early 1924 did repeatedly express expectation of international disaster. This he usually saw as arising from the failed German revolution of late 1923, in which the Russian Communists were centrally involved.[79] He perceived, moreover, that their foreign meddling—like Rokk's tampering with nature (involving eggs sent from Germany)—also had unintended monstrous consequences: "In Germany, instead of the expected Communist revolution, evident and widespread Fascism has resulted."[80] The writer even speculates on a possible deadly struggle between Fascism and Communism: "It is possible that the world really is on the eve of a general skirmish between Communism and Fascism."[81] The significance of the snake infestation, however, is probably not limited to the Fascist danger alone but applies to foreign threat in general. Thus, on August 6, 1924, shortly before he wrote *The Fatal Eggs*, Bulgakov comments on the potentially dire consequences of another foreign policy failure, the breakdown of an Anglo-Soviet conference: "It would be interesting to know how long the 'Union of Socialist Republics' will exist in such a situation."[82]

Domestically, the fact that the monsters are hatched in the countryside suggests an allusion to the danger of peasant uprising. There are signs of peasant dissatisfaction in the novella. A "prophet" turns up in Volokolamsk, "who proclaimed that the chicken plague was caused by none other than the commissars" (2:77), after which the peasants beat some policemen and smash windows. Then there is the threat to kill Rokk. In a diary entry of late 1923, Bulgakov notes that "hooliganism is developing among the young people in the villages" and comments: "We are a savage, dark, unfortunate people."[83] There were numerous cases of rural rioting in 1924 and occasional murders of *sel'kory*, village correspondents, whose often ardent Bolshevism, like Rokk's, aroused antagonism among the peasants.[84] That Bulgakov was aware of such cases and linked them to a future disaster is shown in a diary entry of December 1924, in which he writes of a *sel'kor* murder: "Either I have no intuition [*chut'e*] . . . or this is the introduction to a totally unbelievable opera."[85]

As the giant snakes approach Moscow, incredible telegrams pour into the *Izvestia* office and create "unbelievable commotion and confusion" (2:105). A reddish light illuminates the scene, indicating the broadening reach of the red ray: "The sharp hat of Alfred Bronsky flashed in the blinding pink light flooding the printing press room" (2:106). Here again the beam is not a "ray of life" but a hellish destructive force, which "created the impression that the gray, unsightly building was blazing in an electric fire." The "electric fire" soon spreads throughout the city: "A mad electric night blazed in Moscow. All the lights were burning and in apartments there was no place where lamps with their shades thrown off were not burning" (2:109). On the street giant projectors cut through the night sky and posters are illuminated by "burning raspberry-colored reflectors." Like the amoebae under the red ray, the crowds under these agitating lights grow in number and aggressiveness: "On Tverskaya-Yamskaya Street they were running in a thick brew, riding in buses, riding on trolley car roofs, crushing one another, and falling under the wheels."

The shadeless lamps in Moscow apartments recall Civil War Kiev of *The White Guard*, and now as then combat is imminent. There are in fact associations both with the Napoleonic war of 1812 (the conflagration of Smolensk)[86] and with the Civil War, as Budenny's horse army is summoned to struggle against the alien monsters. Significantly, although sent to battle snakes, the soldiers are also described in reptilian terms, as a "many-thousandfold . . . snake" (2:110). The crowd initially welcomes the troops, but cries of enthusiasm imperceptibly shift to acoustically similar cries of pain. The army, like the snakes it has been called to combat, is crushing people:

> "*Da zdravstvuet* [long live] the horse army!" cried frenzied women's voices.
>
> "*Da zdravstvuet!*" echoed the men.
>
> "*Zadaviat!!. Daviat!* [They'll crush us!! They're crushing us!]" people were howling somewhere. (2:110)

Thus the revived revolutionary ethos brings death and destruction from both parties to the conflict.

A concrete scapegoat is sought, however, and this results in Persikov's end. Even before his violent death, the professor, devastated by news of the catastrophe, has suffered a total collapse, both physical and mental. As the monsters approach, he, in stark contrast to the frenzied Muscovites, sits motionless in his dimly lit institute, guarding "his only remaining extinguished box" (2:112). He has not gone home for three nights, has instead brought his housekeeper, Maria Stepanovna, to the institute, and they, together with the ever-faithful Pankrat, are the only inhabitants of the building.

Persikov is indeed soon called upon to defend his laboratory, as an enraged crowd storms the institute. Maria Stepanovna tries to convince him to follow the usual path of Bulgakov's heroes and run away, but he refuses: "'I will not go anywhere . . . this is simply stupidity,—they're running around like madmen . . . What do I have to do with it. Pankrat!' he called and pressed a button" (2:113). Persikov, deluded by his conviction that elemental natural forces can always be controlled, exaggerates the "all-powerful" Pankrat's ability to bring order. Moreover, his words, "what do I have to do with it," reveal that even now he acknowledges no responsibility for the consequences of his experiments. Therefore, displaying once more his combination of admirable devotion to science and lamentable naiveté, he refuses to run. Standing up "to his full height" (2:113), like Korotkov at the end of *The Diaboliad,* he heroically guards the door, stretching out his arms "like one crucified" (2:114).

Trotsky, in a visionary passage, imagines humanity's evolutionary advance under socialism: "Man will make it his purpose to master his own feelings, to raise his instincts to the heights of consciousness, to make them transparent, to extend the wires of his will into hidden recesses, and thereby to raise himself to a new plane, to create a higher social biologic type, or, if you please, a superman."[87] The end of *The Fatal Eggs,* however, indicates that Bolshevik attempts to transcend nature have produced not an evolutionary leap forward but regression. This is especially clear in the simian appearance of Persikov's murderer: "A short man, on bowed ape's legs, in a torn jacket" (2:114). This subhuman apparition gives vent to his elemental rage and kills one who, if not the higher evolutionary type Trotsky envisages, is at the peak of intellectual achievement of his time. The crowd then proceeds to kill Maria Stepanovna, who is "not guilty of anything." She is torn to bits, as is Pankrat (*"rvanyi v kloch'ia,"* 2:114), recalling how the amoebae under the red ray "tore [each other] to bits" [*"rvali v kloch'ia,"* 2:54). They then subject the animals to a horrible death and set the institute ablaze.

A nagging question that has not yet been satisfactorily answered is the degree to which Persikov is actually responsible for the disaster. On the very first page of the story the narrator labels him the "original cause" (2:45), but the mere fact that Persikov discovered the ray surely does not in itself make him culpable. And although he does yield to pressure from above when he "washes his hands," he does so only after fulfilling the intellectual's duty to speak out. He cannot be blamed too much, after all, for doing what most would have under the circumstances. Yet one barely perceptible plotline hints that Persikov cannot be so easily condoned.

This has to do with his plan to conduct "mysterious and complex experiments" (2:79) with the red ray on eggs ordered from abroad. He obtains diving suits, helmets, and poison gas for the "mysterious and extremely dangerous experiments" (2:105), and Ivanov even suggests they borrow an electric revolver from the GPU. Only then do we discover that Persikov's order consisted of the very snake and ostrich eggs sent mistakenly to Rokk, that the scientist was planning what Rokk does unwittingly: to subject the eggs to his red ray, and not in a sparsely populated rural area but in the heart of Moscow. The experiment would have been conducted, of course, under tight and highly competent scientific control, but, given the ghastly experience on the *sovkhoz,* it is doubtful that any control would have been sufficient. (One recalls Persikov's difficulty in exterminating even the irradiated frogs.) The fact that the scientists have the same means of defense that fail against the snakes—an electric revolver, with which the ill-fated GPU men were armed, and poison gas, which cannot stop the snakes' advance on Moscow—does not increase one's confidence.[88] Even the detail that Persikov plans to seal the door but open the window recalls the shut door and broken upper panes of the greenhouse through which the monsters escape at the *sovkhoz.*

Here the brilliant scientist Persikov again reveals his fatal flaw: excessive faith in science makes him underestimate nature's ungovernable power. His indifference to the surrounding world, implicit in planning so dangerous an experiment in the midst of a vast metropolis, only increases his culpability. Therefore, while one cannot justify Persikov's murder, neither is he a mere scapegoat. On the deepest level the brilliant professor, by exceeding the proper bounds of science, shares the guilt with his apparent opposite, the semieducated Bolshevik, Rokk.[89] It is significant in this regard that, whereas Persikov is "crucified," it is the housekeeper who is "not guilty of anything."

The final chapter of *The Fatal Eggs* tells of the extraordinary halt of the invading snakes. Here as elsewhere the latest technology is incapable of stopping the incursion. Only nature, the harsh Russian climate, which has been the nemesis of Napoleon and other invaders, succeeds in killing off the beasts.[90] The "frosty god on a machine," as the final chapter heading calls it (2:114—a mistranslation of *deus ex machina*), earns its supernatural designation by arriving in August and thus violating the ordinary laws of nature. Even this superhuman intercession does not bring a complete end to the disaster, however, for the rotting corpses create a lingering epidemic. Only in the spring of 1929 have the last effects of the catastrophe disappeared.

Thus the story ends approximately a year after it began, on that fateful April evening in 1928. Moscow has by now returned to normal, is again aglitter with artificial lights and filled with speeding mechanical carriages. Now, too, as on the morning after Persikov's discovery, the only hint of an alternative world is the Cathedral of Christ the Savior, this time illuminated by the moon instead of the sun. The repeated linkage of religious monument and heavenly body hints, perhaps, at an eternal spiritual presence, the Christian God, whose yearly rebirth is celebrated at approximately the time of year the novella begins and ends. The false god Persikov, in contrast, has disappeared, as has his ray. Like the materialist Berlioz in *The Master and Margarita,* Persikov has been "given according to his belief" and "sinks into nonbeing" (5:265): "The name of Vladimir Ipatievich Persikov became clothed in mist and was extinguished, as was extinguished the red ray discovered by him on an April night" (2:115–116). A new "zoological palace" (2:115), headed by Persikov's former assistant, has been built on the site of the old institute, but try as he might, Ivanov cannot capture the red ray. The narrator comments in conclusion: "Evidently something special was necessary for that besides knowledge, which only one person in the world possessed: the late Professor Vladimir Ipatievich Persikov" (2:116). Thus, even in Persikov's materialistic world, an ineffable "something" distinguishes the genius from the ordinary, even highly competent, remainder of humanity.

In his diary, in his usual tone of harsh self-criticism, Bulgakov wonders about *The Fatal Eggs:* "What is it? A feuilleton? An impertinence? But perhaps it's something serious? If so, it's half-baked [*ne vypechennoe*]."[91] This judgment of his glittering, talented novella is certainly overly severe, although the work *is* excessively convoluted and complicated, the symbolism and overall structure not worked out with the clarity and virtuosity of its successor, *Heart of a Dog*. If the latter therefore is indisputably the best of Bulgakov's shorter prose works, *The Fatal Eggs* remains the most intricate and many-layered, synthesizing many of the features of Bulgakov's early writings: the theme of the intellectual and the revolution in the early autobiographical works; the panoramas of Moscow from the *Nakanune* feuilletons; *Gudok*'s depiction of provincial Russia, where old superstitions thrive under Soviet cover. It also has formal links to two other works in *The Diaboliad* collection: "No. 13. The Elpit-Workommune House," which ends with the destruction by fire of its principal edifice, and *The Diaboliad*, where the hero himself comes to a violent end. A similar paradox, moreover, underlies the tragic fates of the heroes of *The Diaboliad* and *The Fatal Eggs*. Korotkov, who seeks no more than bureaucratic happiness, is in the end destroyed by the bureaucracy, while Persikov, a practitioner of scientific control, is a victim of untamable forces he unleashes in the pursuit of scientific knowledge.

The similarities to the other *Diaboliad* stories, however, only underline the greater moral complexity of *The Fatal Eggs*. If in the earlier works Bulgakov directs his destructive satire at rather easy targets—the housing crisis and the bureaucracy, respectively—here his subject is the realm of science, in which he had labored for many years and to which he had always felt great intellectual and emotional affinity. Persikov, moreover, is a much deeper, more complex figure than Korotkov. An isolated man of genius with a unique vision, hounded by the press, coerced by the government, and finally "crucified" by social forces, he (in a much more fundamental way than Korotkov) is a precursor of the Master and Yeshua in *The Master and Margarita*. He differs from the later heroes, however, in that he shares the materialistic, rationalistic assumptions of his society. In this sense, he is akin to the more negative characters of the novel: like Berlioz he embodies his milieu's ideological underpinnings, and like Pilate he yields to government pressure and "washes his hands." And both of these factors figure in his downfall.[92]

The Fatal Eggs is also clearly influenced by the formal breakthroughs of *The White Guard*, with the narrator, in contrast to other early works, freeing himself from the point of view of his main hero, ranging from the protagonist's dwelling to the city and to the countryside beyond. In both works, moreover, Bulgakov places humanity within an extrahuman context. In *The White Guard* the human drama is played out against the transcendent sphere, which delimits man's control over his own destiny, whereas in *The Fatal Eggs* human endeavors are circumscribed by the world of nature, with the apocalyptic mood that colors Bulgakov's first novel also apparent.

Both in its centrifugal structure and in the collision it portrays between hubristic humanity and the nonhuman world, *The Fatal Eggs* also anticipates *The Master and Margarita*. There too powerful nonhumans (the devils) upset the modern secular assumption that humanity controls its own destiny, cause chaos and destruction, and then disappear. Soon after life returns to normal, but the one person with a special gift, earlier tormented by his society, disappears, together with his contribution to mankind (the red ray, the Master's novel).

Heart of a Dog

Early 1925 was a promising time for Bulgakov, with his two most ambitious works thus far, *The White Guard* and *The Fatal Eggs*, about to come out in prominent periodicals.[93] In January, within this atmosphere of anticipation, he undertook two new projects, both outgrowths of those recently completed and in very different ways precursors of his future course. The first was his dramatization of *The White Guard*, which in its final version, *Days of the Turbins*, brought his first sensational, although highly controversial, stage success and led to his increased involvement in the theater in the second half of the 1920s.[94] The second, *Heart of a Dog*, which treats some of the same themes as *The Fatal Eggs*, was to suffer a very different fate. It was Bulgakov's first work to be banned outright, thus foreshadowing his total disappearance from print within a few years.[95]

At the hopeful beginning of 1925, however, no one could predict that the writer's first major publications were to be virtually his last during his lifetime. On the contrary, completion of a new satiric novella by the author of *The Fatal Eggs* was impatiently awaited by the literary world. By February 14, he had already received a request from *Nedra* to read a draft to its editor-in-chief, Angarsky, and within a few weeks he read a second draft to the eminent literary grouping, *Nikitinskie subbotniki*.[96] The extant opinions of those present were extremely positive. Singling out, like earlier critics, Bulgakov's talent for combining the fantastic and the quotidian, they also noted the work's special relevance. Yu. N. Potekhin, for example, commented: "Mikhail Afanasievich's fantasy is organically fused with sharp realistic *(bytovoi)* grotesque. This fantasy acts with extreme power and conviction. Many will sense the presence of Sharikov [the novella's antihero] in everyday life." Another listener declared even more categorically: "This is the first literary work that dares to be itself. The time has come for giving full expression [*realizatsiia*] to one's attitude toward current events."

This very daring, however, aroused misgivings about getting *Heart of a Dog* past the censors. The *Nedra* editors warned Bulgakov in February that if he did not complete the work before the influential Angarsky went abroad in a couple of weeks, "we won't have time to drag it through *Glavlit* [the censors]." In April, Angarsky himself expressed qualms to the poet, Maksimilian Voloshin: "I'm not sure his new story *Heart of a Dog* will pass. In general things are bad with literature." He proved correct, for in May *Glavlit* rejected the work with the comment: "it isn't even worth cleaning up [*chistit'*] *Heart of a Dog*. The piece as a whole is not permissible." This was not the end of *Nedra*'s attempt to get the novella published, for Angarsky asked Bulgakov to send the manuscript, accompanied by a "tearful" letter, to no less than Lev Kamenev, member of the ruling triumvirate from 1922 to 1925. When Bulgakov refused (apparently indignant at the word "tearful"), *Nedra* itself sent Kamenev the work, but their hopes proved unfounded. He declared *Heart of a Dog* "a sharp lampoon on contemporary life . . . [which] cannot under any circumstances be published."

Frustrated in his efforts to publish *Heart of a Dog*, Bulgakov signed a contract with the Moscow Art Theater for a dramatization, but this did not come to fruition either.[97] Then in May 1926 an incident occurred that shows vividly Bulgakov's worsening position in general and the particular hostility *Heart of a Dog* aroused: the secret police conducted a search of his apartment and confiscated the novella and his diary. (With Maksim Gorky's help, Bulgakov succeeded in getting back *Heart of a Dog*—but not the diary—a couple of years later.)[98] The vicissitudes of the novella were not soon to end, for it remained unpublished for over forty years, and even then appeared only abroad. Soviet readers had to wait until 1987 for the work, a beneficiary of glasnost, to appear in the author's homeland.[99]

The Stray Dog and the Bourgeois

Heart of a Dog, like *The Fatal Eggs*, is a tale of scientific research run amok. Its hero, Filipp Filippovich Preobrazhensky, an eminent professor and doctor, lures home a stray mutt on a stormy winter night and, in pursuit of his research on rejuvenation, transplants in it a human pituitary gland and testes. (Similar experiments, Chudakova discovered, were widespread at the time, both in Western Europe and the Soviet Union, and received much publicity in the popular press.)[100] The operation results in a far more radical change than the professor planned, for the dog undergoes total transformation into a human being. Much as Persikov's "ray of life" gets out of control and works against him, so does the humanoid turn on Preobrazhensky and threaten disaster. The hero of *Heart of a Dog*, however, succeeds where Persikov fails, for in the end he reverses his operation, turning the monstrous human back into a lovable pooch.

As in *The Fatal Eggs*—and again, probably, under the influence of H. G. Wells—Bulgakov has turned to the genre of science fiction.[101] Many of the same themes, moreover, are played out in both works: the permissible limits of scientific research, the scientist's moral responsibility for his discoveries, the parallels between scientific and social-political experimentation. Bulgakov, indeed, may have felt the need to treat these themes once more, because *The Fatal Eggs*, for all its vividness and depth, is a very complex and tangled work, and in *Heart of a Dog* he achieves a simpler, more unified plot structure and clearer thematic exposition. The plot kernel and attendant moral conflict of the later novella, indeed—involving the sacrifice of an animal subject in the name of science—is an elaboration of one small episode of *The Fatal Eggs:* Persikov's half-comic "crucifixion" of his frog. By simplifying the plot line, Bulgakov is able to magnify and deepen the psychological and moral dimensions of the conflict and offer far more detailed and interesting portraits of both parties to the uneven duel of man and beast. Thus, Preobrazhensky is not simply an obsessive eccentric like Persikov, whose moral limitations stem from his one-sided devotion to science. He is a strong, well-rounded character, who combines scientific pursuits with a satisfying domestic life and outside interests. The dog is also far more complex than the lowly frog of *The Fatal Eggs*. The writer, indeed, goes to all lengths to humanize him, thus sharpening the moral conflict.

The primary means of establishing sympathy with the animal is by telling the tale from its point of view (at least, paradoxically, until the second half of the novella, when the dog is transformed into an "inhuman" human being).[102] The narrative perspective is especially striking in the opening episode, which takes the form of a canine monologue. (Later a third-person narrator takes over, although events continue to be seen mostly through the dog's eyes.) Like such celebrated works with dog heroes as Chekhov's "Kashtanka" and Virginia Woolf's *Flush*,[103] *Heart of a Dog* exploits the peculiarities of canine perception, especially dependence on the sense of smell. For example: "It's about four in the afternoon, judging by the onion smell coming from the Prechistenka fire station"(2:119).[104] Bulgakov, however, does not confine his hero's psyche within canine limits; he gives him a level of awareness close to human. The dog, for example, knows about the human class system, expressing a preference for the upper orders. He calls a cook who scalded him with boiling water "a louse [*gadina*] and a proletarian to boot" and says of another, from the good old days: "May he rest in peace for being a real person, a gentleman's chef for the Counts Tolstoy" (2:120). His cognitive limits are especially stretched in his musings on the sad life of a "little typist" [*mashinistochka*] he sees: "Some little typist gets a ninth rank salary of forty-five rubles, well, granted, her lover gives her *fil de Perse* stockings. But you know, how much humiliation she has to go through for that *fil de Perse*. You see, he doesn't make her do it the usual way, he puts her through French love" (A3:120).[105]

At times Bulgakov gives the pooch powers of cognition even beyond the ordinary human, approaching that of the omniscient narrator. Thus, at very first sight the dog knows Filipp Filippovich's name and his status as "world-renowned figure, thanks to male sex glands" (2:123). Occasionally the canine hero even takes over the function of principal narrator, addressing the reader directly, as in: "I can very easily catch pneumonia and once I've caught it, *citizens*, I'll croak from hunger" (2:120; emphasis mine). The rapprochement of dog and human narrator is also apparent in occasional imperceptible shifts from third to first person, for example: "The dog gathered the remains of his strength . . . The blizzard began banging from a rifle over his head, swept up the immense letters of a canvas placard, 'Is rejuvenation possible?' Naturally, it's possible. The smell [of sausage] has rejuvenated me, has lifted me from my belly" (2:122).[106]

The blurred line between the dog and the omniscient narrator, the authorial surrogate in the text, establishes a link between the animal and the writer himself. This is supported by biographical parallels, for in his early days in Moscow Bulgakov also found himself bereft of home and close to starvation, and he too feared that he would perish in a world dominated by the hostile and cruel proletariat.[107] In *Notes on the Cuff* the authorial persona even refers to himself as a "stray dog [*bezrodnyi pes*]."[108] In *Heart of a*

Dog, Bulgakov makes literal this common figure of speech, taking a homeless mutt as his hero and offering him a shelter of which he himself could only dream.

The opening episode yields another level of meaning, deriving from its parodic relationship to Aleksandr Blok's narrative poem "The Twelve" (1918), a literary work whose influence on Soviet literature can hardly be overestimated.[109] The poem tells of twelve members of the Red Guard who wander through the cold and snow-driven nocturnal streets of Civil War St. Petersburg, wreaking death and havoc in their wake. Both the blizzard and the twelve themselves are linked to the elemental destructiveness of revolution. At the same time, numerous personifications of the old world appear, including a bourgeois *(burzhui)* and his dog: "A bourgeois stands at a crossroads and hides his nose in his collar. And alongside a mangy dog with coarse hair skulks, his tail between his legs. The bourgeois stands, like a hungry dog. He stands speechless, like a question. And the old world, like a stray dog, stands behind him, his tail between his legs."[110] Later the dog, identified with the old world, trails the twelve and they threaten to thrash him.

In *Heart of a Dog*, the snow, wind, and darkness of "The Twelve" have not disappeared from the urban landscape. There are changes, to be sure, in keeping with the spirit of NEP. Blok's wind-torn placard, "All power to the Constituent Assembly" (Blok, pp. 233, 234), has been replaced by another windswept sign, asking a question relevant to the pleasure-loving NEP—and of course, to Bulgakov's tale: "Is rejuvenation possible?" (2:122).[111] The proletariat, moreover, no longer takes the form of anarchic Red Guard soldiers, who "fan the worldwide fire" (Blok, p. 237), but of firemen and other urban workers, whose task is to *extinguish* fires and maintain domestic order. For all the changes, however, the homeless mutt's situation is essentially unchanged, for the working class continues to treat him with unvarying cruelty.

Crucial to Bulgakov's polemic with Blok is the shift in point of view, for the dog, no longer seen from without, is not now an abstract symbol of the old world but a concrete suffering creature. Bulgakov works a similar reversal in the principal feminine character of "The Twelve," the seductive whore, Katya, killed by one of the Red Guards for sexual betrayal. In the poem, Katya is seen purely through the eyes of the twelve; she is treated, despite the abuse she suffers, more as temptress than victim—and, indeed, becomes a symbol of fatally corrupt old Russia, triumphantly killed off by the revolution. The only reservation expressed about the soldiers' violence is the hint that it stems from loss of religious faith: "Freedom, freedom,/ Ekh, ekh, without the cross!" (Blok, p. 236).

In contrast, Bulgakov's "fallen woman," the "little typist," is viewed sympathetically through the eyes of her fellow victim, the dog. She, like him, is not a symbol but a concrete being, whose sufferings are emphasized (her infected lung, her "woman's disease" [2:121]), not her debauchery. Thus, if Katya's "lace linen" (Blok, p. 237) is a sign of her love of luxury, the typist would gladly replace her lace pants (described as "rags for her lover" [2:121]) with warm flannel. The typist's lover, true to the spirit of NEP, is a pleasure-loving official, but if his social position differs from the twelve's, he is of similar humble origin: "I had my fill of hunger when I was young." And the underlying reason for his unbridled behavior is, like theirs, loss of faith: "life beyond the grave doesn't exist."

Most important for the thematic development of *Heart of a Dog* are ironic echoes of the conclusion of "The Twelve." In the poem, the young toughs follow and threaten a mysterious man, who at the very end is identified as Christ: "Behind is the hungry dog, ahead—with a bloody flag, . . . ahead is Jesus Christ" (Blok, p. 243). In Bulgakov's work, in a reversal that characterizes the historical moment, it is the dog who finds a savior, the "gentleman" (*gospodin*, 2:122), Dr. Preobrazhensky—one of those bourgeois whom Blok doomed to extinction but who were thriving during NEP.[112] The doctor appears as a higher being to the dog, who at once calls him "my lord" (*moi vlastitel'*) (2:123). When the stranger, having "christened [him] Sharik," gives him a piece of abominable sausage, the dog's devotion knows no bounds: "Again, again, I lick your hand. I kiss your trousers, my benefactor!" Preobrazhensky then calls to him, "Follow me," and Sharik runs after him—as the twelve pursue Christ—in order "not to lose the miraculous vision in a fur coat in the hubbub."

If Bulgakov thus parodies Blok's naive expectation of Christian renewal arising from bloody revolution, his irony is double-edged. For it is also directed at the materialistic NEP period, when a "miraculous vision in a fur coat," using rotten meat to lure a "slavish" dog (2:123), has replaced the Christian ideal. There is, moreover, much self-irony here, insofar as Bulgakov himself dreamed, especially in his early days in Moscow, of the kind of canine "salvation" promised Sharik—a comfortable, well-ordered home, excellent food and drink, and refuge from the harsh Soviet "blizzard" and cruel proletariat.

A Dog's Happiness

Sharik's new master, while portrayed with characteristic Bulgakovian ambivalence, on the whole makes a more positive impression than do the
heroes of the two earlier novellas.[113] One reason is that—religious symbolism aside for the moment—he really is Sharik's savior, at least at first. He
not only offers the dog food and shelter but heals his badly scalded side, the
latter despite the violent opposition of Sharik himself, who is sure death
awaits him.

In curing the unruly mutt, Preobrazhensky, like the protagonist of *Notes
of a Young Doctor* (written, or rewritten, at about the same time as *Heart of
a Dog*), thus battles not only a physical malady but the ignorant resistance
of his patient. The two doctors also share the trait of courage, for while the
young hero of the stories gradually grows brave in his fight against disease
and ignorance, the elderly Preobrazhensky exhibits a high degree of fear-
lessness from the very first. One might, indeed, call his portrayal a "portrait
of the young doctor as an old man." The fact that he is modeled at least in
part on the author's uncle[114] by no means contradicts this role, for it is
plausible that Bulgakov took his relative—an eminent physician who often
fed him in his early Moscow days, as Preobrazhensky does Sharik—as a
model for what he might have become had he remained in medicine.

In his role as valiant doctor, the "first—unrealized—variant of . . . [Bul-
gakov's] biography," as Chudakova calls him,[115] Preobrazhensky performs
feats of courage that eluded the author himself. Thus, in his pursuit of
the Bulgakovian aim of establishing a norm of civility and comfort in his
life,[116] he effortlessly vanquishes the house committee chairman, Shvonder,
whose ilk tormented authorial personae throughout the early fiction. He
defends his ideal of domestic harmony, declaring: "I will eat dinner in the
dining room and operate in the operating room! . . . I most humbly request
that you . . . grant me the opportunity to ingest food where all normal
people ingest it, that is, in the dining room, and not in the entrance room
and not in the nursery" (2:137). In general, he fulfills the duty of the
intellectual by courageously speaking out on various aspects of the new
society. He even admits at one point that he does "not like the proletariat"
(2:140). Then when his assistant, Bormental, attributes the encroaching
disorder to *"razrukha,"* or "ruin" (2:144)—a word commonly used to denote the destruction wrought by the Civil War and its aftermath—the
professor denies that ruin is an "old woman with a crutch" (a polemical

allusion to Mayakovsky's "*razrukha* is an accursed old woman").[117] For him *razrukha* is not an abstract symbol but the result of concrete uncouth behavior: "If when I go to the bathroom I start urinating past the toilet, if you'll excuse the expression, . . . *razrukha* will begin in the bathroom" (2:144–145). Of particular thematic significance is Preobrazhensky's opposition to terror and violence, be they against man or beast: "It is impossible to do anything with an animal through terror, no matter at what stage of development it may stand . . . No, sir, no, it will not help, whoever it might be: white, red, and even brown! Terror entirely paralyzes the nervous system" (2:129). Later he adds: "One must not whip anyone . . . One can affect a person or animal only through suggestion!" (2:148).

Dr. Preobrazhensky thus seems the perfect master for Sharik, a fearless protector from the proletarian blizzard without. From the first, however, he arouses certain misgivings. There is, first of all, the very nature of the domestic values he so eloquently defends. Although comfort is obviously important to Bulgakov, it is significant that those for whom the ideal of home is limited to material well-being, who do not value family life, tend to come to a bad end in his works. Especially relevant is the barrister in "Moscow Scenes" (like Preobrazhensky apparently modeled, at least partly, on Bulgakov's uncle),[118] who, in his efforts to hold on to his living space, perverts the function of home.

As often in Bulgakov, perversion of the domestic ideal in *Heart of a Dog* is signaled by an interweaving of divine and diabolical imagery. Thus, whereas for Sharik Preobrazhensky's kitchen is the "main department of paradise" (2:149), the hot stove makes of it a "terrible hell" (2:150), where the face of the cook, Darya Petrovna, burns "with eternal fiery torment and unquenched passion" (2:149).[119] The cook's sexual proclivities add to the demonic ambience, for when embraced by a visiting fireman (whose presence signifies, perhaps, a shift from Blok's "fire" of revolution to the private self-gratification of NEP), her face again burns "with torment and passion" (2:150). She protests: "You've latched on to me like a demon . . . What are you doing, have you been completely rejuvenated too?"

Darya Petrovna's mention of rejuvenation links the "hellish" goings-on in the kitchen and Preobrazhensky's scientific work, which also has diabolical overtones. Although the doctor's field, eugenics, is avowedly devoted to "the improvement of the human race" (2:194), his patients all want returned youth and sexual prowess for the most unsavory reasons. A middle-aged woman, for example, longs to win over a "devilishly young" (2:133) cardsharp, while a prominent official plans to seduce a fourteen-year-old girl. (One recalls here the increased sexual capacity of Persikov's terrifying amoebae and frogs.) The moral degeneration resulting from the scientist's purely material attempts to improve humanity is underlined by Sharik's embarrassed reaction: "An obscene [*pokhabnaia*] apartment" (2:135).[120]

If "obscene" activities occur both in Darya Petrovna's kitchen and in Dr. Preobrazhensky's clinic, however, the parallel is only partial. The cook's passion and the fireman's devilish "rejuvenation," after all, have natural causes, while Preobrazhensky's scientific work is more truly hellish, stemming from his urge to transform the God-given order (see his name: *preobrazhenie* = *transformation*). Although superficially associated with Darya Petrovna's NEP-time excesses, on a deeper level the operations are analogous to the radical transformations propounded by the extreme Bolsheviks, despite the professor's hostility toward them. (One recalls Trotsky's eugenic visions, outlined in the analysis of *The Fatal Eggs*.) Moreover, as we shall see in the operation on Sharik, Preobrazhensky shares the radicals' readiness to subordinate the individual living creature and traditional ethics to the abstract goal of improving humanity.

The doctor's materialism, finally—and his tie to the Communists—take another, more mundane form: a quest for money and influence. Thus he accepts "a packet of white money" from one patient (2:132) and agrees to operate on another at home only for five hundred rubles. Even more important than pecuniary gain, however, is the protection from above the operations afford him and to which he resorts when threatened by the house committee. The existence of powerful defenders, in fact, somewhat tempers one's admiration for his courage, since in any case he is untouchable.

This link between the scientist and Communist officialdom is one of those unholy alliances of NEP, with the doctor a *spets,* apparently independent, but in fact beholden to the powers that be for his privileges.[121] His position, essentially, is not so very different from Sharik's once he acquires his shiny collar. When first taken out on a leash, the dog feels like a prisoner, but once he sees the burning envy of the street mutts and the respect accorded him by the policeman and doorman, he happily accepts his bondage. Much as a powerful master shields Sharik, so do the professor's protectors allow him to ignore the impotent growling of the house committee—while at the same time limiting his autonomy and compromising his integrity. If it would be an exaggeration to say that the doctor has the "heart of a dog" (he remains too insubordinate for that), his is very much a "dog's happiness" (the original title of the work).

Heart of a Man

Sharik, meanwhile, remains blissfully unaware of the more disturbing side of his master's character. Seduced by the material delights of his new life, he experiences ever greater quasi-religious adoration of Preobrazhensky. The doctor becomes for him "a wizard, magician, and sorcerer from a dog's fairy tale" (2:147) and is soon accorded "the status of a divinity" (2:147–148). Shortly before the operation, however, the dog gets a far more disquieting view of his master: "Sharik lay on the rug in a shadow and, not tearing himself away, watched terrible deeds. Human brains lay in repulsive, caustic, and turbid muck, in glass vessels. The hands of the divinity, bared to the elbow, were in rust-colored rubber gloves, and his slippery, stubby fingers were puttering about in the convolutions. At times the divinity armed itself with a small, glittering knife and slowly sliced the yellow elastic brains" (2:150–151).

This sinister apparition, again joining the divine and diabolical, is reinforced by the words Preobrazhensky sings—"To the sacred banks of the Nile" (2:151)—the beginning of the grand march from *Aida,* which bids the gods to bring "death without mercy" to the foe.[122] The aria prefigures the mercilessness of the "divinity" Preobrazhensky, who in his operation on Sharik usurps the godlike power over life and death. That science raised in this way to a religion becomes an evil can be seen in the odd mixture of imagery—pagan and Christian, supernatural and subhuman—used to describe the operation.[123] Thus the doctor is called a "pagan priest" (*zhrets,* 2:153), but his surgeon's garb is likened to a "patriarch's skullcap" (*skufeika*) and a monk's outer dress (*epitrakhil'*). Before operating he utters a Christian prayer—an uncharacteristic moment of humility, figuring, perhaps, in Sharik's survival: "Well, Lord, give me Your blessing" (2:155). During the operation, however, divine imagery shifts more and more to the subhuman, Preobrazhensky and/or his assistant Bormental being likened to criminals ("murderers," 2:156, "an inspired robber," 2:157); a wild beast ("a tiger," 2:157); and a demonic being ("a satiated vampire," 2:158). At the end sacred imagery returns, but within the context only arouses horror: "The pagan priest took off the bloodied cowl with his chalky hands" (2:158).

The dog's humanization following the operation (related through the admiring Bormental's diary) appears to confirm Preobrazhensky's super-human powers. Like Ivanov in *The Fatal Eggs,* Bormental regards his mentor as "a creator" (2:164) and imagines that Preobrazhensky also possesses the godlike power to transform the new creature "into a psychically lofty personality" (2:165). Another and less exalted interpretation of the operation, however, can be culled from the text, for the new man's formation was not the result of godlike omnipotence but of scientific miscalculation. Preobrazhensky, older and wiser than his enthusiastic assistant, is, indeed, aware from the first of his limited power and suspects that, far from a *tabula rasa,* the newly formed being has a fully developed moral nature, derived from the man whose pituitary gland he has inherited:

> "Klim Grigorievich Chugunkin, twenty-five years old, bachelor. Non-Party member, sympathizer. Tried three times and acquitted: the first time due to lack of evidence, the second time saved by his class origin, the third time—sentenced to fifteen years of hard labor, on probation. For stealing. Profession—playing the balalaika in taverns.
>
> "Short in height, badly built. Enlarged liver (alcohol).
>
> "Cause of death—knife stab to the heart at the Stop Signal Beer Hall, by the Preobrazhensky Gate." (2:165)

The professor is of course correct, for the former engaging mutt has turned into a vile human being, retaining only such vestiges of canine instincts—natural in an animal, but revolting in a human—as pursuing cats and catching fleas with his teeth. The scientist's greatest misfortune, however, is not his failure to achieve godlike control over nature but his inability even to maintain his hard-won mastery over his own life. For Sharikov (as the new human calls himself) succeeds where the house committee failed, forcing the professor to settle more people into his apartment and to subvert the function of its rooms. Bormental writes: "I have moved to Preobrazhensky's at his request and sleep in the reception room with Sharikov. The examining room has been turned into a reception room. Shvonder has proven right. The house committee is gloating" (2:165). Sharikov not only brings crowding to the apartment, moreover; he also introduces the dreaded *razrukha:* "There isn't a single pane of glass in the cupboards, because he jumped." This *razrukha* continues to grow throughout the novella, making Preobrazhensky's life ever more intolerable.

Heart of a Dog has most commonly been interpreted as an allegory of revolution, the operation and its aftermath paralleling the revolution's mis-guided attempt to radically transform mankind.[124] Although this view has much validity, of more interest than this simple analogy is the double-pronged parable the novella presents. In its two halves, centering on the dog Sharik and the humanoid Sharikov, respectively, Bulgakov juxtaposes two types of change, "beloved and Great Evolution" and "the revolutionary process," to borrow words he would later write in a letter to the Soviet government (4:446).

Thus, in the first half, Sharik, repelled by the harsh life of the streets, eagerly follows the professor home. Psychologically prepared to accept new restraints in return for his privileges, the dog quickly evolves from a scrappy mutt into an acceptable member of civilized society. He does, it is true, give up his former freedom grudgingly and right before the opera-tion nostalgically recalls his old life: "For some reason he suddenly and clearly recalled a fragment of his earliest youth—a boundless sunny yard by the Preobrazhensky Gate [*zastava* = gate to the city], splinters of sun in bottles, a broken brick, free stray dogs" (2:152–153). He immediately rec-onciles himself, however: "'No, what for, you won't leave here for any freedom, why lie,' the dog pined, sniffling, 'I've gotten used to it. I'm a gentleman's dog, a cultivated [*intelligentnoe*] creature, I've had a taste of a better life. And besides, what is freedom? Here's what, smoke, a mirage, a fiction...'" (2:153). When Sharik follows the doctor home, therefore, he not only crosses Dr. Preobrazhensky's threshold in the literal sense; he also, figuratively speaking, enters the Preobrazhensky Gate to the city (with all the connotations that word contains in early Bulgakov), forsaking elemen-tal freedom for the civilized life.

Bulgakov, to be sure, portrays Sharik's acculturation—his acceptance of bondage in exchange for comfort—with a note of characteristic irony. The dog's false sense of bliss in the doctor's apartment is reminiscent, indeed, of Korotkov's delight with his bureaucratic haven at the beginning of *The Diaboliad*. (One notes that Sharik compares his collar to a bureaucrat's briefcase [2:149] and that he, like Korotkov, fancies he is of royal descent, an "unknown canine prince-incognito" [2:147].) The operation, moreover, proves Sharik's expectations as misplaced as Korotkov's, for just as the new world replaces the head clerk with his morally repellent double, Kolobkov, so is Sharik transformed by Preobrazhensky's experiment into the loath-some Sharikov (like Kolobkov, a thief and a womanizer).[125]

Sharikov, whose soul comes from one who died by the same Preobrazhensky Gate near which Sharik used to roam, refuses, spiritually speaking, to cross the threshold. Unlike the dog, he did not enter this civilized world voluntarily; wrenched here by a violent, terrible operation, he now refuses to live by its standards. As he says to Preobrazhensky: "Why don't you let me live? . . . Did I really ask you to operate on me . . . They grabbed an animal, slashed up his head with a knife, and now they loathe him. Maybe I didn't give my permission for the operation" (2:169). When asked if he would prefer running around rubbish heaps, he retorts: "Why do you keep reproaching me—rubbish heap, rubbish heap. I got my piece of bread!"

Thus the revolution of Preobrazhensky's operation cannot achieve what evolution has not. From the very beginning all the scientist's attempts to change Sharikov's ways—to rid him of his atrocious manners and slovenly personal hygiene, his constant swearing and unconscionable womanizing—fail miserably. Most galling to the doctor is the arrogant ignoramus's failure even to acknowledge that he has something to learn from his betters: "You stand at the lowest stage of development! . . . you are still a creature only in the process of formation, weak in intellectual terms, all your actions are purely bestial and you, in the presence of two people with a university education, allow yourself with absolutely unbearable impudence to offer some kind of advice on a cosmic scale and of equally cosmic stupidity" (2:185–186).

Preobrazhensky is not the only one incapable of molding Sharikov in his own image; the ex-dog's natural class ally, the house manager Shvonder, also fails. Shvonder does get Sharikov the proper documents, "the most important thing in the world" (2:173), and these give the humanoid a proletarian identity and the right to sixteen square arshins in Preobrazhensky's apartment. But, as the odd first name and patronymic Sharikov chooses for himself suggest (Poligraf Poligrafovich, based upon the name of a publishing house, Mospoligraf),[126] he remains a proletarian on paper only: whatever his documents might claim, Sharikov stubbornly resists becoming the exemplary worker of Soviet literature. He even speaks slightingly of the cofounder of Communism, Friedrich Engels, and a correspondent: "They write, write... a congress, some Germans or other... My head is splitting! Just take everything and divide it up..." (2:183). When, finally, Sharikov practices this thief's brand of Communism ("take everything") by stealing from the house committee itself, even Shvonder recognizes that Poligraf has "turned out to be a scoundrel" (2:197).

Near the end the professor concludes that all attempts to raise Sharikov's level have been futile, that his biological heritage is immutable: "In a word, the hypophysis is a closed box, determining a given human image [*litso*]. A given one! . . . and not a general human one! It is the brain itself in miniature" (2:194). Ironically, the man—at least one of Sharikov's breed—has proven a far wilder and more intractable creature than the dog. In this sense, as Preobrazhensky concludes, Sharikov "no longer has a dog's heart, but precisely a human one" (2:195).

Fathers and Sons

Heart of a Dog returns to a subject that long occupied Bulgakov: enlightenment of the masses. Preobrazhensky's prognosis here is unusually gloomy, however, for whereas earlier works, beginning with "A Week of Enlightenment," question the efficacy of the Bolsheviks' "instant" enlightenment, the doctor's critique casts doubt on the very possibility of reeducating society's dregs.[127] It would be risky, however, to accept this view uncritically, for although the scientist's materialistic creed has given him the means to change Sharik's *physical* shell, it is powerless to modify the inner essence of the new man (in contrast to the *spiritual* transformation that the Master and Yeshua later work on the proletarian poet, Ivan Bezdomny). One might go further, for a fundamental reason for Preobrazhensky's inability to enlighten Sharikov is that, for all their differences in intelligence and breeding, the two are spiritually cut from the same cloth.[128]

The first hint of kinship are rumors, spread by Shvonder, that Sharikov is the professor's illegitimate son. This is a relationship that Sharikov apparently accepts—he repeatedly calls Preobrazhensky "daddy" *(papasha)*— but that the old bachelor, understandably, squeamishly denies. There is no question, however, that Sharikov is in a way the doctor's offspring, albeit engendered by scientific rather than natural means. One indication of Preobrazhensky's odd paternity is Sharikov's first name and patronymic, which offer a virtual backward echo of his creator's: *Filipp Filippovich—Poligraf Poligrafovich*.[129] The link in fact exists on several levels. The novella's religious imagery, first of all, as Diana Burgin has persuasively shown, contains a parody of the father-son relationship between God and Christ.[130] Thus Sharikov is born during the Nativity season, on December 23, but the obscenities and philistine clichés he spews forth—and perhaps the fact that he almost dies on December 25—underline the parodic intent.[131] Similarly, in a variation on the Transfiguration (*preobrazhenie,* the root of the professor's name, means both *transformation* and *transfigura-tion*), Jesus's "face [which] did shine as the sun" (Matt. 17:2) is replaced by Sharikov's "unpleasant" face, barely visible through "unshaven down," thick eyebrows and low hairline. The "sun" has degenerated to Sharikov's "fake ruby stickpin," shining out from his "venomously sky-colored tie" (2:167). And in reverse of God's declaration, "This is my beloved Son, in whom I am well pleased" (Matt. 17:5), Preobrazhensky, anything but pleased, denies paternity. The implication that this new "man" is the Anti-christ is reinforced by the apocalyptic rumors his unholy birth gives rise to, "about the end of the world, which the Bolsheviks have brought on" (2:165). Such intimations are supported by the growing chaos he intro-duces into Preobrazhensky's harmonious existence, culminating in a flood (an apocalyptic symbol). The episode begins with Zina calling Sharikov a "cursed devil" (2:175) and ends with the professor exclaiming: "The devil knows what this is!" (2:179).

Sharikov is also akin to Preobrazhensky on a purely human level. Osten-sibly the diametric opposite of his learned and cultivated "daddy," the ex-dog is in fact his negative double, in rather the same way that Smerdyakov and the devil are Ivan Karamazov's doubles.[132] (One also recalls the Dosto-evskian devil who haunts Aleksei in *The White Guard*.) Like Dostoevsky's antiheroes, Sharikov is a degenerate version of the materialist hero: he embodies the negative ramifications of the latter's apparently lofty ideas and aims. Thus, if Preobrazhensky during the operation seems to tran-scend human laws, his "offspring"'s lawlessness takes the prosaic forms of petty thievery and drunkenness. (The fact that the professor's presumably godlike act is described in largely criminal and bestial terms only under-lines the connection.) Sharikov, moreover, offers a debased version of his "daddy's" love of the good life. Whereas Preobrazhensky dresses elegantly and expensively and wears a "heavy fur coat of black and red fox with a bluish sheen" and a "black suit of English broadcloth" (2:127), Sharikov sports unkempt but flashy dress. And whereas the doctor loves fine food, drink, and tobacco, Sharikov vulgarizes and carries to excess these hedonis-tic tendencies, especially with regard to the bottle. Even Preobrazhensky's love of opera degenerates in Sharikov to balalaika playing and fondness for the circus. Within a political context, Preobrazhensky and Sharikov repre-sent the two faces of NEP. The professor is a high class *spets* who revives the refined tastes of the *haute bourgeoisie,* while Sharikov reflects the love of easy living among the lower orders. Although in terms of taste and culture the two faces contrast, the spiritual underpinnings are the same.

Shvonder's rival "paternity" of Sharikov also has a topical political dimension: the heightened struggle in the mid-twenties between defenders of NEP and advocates of a return to purer socialism, already an important theme in *The Fatal Eggs*. Shvonder's growing influence is apparent when Sharikov casts off his NEP finery for standard revolutionary garb. The fact that his new outfit is secondhand, "a leather jacket off somebody else's back, the same kind of leather scuffed pants" (2:198—one recalls Rokk's "old-fashioned" leather jacket in *The Fatal Eggs*)—suggests a throwback to the revolutionary ardor of the Civil War period. The work Shvonder finds for Sharikov, moreover, as "head of the subdepartment for purging the city of Moscow of stray animals (cats, etc.)," also reflects a return to the terror of that earlier time. The ex-dog's subsequent denunciation of the professor indicates that cats will not be the only object of his purge.[133] As the perceptive Preobrazhensky recognizes, indeed, the ardent Communist Shvonder ultimately has even more to fear than he: "Shvonder is the biggest fool. He doesn't understand that Sharikov is a graver menace to him than to me" (2:95).

Thus toward the end of the novella Preobrazhensky's creation, like Persikov's before him, threatens to bring about his destruction. The doctor, almost a broken man, has, ironically, aged as a result of his experiment in rejuvenation, "has become stooped and even, apparently, has grown grayer in recent days" (2:203). If Preobrazhensky nevertheless succeeds in vanquishing the subhuman monster (who in one form or another has been pursuing Bulgakov's heroes through the early works), the principal reason is the genuine relationship he forms with another human being: Bormental. His assistant, indeed, emerges as a second "son" (although never explicitly called such)—one who possesses precisely the character traits Sharikov lacks, but which, oddly, Sharik displayed to a high degree. Thus, like the dog, Bormental is "loyal and attached" to the professor (2:189); he is, as he avows late one night, deeply grateful for the refuge he received when hungry and homeless: "I shall never forget how I, a half-starving student, appeared to you and you gave me shelter in the department" (2:191).[134] Bormental's attachment, moreover, is not purely utilitarian, as the professor's own relations have been heretofore: "Believe me, Filipp Filippovich, you are much more to me than a professor, a teacher... My unbounded respect for you... Allow me to kiss you, dear Filipp Filippovich."

By offering Preobrazhensky the human equivalent of the love and devotion Sharik gave his master, the assistant stirs the previously imperious professor's feelings: "'You have moved me so much, moved me so much...

Thank you,' said Filipp Filippovich, '. . . I am, in essence, so alone, you know...'" (2:191). Preobrazhensky now takes Bormental into his confidence and with an unprecedented note of humility confesses his error: "I'll tell you in secret, as a friend . . . the old ass Preobrazhensky pulled a boner with this operation, like a third-year student" (2:193). He admits to Bormental that he overstepped scientific limits ("Here, doctor, is what happens when a researcher, instead of going gropingly and parallel with nature, forces the question and lifts the curtain") and acknowledges the superiority of natural evolution to human intervention: "Explain to me, please, why it is necessary to manufacture Spinozas artificially when any peasant woman can give birth to one whenever she likes!..." (2:194). He also repents having sacrificed Sharik, saying that even if he had the brain of Spinoza, he would perform such operations again "only if the ill-fated dog would not die under my knife" (2:193).

If Bormental, the surrogate son, thus becomes the professor's confidant, he is determined to render him more active aid—and by the most extreme means: murder. In his determination to kill Sharikov the assistant evinces an almost religious readiness to sacrifice himself. The professor, however, manifesting his heightened humanity, refuses a sacrifice due a *super*human and thereby distinguishes himself from the *sub*human Sharikov: "But to abandon a colleague in case of catastrophe and to get out of it myself because of my worldwide significance, excuse me... I am a Moscow student and not Sharikov" (2:192). Preobrazhensky also tries to prevent the murder by instilling sound principles in Bormental: "Never resort to crime, no matter whom it is directed against. Live until old age with clean hands" (2:195). His advice, however, hardly registers. This points to a subtle shift in the balance of strength between professor and assistant, also apparent in Preobrazhensky's exhausted pose when uttering his wise words: "Filipp Filippovich faded out, grew flabby, collapsed in an armchair" (2:195). From now on, indeed, he will hardly exercise more control over his second "son," the "fiery" Bormental (2:191), than over his first.

As the novella approaches its climax, Bormental comes closer and closer to committing violence against Sharikov, while the professor appears ever more helpless. Already later that night the assistant, responding to an attempted assault on Zina, shakes Sharikov, while Preobrazhensky helplessly "lifted up his arms and eyes to the ceiling lamp in the corridor and murmured, 'Well, well...'" (2:197). A couple of days later, while the professor stands "huddled pitifully" (2:200), Bormental again grabs the ex-dog, his eyes resembling "two black gun muzzles aimed point-blank at Sharikov" (2:199). And another time, after Sharikov threatens to fire a typist (the same one Sharik earlier pitied?) for rejecting his marriage proposal, Bormental's threat becomes explicit: "If I find out you've fired her, I'll shoot you right here with my own hands" (2:202). The conflict culminates after the doctors find out about Sharikov's denunciation of Preobrazhensky. Again "gun muzzles [appear] in the face" (2:203) of Bormental, who now does commit a "crime"—although not quite the murder the professor warned against. He knocks Sharikov down and smothers him, after which the doctors perform a reverse operation, turning the vile man back into a dog.

Bormental's violent behavior evokes much ambivalence. On the one hand, there are grounds for condemnation because he ignores the professor's wise counsel against committing a crime. In addition, his actions once again involve scientific hubris—usurpation of the power over life and death, this time of a human being, whom Bormental regards as no more than Preobrazhensky's "experimental creature" (2:195). By resorting to the same violent means as Sharikov, moreover, Bormental reveals his kinship to Preobrazhensky's other "son."

If most critics have nevertheless looked favorably upon Bormental's actions and their bloody denouement,[135] it is because the need to save Preobrazhensky seems reason enough for destroying so detestable a creature as Sharikov. A link exists, indeed, between Bormental and the Civil War heroes, especially Aleksei Turbin of *The White Guard*. For in defending his mentor from a bestial and dangerous member of the lower orders, the assistant is doing in microcosm what Aleksei views as the mission of his circle: saving the City and its culture from the barbarous hordes. Aleksei, moreover—and even more Yashvin of "I Killed"—resorts to violence, thus overcoming the ethical inhibitions of the earlier Civil War heroes (and Preobrazhensky), which made them powerless to oppose evil. The tie of Bormental to the stronger Civil War heroes suggests that he, like Sharik and Preobrazhensky, has autobiographical roots—a connection reinforced by the consonance of names: *Bormental—Mikhail Bulgakov*.

The ambivalence toward Bormental's—and Preobrazhensky's—violence at the end of *Heart of a Dog* is in fact never resolved. Bulgakov instead mutes the moral dilemma by surrounding the "crime" with mitigating circumstances. Thus it is said that Sharikov brings about his own end, when, possessed by an "impure spirit" (2:204), he refuses to leave the apartment peacefully. And it is he who initiates the violence: "Sharikov himself invited his death . . . with his right hand he took a revolver from his pocket and aimed it at the dangerous Bormental." Finally, the narrative strategy minimizes the horror of the operation itself, the coy narrator developing partial vision, thus preventing the reader this time from directly witnessing the bloody goings-on.

A sense of wrongdoing is not entirely obliterated, however. Zina testifies that after the operation Bormental "scared her to death," his face "entirely green and all, well, all, scratched to bits," while the professor "was not at all himself" either (2:205). The narrator questions the maid's veracity, but he himself notes that before the operation Bormental's "face is not his own" ("*s ne svoim litsom*", 2:204) and that afterward "the most total and most terrible silence" reigns in the apartment (2:205). Thus extenuating circumstances do not entirely eliminate the moral question. Violence, however justified, still horrifies, and the violation of ethical rules, whatever the cause, still has troubling consequences.

A Dog's Life

The epilogue begins ten days later, when the police come to investigate Sharikov's murder. Preobrazhensky, his youth and vigor restored (and by natural means) now that he is rid of his ungodly offspring, declares coolly that no one killed Sharikov. As proof he produces a strange hybrid creature, no longer human, but not entirely dog either. To the police's objection that Sharikov was a man, the doctor replies: "That is, he talked? . . . that is not what it means to be a man" (2:206). When asked the reason for Sharikov's reversion to a dog, Preobrazhensky sums up his own vain efforts: "Science does not yet know the way to turn beasts into people" (2:207). These clever double entendres are actually fraught with moral ambiguity. In the figurative sense they contain a fundamental truth—they could, indeed, serve as mottoes for the story. On the literal level, however, the professor is involved in a self-serving lie, since he attributes Sharikov's regression not to a willful act but to the impersonal workings of nature: "Now I tried, only it was unsuccessful, as you see. He talked a little and began to revert to a primeval state. Atavism!" Preobrazhensky's crime thus involves him in uncharacteristic duplicity, one moral compromise leading ineluctably to another.

The novella concludes some time later, with the pre-Sharikov harmony ostensibly restored. The point of view reverts to the dog Sharik, who, unaware of his strange stint as a human being, is again delighted with his life and again regards Preobrazhensky as a "higher creature, an important canine benefactor" (2:208). As for the professor, he is once more a "wizard," totally engrossed in his scientific work now that, with Bormental's crucial aid, he has eliminated Sharikov, a latter-day embodiment of those destructive, primitive impulses so powerful in different ways in the Civil War and satirical works.

For all this, *Heart of a Dog* ends on a discordant note:[136] "The dog saw terrifying things. The important man was immersing his hands in their slippery gloves into a vessel, was reaching for brains. The stubborn man kept trying persistently to get hold of something, was cutting, examining, squinting, and singing: 'To the sacred banks of the Nile...'" (2:208). Preobrazhensky has thus again become a priest of science, and this clouds the significance of his final victory. Although he has triumphed over Sharikov, the transformation of that unruly member of the lumpen proletariat back into a sweet but "slavish" dog and the scientist's resumption of his theurgic role offer another disturbing—and prophetic—model for the future: total control from above and the disappearance of any trace of that elemental freedom, which, for good or ill, Sharikov alone of all the characters stubbornly refused to relinquish. It was the dreadful Sharikov, after all (in what is surely one of the most disconcerting examples of Bulgakov's quest for moral balance), who rejected the "dog's happiness" of subservience and who, in this sense at least, preserved a "human" heart.

Heart of a Dog's happy ending is thus fraught with disquieting moral implications. Sharik has achieved domestic bliss, but at the cost of his freedom; the doctors have successfully defended their values from the barbaric threat from below, but only through violence, the means of their enemy. Their sacrifice of another contrasts with the *self*-sacrifice of the most heroic of Bulgakov's early protagonists. Yet to give the doctors their due, self-destruction within the context of the new society would hardly have been a helpful alternative. As the valiant but futile deaths of Korotkov and Persikov show, this would have led only to the total triumph of the hellish Kalsoners, Rokks, and Sharikovs. And so the scientist-heroes of *Heart of a Dog* are caught in an ethical bind—one from which Bulgakov himself found escape only by abandoning medicine for literature. For as a writer he could engage in a *bloodless* struggle against the likes of Sharikov and strive to bring about that genuine, spiritual improvement of humanity of which Preobrazhensky proves incapable.

Zoika's Apartment

The theme of the "caninization" of Soviet society—moral compromise and surrender of freedom in the name of material comfort—soon reappears in Bulgakov's works in the comedy *Zoika's Apartment*.[137] While the play presents a much more corrupt, decadent version of NEP, there are many parallels with *Heart of a Dog*, of which I will point out a few.

The protagonists of both works, first of all, are representatives of the old world, defending their spacious living quarters from incursions by the new order. The heroine of the play, the adventuress, Zoika Pelts, is, like Preobrazhensky, threatened by a bothersome house committee chairman, the bribe-taking Alliluya;[138] but at the same time she enjoys protection from her neighbor, Gus, the trust director. The one with deepest ties to the old order is Zoika's lover, Obolyaninov, a "former count" (3:88) and present-day cocaine addict. He, like Preobrazhensky, bemoans certain aspects of Bolshevism but, in an interesting twist, singles out for reproach a phenomenon strikingly similar to the experiments of the scientist-heroes of the novellas. Thus he recalls seeing a notice outside a zoo announcing the demonstration of a "former chicken." Told that the chicken is now a rooster, he comments: "It turns out one of those bandits, a Communist professor, did some disgusting thing to the unfortunate chicken, as a result of which it turned into a rooster . . . I rode on and began to imagine: a former tiger, now it is probably an elephant. What a nightmare!" Although Obolyaninov expresses horror at such Bolshevik transformations, he and Zoika have brought about a similar radical alteration in the function of home. For if Preobrazhensky's apartment is "obscene" only in the figurative sense, in the play the word takes on literal meaning: Zoika's apartment is turned into a bordello.

Joining in the shady enterprise is the cardsharp and rogue, Ametistov, who, although more likable than Sharikov, shares some of his traits: he too has undergone startling transformations, having once taken on the identity of a deceased Communist; and he too, in a sense, returns from the dead, for he was supposedly executed in Baku. The vulgar philistine, Ametistov, moreover, refers to the aristocratic Obolyaninov as "daddy" (*papasha*, 3:122). Like the "father-son" pair of Sharikov and Preobrazhensky, this one points to the two sides of NEP, apparently contrasting, but spiritually joined.

Through their obscene activities, Zoika and her cohorts succeed, like

Preobrazhensky, both in preserving their living space and in earning large sums of money. The novella and play end differently, however: while the professor is victorious, his "crime" concealed from the police, Zoika's illegal operations—which lead to a more unambiguous murder than the one in *Heart of a Dog*—are exposed, and she and her lover (but not Ametistov or the murderer, Kheruvimov) are arrested.[139]

Zoika's and, to a lesser extent, Preobrazhensky's "obscene" apartments are outgrowths of the incongruities and excesses of NEP. In the later time frame of *The Master and Margarita*, however, the impulse to choose comfort over freedom, to prostitute oneself for material privilege, has, if anything, grown more marked. For here the entire literary-theatrical establishment has given up freedom and independence of thought for good apartments and good food—in other words, to lead a "dog's life."[140] It is significant that the head of MASSOLIT, the learned and courteous Berlioz, would not be out of place at Preobrazhensky's table, while those who come to upset the canine paradise of comfort and bondage—the devils—are a bunch of ruffians, who take over Berlioz's apartment and, like Sharikov, create *razrukha* wherever they go.

Among the Muscovites only Margarita joyfully exchanges her easy life for freedom. When enlisted as a witch by the devils, she flies off from her splendid apartment, crying: "Invisible and free! Invisible and free!" (5:227). She then proceeds to ruin the flat of the critic Latunsky, flooding it as Sharikov does Preobrazhensky's dwelling.[141] Finally, while the gifted scientist Preobrazhensky lives in luxury, the talented writer, the Master, is an outcast, robbed of his modest basement flat and residing in a mental hospital. And at the very end he and his beloved watch joyfully as their former refuge burns and they depart for a higher, spiritual dwelling.

Conclusion

Bulgakov's Early Works: The Knight and the Dragon

At the very beginning of this study there sits a knight astride a horse—the subject of Bulgakov's first literary effort at the age of seven. The bright chivalric figure Svetlan (*svet* = light), setting out to vanquish the dark forces of evil, encapsulates the ideals of Bulgakov's childhood, culled both from his religious upbringing and, on quite another level, his adventure reading.

Traces of this ideal can occasionally be detected in Bulgakov's writings, for example in *Flight*, originally entitled *Serafima's Knight*. On the whole, however, the Civil War experience eclipsed the knightly model, replacing it (to extend the chivalric imagery) with another horrifying emblem: the dragon of revolution wreaking terrible destruction and the knight—the weak hero—reduced to helpless and self-recriminating bystander. Paradoxically, however, it is precisely this image of death that led to the birth of Bulgakov the writer, for if he was powerless to fight evil with guns or lances, he could wield the powerful weapon of words. These words, moreover, not only castigated misdeeds, but gradually made visible, within the palimpsest of Bulgakov's life and times, the outlines of the chivalric ideal buried beneath the dreadful image of civil strife.

The earliest Civil War works present variants of the reversed chivalric emblem, depicting (to use more conventional terminology) the confrontation of the intellectual and revolution, the latter taking the form of the anarchic uprising of the common people (the *narod*) and often personified by a brutal military commander slaying or maiming a defenseless victim (typically a Jew). Faced with such unfettered violence, the civilized hero, for all his moral superiority—indeed, *because* his moral superiority prevents

228

him from descending to the bestial level of the forces of revolution—is helpless. All he can do is cringe in silent fear or at most *imagine* himself annihilating the source of evil. And, when the opportunity presents itself, he runs away.

In Bulgakov's successive fictions both parties to this confrontation evolve. On the one hand, the autobiographical "deserters" gradually grow stronger. The critical point is reached when Aleksei Turbin of *The White Guard* shoots back at his Petlyurite pursuers, after which other personae come close to the chivalric ideal: Dr. Yashvin of "I Killed" literally, by killing the brutal colonel to defend a helpless woman; the hero of *Notes of a Young Doctor* figuratively, in his indefatigable battle against disease and ignorance, armed "with something like a sword, or perhaps a stethoscope" (1:121). At the same time, Bulgakov comes to terms with his personae's failures of courage by flanking them with two other types, who represent the extremes of cowardice and valor: the *moral* deserters and the selfless martyrs. The former (who include Talberg and Shpolyansky in *The White Guard* and Korzukhin in *Flight*) stand at the negative pole, for they do not simply flee in instinctual terror, like the autobiographical heroes, but betray family and comrades out of rational self-interest. The martyrs, in contrast (Streltsov of "The Raid," Nai-Turs of *The White Guard*, Aleksei of *Days of the Turbins*), achieve the genuine heroism of which the authorial personae are incapable by giving their lives in defense of others. They do not slay the "dragon"— they are slain instead—but by upholding their values to the highest degree, they fulfill the chivalric ideal. This becomes explicit in *The White Guard*, where in Aleksei's dream Nai-Turs appears in knightly raiment, "the likes of which had not existed in a single army since the Crusades" (1:233).

The antagonists of the Civil War heroes—the *narod* and the commander—also go through various transmutations in the early work. The unbridled mob, to be sure, never ceases to horrify. Even the occasional individual who arises momentarily from the undifferentiated mass is invariably portrayed as a subhuman, nightmarish being, like the "broad-cheekboned something" in "On the Night of the Second" (1:513). And when gathered together, the mob reveals its true identity as the knight's eternal foe, the dragon or snake (the "snake's belly" of *The White Guard* [1:386], the "snake of the horse army" in *The Fatal Eggs* [2:110]). Precisely because of its lack of individuation, however, the mob gradually ceases to be the main issue. As the narrator of *The White Guard* concludes, peasant rage, although horrifying, is a constant given, an impersonal natural force that erupts from time to time but has little relevance to human civilization.

If the anarchic *narod* decreases in significance, the most highly developed embodiment of the revolutionary ethos, the brutal military commander, grows in importance and complexity. Thus, in the "The Red Crown," the hero-narrator views the brutal White general with unalloyed horror and wishes that the perpetrator of atrocities would at least once experience suffering equal to his own. By the time Bulgakov wrote "I Killed," there are signs that the constant violence has indeed had an effect on the bestial Cossack colonel, who is "sickly" and "nervous" (2:653). And in *Flight* the equally violent Khludov is "sick with something . . . entirely sick, from head to foot."[1] He therefore arouses pity as well as revulsion and is finally forgiven because of his suffering.[2] Thus sympathy gradually brings reconciliation and at least partial resolution of the conflict of knight and dragon.

If Bulgakov thus makes rather uneasy peace with both the Civil War masses and the brutal commander, postrevolutionary society brought forth other inimical forces, depicted in the satiric works. There the evil against which the hero struggles stems not so much from *dis*order, as during the Civil War, as from what one might term *mis*order—an organizational structure that fosters people's basest impulses. The new system ushered in the institutionalized rule of the dreaded masses, both in domestic arrangements (the communal apartment) and in the political-economic-artistic apparatus (the bureaucracy). The hero, indeed, is not much better off now than during the Civil War, especially on the housing front. Once more he is a lone intellectual confronted by the dark *narod,* to whom reptilian and bestial imagery is at times applied, as in "No. 13. The Elpit-Workommune House" (2:244, 249). Now he again imagines that he will "rout" the foe ("Moonshine Lake," 2:325), who in reality proves too strong for him. If he does not succeed in slaying the "dragon," however, the persona does grow more heroic in the struggle: he is "tempered" ("Forty Times Forty," 2:279), becomes "iron" ("Moonshine Lake," 2:324), and turns into a "remarkable person" ("Moscow of the Twenties," 2:443).

The attitude toward the masses, moreover, imperceptibly shifts in the satirical works, as in the Civil War writings. While drunkenness, boorishness, and dishonesty still abound, the common people gradually emerge as much victims as victimizers, whether of the bureaucracy, as in the *Gudok* feuilletons, or of the radical experimenters in *The Fatal Eggs* and *Heart of a Dog.* Increased tolerance of the *narod,* however, does not extend to its leaders, as it does eventually even to the commanders of the Civil War works. These leaders fall into two categories: the "Vasily Ivanoviches"—the house committee chairmen and bureaucrats who make Soviet society a hell on earth—and the ideological champions of the new system, the Bolshevik *intelligenty* (the young poets in *Notes on the Cuff,* Antonov in "The Khan's Fire," the many false educators of the *Gudok* feuilletons). It is the latter who are ultimately the more formidable, for as rival *intelligenty,* they do not simply threaten the persona with literal homelessness, like the administrators, but attempt a *spiritual* eviction, dislodging the heroes' traditional values from the domicile of Soviet life.

In Bulgakov's most significant satiric works of the 1920s, the novellas *The Fatal Eggs* and *Heart of a Dog,* the antagonists of the scientist-heroes actually fulfill the negative functions of both administrator and Bolshevik *intelligent:* Rokk is not only a *sovkhoz* director, but also a flutist and former newspaper editor; Shvonder is both house committee chairman and journalist. At the same time, however, in both works a new and unsettling truth emerges—namely, that underlying the enmity of scientist and Bolshevik— and despite their differences in ability, educational level, and cultural heritage, they share fundamental intellectual assumptions: their materialism and their belief in humanity's ability to transform and improve nature. It is significant, therefore, that the scientists' efforts, like the Bolsheviks', not only fail to annihilate the dragon but lead to the creation of *new* destructive monsters (giant snakes, Sharikov).

In *The Fatal Eggs* the snakes arouse the latent bestial instincts of the masses, and—in a reversal of the knight-dragon archetype—an apelike rioter slays Persikov. In *Heart of a Dog* Preobrazhensky does succeed in eliminating the monstrous Sharikov, but this literal realization of the chivalric imperative—involving as it does the adoption of the violent means of the foe—in itself raises serious moral questions. Then, after one more murder by an autobiographical hero, Yashvin in "I Killed," Bulgakov forever closed the path of physical violence to his personae. Indeed, he abandoned the strong hero entirely almost as soon he had created the purest examples, in 1925–1926 (*Heart of a Dog, Notes of a Young Doctor,* "I Killed"), and by 1927 he had returned to the weaker type: Doctor Polyakov of "Morphine," who retreats into his drug-induced hallucinations, and Golubkov of *Flight,* who out of terror betrays the woman he loves.

These figures in some ways hearken back to the weak authorial personae of the early stories, although a new spirit of sympathy and forgiveness modifies the former self-recrimination. This is not only a matter of regression, moreover, for by creating ever more valorous variants of the authorial personae in his early writings, Bulgakov was moving further and further from the image of self as artist. Then, once the doctor persona gave way to the writer (Maksudov in *Notes of a Dead Man,* the Master), what had seemed weaknesses in the men of action—their solitude and acute sensitivity, their alienation from the everyday "real" world—proved essential attributes. In their private spiritual sphere, indeed, the writers, like the scientists of the novellas, are masters. They succeed in their literary works—as the scientists do *not* in their laboratories—in creating entire alternative worlds superior to the hell on earth without. Their works inevitably place them at odds with the powers that be and they pay for their utterances with their lives. Thus the authorial personae in the late fiction are a synthesis of three disparate types in the early works: the timid intellectual, the masterful creator, and the martyr. As such, they are incapable of slaying the dragons of Soviet society in the material sense, but they win the ultimate spiritual battle.

The Early Fiction and *The Master and Margarita*

Just as the Master combines ostensibly incompatible traits from characters in the early works, so does *The Master and Margarita* as a whole join in a new way former oppositions, achieving, if not total resolution of former moral and psychological conflicts, then at least a high level of reconciliation. In Yeshua, first of all, one finds traits of two of the early heroes: the martyrs and the meek authorial personae. In contrast to such valiant warriors as Nai-Turs and the Aleksei Turbin of *Days of the Turbins,* Yeshua is physically weak and appears naive and vulnerable in his initial confrontation with the menacing Pilate. Indeed, with his mild and even slightly comic demeanor, he bears some resemblance to the deceptively fragile Abram in "The Raid" and even the hapless, but kind and generous, Lariosik of *The White Guard.* Yeshua's physical weakness, however, belies his great spiritual strength, for even when threatened with death he does not betray his higher vision. By speaking out, declaring that "it is easy and pleasant to tell the truth" (5:31), he fulfills to the highest degree the duty of the intellectual.

Yeshua confronts inimical forces analogous to those facing the early heroes—the mob, the cruel military commander (Pilate), the ideological foe (Kaifa), the moral deserter (Iuda)—but these too have continued to evolve. The people, first of all, who already played a diminishing role in Bulgakov's previous writings, figure little in Yeshua's fate. In contrast to the Gospel accounts, a crowd is not even present at Pilate's judgment and exerts no pressure on the procurator to condemn Christ. The masses do appear to hear Pilate's decision, but even then they do not unambiguously support him, their "roaring, squeals, groans, guffaws, and whistling" (5:42) conveying a whole range of disparate reactions. The irrelevance of the mob—both in ancient Jerusalem and in the Soviet Union—is made explicit in one of the earliest extant drafts of the novel, in a dialogue between Berlioz (then named Vladimir Mironovich) and Woland (the engineer):

> "Tell me please," Berlioz asked unexpectedly, "that means that according to you there were no cries 'crucify him!'?"
>
> The engineer smiled condescendingly: "For pity's sake! I would like to see how some crowd could meddle in a trial carried out by a procurator and, furthermore, such a one as Pilate! I'll clarify it with an example, finally. A trial is in session at the revolutionary tribunal on Prechistensky Boulevard, and suddenly, imagine, the public begins to howl. 'Shoot, shoot him!' They would be cleared from the hall immediately, that's all there is to it. And why would they start howling? They don't care at all if someone gets hanged or shot. A crowd, Vladimir Mironovich, is in all periods a crowd—a mob [*chern'*], Vladimir Mironovich!"[3]

If the people do not collectively condemn Yeshua, however, neither do they follow him in large numbers, as they do in the Biblical accounts. Yeshua himself states that no crowd greeted his entrance into Yershalaim (5:28). And later the curious mob finds "absolutely nothing interesting" at the crucifixion (5:169) and is dispersed well before the end by the unbearable heat.

If the collective rage so prominent in the Civil War works no longer plays a role, the brutal commander has become all important. Thus it is significant that Pilate's military background, not even mentioned in the Bible, is given considerable prominence in the novel,[4] and as procurator of Judaea he still controls a considerable military force. The horrifying brutality inherent in martial might is personified by the gigantic centurion, Krysoboi, whose maimed, noseless face recalls the "something, vaguely reminiscent of a human face" in "On the Night of the Second" (1:513–514).

Pilate, moreover, immediately uses the brute power at his disposal, ordering Krysoboi to strike Yeshua, and later explicitly confirms his own cruelty, calling himself a "vicious monster" (5:21).

Horror at Pilate's use of force, however, is balanced by pity, for like Khludov in *Flight* the procurator is a sick man, tormented by excruciating headaches. He arouses further sympathy because he is a rounded and complex figure, who has roots not only in the brutal commanders but in the autobiographical heroes of the Civil War prose. Thus he, like them, earlier witnessed a war atrocity: the maiming of Krysoboi by German troops, who "threw themselves at him like dogs at a bear" (5:28). The procurator was in a sense more fortunate than the Civil War heroes, for as commander he was able to save the victim of barbaric hordes. His opposition of force by force, however, has proved a curse, for Pilate himself has become a "vicious monster," who, although representative of the most advanced civilization of his time, hardly rises above the bestial Germans. The military ethic of might, dooming humanity to an unending violent struggle, with the strong ever victimizing the weak (like the vicious amoebae under Persikov's red ray), accounts, furthermore, for Pilate's low opinion of the human race, diametrically opposed to Yeshua's.

Yeshua insists that all people are good, even the Germans who maimed Krysoboi. By answering force and hatred with good will—by extending the spirit of understanding and forgiveness first apparent in "Morphine" and *Flight* to its furthest limit—he succeeds in breaking the vicious circle of violence. His ideas, for all their apparent naiveté, have great power, winning over such unlikely people as the tax collector Levi Matvei. Yeshua even asserts that the brutal Krysoboi—a type regarded with unmitigated horror in the early works—is good, and the reader does not doubt his assertion that he could change the centurion if given the chance. Yeshua's positive influence is especially apparent on Pilate, for by the end of their conversation the procurator ceases to be an enemy and even tries to save the mild-mannered philosopher.

Preventing the full reconciliation of the brutal commander and "weak" martyr, however, are two other characters, also related to types from the early works. The first, the high priest, Kaifa, is a dogmatic ideologue, and as such is generically related to the Bolshevik *intelligent*. The second, Iuda, is heir to the unprincipled deserters of the Civil War fiction. While they *literally* fled for self-serving reasons, Yeshua's false disciple is a *spiritual* deserter, who betrays for material gain. Pilate yields to Kaifa's demand that

Yeshua be executed when it becomes clear that he would otherwise sacrifice his own position and perhaps his life. He, like the Civil War heroes, thus fails to prevent an unjust death, but the procurator is morally more culpable because he has the power to save the blameless victim. He does, to be sure, soon try to make up for his moment of weakness by wreaking revenge upon Iuda. But this—yet one more instance of countering violence with violence—cannot compensate for his earlier failure of courage. And so the mighty procurator acts the coward, whereas the "weak" Yeshua displays the highest level of valor, choosing death over betrayal of his beliefs.

Pilate, as Bulgakov's final rejection of the martial model of courage, serves partially to absolve the early heroes of their shortcomings in battle. The authorial personae, however, failed just as often to live up to Yeshua's example of *spiritual* steadfastness, and this occurs once more in the main plot of *The Master and Margarita*. The Master's position in his oppressive society is, to be sure, even more terrible than that of the Civil War personae. For if they helplessly witnessed the murder of a defenseless person, an analogous configuration, but one of far vaster import, underlies the Master's plight: as creator of the quintessential innocent victim, Yeshua, he witnesses his hero's crucifixion both in the Judaean setting of his novel and in the "real" life of the frame novel, where his fictionalized Christ is pilloried anew by the literary critics. The Master, like the early heroes, is unable to oppose the onslaught, but, as creator of Yeshua, cannot so easily dissociate himself from the victim. Attacks on the novel ineluctably shift to persecution of its author, leading finally to the Master's arrest and his later confinement in a mental hospital.

In the persecution of the Master, the main enemy is not the anarchic mob any more than it is in the Judaean chapters. As in the early satiric works, the main problem is not *dis*order but *mis*order, which manifests itself in the same two spheres as before: the bureaucracy (primarily within the literary and theatrical organizations) and the dwelling place (the "hellish" 302B Sadovaya Street). The gravest threat to the Master and his novel, the literary grouping MASSOLIT, not only exemplifies the general horrors of mass bureaucratized society but, as a collective of writers, also represents a terrifying multiplication of the early authorial persona's most serious and constant foe: the Bolshevik *intelligent*. Here the solitary writer with his private vision is opposed not simply by an individual or by one grouping out of the many that existed during NEP but by an entire monolithic organization espousing official truth and denying any other. The organization is best personified by Berlioz, chairman of its board and editor of its journal. Heir to the false enlighteners of the early prose, he distills the nihilistic views and coercive function of the new intellectual, instructing the ignorant young poet, Ivan Bezdomny, that Christ—and the spiritual realm as a whole—does not exist at all. Berlioz, as watchdog of Communist orthodoxy, occupies a position analogous to Kaifa's in the Judaean plot, and MASSOLIT also has its Iuda, or self-interested betrayer: Aloisy Mogarych, the Master's neighbor and supposed friend, who informs on the writer in order to get his better apartment.

The Master, a weak intellectual, is incapable of following Yeshua's path to the end, and as his persecution intensifies he grows terrified, becomes afraid of the dark, and suffers a mental breakdown. In his deranged imagination the evil and darkness by which he is surrounded crystallizes into a repulsive, slimy creature, not a dragon or snake, to be sure, but an octopus, whom he imagines crawling into his room one autumn night. The Master, who does not have the knightlike strength to battle the beast, surrenders to his terror and burns his manuscript. Thus, despite his artistic and spiritual achievements, he remains in the line of the psychologically weak heroes, abandoning a defenseless victim—his own creation, Yeshua. The Master's message does, to be sure, reach one other writer, the proletarian poet, Ivan Bezdomny (a proletarian thereby joins two of the other most hated types of the early fiction—the brutal commander, Pilate, and the mercenary money lender, Levi Matvei—as Christian "converts"). Upon departing from the earthly realm, the Master commands Bezdomny to continue his novel. Thus it appears likely that the Master's spiritual message, like Yeshua's, will survive, despite his own destruction.[5]

Ivan Bezdomny, however, can no more struggle in a direct way against the evil surrounding him than can the Master. The only force capable of upsetting this oppressive hell on earth is a still stronger hellish force: Satan/Woland and his cohorts. That the devils are highly ambivalent figures is apparent from the unending polemic surrounding them. Like their human precursors, the scientist-heroes of *The Fatal Eggs* and *Heart of a Dog*, they exercise extraordinary control over the material world and have the potential to wreak great destruction. There is an important difference, however; for whereas Persikov's and Preobrazhensky's use of their almost supernatural powers is a hubristic assumption of a divine function, the devils actually *are* part of the supernatural order, their violent behavior, therefore—the just wrath that complements Yeshua's bright mercy and love—serving a transcendent purpose.[6]

Near the beginning of *The White Guard*, the narrator declares that "whatever might happen is . . . only for the best" (1:180). This promise of final justice is not achieved within the bounds of the novel but, it is said, will occur at the apocalyptic end of history, when all will be "judged according to their works" (1:179, 426). In *The Master and Margarita* Bulgakov belatedly fulfills the Turbins' wish for swift justice, if only for a few days. For the most part the devils behave as princes of disorder, raining down the kind of *razrukha* so bemoaned in *Heart of a Dog* and in general so dreaded by the early Bulgakov. The writer's attitude toward such *diablerie*, however, has changed fundamentally, for whereas the chaos in the works of the twenties threatened the old beloved civilization, here it is directed against coercive, stifling *mis*order, and therefore has a liberating function. The devils, moreover, although they turn Moscow society topsy-turvy and set numerous buildings ablaze, are not merely agents of wanton destruction. As a conversation between Woland and Koroviev makes clear, they are demolishing the old system in order to clear the way for a new, more harmonious order:

> "Of course it will be necessary to build a new building."
>
> "It will be built, messire," Koroviev responded, "I make bold to assure you of that."
>
> "Well, all right, one can only wish it will be better than the former," Woland noted.
>
> "So it will be, messire," said Koroviev. (5:352)

The devils' harsh exposé of human foibles seems to contradict Yeshua's belief in man's essential goodness, but people, after all, are contradictory creatures, combining that light and dark, which, according to Woland, are necessary for life itself. Although *The Master and Margarita* takes place at a time when the dark side predominates, the fierce attacks on the Master's novel indicate the continuing threat to the status quo of Yeshua's appeal to people's better nature. Even in the midst of that most vivid exposé of the modern Muscovites' petty foibles, the magic show, human goodness makes a fleeting appearance when the audience begs forgiveness for the beheaded emcee, Bengalsky. Complying with their wish, Woland comments quite equably on the crowd sitting before him: "They're people like any other.

They love money, but that, after all, has always been the case... Mankind loves money . . . Well, they're frivolous ... well, all right... mercy also knocks sometimes at their hearts... ordinary people..." (5:123).

The intertwining of dark and light is most apparent in the character of Margarita, who as witch wreaks destruction on the critic Latunsky's apartment but who also embodies the spirit of mercy, attaining forgiveness for the child murderer, Frieda, and winning the Master's freedom from the mental hospital and from the larger prison of earthly life. There have been female saviors before in Bulgakov—Elena and Yuliya in *The White Guard,* Serafima in *Flight.* The love that moves Margarita, however, played only a marginal role in Bulgakov's early works. Its centrality in his final novel springs from a biographical source: the writer's liaison with the woman who was to become his third wife, Elena Sergeevna Shilovskaya.[7]

Like Bulgakov, beginning in 1932, the Master is not alone, as the early heroes typically were, but shares his life with a kindred being, whose indomitable spirit compensates for his own weakness. Margarita, indeed, by throwing in her lot with the devils—risking damnation to rescue the Master—is allied to such self-sacrificing heroes as Nai-Turs and the Aleksei Turbin of *Days of the Turbins.* She thus comes far closer to the chivalric ideal than the Master himself. Her exploit, to be sure, does not save her beloved's life; rather, it leads to his—and her own—death. But it also brings them refuge from the hellish Soviet world and delivers them to an idyllic and peaceful "eternal home" (5:372). Thus, through Margarita's intercession, the fervent wishes of so many of Bulgakov's personae—for escape, peace, home—come true for his last hero.

The Master and Mikhail Afanasievich

The autobiographical sources for the Master's literary woes have been noted by many.[8] Bulgakov too was repeatedly attacked by critics and was hounded from literature and the theater altogether in 1929. Although after Stalin's surprise telephone call of 1930 he was allowed to work for the Moscow Art Theater as literary consultant, assistant director, and even actor,[9] on the whole the writer's life in the thirties was marked by one frustration after another and by ever-increasing fear. Except for his successful stage adaptation of Gogol's *Dead Souls* (1932) and a revival that same year of *Days of the Turbins,* all his attempts to publish and to get his plays produced ended in failure.[10]

The only other partial exception was *The Cabal of Hypocrites (Molière)*, first written in 1929 and staged at the Moscow Art Theater in February 1936 after many harrowing years of rehearsal, revision, and conflicts with Stanislavsky and others. Although the play enjoyed immediate popular success, it was attacked by the press, and after a vituperous article, "External Glitter and False Content," appeared in the authoritative *Pravda* (a very ominous sign during this time of high Stalinism), it was closed after only a few performances. Because of what Bulgakov considered a capitulation by the Moscow Art Theater, he severed his long-standing tie with that institution and went to work as a librettist for the Bolshoi Opera.

Not only was Bulgakov hounded into silence like the Master, but he also reacted in similar ways to the intolerable pressure. In March 1930 he burned the first draft of *The Master and Margarita,* as well as some other works. Then through much of the last decade of his life he suffered from mental problems. Elena Sergeevna's diary repeatedly describes his attacks of fear and depression, his phobias, and attempts to treat his illness by such means as electric shock and hypnotism.[11]

If the autobiographical roots of the Master's character are thus incontestable, one must hasten to add that Bulgakov's last hero, like so many before him, reflects primarily the writer's weaker side. In contrast to the Master, after all, his creator did not abandon literature, and, despite periods of despair verging on mental breakdown, he continued to write and revise *The Master and Margarita* until his death from a kidney ailment in 1940. Nor did Bulgakov, like so many gifted artists, seriously compromise his talent by joining in the paean to Stalinist Russia, in spite of almost unbearable pressure to do so.[12] One indication of his exceptional position occurred in 1935, when Boris Pasternak, at a name-day party for Veresaev, proposed a toast to Bulgakov. The hostess suggested they first toast Veresaev, but Pasternak retorted: "No, I want to toast Bulgakov! Veresaev, of course, is a very major figure [*ochen' bol'shoi chelovek*], but he is a lawful phenomenon. Bulgakov is an unlawful one!"[13]

Even *Batum,* Bulgakov's play on Stalin (1939), although no doubt written partly in response to the immense pressure, does not represent full capitulation.[14] As Chudakova has persuasively demonstrated, Bulgakov had been obsessed by the dictator ever since the telephone call of 1930. Moreover, the work's juxtaposition of the young, revolutionary Stalin to organs of coercive authority—the tsarist government and the organized church— offers a variant of a pattern that appears in one form or another in many of the writer's works of the 1930s, including *The Master and Margarita*. The fact that the play is set before the revolution also allowed Bulgakov to avoid eulogizing contemporary reality. This may have contributed, indeed, to Stalin's dissatisfaction with the work and to its prohibition, a very grave matter in those years of mass arrests.

Bulgakov also differs from the Master and Maksudov in the nature of his literary gifts. The romantic image of the artist to which these characters conform—the impractical dreamer destroyed by the cruelty of the real world—is hardly compatible, after all, with the description of E. T. A. Hoffmann that Bulgakov applied to himself: the artist as fighter, who "transforms literature into a battle tower." What is characteristic of Bulgakov, and what underlies his originality, is that he is both self-absorbed romantic and acerbic social critic. Whereas in his early autobiographical writings he, like Maksudov, conjured up lyrical images of a lost family life in Civil War Kiev, his satirical works waged a spirited attack against the evils of Soviet Russia during NEP. In *Notes of a Dead Man* itself Bulgakov not only portrays Maksudov's torments but subjects the tormenters to biting mockery. Similarly, in *The Master and Margarita,* coexisting with the story of the "thrice romantic Master" and his creation, the gentle Yeshua, there is the embodiment of the other side of the author's psyche, the retribution-dealing Woland, who reduces to chaos, at least for a while, the sham world of Moscow in the thirties.

Bulgakov, like his writer-heroes, suffered from persecution by the literary-theatrical establishment, but rather than committing suicide or retreating into an insane asylum as they do, he—like his alter egos, Tugai-Beg of "The Khan's Fire," Yashvin of "I Killed," and Woland of *The Master and Margarita*[15]—fought back, wielding, however, the nonmaterial weapon of the word. By thus continuing his battle against evil to the very end, he remained true to the knightly ideal of his childhood.

Notes

Introduction

1. Bulgakov to I. V. Stalin, May 30, 1931, *Sob. soch.*(M) 5:455. Page references to this edition are in the text, with volume number followed by page number.
2. For the fullest treatment of the period, see Edward J. Brown, *The Proletarian Episode in Russian Literature* (New York: Columbia University Press, 1953).
3. Quoted by Bulgakov in his letter to the Soviet government of March 25, 1930 ("Pravitel'stvu SSSR," *Sob. soch.*(M) 5:448).
4. For a succinct, lucid account of events of 1929, see J. A. E. Curtis, *Bulgakov's Last Decade: The Writer as Hero* (Cambridge: Cambridge University Press, 1987), 8–12.
5. On April 18, 1930, Bulgakov received a surprise telephone call from Stalin, and the day after he was "greeted with open arms at the Moscow Art Theater." See V. V. Gudkova and E. A. Zemskaia, "Kommentarii," *Sob. soch.* (M) 5:697.
6. For a description of the first steps toward turning the apartment into a museum, see Jean MacKenzie, "Bulgakov's Haunt Gains New Aura," *The Moscow Times,* June 18, 1995, p. 41. I am grateful to Marshall Goldman for providing me with this article. For a perceptive interpretation of the graffiti, see John Bushnell, *Moscow Graffiti: Language and Subculture* (Boston: Unwin Hyman, 1990), chap. 5. I owe information on a 1989 Bulgakov festival to Jacqueline Decter. For a description of one Bulgakovian eating place, see Steven Erlanger, "Speaking of the Devil," Sophisticated Traveler, *New York Times,* Nov. 13, 1994, 10. On Satan's Ball, see Marina Medvedeva-Khazanova, *Rossiia: smutnoe vremia* (St. Petersburg: Astra-Liuks, 1994), 60.
7. M. O. Chudakova, *Zhizneopisanie Mikhaila Bulgakova* (Moscow: Kniga, 1988).
8. Boris Myagkov has been particularly active in this area. See especially his *Bulgakovskaia Moskva* (Moscow: Moskovskii rabochii, 1993).
9. V. I. Nemtsev, ed., *Tvorchestvo Mikhaila Bulgakova v literaturno-khudozhestvennom kontekste: Tezisy dokladov Vsesoiuznoi nauchnoi konferentsii*

241

(16–21 sentiabria 1991 goda) (Samara, Russia: Samarskii Gos. Ped. Institut im. V. V. Kuibysheva, 1991), 2; Viktor Losev, "K chitateliu," in Mikhail Bulgakov, *Neizvestnyi Bulgakov,* ed. Viktor Losev (Moscow: Knizhnaia palata, 1993), 5; "To Stand for a Foreword," in Viacheslav Vozdvizhenskii, comp., *Mikhail Bulgakov and His Times: Memoirs, Letters,* trans. Liv Tudge (Moscow: Progress Publishers, 1990), 7.

10. Sergei Kiselev, "Sergeevskii spusk, 13: Realii i mistika," *Literaturnaia gazeta,* May 22, 1991, 1.

11. For a thoughtful, balanced overview of these questions, see Lesley Milne, "Nationalism, Anti-Semitism and Bulgakov," in Lesley Milne, ed., *Bulgakov: The Novelist-Playwright* (Luxembourg: Harwood Academic Publishers, 1995), 61–73.

12. G. El'shevskaya, "Iskusstvo pisat' pis'ma: Vystavka 'Pis'mo M. A. Bulgakovu,'" *Novoe literaturnoe obozrenie,* no. 2 (1993), 354.

13. See especially Anatoly Smeliansky, *Mikhail Bulgakov v Khudozhestvennom teatre* (Moscow: Iskusstvo, 1986). Translation: *Is Comrade Bulgakov Dead? Mikhail Bulgakov at the Moscow Art Theatre,* trans. Arch Tait (London: Methuen, 1993).

14. Gerard Genette, *Figures III,* trans. Paul de Man (Paris: de Seuil, 1972), 50. Quoted by Anna Lisa Crone, "Rozanov and Autobiography: The Case of Vasily Vasilievich," in Jane Gary Harris, ed., *Autobiographical Statements in Twentieth-Century Russian Literature* (Princeton, N.J.: Princeton University Press, 1990), 44.

15. Harris, "Diversity of Discourse: Autobiographical Statements in Theory and Praxis," in Harris, *Autobiographical Statements,* 25.

16. As Svetlana Boym reminds us, it is an oversimplification to say that the formalists totally divorced biography from literary study. See her *Death in Quotation Marks: Cultural Myths of the Modern Poet* (Cambridge, Mass.: Harvard University Press, 1991), 21–25.

17. Aleksandr Zholkovsky, "Vvedenie," in A. K. Zholkovsky and Yu. K. Shcheglov, *Mir avtora i struktura teksta: Stat'i o russkoi literature* (Tenafly, N.J.: Hermitage, 1986), 15.

18. Georges Gusdorf, "Conditions and Limits of Autobiography," trans. James Olney, in James Olney, ed., *Autobiography: Essays Theoretical and Critical* (Princeton, N.J.: Princeton University Press, 1980), 44.

19. Harris, "Diversity of Discourse," 15; Roy Pascal, *Design and Truth in Autobiography* (Cambridge, Mass.: Harvard University Press, 1960; reprint, New York: Garland Publishing, 1985), 173–174.

20. William L. Howarth, "Some Principles of Autobiography," in Olney, ed., *Autobiography,* 105, 110.

21. William C. Spengemann, *The Forms of Autobiography: Episodes in the History of a Literary Genre* (New Haven, Conn.: Yale University Press, 1980) 120.
22. Ibid., 130. Anna Akhmatova (who befriended Bulgakov in the 1930s) sees a similar phenomenon in Pushkin: a "dramatic embodiment of . . . [his] inner personality" in "finished and objective characters" ("'Kamennyi gost' Pushkina," in Akhmatova, *O Pushkine: Stat'i i zametki* [Leningrad: Sovetskii pisatel', 1977], 108–109.)
23. Gusdorf, "Conditions," 44.

1. The Earliest Years

1. M. A. Bulgakov, "Zametki avtobiograficheskogo kharaktera," rukoi P. S. Popova, Otdel rukopisei Rossiiskoi Gosudarstvennoi Biblioteki, fond 218, karton 1269, ed. khran. 6. The name Svetlan has been variously spelled in other publications. These autobiographical remarks were jotted down by Bulgakov's friend, Pavel Popov, in 1926 or 1927. Elena Sergeevna, the writer's widow, attested to their accuracy but added that the style was not Bulgakov's.
2. Ibid.
3. Konstantin Paustovsky, *The Story of a Life*, trans. Joseph Barnes (New York: Pantheon-Random House, 1964), 166–167.
4. Konstantin Paustovsky, "Bulgakov i teatr," *Mosty*, no. 11 (1965), 380.
5. Paustovsky, *Story of a Life*, 156, 158. Another of Bulgakov's schoolmates, E. B. Bukreev, claims that Paustovsky exaggerated the writer's role in school battles. He adds, however, that "Bulgakov was an indispensable participant in fights" (Chudakova, *Zhizneopisanie*, 19–20).
6. Bulgakov, "Zametki."
7. Paustovsky, *Story of a Life*, 166.
8. Konstantin Paustovsky, *Povest' o zhizni* (Moscow: Sovetskaia Rossiia, 1966), 2:557; Pamela Davidson, "The House of the Bulgakovs," *RLT*, no. 15 (1978), 111.
9. Quoted by Sergei Ermolinsky in "O Mikhaile Bulgakove," *Teatr*, no. 9 (1966), 88.
10. Ibid., 80.
11. For a fuller treatment of A. I. Bulgakov's life, ideas, and influence on his son, see Edythe C. Haber, "The Lamp with the Green Shade: Mikhail Bulgakov and His Father," *RR* 44 (1985), 333–350. See also "Professor Afanasii Ivanovich Bulgakov (Nekrolog)," *TKDA*, no. 5 (May 1907), 132–144; Lidiya Yanovskaya, "Neskol'ko dokumentov k biografii Mikhaila Bulgakova," *VI*, no. 6 (June 1980), 305, 308; Yanovskaya, *Tvorcheskii put' Mikhaila Bulgakova* (Moscow: Sovetskii pisatel', 1983), 5–6, 13–14, 22–23; A. S. Burmistrov, "K biografii

M. A. Bulgakova (1891–1916)," *Kontekst-1978* (Moscow: Nauka, 1978), 250–252; E. I. Kolesnikova, "Kratkii obzor dokumental'nykh materialov M. Bulgakova," in N. A. Groznova and A. I. Pavlovsky, *Tvorchestvo Mikhaila Bulgakova: Issledovaniia i materialy,* bk. 1 (Leningrad: Nauka, 1991), 196–198. There is disagreement about certain details of the elder Bulgakov's life, in particular as to whether he was related to the eminent religious thinker, Father Sergei Bulgakov. Since the fact is much disputed, I have not included it in my account.

12. Burmistrov, "K biografii (1891–1916)," 252–253.

13. A. I. Bulgakov, "'O prosveshchenii' narodov," *TKDA,* no. 4 (1904), 476.

14. A. I. Bulgakov, "Ideal obshchestvennoi zhizni, po predstavleniiu katolicheskogo, reformatskogo i liuteranskogo veroispovedanii," *TKDA,* no. 9 (1891), 102.

15. E. A. Zemskaya, "Iz semeinogo arkhiva: Materialy iz sobraniia N. A. Bulgakovoi-Zemskoi," in E. S. Bulgakova and S. A. Lyandres, comp., *Vospominaniia o Mikhaile Bulgakove* (Moscow: Sovetskii pisatel', 1988), 68–69, 71, 72.

16. Bulgakov, "Zametki."

17. Quoted by Yanovskaya, *Tvorcheskii put',* 28.

18. Mikhail Bulgakov, "Ia mogu byt' odnim—pisatelem" (edited by G. S. Faiman and K. N. Kirilenko), *Teatr,* no. 2 (1990), 148.

19. Sergei Ermolinsky, "Mikhail Bulgakov: Iz zapisok raznykh let," in Ermolinsky, *Dramaticheskie sochineniia* (Moscow: Iskusstvo, 1982), 623, 626.

20. Bulgakov, "Zametki."

21. See Lesley Milne, *The Master and Margarita—A Comedy of Victory* (Birmingham, England: University of Birmingham, 1977), no. 3, 33; Ellendea Proffer, *Bulgakov: Life and Works* (Ann Arbor, Mich.: Ardis, 1984), 525.

22. For a stimulating inquiry into the role of Nietzscheanism in *The Master and Margarita,* see Boris Grois, "Nitssheanskie temy i motivy v sovetskoi kul'ture 30kh godov," in D. Kuyudzhich and V. L. Makhlin, ed., *Bakhtinskii sbornik II: Bakhtin mezhdu Rossiei i zapadom* (Moscow, 1991), 120–123.

23. For a full transcript of Bulgakov's graduation certificate *(attestat zrelosti),* see Leonid Khinkulov, "Mikhail Bulgakov i Aleksei Turbin," *Raduga,* no. 5 (1981), 173. For more details on the writer's school years and his teachers, see Burmistrov, "K biografii (1891–1916)," 253–257.

24. Bulgakov, "Zametki."

25. Chudakova, *Zhizneopisanie,* 17.

26. Burmistrov, "K biografii (1891–1916)," 256. According to Bukreev, Chelpanov taught psychology and logic to the seventh and eighth grades of the gymnasium (Chudakova, *Zhizneopisanie,* 18). By the time Bulgakov was in the seventh grade, in 1907–1908, Chelpanov would have just left Kiev for

Moscow. It is plausible to assume, however, that his replacement would have retained his curriculum.

27. V. V. Zenkovsky, *A History of Russian Philosophy*, trans. George L. Kline (New York: Columbia University Press, 1953), 1:695.

28. G. I. Chelpanov, *Mozg i dusha: Kritika materializma i ocherk sovremennykh uchenii o dushe*, 6th ed. (Moscow: Izd. T-va V. V. Dumnov-nasledn. Br. Salaevykh, 1918); *Vvedenie v filosofiiu. S prilozheniem voprosnika i konspektivnogo obzora istorii filosofii*, 7th ed. (Riga: Izd. Davida Gliksmana, 1923).

29. Chelpanov, *Mozg i dusha*, 209. Emphasis in the original.

30. Quoted by Burmistrov, "K biografii (1891–1917)," 252.

31. Ibid., 258–259. See also Yanovskaya, *Tvorcheskii put'*, 23–24.

32. Davidson, "House of the Bulgakovs," 112–113.

33. Burmistrov, "K biografii (1891–1916)," 252.

34. Yanovskaya, *Tvorcheskii put'*, 25.

35. Paustovsky, *Povest' o zhizni*, 2:558.

36. Lidiya Yanovskaya, "Kuda ia, tuda i on so svoim trombonom," *Iunost'*, no. 8 (1975), 106.

37. Bulgakov, "Zametki."

38. Quoted by T. A. Ermakova, "Dramaturgiia M. A. Bulgakova," Dissertatsiia na soiskanie uchenoi stepeni kandidata, Moskovskii Pedagogicheskii Institut Filologicheskikh Nauk im. N. K. Krupskaia (1971), 22.

39. Yanovskaya, "Kuda ia," 106; T. N. Kisel'gof, "Gody molodosti," E. S. Bulgakova and S. A. Lyandres, Comp., in *Vospominaniia o Mikhail Bulgakove*, (Moscow: Sovetskii pisatel', 1988), 111. Kisel'gof was Bulgakov's first wife.

40. Yanovskaya, "Kuda ia," 106.

41. Bulgakov, "Zametki."

42. Quoted by Burmistrov, "K biografii (1891–1916)," 259.

43. Ermakova, "Dramaturgiia," 22; Burmistrov, "K biografii (1891–1916)," 259.

44. Ermakova, "Dramaturgiia," 22.

45. M. O. Chudakova, "Arkhiv M. A. Bulgakova: Materialy dlia tvorcheskoi biografii pisatelia," *Zapiski Otdela rukopisei Vsesoiuznoi Biblioteki imeni Lenina*, no. 37 (1976), 35.

46. Leonid Parshin notes the connection between "The Fiery Serpent" and *The Fatal Eggs* and attempts a Freudian explanation of the recurring image. See *Chertovshchina v amerikanskom posol'stve v Moskve, ili trinadtsat' zagadok Mikhaila Bulgakova* (Moscow: Knizhnaia palata, 1991), 55–58.

47. Quoted by Ermakova, "Dramaturgiia," 26.

48. See, for example, Burmistrov, "K biografii (1891–1916)," 260.

49. Bulgakov, "Zametki." Kisel'gof recalls that Bulgakov "was interested in all medical issues" (Parshin, *Chertovshchina*, 37).

50. See Burmistrov, "K biografii (1891–1916)," 262–263, 266.
51. See Parshin, *Chertovshchina*, 27, 37.
52. Bulgakov, "Zametki."
53. For a citation from the official marriage document, see Khinkulov, "Mikhail Bulgakov and Aleksei Turbin," 174–175. For the most detailed, if inevitably one-sided, description of the relations of Lappa and Bulgakov, see Parshin's lengthy interview, "Iz semeinoi khroniki," in *Chertovshchina*, 13–113.
54. Kisel'gof, "Gody molodosti," 111.
55. Ibid., 112.
56. Three unspaced dots indicate Bulgakov's punctuation. Spaced dots indicate an ellipsis.
57. Chudakova, *Zhizneopisanie*, 52.
58. Ibid., 52. See also Yanovskaya, *Tvorcheskii put'*, 27–28. Much of the following narration is based on these two sources.
59. Kisel'gof, "Gody molodosti," 114. For additional information on Nikolskoe, see A. S. Burmistrov, "K biografii M. A. Bulgakova (1916–1918)," in Groznova and Pavlovsky, ed., *Tvorchestvo Mikhaila Bulgakova*, bk. 1, pp. 5–23.
60. Yanovskaya, *Tvorcheskii put'*, 28–29. The certificate is quoted in Ellendea Proffer, ed., *Neizdannyi Bulgakov: Teksty i materialy* (Ann Arbor, Mich.: Ardis, 1977), 13.
61. M. O. Chudakova, "K tvorcheskoi biografii M. Bulgakova," *Vl*, no. 7 (1973), 234.
62. Quoted by Yanovskaya, *Tvorcheskii put'*, 28. The letter, which did not survive, was paraphrased by its addressee, A. P. Gdeshinsky, for Bulgakov's sister, Nadezhda, after the writer's death in 1940. See M. O. Chudakova, "Vesnoi semnadtsatogo v Kieve," *Iunost'*, no. 5 (1991), 72.
63. Bulgakov, letter to K. P. Bulgakov, February 1, 1921, *Sob. soch.*(M) 5:391.
64. Parshin, *Chertovshchina*, 48.
65. Chudakova, *Zhizneopisanie*, 55, 59, 64. For a more detailed account, see Parshin, *Chertovshchina*, 47–57.
66. Chudakova, *Zhizneopisanie*, 54. In "Vesnoi semnadtsatogo," Chudakova offers evidence that Bulgakov was in Kiev during the February Revolution (p. 72).
67. Based on his interview with Kisel'gof, Parshin claims the letter conveys Bulgakov's impressions of the February, not the October, Revolution (Parshin, *Chertovshchina*, 46–47, 51).
68. Letter from V. M. Bulgakova to N. A. Bulgakova-Zemskaia, November 10, 1917. Quoted in Anatoly Shvarts, *Zhizn' i smert' Mikhaila Bulgakova* (Tenafly, N.J.: Ermitazh, 1988), 11. The letter has been translated almost in full in E. A. Zemskaya, "Nikolka Turbin and the Bulgakov Brothers (From the Family Archive)," trans. Lesley Milne, in Milne, ed., *Bulgakov: The Novelist-Playwright*, 31–33.

69. Shvarts, *Zhizn' i smert'*, 12.

70. Bulgakov says that they lived in Kiev from February 1918 ("Zametki"). Kisel'gof, however, remembers that by the time they arrived in Kiev, the Germans, who occupied the city on March 1, were already there ("Gody molodosti," 115).

71. For a full account of Kiev during the Civil War, see John S. Reshetar, Jr., *The Ukrainian Revolution, 1917–1920* (Princeton, N. J.: Princeton University Press, 1952).

72. Viktor Nekrasov, "Dom Turbinykh," *Nm*, no. 8 (1967), 137.

73. Chudakova, "Arkhiv," 35.

74. Bulgakov, "Zametki."

75. Chudakova, *Zhizneopisanie*, 76–77; Kisel'gof, "Gody molodosti," 118.

76. Kisel'gof, "Gody molodosti," 118.

77. This coincides with the general mood in Kiev at the time, as Reshetar describes it. One of the principal causes of the ouster of Petlyura's forces, he says, was the incredible chaos and inefficiency that reigned during their time. This resulted "in the growing demand for soviet order, the fulfillment of which the Bolsheviks advocated" (*The Ukrainian Revolution*, 258).

78. Chudakova, *Zhizneopisanie*, 89.

79. "Sovetskaia inkvizitsiia (Iz zapisnoi knizhki reportera)," Grigory Faiman, ed., *Konets veka*, no. 4 (1992), 14. Originally published in *Kievskoe ekho*, August 29 (September 11), September 3 (16), September 6 (19), 1919.

80. Mikhail Bulgakov, "Belaia gvardiia," with afterword by Igor' Vladimirov, *Slovo*, no. 7 (1992), 63–70.

81. Kisel'gof, "Gody molodosti," 118. See also Chudakova, *Zhizneopisanie*, 93–94. This account of events differs very substantially from that given by the late Devlet Gireev in *Mikhail Bulgakov na beregakh Tereka: Dokumental'naia povest'* (Ordjonikidze, USSR: Ir, 1980). Gireev, while providing some useful documentary information, fills in the gaps in his narrative by borrowing freely either from Bulgakov's fiction or from his own imaginings. Whereas in the recently published correspondence between Gireev and Kisel'gof she praises him for having "faithfully conveyed Mikhail's inner world of that time," Gireev himself admits that his narrative contains "quite a few deviations from the facts" (T. D. Gireeva, "'Vy ochen' verno peredali mir Mikhaila togo vremeni . . .': Perepiska pervoi zheny M. A. Bulgakova T. N. Bulgakovoi [Kisel'gof] s D. A. Gireevym. 1980–1981 gg.," *IAN, Ser. literatury i iazyka*, 53, no. 1 [1994], 52, 54). In Kisel'gof's interview with Parshin, moreover, she emphatically refutes Gireev's book (*Chertovshchina*, 72–73, 79–80). Unfortunately, many of Gireev's mistakes have found their way into later works on Bulgakov. I have used his book sparingly, adopting only data that are well documented or supported by other sources.

82. Bulgakov's statement in "Zametki" that he left Kiev in August 1919—that is, before Denikin's troops had arrived in Kiev—implies that he volunteered. Kisel'gof, however, has said repeatedly that he was mobilized after the White occupation of Kiev in September. (See, for example, Yanovskaya, *Tvorcheskii put'*, 45, 48.) If Bulgakov was indeed the author of the article discussed above, written after the Bolsheviks' departure , this would indeed support Kisel'gof's assertion.

83. Mikhail Bulgakov, "Griadushchie perspektivy," *Izbrannye proizvedeniia,* ed. Viktor Losev (Kiev: Dnipro, 1990), 39. Also in *Sob. soch.* (1995) 1: 85–87. Originally published in the newspaper *Groznyi* on November 26, 1919.

84. G. S. Faiman, "Pered prem'eroi: 1926 god v zhizni Mikhaila Bulgakova," *Nezavisimaia gazeta,* Nov. 17, 1993, 5. Bulgakov's KGB file, from which Faiman quotes, was declassified on November 11, 1993. See Vladimir Vinogradov, "'Glazami VChK-OGPU-NKVD': novye nakhodki v arkhive gosbezopasnosti," *Nezavisimaia gazeta,* Nov. 12, 1993, 7.

85. See Lidiya Yanovskaya, commentary to "Krasnaia korona," *Avrora,* no. 6 (1977), 51. Kisel'gof says she has no recollection of this (Parshin, *Chertovshchina,* 76–77).

86. "Griadushchie perspektivy," 39. Chudakova points out the first appearance here of the themes of madness, retribution, and flight (*Zhizneopisanie,* 95).

87. "Mikhail Bulgakov," in V. G. Lidin, ed., *Pisateli: Avtobiografii i portrety sovremennykh russkikh prozaikov* (Moscow: Kn-vo "Sovremennye problemy" N. A. Stolliar, 1926), 55.

88. Another recently found sketch from this period, "In the Café," was published in the Vladikavkaz newspaper, *Kavkazskaia gazeta,* January 18, 1920. See M. Bulgakov, "V kafe," preface by A. Kruchinin, *Moskva,* no. 4 (1993), 120–123. Also in *Sob. soch.* (1995) 1: 88–91.

89. Bulgakov, "Zametki."

90. Gireev's version of events (*Na beregakh Tereka,* 24–26, 30) has Bulgakov's brother Nikolai and cousin Konstantin disappearing with Denikin's army at the time of the Petlyura invasion in December 1918. Kisel'gof has dismissed Gireev's assertion as a fabrication, stating unequivocally that the brothers left Kiev after Bulgakov (Parshin, *Chertovshchina,* 71, 82).

91. See commentary by E. A. Zemskaya, ed., M. A. Bulgakov, "Pis'ma k rodnym (1921–1922 gg.)," *IAN, Ser. literatury i iazyka,* 35, no. 5 (1976), 451.

92. According to Gireev (*Na beregakh Tereka,* 137–138, n. 13), the story was published in the Vladikavkaz newspaper, *Kavkazskaia gazeta,* on February 5, 1920. The full text has not been found.

93. The first and third fragments are quoted by Vera Chebotareva in "K istorii sozdaniia 'Beloi gvardii,'" *Rl,* no. 4 (1974), 149. The second fragment appears in Zemskaya, "Iz semeinogo arkhiva," 88.

94. Gireev, *Na beregakh Tereka,* 62–63. See also Yanovskaya, *Tvorcheskii put'*, 58.

95. Gireev identifies the editor as Nikolai Nikolaevich Pokrovsky, the son of a cousin of Bulgakov's mother, Nikolai Ivanovich Pokrovsky (*Na beregakh Tereka*, 60). Kisel'gof, however, states categorically that neither she nor Bulgakov had any relatives in the Caucasus (Parshin, *Chertovshchina*, 80).

96. Chudakova makes a supposition similar to mine (*Zhizneopisanie*, 99). For further speculations along the same line, see Marianne Gourg, "The Story 'Morphine': An Attempt at Analysis of Mikhail Bulgakov's Creative Biography," trans. Lesley Milne, in Milne, ed., *Bulgakov: The Novelist-Playwright*, 111.

97. Kisel'gof, "Gody molodosti," 119, 120.

98. Yury Slezkin, *Devushka s gor* (Moscow: Kn-vo "Sovremennye problemy" N. A. Stolliar, 1925), 38–39. The first to discover this fictionalized portrait was Vera Chebotareva, "Mikhail Bulgakov na Kavkaze," *Ural'skii sledopyt*, no. 11 (1970), 76.

99. Some details of my account of this period are taken from Yanovskaya, *Tvorcheskii put'*, 58–59.

100. Yury Slezkin, "'Poka zhiv—budu verit' i dobivat'sia," *VI*, no. 9 (1979), 212, n. 1.

101. Yanovskaya, *Tvorcheskii put'*, 61.

102. Ibid., 60. See also Lidiia Ianovskaia, "Vstupitel'noe slovo skazhet pisatel' t. Bulgakov," *Nauka i zhizn'*, no. 3 (1978), 61.

103. Slezkin, *Devushka s gor*, 87–88.

104. For the fullest documentation of Bulgakov's activities in Vladikavkaz and the polemics surrounding them, see G. S. Faiman, "'Mestnyi literator' Mikhail Bulgakov," *Teatr*, no. 6 (1987), 134–169. See also Gireev, *Na beregakh Tereka*, chaps. 6–8; Yanovskaya, "Vstupitel'noe slovo"; Bulgakov, "Zapiski na manzhetakh," *Sob. soch.*(M) 1:482–484.

105. Faiman, "'Mestnyi literator,'" 140. Kisel'gof describes in some detail the danger of being an ex-White in Communist Vladikavkaz (Parshin, *Chertovshchina*, 81, 88; Chudakova, *Zhizneopisanie*, 101).

106. Quoted by Sheila Fitzpatrick, *The Commissariat of Enlightenment: Soviet Organization of Education and the Arts under Lunacharsky, October 1917–1921* (Cambridge: Cambridge University Press, 1970), 125.

107. Gireev, *Na beregakh Tereka*, 91–94; 139, n. 22. See also Faiman, "'Mestnyi literator,'" 150–158.

108. Gireev, *Na beregakh Tereka*, 93–94. Gireev paraphrases Bulgakov here.

109. Ibid., 95.

110. Ibid., 77.

111. Kisel'gof, "Gody molodosti," 120.

112. Yanovskaya, *Tvorcheskii put'*, 64.

113. Zemskaya, "Pis'ma k rodnym," 452.

114. Gireev, *Na beregakh Tereka*, 108–109.

115. Slezkin, "'Poka zhiv,'" 212.
116. Faiman, "'Mestnyi literator,'" 161.
117. Yanovskaya found a program of a Pushkin evening dated October 26, 1920. Bulgakov was scheduled to read an article, once again entitled "Revolutionary of the Spirit" ("Vstupitel'noe slovo," 61).
118. Gireev, *Na beregakh Tereka*, 138–139, n. 22. There is a discrepancy between the date Gireev gives for this occurrence, October 28, and that contained in Faiman, November 24 ("'Mestnyi literator,'" 161). Others, including Slezkin, were also dismissed from the Subdepartment of the Arts at this time.
119. See Chudakova, "K tvorcheskoi biografii," 242–247.
120. Quoted by Yanovskaya, *Tvorcheskii put'*, 88.
121. Gireev, *Na beregakh Tereka*, 111. The review of the play, untypically, was not entirely negative. (See Faiman, "'Mestnyi literator,'" 162–163.)
122. All three works were published in a Vladikavkaz newspaper, *Kommunist* (see Gireev, *Na beregakh Tereka*, 113–114, 141, n. 30.) The feuilleton, "Nedelia prosveshcheniia," is in *Sob. soch.*(M) 2:211–216. The review, of A. K. Tolstoy's *The Death of Ivan the Terrible*, is published in Faiman, "'Mestnyi literator,'" 63–64. The article on the actor, "S. P. Aksenov," appears in *Sob. soch.*(A) 2:350–351.
123. Gireev, *Na beregakh Tereka*, 118; Faiman, "'Mestnyi literator,'" 166.
124. Yanovskaya, *Tvorcheskii put'*, 72–78.
125. See also "Notes on the Cuff," *Sob. soch.*(M) 1:488.
126. Lidin, ed., *Pisateli*, 55.
127. Lidiya Yanovskaya, "Mikhail Bulgakov—fel'etonist," *Iunost'*, no. 7 (1974), 109.
128. "Synov'ia mully. P'esa iz zhizni ingushev v 3-kh aktakh," Suflerskii ekzempliar s pometami rezhissera (1921), Otdel rukopisei Rossiiskoi Gosudarstvennoi Biblioteki, fond 562, karton 11, ed. khran. 2.
129. Kisel'gof, "Gody molodosti," 120. She mistakenly remembers the date of these occurrences as the summer of 1921. By then the Bulgakovs had in fact left Vladikavkaz.
130. Parshin, *Chertovshchina*, 88.
131. Zemskaya, ed., "Pis'ma k rodnym," 451–452, 455–459. Bulgakov had submitted *The Paris Communards* to an All-Russian Competition, and, according to a Vladikavkaz newspaper report of May 8, 1921, it had actually been accepted for production in Moscow. It was never staged, however, perhaps because Bulgakov would not agree to demanded changes. (See Ianovskaia, *Tvorcheskii put'*, 71–72.)
132. Kisel'gof, "Gody molodosti," 120.
133. Chudakova, *Zhizneopisanie*, 114.
134. Zemskaya, ed., "Pis'ma k rodnym," 452.
135. Chudakova, "Arkhiv," 48.

2. Looking Backward

1. Zemskaya, ed., "Pis'ma k rodnym," 452. For more detailed biographical information, see Chudakova, *Zhizneopisanie*, chap. 2.

2. For a recollection by Bulgakov's neighbor, see V. Levshin, "Sadovaia 302-bis," *Teatr*, no. 11 (1971), 110–120. See also Chudakova, *Zhizneopisanie*, 130–132. The letter to Krupskaya is the subject of a story by Bulgakov, "Vospominanie . . .," published in *Zheleznodorozhnik*, no. 1–2 (1924), 9–12. See *Sob. soch.*(M) 2:378–383.

3. For the fullest account of Bulgakov's activities at Moscow Lito, see R. Yangirov, "M. A. Bulgakov—sekretar' Lito Glavpolitprosveta," in A. A. Ninov and V. V. Gudkova, ed., *M. A. Bulgakov-dramaturg i khudozhestvennaia kul'tura ego vremeni* (Moscow: Soiuz teatral'nykh deiatelei RSFSR, 1988), 225–245. For the text of "The Muse of Vengeance" ("Muza mesti"), see *Sob. soch.*(A) 2:352–355. For a detailed analysis of the work, see Chudakova, *Zhizneopisanie*, 126–128.

4. Chudakova, *Zhizneopisanie*, 141.

5. One article originally published in *Rabochii* on May 30, 1992 appears in *Sob. soch.* (1995) 1:102–104: "Rabochii gorod sad (Zakladka 1-go v Respublike rabochego poselka)." Kisel'gof recalls that he never actually worked as master of ceremonies. (See Parshin, *Chertovshchina*, 98.)

6. By late 1922 Bulgakov also undertook a project, never carried out, of compiling a bibliographical dictionary of contemporary Russian writers. (See Chudakova, *Zhizneopisanie*, 167–168.)

7. Some of my remarks on these and subsequent works expand upon and modify Chudakova's observations, especially in "Arkhiv," 60–63. The main focus of my analysis, however, on the evolution of the autobiographical hero, is my own.

8. "Tainomu drugu" ("To a Secret Friend"), *Sob. soch.*(M) 4:559.

9. Part One of *Notes on the Cuff* ("Zapiski na manzhetakh") appeared in *Nakanune (Literaturnoe prilozhenie)*, June 18, 1922, 5–7, and *Vozrozhdenie*, no. 2 (1923), 15–19. Part Two was published in *Rossiia*, no. 5 (1923), 20–25. Excerpts from Part One also came out in *Bakinskii rabochii*, Jan. 1, 1924.

10. For a discussion of this stylistic feature of early Soviet prose, see M. O. Chudakova, "Zametki o iazyke sovremennoi prozy," *Nm*, no. 1 (1972), 214–216.

11. Quoted by Ermakova, "Dramaturgiia." For more on the influence of the *Satyricon* writers, see Miron Petrovsky, "Smekh pod znakom Apokalipsisa (M. Bulgakov i 'Satirikon')," *Vl*, no. 5 (1991), 3–20.

12. Quoted by L. F. Ershov, *Iz istorii sovetskoi satiry: M. Zoshchenko i satiricheskaia proza 20–40-kh godov* (Leningrad: Nauka, 1973), 12.

13. Ibid., 11–12.

14. Ibid., 11.
15. *Izb. pr.,* 1:665. *Sob. soch.*(M) has the incomplete version of Part One originally published in *Vozrozhdenie.* The fullest text can be found in *Izb. pr.* Page references to this edition, preceded by *Iz* and the volume number, will be included in the text.
16. *Bozhestvennaia Liturgiia sv. Ioanna Zlatoustago* (New York: Alumni Association of the Russian Theological Seminary of North America, 1954), 40–42.
17. The refrain, "Mama! Mama! What will we do" is from a popular song of the time. See Ya. S. Lur'e, M. O. Chudakova, "Kommentarii," *Sob. soch.*(M) 1:610.
18. Bulgakov quotes the less familiar variant of the poem included in Pushkin's late unfinished play, *Scenes from Knightly Times (Stseny iz rytsarskikh vremen).* I am grateful to Gene Barabtarlo for calling my attention to the existence of this variant. Some of my remarks on Pushkin are incorporated in my article, "Bulgakov's Pushkin: Poor Knight or Poor Evgenii?" in *Alexander Lipson: In Memoriam,* ed. Charles E. Gribble, et al. (Columbus, Ohio: Slavica, 1944), 73–78.
19. A. S. Pushkin, *Sobranie sochinenii v 10-i tomakh* (Moscow: Khudozhestvennaia literatura, 1959–1962), 4:428.
20. Ibid., 3:298.
21. The three rows of dots following the words "Ia golodaiu" suggest that the chapter was originally longer. In the *Rossiia* edition, even the two words are missing, leaving only the title and three rows of dots.
22. Rita Giuliani, in "Demonicheskii element v *Zapiskakh na manzhetakh* M. A. Bulgakova," *RÉS* 65, no. 2 (1993), 271–279, notes another demonic allusion. The narrator's words, "Moscow is not as terrifying as its children" *("An Moskva ne tak strashna, kak ee maliutki"),* rephrases the saying, "The devil is not as terrifying as his children" *("Chert ne tak strashen, kak ego maliutki")* (p. 276).
23. For a fuller examination of the influence of Gogol and Dostoevsky on *Notes on the Cuff,* see Jane E. Knox, "Zapiski na manzhetakh: Bulgakov's Defiant 'Sideward Glance,'" *RLJ* 38, nos. 129–130 (1984), 133–141.
24. Lesley Milne argues persuasively that the model for Kritskaya is Nadezhda Krupskaya. See her *Mikhail Bulgakov: A Critical Biography* (Cambridge: Cambridge University Press, 1990), 38.
25. Slezkin, *Devushka s gor,* 94.
26. Bulgakov, "Neobyknovennye prikliucheniia doktora," *Rupor,* no. 2 (1922), 10–12.
27. First noted by Chebotareva, "K istorii sozdaniia," 149–150.
28. Bulgakov, "Krasnaia korona," *Nakanune (Literaturnoe prilozhenie),* October 22, 1922, 28–33.
29. See, for example, Proffer, *Bulgakov,* 140–141; M. O. Chudakova, "Tvor-

cheskaia istoriia romana M. Bulgakova 'Master i Margarita,'" *VI*, no. 7 (1976), 239, 243–244, 249.

30. Many critics have noted this connection. See especially Chudakova, "Arkhiv," 60–61; Proffer, *Bulgakov*, 280.

31. The similarity is noted by Chudakova, "Tvorcheskaia istoriia," 243–244.

32. Bulgakov, "V noch' na tret'e chislo," *Nakanune (Literaturnoe prilozhenie)*, Dec. 10, 1922, 3–6.

33. A later variant, closer to the final ending of the novel, appeared in the Odessa magazine *Shkval*, no. 5 (1924). See Mikhail Bulgakov, "Konets Petliury (Iz romana 'Belaia gvardiia')," afterword by Natal'ya Kuzyakina, *Avrora*, no. 12 (1986), 95–100. The complicated creative history of *The White Guard*, which is still far from clear, is outlined in Chapter 3.

34. Bulgakov, "Nalet (V volshebnom fonare)," *Gudok*, December 25, 1923, 2–3.

35. Bulgakov, "Khanskii ogon'," *Krasnyi zhurnal dlia vsekh*, no. 2 (1924), 101–111. A variant of my analysis of the story appears in Edythe C. Haber, "Dwellings and Devils in Early Bulgakov," *SEEJ* 37, no. 3 (1993), 331–336.

36. Lidiya Yanovskaya, in "O rasskaze Mikhaila Bulgakova 'Khanskii ogon','" *Nash sovremennik*, no. 2 (1974), 124–126, notes that the palace and Tugai-Beg were modeled upon Arkhangelskoe and Prince F. Yusupov, respectively (p. 125). Some of Yanovskaya's observations on the connections between the story and *The White Guard* coincide with mine.

37. Quoted by M. O. Chudakova, "O rasskazakh," in Mikhail Bulgakov, *Izbrannoe* (Moscow: Khudozhestvennaia literatura, 1980), 398. As summarized in the memoir from which Chudakova quotes, the story Bulgakov read at *Gudok* differed substantially from "The Khan's Fire," although the denouements are similar. The memoirist might have heard an earlier version of the work. (See I. Ovchinnikov, "V redaktsii 'Gudka,'" in Bulgakova and Lyandres, ed., *Vospominaniia o Bulgakove*, 140–141.)

38. Bulgakov, "Zametki avtobiograficheskogo kharaktera."

39. For a different interpretation of the role of Asia and Europe from mine, see M. O. Chudakova, "Pushkin u Bulgakova: 'soblazn klassiki,'" in E. V. Permyakov, ed., *Lotmanovskii sbornik* (Moscow: ITs-Garant, 1995), 1:542.

40. Chudakova also notes the connection ("Pushkin u Bulgakova," 544–555).

41. Proffer, "Kommentarii," *Sob. soch.*(A) 2:533.

3. *The White Guard*

1. Mikhail Bulgakov, "Zametki avtobiograficheskogo kharaktera." See also Lidiya Yanovskaya, "Kogda byla napisana 'Belaia gvardiia'?," *VI*, no. 6 (1977), 302–307. For somewhat different reconstructions of the creative history of the novel, see Chudakova, "Arkhiv," 47–52; Chebotareva, "K istorii," 148–152;

N. V. Petrova, "Kogda i kak byl napisan roman M. Bulgakova 'Belaia gvardiia,'" *Trudy Irkutskogo Gosudarstvennogo Universiteta im. A. A. Zhdanova, Seriia literaturovedenie i kritika*, 71, no. 7 (1969), 57–77. My account is closest to Yanovskaya's.

2. The information appeared in the journal *Rossiia*. Quoted by Yanovskaya, "Kogda byla napisana," 303.

3. Bulgakov informed his sister in a letter written no earlier than April 1923: "I am urgently trying to finish the first part of my novel; it is called 'The Yellow Banner.'" Quoted by Yanovskaya, ibid., 303.

4. My observations on the significance of the Kiev trip essentially follow Yanovskaya, "Kogda byla napisana," 304–305. For additional interesting observations on the subject, see N. V. Petrova, "Ot 'Kieva-goroda' k 'Beloi gvardii' (M. A. Bulgakov—publitsist i khudozhnik)," in O. I. Fedotov, ed., *Zamysel i ego khudozhestvennoe voploshchenie v proizvedeniiakh sovetskikh pisatelei*, (Vladimir, USSR: Vladimirskii Gosudarstrennyi Pedagogicheskii Institut imeni P. I. Lebedeva-Polianskogo, 1979), 3–15.

5. Bulgakov, "Zametki avtobiograficheskogo kharaktera." This source also reveals that Glagolev was the prototype for the priest in the novel.

6. Yanovskaya, "Kogda byla napisana," 306; Chudakova, "Arkhiv," 52, n. 6.

7. The first two parts of *The White Guard* appeared in *Rossiia*, no. 4 (1925), 3–100; no. 5 (1925), 1–82. The French edition was published under the title *Dni Turbinykh (Belaia gvardiia)* (Paris: Concorde, 1927 [Part One], 1929 [Part Two]). The first full Soviet edition came out in Mikhail Bulgakov, *Izbrannaia proza* (Moscow: Khudozhestvennaia literatura, 1966), 111–348.

8. Mikhail Bulgakov, "Glava iz romana i pis'ma" (introdution by M. O. Chudakova), *Nm*, no. 2 (1987), 150–163. Reprinted in *Sob. soch.*(M) 1:529–546; henceforth referred to as "1925 proofs."

9. Lidiya Yanovskaya, commentary to "Belaia gvardiia," in Bulgakov, *Izb. pr.*, 1:747.

10. See Bulgakov, "Belaia gvardiia" (edited by Igor' Vladimirov), *Slovo*, no. 7 (1992), 63–71. This text (henceforth referred to as "early draft") has been published together with the 1925 proofs as "Okonchanie romana 'Belaia gvardiia' (Ranniaia redaktsiia)," in Mikhail Bulgakov, *Iz luchshikh proizvedenii*, ed. Viktor Losev (Moscow: Izofaks, 1993), 404–450. My information on Vladimirov is from M. O. Chudakova, "Neobyknovennye prikliucheniia rukopisi: Mikhail Bulgakov v Moskve, 1991–92 gg.," *Lg*, March 18, 1992, 6.

11. See Ya. S. Lur'e, "K istorii napisaniia romana 'Belaia gvardiia,'" *Rl*, no. 2 (1995), 236–241; Lidiya Yanovskaya, letter to "The Bulgakov Forum: Ruminations on the State of the Field," *The Newsletter of the Mikhail Bulgakov Society*, no. 1 (1995), 16.

12. For a good account of the development of the novel during this period, see V. Gura, *Roman i revoliutsiia: Puti sovetskogo romana, 1917–1929* (Moscow: Sovetskii pisatel', 1973).

13. The "classic" Soviet novels, *The Iron Flood* by Alexander Serafimovich, *Cities and Years* by Konstantin Fedin, and *The Rout* by Alexander Fadeev, all appeared in 1924, too late to influence Bulgakov. The only earlier novel of the period that had some peripheral influence is the first part of Aleksei Tolstoy's celebrated trilogy *The Road to Calvary (Khozhdenie po mukam), The Sisters,* first published in Berlin in 1922. Bulgakov was certainly acquainted with the work, which, while bearing some thematic resemblance to *The White Guard,* is a much more conventional novel. See Yanovskaya, *Tvorcheskii put',* 111–115; V. Pertsov, *Poety i prozaiki velikikh let,* 2nd ed. (Moscow: Khudozhestvennaia literatura, 1974), 98–107; Proffer, *Bulgakov,* 160.

14. Ya. S. Lur'e has written extensively on Tolstoy and *The White Guard.* See, for example, "Istoricheskaia problematika v proizvedeniiakh M. Bulgakova (M. Bulgakov i 'Voina i mir' L. Tolstogo)," in Ninov and Gudkova, ed., *Bulgakov-dramaturg,* 190–201; J. Luria, "Mikhail Bulgakov and Lev Tolstoy," in, *Oxford Slavonic Papers,* 23 (1994), 67–78. Another very good discussion appears in the unpublished dissertation of A. M. Al'tshuler (Smelyansky), "'Dni Turbinykh' i 'Beg' M. A. Bulgakova v istorii sovetskogo teatra 20-kh godov," Dissertatsiia na soiskanie uchenoi stepeni kandidata, Institut Istorii Iskusstv (Moscow, 1972). See also Sydney Schultze, "The Epigraphs in *White Guard,*" *RLT,* no. 15 (1978), 214–215.

15. Vladimir Lakshin mentions the "lures of expressionism and 'ornamental prose'" to which the author to some extent succumbed ("O proze Mikhaila Bulgakova i o nem samom," in Mikhail Bulgakov, *Izbrannaia proza* [1966], 24). Proffer is very good on the influence of modernism—especially of Bely— on the novel's style (*Bulgakov,* 156, 605, n. 27).

16. Al'tshuler, "'Dni Turbinykh'i 'Beg,'" 111.

17. For an interesting discussion of Bulgakov's use of leitmotifs, see two articles by N. A. Kozhevnikova, both published in *Uchenye zapiski Azerbaidzhanskogo Pedagogicheskogo Instituta Russkogo Iazyka i Literatury im. M. F. Akhundova:* "Slovo i siuzhet v romane M. Bulgakova 'Belaia gvardiia,'" seriia 12, no. 3 (1973), 119–124; "O priemakh organizatsii teksta v romane M. Bulgakova 'Belaia gvardiia,'" seriia 12, no. 3 (1974), 109–114.

18. For the role of the *Satyricon* in *The White Guard,* see Petrovsky, "Smekh pod znakom," 3–8; 13–20.

19. M. A. Bulgakov, "Iurii Slezkin (Siluet)," in Slezkin, *Roman baleriny* (Riga, 1928), 9. This article was originally published in the Berlin émigré journal, *Spolokhi,* no. 12 (1922).

20. Yevgeny Zamyatin, "On Literature, Revolution, Entropy, and Other Matters," in Yevgeny Zamyatin, *A Soviet Heretic,* ed. & trans. Mirra Ginsburg (Chicago: University of Chicago Press, 1970), 111.

21. Zamyatin, "The Day and the Age," in Zamyatin, *Soviet Heretic,* 116.

22. Barbara Kejna Sharratt, "In Defense of Bulgakov's *Belaja gvardija,*" *RLJ* 36, no. 123–124 (1982), 137–138.

23. This is noted by Sharratt, "Bulgakov's *Belaja gvardija,*"134.

24. Most commentators have noted *The White Guard*'s apocalyptic ambience. See especially Boris Gasparov, "Novyi zavet v proizvedeniiakh M. A. Bulgakova," *Neue russische Literatur. Almanach,* no. 4–5 (1981–1982), 166–171. Two other interesting interpretations are: Andrew Barratt, "Apocalypse or Revelation? Man and History in Bulgakov's *Belaya gvardiya,*" *New Zealand Slavonic Journal,* (1985), 105–131; David M. Bethea, *The Shape of Apocalypse in Modern Russian Fiction* (Princeton, N. J.: Princeton University Press, 1989), 191, 193–200.

25. Al'tshuler shows that this opposition between the city, representing the embodiment of human culture, and the country, the elemental rage of the masses, was characteristic of such contemporaries of Bulgakov as Esenin, Pilnyak, and Goky ("'Dni Turbinykh' i 'Beg,'" 113–114).

26. The allusion to this once-popular children's novel by Petr Romanovich Furman was first unearthed by Lidiya Yanovskaya, "'Saardamskii plotnik,'" *V mire knig* (January 1977), 92.

27. For a discussion of the function of the portrait of Alexander I, see Schultze, "Epigraphs," 215. For another interpretation of the royal images in the novel, see Maya Kaganskaya, "Beloe i krasnoe," *Lo,* no. 5 (1991), 98–99.

28. I. F. Belza was told by Bulgakov's friend, P. A. Markov, that the author considered "The Bronze Horseman" a "model of poetic mystery." See Belza, "K voprosu o pushkinskikh traditsiiakh v otechestvennoi literature (na primere proizvedenii M. A. Bulgakova)," *Kontekst-1980* no. 9 (1981), 231, 233. For a fuller treatment of Pushkinian allusions in the novel, see Edythe C. Haber, "Bulgakov's *White Guard* and Pushkin," in Elena Semeka-Pankratov, ed., *Studies in Poetics: Commemorative Volume, Krystyna Pomorska (1928–1986),* (Columbus, Ohio: Slavica, 1995), 261–273.

29. See Gura, *Roman i revoliutsiia,* 111–118. For a fine recent discussion of the snowstorm image in Blok and Bulgakov, see Vladimir Lakshin, "Home and Homelessness (Aleksandr Blok and Mikhail Bulgakov)," trans. Lesley Milne, in Milne, ed., *Bulgakov: The Novelist-Playwright,* 1–11.

30. The allusion to "The Lay of Igor's Campaign" is mentioned by Lakshin, "O proze," 16–17.

31. I have adopted here the succinct and lucid description by Katerina Clark, "The City Versus the Countryside in Soviet Peasant Literature of the Twenties:

A Duel of Utopias," in Abbott Gleason, Peter Kenez, Richard Stites, eds., *Bolshevik Culture: Experiment and Order in the Russian Revolution,* Special Study of the Kennan Institute for Advanced Russian Studies, The Wilson Center, No. 5 (Bloomington: Indiana University Press, 1985), 178.

32. Yanovskaya regards the watchman's wife in "The Raid" as a precursor to Yuliya (*Tvorcheskii put',* 102–103). Although there are some parallels, the former does not actively rescue Abram, only reluctantly lets him into her hut, and therefore cannot truly be included among the saviors.

33. Al'tshuler remarks on the symbolic significance of the doctor ("'Dni Turbinykh' i 'Beg,'" 139).

34. Lesley Milne makes much the same point (*Mikhail Bulgakov,* 91).

35. Al'tshuler, "'Dni Turbinykh'i 'Beg,'" 136–138; 161–180.

36. In the 1925 proofs, Lariosik's parodic doubling of Aleksei continues to the final chapter, which begins on the eve of the Epiphany. The convalescing Aleksei joins the family celebration dressed in a dinner jacket, and right behind him appears Lariosik, also in a dinner jacket, but an ill-fitting one. Lariosik has acquired the jacket, with considerable difficulty, as a "matter of principle," an outward sign that life behind the Turbins' walls will remain untouched by the "rascal" (*kanal'ia*) Petlyura (1:525). His absurd appearance, however, undercuts his words.

37. Anatoly Smelyansky notes an internal pun here: *Aid* is Russian for Hades (*Bulgakov v Khudozhestvennom teatre,* 21).

38. Aleksandr Blok, "Intelligentsiia i revoliutsiia," *Sobranie sochinenii v shesti tomakh* (Moscow: Izd. "Pravda," Biblioteka "Ogonek," 1971) 5:402. Al'tshuler talks at some length about the importance of Blok's ideas on "culture and the elements" for early Soviet art as a whole and for Bulgakov in particular ("'Dni Turbinykh'i 'Beg,'" 140–161).

39. Milne notes the extension of the family theme to this line of the novel (*Mikhail Bulgakov,* 91).

40. Milne traces the celestial image to Cicero's *Republic,* in which the Milky Way is "the place 'where eminent and excellent men find their true reward.'" Cicero defines "the best tasks" of such men as "those undertaken in defence of [their] native land" (ibid., 85).

41. In the 1925 proofs, Nikolka's closeness to Nai is reinforced by his love for Irina Nai, whose funereal visage so resembles her brother's. Thus, when she appears at the Turbins' Epiphany eve party, her dark, pale figure is much in contrast to the vital, "golden" Elena: "Irina Nai, all in black and mourning, was thin, muted, alongside the luxuriant Elena, who was shot through with gold, and in the fir tree lights, she [Irina] seemed like a crape candle" (p. 526).

42. Chudakova, "Glava iz romana," 141–142.

43. For more details, see Edythe C. Haber, "Bulgakov and Šklovskij: Notes on a

Literary Antagonism," in Anna Lisa Crone and Catherine V. Chvany, ed., *New Studies in Russian Language and Literature* (Columbus, Ohio: Slavica, 1986), 151–158. The Shklovsky-Shpolyansky connection has also been noted by several other investigators. See especially Chudakova, *Zhizneopisanie,* 260–264.

44. Ilya Ehrenburg, *People and Life: 1891–1921,* trans. Anna Bostock and Yvonne Kapp (New York: Alfred A. Knopf, 1962), 314. (I preserve the transliteration used in this edition.) For more about *Khlam,* see Chudakova, the journal edition of *Zhizneopisanie, Moskva* no. 7 (1987), 7–8.

45. For Shpolyansky's dandyism, there is also a second likely prototype, the Kievan poet and son of a friend of Bulgakov's father, Vladimir Makkaveisky. See Haber, "Bulgakov and Šklovskij," 155–156.

46. Al'tshuler interprets the Futurist theme in the novel as a symbol of the degeneration of twentieth-century culture. He notes the similarity here to Blok's views in his essay, "Russian Dandies" ("'Dni Turbinykh'i 'Beg,'" 116).

47. Aleksandr Blok, "Narod i intelligentsiia," *Sobranie sochinenii* 5:267.

48. See, for example, Barratt, "Apocalypse or Revelation?" 110.

49. Early draft, "Belaia gvardiia," 68.

50. "Griadushchie perspektivy," 439.

51. "The End of Petlyura," the excerpt from an early draft of *The White Guard* that Bulgakov published in the Odessa magazine *Shkval* in 1924, is practically identical to parts of the manuscript found by Vladimirov but omits most of the domestic episodes. See Bulgakov, "Konets Petliury," Afterword by Nateliya Kuzyaking, *Avrora* no. 12 (1986), 95–100.

52. See for example Belza, "O pushkinskikh traditsiiakh," 198.

4. More Versions of the Autobiographical Hero

1. See Chudakova, "Arkhiv," 58.

2. For the text of the letter, see Lidiya Yanovskaya, "Mikhail Bulgakov datiruet 'Dni Turbinykh,'" *Vl,* no. 7 (1976), 312–313. Yanovskaya states that Bulgakov was simultaneously invited by the Vakhtangov Theater to dramatize *The White Guard* (p. 313).

3. For a full explication of the theater's position in the early Soviet period, see Smelyansky, *Bulgakov v Khudozhestvennom teatre,* 45–60.

4. See P. A. Markov, *Kniga vospominanii* (Moscow: Iskusstvo, 1983), 220–266.

5. For full textological details, see Ya. S. Lur'e, "Primechaniia," in M. A. Bulgakov, *P'esy 20-kh godov,* ed. A. A. Ninov (Leningrad: Iskusstvo, 1989), 514–519. There were actually two variants of the first redaction, the second published in full for the first time in this edition. Scenes from the first variant that were later omitted are also published here. Page references to this edition of the first version will be included in the text.

6. The original play consisted of 266 pages and either thirteen or sixteen scenes, depending on how they are counted. See Chudakova, "Arkhiv," 88; Lesley Milne, "Mikhail Bulgakov and *Dni Turbinykh*: A Case of Censorship," in William Harrison and Avril Pyman, eds., *Poetry, Prose, and Public Opinion: Essays presented in memory of Dr. N. E. Andreyev* (Letchworth, England: Avebury, 1984), 234, n. 12. The fact that the first draft is dated "June–September 1925," whereas Bulgakov claimed he began the play in January, has led to speculation that an earlier draft existed and was destroyed (see Milne, 215; Proffer, *Bulgakov*, 184).

7. The Petlyurite episode is part of Aleksei's nightmare only in the earlier version of the first redaction. (See *P'esy 20-kh godov*, 351–353.) Later it is presented as an objective occurrence, beyond Aleksei's consciousness (pp. 57–61).

8. By the second variant of the first redaction, Nai-Turs has been eliminated, his heroic action and death transferred to Malyshev (see pp. 81–82; 354).

9. Bulgakov, "Zametki avtobiograficheskogo kharaktera."

10. For an alternative interpretation of the time setting of the final act, see Gail Lenhoff, "Chronological Error and Irony in Bulgakov's *Days of the Turbins*," in Kenneth N. Brostrom, ed., *Russian Literature and American Critics: In Honor of Deming B. Brown*. Papers in Slavic Philology, 4 (Ann Arbor, Mich.: Michigan State University, 1984), 149–160.

11. For a brief summary of "Change of Landmarks," see Nikolai P. Poltoratsky, "Smena vekh," in Victor Terras, ed., *Handbook of Russian Literature* (New Haven, Conn.: Yale University Press, 1985), 427–428. For Bulgakov's association with the group and the troubles it later caused him, see Proffer, *Bulgakov*, 63–65; 595, n. 22.

12. I. Grossman-Roshchin, "Stabilizatsiia intelligentskikh dush i problemy literatury," *Oktiabr'*, no. 7 (1925), 124–125.

13. In a diary entry of October 26, 1923, Bulgakov expresses strong disdain for some of his associates at *Nakanune* and adds: "Oh, I will be really be in trouble later, when I will have to scrape the accumulated mud off my name" ("Ia mogu byt' odnim," 149).

14. L. E. Belozerskaya-Bulgakova, *O, med vospominanii* (Ann Arbor, Mich.: Ardis, 1979), 45, 46.

15. Mikhail Bulgakov, *'Belaia gvardiia': P'esa v chetyrekh deistviiakh. Vtoraia redaktsiia p'esy 'Dni Turbinykh,'* ed. Lesley Milne (Munich: Otto Sagner, 1983), 45. Page references to this edition will be included in the text preceded by the name Milne.

16. Ibid., 120, n. 168. See also E. Polyakova, *Teatr i dramaturg: Iz opyta Moskovskogo Khudozhestvennogo Teatra nad p'esami sovetskikh dramaturgov, 1917–1941 gg.* (Moscow: Vserossiiskoe teatral'noe obshchestvo, 1959), 64.

17. The shift in Shervinsky had already occurred by the first redaction, where much of his dialogue is identical to that of the second.
18. "Iz zhurnala repetitsii p'esy 'Belaia gvardiia,'" in Proffer, ed., *Neizdannyi Bulgakov*, 77.
19. The best accounts of the complex interplay of forces that produced the final text of *Days of the Turbins* are: Milne, "Mikhail Bulgakov and *Dni Turbinykh*," 214–240; and Anatoly Smelyansky, "'Volshebnaia kamera,'" *Sovremennaia dramaturgiia*, no. 4 (1983), 266–279. See also Smelyansky, *Bulgakov v Khudozhestvennom teatre*, 59–145. An early but still valuable article is Ya. S. Lur'e and I. Serman, "Ot 'Beloi gvardii' k 'Dniam Turbinykh,'" *Rl*, no. 2 (1965), 194–203.
20. See Bulgakov's letter to Stanlislavsky in Proffer, ed., *Neizdannyi Bulgakov*, 80.
21. "Vypiska iz protokola soveshchaniia glavnogo repertuarnogo komiteta s predstaviteliami MKhAT 1-go ot 25 iunia 1926 goda," in Proffer, ed., *Neizdannyi Bulgakov*, p. 81.
22. Smelyansky quotes from a letter of July 2, 1926, written by the play's starring actor, N. Khmelev, which indicates support in high places: "The first scene of the third act met with a rebuff from the *Glavrepertkom* and support by a higher authority" ("Volshebnaia kamera," 275). Grigory Faiman speculates that the higher authority in question was Stalin himself. See his "Bulgakovshchina," *Teatr*, no. 12 (1991), 84.
23. "Iz zhurnala repetitsii," 77.
24. Although Lunacharsky had supported the production, he considered the play very weak. See Smelyansky, *Bulgakov v Khudozhestvennom teatre*, 63–64. For minutes of a meeting at which Lunacharsky discussed the play at length, see Faiman, "Bulgakovshchina," 87–102. For more details on the polemics surrounding the play, see A. Colin Wright, *Mikhail Bulgakov: Life and Interpretations* (Toronto: University of Toronto Press, 1978), 87–95; Proffer, *Bulgakov*, 195–204; Faiman, "Bulgakovshchina," 82–102.
25. The more negative image of the troops and the consequent isolation of Colonel Turbin were emphasized in the play's first staging. See Polyakova, *Teatr i dramaturg*, 62–64.
26. *Dni Turbinykh*, in Mikhail Bulgakov, *P'esy* (Moscow: Sovetskii pisatel', 1986), 98. Further page references to this edition will be included in the text. In *Sob. soch.*(M) and *P'esy 20-kh godov* there appears a version of the play prepared for publication by Bulgakov's widow in 1940 and based on the writer's own preferred text without some of the late forced changes. Since one of my purposes is to trace the outside pressures resulting in the final produced version, I use that version but indicate significant variations.
27. The last two sentences are omitted in the *Sob. soch.*(M) version. See 3:72.
28. See Milne, "*Belaia gvardiia*," 111, n. 55.
29. A similar observation is made by Smelyansky, "Volshebnaia kamera," 277. In

the *Sob. soch.*(M) the musical sequence is missing. Only Nikolka's quiet singing of one of Pushkin's foreboding lines remains, creating a far more muted mood at the end.

30. A. Orlinsky, "Perspektivy teatral'nogo sezona," *Novyi zritel'*, no. 40 (1926), 12.

31. *Days of the Turbins* was reportedly one of Stalin's favorite plays. According to the Art Theater records, he saw the production fifteen times. See V. Petelin, "M. A. Bulgakov i 'Dni Turbinykh,'" *Ogonek*, no. 11 (March 1969), 27.

32. "Stal'noe gorlo," *Krasnaia panorama*, August 15, 1925. The other stories were published in *Meditsinskii rabotnik* in the following order: "Baptism by Rotation" ("Kreshchenie povorotom"), October 25, November 2, 1925; "The Blizzard" ("V'iuga"), January 18, 25, 1926; "The Starry Rash" ("Zvezdnaia syp'"), August 12, 19, 1926; "Towel with a Rooster" ("Polotentse s petukhom"), September 12, 18, 1926; "The Missing Eye" ("Propavshii glaz"), October 2, 12, 1926.

33. The first publications (which omitted "A Starry Rash," presumably because it is about syphilis) were: Mikhail Bulgakov, *Zapiski iunogo vracha* (Moscow: Biblioteka *Ogon'ka*, no. 23, 1963); Mikhail Bulgakov, *Izbrannaia proza* (Moscow: Khudozhestvennaia literatura, 1966), 47–108.

34. See Chudakova, "K tvorcheskoi biografii," 236. Yanovskaya gives the title of the early draft as *Notes [Zapiski] of a Zemstvo Doctor* (*Tvorcheskii put'*, 37).

35. See Yanovskaya, *Tvorcheskii put'*, 38; Proffer, *Bulgakov*, 92.

36. See Chudakova, "O rasskazakh," 398; Anatoly Al'tshuler, "Bulgakov-prozaik," *Lg*, Feb. 7, 1968, 5; Milne, *Mikhail Bulgakov*, 125–140. Milne's insightful observations overlap with mine in places and complement them in others. See also the article by Natalia Pervukhina, which appeared too late for me to incorporate it into my analysis: "*Notes of a Young Doctor:* A Haven in the Limelight," *SEEJ* 40, no. 4 (Winter 1996), 685–699.

37. Al'tshuler, in "Bulgakov-prozaik," writes briefly but much to the point about the imagery of the cycle. See also Michael Glenny, "Introduction," in Mikhail Bulgakov, *A Country Doctor's Notebook*, trans. Michael Glenny (Glasgow: William Collins Sons, Fontana Books, 1976), 9; Milne, *Mikhail Bulgakov*, 127–128.

38. The first to note the importance of the theme of faintheartedness was Lakshin, "O proze," 28.

39. In a different context from mine, Efim Etkind notes the "several layers of the 'inner man'" in *Notes of a Young Doctor*. See "Sumerechnyi mir doktora Bomgarda," *Vremia i my*, no. 81 (1984), 127–130. See also Gasparov, "Novyi zavet," 153; Kalpan Sahni, *A Mind in Ferment: Mikhail Bulgakov's Prose* (New Delhi: Arnold-Heinemann, 1984), 31–32.

40. For my interpretation of the story's symbolism I am indebted in part to Al'tshuler, "Bulgakov-prozaik," 5.

41. Bulgakov, "Ia ubil," *Meditsinskii rabotnik*, no. 44, 45 (November 18, December 12, 1926).

42. Markov remembers Bulgakov in the mid-twenties as "well dressed, even with a shade of a certain dandyism" and adds that he "was a splendid storyteller, bold, unexpected" (*Kniga vospominanii,* 229, 230). Even Yashvin's patent leather shoes are borrowed from his creator. The author's second wife recalls that when they first met in 1924, Bulgakov was wearing "high patent leather shoes [*botinki*] with a bright yellow top" (Belozerskaya-Bulgakova, *O med,* 10).

43. Bulgakov, "Morfii," *Meditsinskii rabotnik,* December 9, 17, 23, 1927.

44. Yanovskaya, *Tvorcheskii put',* 83.

45. The anagram is noted by Gourg, "The Story 'Morphine,'" in Milne, *Bulgakov: The Novelist-Playwright,* 108.

46. Yanovskaya, *Tvorcheskii put',* 86.

47. Yanovskaya assumes this to be the case (ibid., 84–85).

48. For more on the relationship between the author and Polyakov, see Gourg, "The Story 'Morphine,'" 112–114.

49. In 1933, the Moscow Art Theater received permission to stage the play, providing that fundamental revisions, especially in the final scene, be made. Bulgakov complied, and rehearsals actually began in the fall. Apparently the production was almost ready when it was removed from the repertory. Hopes were aroused again in 1934, and Bulgakov once more revised the ending, but in November *Flight* was banned. One scene of the play was published during Bulgakov's lifetime: M. Bulgakov, "*Beg,* Sed'maia kartina," *Vecherniaia Krasnaia gazeta,* Oct. 1, 1932. (See Anatoly Smelyansky, "Kommentarii," *Sob. soch.*(M) 3:647.) For the fullest description of the textological and theatrical history of the play during Bulgakov's lifetime, see V. V. Gudkova, "Primechaniia," *P'esy 20-kh godov,* 550–556.

50. Bulgakov, *P'esy 20-kh godov,* 418. This edition publishes the original version (dated 1927) for the first time, as well as the final redaction of 1937. My analysis is of the 1927 redaction, but with relevant comparisons to the 1937 version contained in the notes. Further page references to *P'esy 20-kh godov* will be included in the text.

51. Khludov is based in large part on a historical personage, the White general, Ya. A. Slashchov-Krymsky, who wrote two highly polemical and vivid memoirs about his role in the Crimean campaign: *Trebuiu suda i glasnosti* (Constantinople: Knigoizd-vo M. Shul'man, 1921); and *Krym v 1920 godu: Otryvki iz vospominanii* (Moscow-Leningrad: Gosudarstvennoe izd., 1923). Some of the realia of the play, especially of life in Constantinople, were provided by the author's second wife, who had been in emigration. (See Belozerskaya-Bulgakova, *O med,* 114–115.) For other probable sources for the play, see Gudkova, "Primechaniia," *P'esy 20-kh godov,* 554.

52. Chudakova, "Arkhiv," 60.

53. By the final version, Serafima's words are yet more forgiving: "Everything has passed! Forget it. I have forgotten, and don't you remember" (p. 292).

54. Wright, *Mikhail Bulgakov,* 136.

55. There are more references to Golubkov as *intelligent* in the original than in the final version. See, for example, Tikhy's remark during his interrogation (p. 433) and Lyuska's disparaging comment when Golubkov turns up in Constantinople (p. 454).

56. In the final redaction, Serafima goes still further and declares: "He has gone crazy." She then places the bulk of the blame on his tormentors: "See what they forced him to write!" (pp. 268, 269).

57. By the final version, Bulgakov makes Khludov's threat vaguer: "Well, I'll settle accounts with him!" (p. 263). He thus tones down the danger to Korzukhin and makes him appear more culpable from the beginning.

58. Wright expresses something of this sort when he states that "the play is about man with all his strengths and weaknesses" (*Mikhail Bulgakov,* p. 139).

59. Bulgakov from the very beginning apparently wavered between the two endings for the play: Khludov's return to Russia or his suicide. Thus, in a letter to his brother in 1933, he justified his compliance with a request that the new redaction end in suicide, saying that this had been his original conception. (See Gudkova, "Primechaniia," 558.) In a second revision in 1934, he retained the new ending, and for the final version of 1937 he wrote two variants, the first entailing Khludov's return to Russia, the second his suicide. In any case, either choice would have had essentially the same result, Khludov's death.

60. The lack of political motivation for the couple's return was a major stumbling block for production of the play. Thus *Glavrepertkom,* in its directive of May 18, 1928, complained about the absence of "an emphasis on the historical correctness of the victories of October" in the decision of the protagonists. (See Proffer, ed., *Neizdannyi Bulgakov,* 84.)

5. The Soviet Human Comedy

1. See Emily Mindlin, *Neobyknovennye sobesedniki* (Moscow: Sovetskii pisatel', 1968), 122–129; Proffer, *Bulgakov,* 62–65.

2. See Belozerskaya-Bulgakova, *O, med,* 9–11.

3. Mindlin, *Neobyknovennye sobesedniki,* 145–147. The friendship between the two writers cooled when Bulgakov opposed Kataev's marriage to his sister.

4. Aron Erlikh, *Nas uchila zhizn'* (Moscow: Sovetskii pisatel', 1960), 35–39.

5. "Chetvertyi den': Vechernee zasedanie. Rabkor, gazeta i chitatel'. Rech' tov. Sosnovskogo. Kak ne nado pisat' fel'etonov," *Gudok,* January 31, 1925, 2; "Vechernee zasedanie 3 fevralia: Nakaz 'Gudku,'" *Gudok,* February 4, 1925, 4.

6. See Chudakova, "Arkhiv," 37; Proffer, *Bulgakov,* 87–89. Kinder evaluations are given by Wright, *Mikhail Bulgakov,* 36–37; L. E. Kroichik, "M. Bulgakov-fel'etonist 'Gudka,'" *Voprosy zhurnalistiki* (Voronezh), no. 1 (1969), 110–123. See also the more recent article by E. A. Kukhta, some of whose observations overlap with mine: "Satiricheskii teatr fel'etonov M. Bulgakova v 'Gudke,'" in Ninov and Gudkova, ed., *M. A. Bulgakov-dramaturg,* 246–259.

A particularly curious case is that of the preeminent scholar of Soviet satire, L. F. Ershov, whose shift in attitude is an exact reflection of the change of Bulgakov's fortunes in his native land. In his earlier works, *Sovetskaia satiricheskaia proza 20-kh godov* (Moscow-Leningrad: Izd. Akademii nauk SSSR, 1960) and *Sovetskaia satiricheskaia proza* (Moscow-Leningrad: Khudozhestvennaia literatura, 1966), Ershov does not discuss Bulgakov's feuilletons at all and denigrates his satire in general, while in his later *Satiricheskie zhanry russkoi sovetskoi literatury* (Leningrad: Nauka, 1977), he dubs Bulgakov the foremost *Gudok* feuilletonist.

7. See, for example, Mindlin, *Neobyknovennye sobesedniki,* 74–75. Other memoirs from which I draw are: Yury Olesha, *Ni dnia bez strochki* (Moscow: Sovetskaia Rossiia, 1965); Valentin Kataev, *Almaznyi moi venets* (Moscow: Sovetskii pisatel', 1979); *Sbornik vospominanii ob Il'fe i Petrove* (Moscow: Sovetskii pisatel', 1963), especially the essays by Konstantin Paustovsky, "Chetvertaia polosa," 80–92, and Mikhail Shtikh, "V starom 'Gudke,'" 93–106.

8. Kataev, *Almaznyi moi venets,* 64.

9. Petrovsky notes the tie between the feuilletons and the comedy in *The Master and Margarita* ("Smekh pod znakom," 9–12). Two books delve into the similarities between Bulgakov and Il'f and Petrov: A. A. Kurdyumov, *V kraiu nepuganykh idiotov: Kniga ob Il'fe i Petrove* (Paris: La Presse Libre, 1983); and Maya Kaganskaya and Zeev Bar-Sella, *Master Gamba i Margarita* (Tel Aviv: Kn-stvo Moskva-Ierusalim, 1984).

10. Viktor Shklovsky, "Zorich," *Zhurnalist,* nos. 6–7 (1925), 16.

11. Il'ya Gruzdev, "Tekhnika gazetnogo fel'etona," in Yu. Tynyanov and B. Kazansky, eds., *Fel'eton: Sbornik statei* (Leningrad: Academia, 1927), 13–14.

12. Ershov, *Satiricheskie zhanry,* 96.

13. For an interesting discussion of the narrative voice in the *Nakanune* feuilletons, see E. I. Orlova, "Avtor-rasskazchik-geroi v fel'etonakh M. A. Bulgakova 20-kh godov," *Nauchnye doklady vysshei shkoly. Filologicheskie nauki,* no. 6 (1981), 24–28.

14. For the influence of Doroshevich on early Soviet prose writers, see Chudakova, "Zametki o iazyke," 214–216; Ershov, *Satiricheskie zhanry,* 101–105.

15. See Ershov, *Satiricheskie zhanry,* 109, 110.

16. The general belle-lettristic tendency in feuilletons of the 1920s, including the

particular case of Bulgakov, is discussed in Ershov, *Satiricheskie zhanry,* 120–129. See also Kroichik, "M. Bulgakov-fel'etonist," 111–112.

17. Percy Lubbock, *The Craft of Fiction* (New York: Viking Press, Compass Books, 1957), 66.

18. For an interesting discussion of dramatic elements in the *Gudok* feuilletons, see Smelyansky, *Bulgakov v Khudozhestvennom teatre,* 41–45. See also Kukhta, "Satiricheskii teatr," 246–259.

19. My remarks on *Nakanune* have appeared previously in a slightly different form in Edythe C. Haber, "Bulgakov's *Nakanune* Feuilletons," *Transactions of the Russian-American Scholars in the U.S.A.,* 24 (1991), 3–19.

20. Bulgakov, "Moskva Krasnokamennaia," *Nakanune,* June 30, 1922.

21. *Sob. soch.*(A) 1:259–262. Further page references to this edition, preceded by A, will be included in the text. I use the Ardis *Collected Works* in this chapter both because the feuilletons are conveniently grouped together and because this edition contains a more comprehensive collection of the *Gudok* feuilletons than does *Sob. soch.*(M).

22. "Pokhozhdeniia Chichikova," first published in *Nakanune,* September 24, 1922, was included in the *D'iavoliada* collection, 147–160.

23. For a similar observation, see Kurdyumov, *V kraiu nepuganykh idiotov,* 72–74.

24. Kataev, *Almaznyi moi venets,* 69.

25. Bulgakov published the four *Nakanune* housing stories ("Psalm" ["Psalom"], "Moscow Scenes" ["Moskovskie stseny"], "Moonshine Lake" ["Samogonnoe ozero"], and "Moscow of the Twenties" ["Moskva 20-kh godov"]) in a separate collection: *Traktat o zhilishche (A Tract on Housing)* (Moscow-Leningrad: Zemlia i fabrika, 1926). "Moscow Scenes" and "Moscow of the Twenties" appear there in revised, abbreviated form, under the titles, "Four Portraits" ("Chetyre portreta") and "A Tract on Housing," respectively.

26. In a diary entry of October 1923, Bulgakov wrote: "Unfortunately I am not a hero. But I have more courage [*muzhestvo*] now. Oh, much more than in 1921" ("Ia mogu byt' odnim," 149).

27. Bulgakov, "No. 13. Dom-El'pit Rabkommuna," *Krasnyi zhurnal dlia vsekh,* no. 2 (December 1922). The story was republished in the *D'iavoliada* collection, 125–134. A version of my remarks on the story has appeared in Edythe C. Haber, "Dwellings and Devils in Early Bulgakov," *SEEJ,* 37, no. 3 (1993), 327–331.

28. See V. Levshin, "Sadovaia, 302-bis," 119–120. One must treat this source cautiously, since much of Levshin's information, as Bulgakov's widow pointed out, is inaccurate. See "Pis'mo v redaktsiiu zhurnala 'Teatr' ot vtoroi zheny M. A. Bulgakova—L. E. Belozerskoi-Bulgakovoi," in Proffer, ed., *Neizdannyi Bulgakov,* 22–24.

29. For another interpretation of the Christian allusions of the story, one which partially overlaps with mine, see Gasparov, "Novyi zavet," 162–163.

30. See Katerina Clark, *The Soviet Novel: History as Ritual* (Chicago: University of Chicago Press, 1981), 23.

31. Bulgakov also wrote several articles on education for the journal *Golos rabotnika prosveshcheniia*, one of which shows the very low level of those seeking teacher certification. See "Kaenpe i Kape," no. 4 (March 15, 1923), 19–21; in *Sob. soch.*(A) 2:383–388.

32. See Peter Kenez, *The Birth of the Propaganda State: Soviet Methods of Mass Mobilization, 1917–1929* (Cambridge: Cambridge University Press, 1985), 145–146.

33. For a recent article on the problem of communication with the peasantry, see Orlando Figes, "The Russian Revolution and Its Language in the Village," *RR* 56, no. 3 (July 1997), 323–345.

34. "Fire Chief Pozharov" ("Brandmeister Pozharov") was published in *Gudok* under the title "Herculean Feats to the Sacred Memory of Fire Chief Nazarov" ("Gerkulesovy podvigi svetloi pamiati brandmeistera Nazarova," (A2:58–59). A later variant appeared in *Nakanune* as the first chapter of "Golden Documents (From My Collection)" ("Zolotye dokumenty [Iz moei kollektsii]," A1:385–388). In Mikhail Bulgakov, *Rasskazy* (Moscow: Smekhach, 1926), the latter is published as the "Fourth Correspondence" of "The Golden Correspondences of Ferapont Ferapontovich Kaportsev" ("Zolotye korrespondentsii Feraponta Ferapontovicha Kaportseva"), 15–29. I quote from the more polished *Nakanune/ Rasskazy* version.

35. The *Nakanune* version has "whales" *(kity)* (A1:385) instead of "bedbugs" *(klopy)*, but *Rasskazy* restores the "bedbugs" of the *Gudok* version (A2:58). Probably "whales" was a misprint.

36. The name of the house is evidently an ironic allusion to the Ligovsky People's House, founded at a railway station in a poor section of St. Petersburg in 1902. By 1913 there were 147 such establishments, considered prototypes for later Soviet houses of culture. See Richard Stites, *Russian Popular Culture: Entertainment and Society since 1900* (Cambridge: Cambridge University Press, 1992), 18.

37. Both quotes are from Ershov, *Sovetskaia satiricheskaia proza*, 39–40.

38. A. Andreichik, "Eshche besposhchadnee borot'sia s nedostatkami," *Gudok*, May 11, 1925, 2.

39. See, for example, the following Kataev feuilletons originally published in *Gudok* (page references to Valentin Kataev, *Sobranie sochinenii v deviati tomakh* [Moscow: Khudozhestvennaia literatura, 1968–1972]), vol. 2: "Pervomaiskaia paskha" (138–141); "Doch' Mironova" (338–341); "Konotopskaia narpytka" (326–328); "Dorogu pokoinikam!" (335–337). An indication of

how similar Kataev's feuilletons sometimes are to Bulgakov's is the fact that the "Main-Polit-Divine Service" is attributed to Kataev in his *Collected Works* (301–303).

40. Other feuilletons involving blood, violence, and death are: "The Toothless Instruction and the Carnage in Accordance with the Foregoing" ("Bezzubyi tsirkuliar i poboishche soglasno onogo"), A2:13–14; "What People Sit On," A2:308; "*The Inspector General* with a Chucking Out" ("'Revizor' s vyshibaniem"), A2:182–184; "The Bookkeeper's Fist," A2:279–281; and "The Musical-Vocal Catastrophe," A2:323. Other examples of the destruction of buildings are: "Fire" ("Pozhar"), A2:284–285 and "First Correspondence. The Fireproof American House," A2:454–455. The latter, published in *Rasskazy* (pp. 15–18) as part of the "Golden Correspondences," did not appear originally in *Gudok* but in the Leningrad newspaper *Krasnaia gazeta*, April 30, 1925.

41. Some other examples of the fake supernatural are: "When the Dead Arise from Their Coffins" (A2:276–278) and "The Mystery of the Safe" (A2:317–322). In "Mademoiselle Zhanna" (A2:219–221), the show with a clairvoyant has certain similarities to the magic show in *The Master and Margarita*.

42. Quoted by A. M. Al'tshuler in "A. M. Gor'kii i problema stilevykh poiskov poslerevoliutsionnoi prozy i dramaturgii (A. M. Gor'kii o M. A. Bulgakove)," in *M. Gor'kii i russkaia literatura, Uchenye zapiski Gor'kovskogo Gosudarstvennogo Universiteta*, no. 118 (1971), 160.

6. The Roads Not Taken

1. Erlikh, *Nas uchila zhizn'*, 37.

2. Aron Erlikh, "Oni rabotali v gazete," *Znamia*, no. 8 (1958), 167. Quoted by Wright, *Mikhail Bulgakov*, 50. Erlikh also describes the matches incident in *Nas uchila zhizn'*, 30.

3. Yangirov, who examined the Lito archive, calls the match incident "mythical" and expresses skepticism about Erlikh's recollections of Bulgakov as a whole. See "Bulgakov—sekretar' Lito," 239–240.

4. The novella was originally published in *Nedra*, no. 4, which, according to Chudakova, came out no later than March 11, 1924 ("Arkhiv," 38). The collection *D'iavoliada* (1925) consists of two novellas (*The Diaboliad* and *The Fatal Eggs*) and three short stories ("No. 13. The Elpit Workkommune House," "A Chinese Story," "Adventures of Chichikov").

5. The connection between *The Diaboliad* and *Notes on the Cuff* is mentioned by Proffer, *Bulgakov*, 79.

6. For a detailed comparison of *The Diaboliad* and *The Double*, see Elena Loghinovski, "*D'iavoliada*—segodnia," *RÉS* 62, no. 2 (1993), 282–286.

7. V. Pereverzev, "Novinki belletristiki," *Pechat' i revoliutsiia*, no. 5 (1924), 134–

139. The connection to Gogol' and Dostoevsky has been pointed out by many critics. See, for example, Wright, *Mikhail Bulgakov*, 51–52; Proffer, *Bulgakov*, 108.

8. Evgeny Zamyatin, "O segodniashnem i o sovremennom," *Litsa* (New York: Chekhov Press, 1955), 217. Originally published in *Russkii sovremennik*, no. 2 (1924).

9. Zamyatin, "O. Henry," in *A Soviet Heretic*, 291.

10. Both Proffer (*Bulgakov*, 108) and V. Novikov ("Ranniaia proza M. Bulgakova," in M. A. Bulgakov, *Povesti. Rasskazy. Fel'etony* [Moscow: Sovetskii pisatel', 1988], 22) see some similarity between the novella and a Chaplin movie. See also Loghinovski, "*D'iavoliada*—segodnia," 283, 286.

11. A survey published in 1924 found that such foreign writers as Jack London, Upton Sinclair, and H. G. Wells were the best sellers, with the Russian classics occupying second place and contemporary Soviet writers well behind. See "Sovetskii pisatel' i kniga v tsifrakh i faktakh," *Zhurnalist*, no. 3 (March 1925), 7–8.

12. Ershov, *Satiricheskaia proza 20-kh godov*, 205.

13. Chudakova, "Arkhiv," 39–40.

14. Ibid., 41, n. 37.

15. Lev Lunts, "Iskhodiashchaia No. 37," in *Rodina i drugie proizvedeniia*, ed. M. Vainshtein (Jerusalem: Seriia Pamiat', 1981), 35.

16. Ibid., 40.

17. Lunts, "Pochemu my Serapionovy Brat'ia," *Rodina*, 282.

18. Zamyatin, "O segodniashnem," 217.

19. The devil, as Chudakova has noted, was a common denizen of early Soviet fiction, appearing in such works as Ilya Ehrenburg's *Unusual Adventures of Julio Jurenito* (1922) and A. V. Chayanov's *Benediktov, or Memorable Events of My Life* (1921), the latter a favorite of Bulgakov's. See *Zhizneopisanie*, 297–300.

20. L. B. Menglinova talks in detail about fantasy and madness growing out of surrounding reality in "Printsip satiricheskogo obobshcheniia v povesti M. Bulgakova 'D'iavoliada,'" *Khudozhestvennoe tvorchestvo i literaturnyi protsess* (Tomsk), no. 7 (1985), 127–141. See also Galina Chernikova, "Satiricheskii grotesk v rannei proze M. Bulgakova," *Analele Universitatii din Timisoara* (Rumania), Seria stiinte Filologice X (1972), 71–73; Loghinovski, "*D'ia-voliada*—segodnia," 286–287.

21. Chudakova places his arrival between September 23 and 26 ("K tvorcheskoi biografii," 245). Milne notes the coincidence of this date and the time frame of *Diaboliad* (*Mikhail Bulgakov*, 43).

22. Translation here and elsewhere is mine, but with occasional borrowings from Carl R. Proffer's translation in: Mikhail Bulgakov, *Diaboliad and Other Stories*,

ed. Ellendea Proffer and Carl R. Proffer (Bloomington/London: Indiana University Press, 1972).

23. Yangirov, "Bulgakov—sekretar' Lito," 230. V. V. Gudkova notes another similarity: Bulgakov's bureaucratic work, like Korotkov's, lasted for approximately eleven months, from March 1921 through January 1922. See "Povesti Mikhaila Bulgakova," in *Sob. soch.*(M) 2:667.

24. Proffer says that Korotkov's "character does seem to reflect one side of Bulgakov's own personality" (*Bulgakov,* 461). Milne notes that "Korotkov has features of Bulgakov's ironic self-image" (*Mikhail Bulgakov,* 43). See also Loghinovski, "*D'iavoliada*—segodnia," 289.

25. There is perhaps an allusion here to Lunacharsky's play *Oliver Cromwell,* which portrays the English Protector as a precursor of later revolutionaries, one who is willing to "walk in blood, to chastise, to execute" in the name of his beliefs. See A. V. Lunacharsky, *Oliver Kromvel': Istoricheskaia melodrama* (Moscow: Gosudarstvennoe izd., 1920), 66.

26. Yangirov considers Sobieski's organization an "undoubted reminiscence of Lito" ("Bulgakov—sekretar' Lito," 244). He also traces the origin of the parodic name, Sotsvossky, to Glavsotsvos (Main Adminstration for Social Upbringing) and the odd surname of his secretary, Persimfans, to the acronym for First Symphony Ensemble without a Conductor.

27. Donald Fanger, *Dostoevsky and Romantic Realism: A Study of Dostoevsky in Relation to Balzac, Dickens, and Gogol* (Cambridge, Mass.: Harvard University Press, 1967), 162.

28. Joseph Frank, *Dostoevsky: The Seeds of Revolt, 1821–1849* (Princeton, N. J.: Princeton University Press, 1976), 304.

29. See, for example, Wright, *Mikhail Bulgakov,* 52; Proffer, *Bulgakov,* 107–108. A notable exception is Chernikova, whose description of Korotkov's development is similar to mine: "And so the timid, modest civil servant, beginning an insignificant comic struggle, grows into a battling epic hero [*bogatyr'*]—one against all, against the whole bureaucracy" ("Satiricheskii grotesk," 74). See also Gudkova, "Povesti," 668.

30. Chudakova, *Zhizneopisanie,* 229–231.

31. Ibid., 231.

32. *Nedra,* no. 6 (1925), 79–149. An abbreviated version, entitled variously *The Red Ray (Krasnyi luch)* and *The Ray of Life (Luch zhizni),* was also serialized in 1925 in the magazine *Krasnaia panorama (Red Panorama),* nos. 19, 20, 21, 22, 24.

33. Chudakova notes that the story aroused the "most lively interest" in readers and editors ("Arkhiv," 43). Reviewers and memoirists also mention the stir it caused. A. Men'shoi, for example, says the work created "a sensation in Moscow" ("Moskva v 1928-m godu," *Zhizn' iskusstva,* no. 18 [May 5, 1925], 3).

34. For the fullest summary of contemporary reviews, see Gudkova, "Povesti," 672–676.

35. M. Lirov, "'Nedra,' kniga shestaia," *Pechat' i revoliutsiia*, no. 5–6 (1925), 519.

36. L-v, "'Nedra,' kniga shestaia," *Nm*, no. 6 (1925), 151–152.

37. Grossman-Roshchin, "Stabilizatsiia intelligentskikh dush," 129.

38. See Chudakova, *Zhizneopisanie*, 232–234; "Arkhiv," 42–43; Al'tshuler, "A. M. Gor'kii," 158–159.

39. Recollection of P. N. Zaitsev. Quoted by Chudakova, *Zhizneopisanie*, 232.

40. Letter from Gor'ky to M. L. Slonimsky, March 31, 1925. Quoted in Al'tshuler, "A.M. Gor'kii," 161.

41. L-v, "Nedra," 151.

42. Bulgakov himself calls attention to his indebtedness to *Food of the Gods* by mentioning it in *The Fatal Eggs* (2:56). Many critics have noted the relationship. See especially Christine Rydel, "Bulgakov and H. G. Wells," *RLT*, no. 15 (1978), 293–311.

43. Zamyatin, "H. G. Wells," in *A Soviet Heretic*, 259.

44. Ibid., 261.

45. Ibid., 270.

46. Belozerskaya-Bulgakova states that her relative, E. N. Tarnovsky, was Persikov's prototype (*O med*, 11, 22), whereas Chudakova shows closer correspondences to the eminent zoologist and father of one of Bulgakov's acquaintances, A. N. Severtsov (*Zhizneopisanie*, 242–244), and Proffer puts forward Pavlov as a model (*Bulgakov*, 113). One more suggestion is the physician and professor A. I. Abrikosov, who worked in a clinic in the same building as the Zoological Museum. (See B. S. Myagkov and B. V. Sokolov, "Kommentarii," Mikhail Bulgakov, *Chasha zhizni* [Moscow: Sovetskaia Rossiia, 1988], 573.)

47. Bulgakov's sister, Nadezhda, notes that he liked to work with a microscope and "as a doctor was inclined to research work" (Zemskaya, "Iz semeinogo arkhiva," 53, 84).

48. Bulgakov, "'Ia mogu byt' odnim," 148. A couple of weeks later, on November 6, Bulgakov's mood was more positive: "Literature is my whole life. I will never again return to medicine" (p. 149).

49. Persikov has elicited the most contradictory reactions from critics. Among those who view him positively are V. A. Chebotareva, "Povesti i rasskazy M. A. Bulgakova 20-kh godov," *Uchenye zapiski Azerbaidzhanskogo Ped. Instituta im. M. F. Akhundova*, seriia 12, no. 4 (1972), 115–116; Nadine Natov, *Mikhail Bulgakov* (Boston: Twayne, 1985), 43. Negative judgments are given by Wright, *Mikhail Bulgakov*, 55, and Sigrid McLaughlin, "Structure and Meaning in Bulgakov's *The Fatal Eggs*," *RLT*, no. 15 (1978), 263–270. Proffer, correctly I believe, considers the portrayal ambivalent (*Bulgakov*, 110).

50. Persikov's obsessive pursuit of his scientific calling at the expense of all else,

his demonic/divine tampering with nature, are best described (although somewhat exaggerated) by McLaughlin, "Structure," 263, 274–275.

51. Lirov, for example, calls the work an "allegory" ("Nedra," 519) and emphasizes the political significance of the ray's color by italicizing it throughout his review. For a more recent allegorical interpretation, see McLaughlin, "Structure," 275–277. In allegorical readings there has been a persistent tendency to equate Persikov with Lenin. For the most persuasive attempt, see Irina Gutkin, "Michail Bulgakov's Novella 'Rokovye jajca' in the Context of Its Mythical Subtexts," *Russian Literature* 31 (1992), 294.

52. The sentence does not appear in *Sob. soch.*(M) or in other published editions. The Ardis version is based upon a typed manuscript dated October 1924 and prints some phrases Bulgakov crossed out, apparently at the command of the censors. (See Proffer, "Kommentarii," A3:213.)

53. L-v, "Nedra," 152; Men'shoi, "Moskva v 1928-m godu," 3.

54. Men'shoi, "Moskva v 1928-m godu," 2. See also S. Osinsky's mention of the "feeling of a 'new America'" created in the novella (*Rabochii zhurnal*, no. 3 [1925], 156. Quoted by Gudkova, "Povesti," 674).

55. Numerous critics have noted this but have seen the parallels with Bolshevism alone. See especially Wright, *Mikhail Bulgakov*, 56; McLaughlin, "Structure," 276.

56. Grossman-Roshchin sees a parallel in the story between laboratory experimentation and the Bolsheviks' attempt to rationalize society from above ("Stabilizatsiia intelligentskikh dush," 128).

57. The agent's reply was crossed out in the typewritten manuscript, replaced there and in the printed version of 1925 by the words "it is impossible" (*D'iavoliada* [1925], 72). In the Moscow *Sob. soch.* even this phrase is absent (2:70).

58. McLaughlin sees here an allusion to the failure of the Soviet antireligious campaign ("Structure," 268).

59. The sexual puns have been pointed out by Wright, *Mikhail Bulgakov*, 57; Proffer, *Bulgakov*, 115.

60. Noted by Myagkov and Sokolov, "Kommentarii," 573.

61. See E. H. Carr, *A History of Soviet Russia: The Interregnum, 1923–1924* (London: Macmillan, 1954), 154, 165–170.

62. Bulgakov, "Ia mogu byt' odnim," 145.

63. Bulgakov, "Benefis lorda Kerzona," *Sob. soch.*(M) 2:295–298. Originally published in *Nakanune*, May 19, 1923.

64. Quoted by Carr, *Interregnum*, 171.

65. E. H. Carr, *A History of Soviet Russia: Socialism in One Country, 1924–1926* (London: Macmillan, 1958–1964), 1:190–191.

66. Ibid., 190.

67. See Vladimir N. Ipatieff, *The Life of a Chemist,* trans. Vladimir Haensel and Mrs. Ralph M. Lusher (Stanford, Calif.: Stanford University Press, 1946), 396–397. Dobrokhim is actually mentioned in *The Fatal Eggs* (2:90), and Trotsky wrote an entire book on the subject: *Zadachi Dobrokhima* (Kharkov, 1924). See Gudkova, "Povesti," 700.

68. Leon Trotsky, "Science in the Task of Socialist Construction," in his *Problems of Everyday Life and Other Writings on Culture and Science,* trans. Z. Vergerova (New York, London, Sydney: Monad Press, 1973), 199. Originally published in *Pravda,* November 24, 1923.

69. For more on apocalyptic allusions, see Phyllis W. Powell, "*The Fatal Eggs* and *Adam and Eve:* Disruption and Restoration of the Natural Order," in Milne, ed. *Bulgakov: The Novelist-Playwright,* 98–102.

70. Bulgakov, "Ia mogu byt' odnim," 150.

71. For a detailed description of the Party battles of 1923–1924, see Carr, *Interregnum,* Part III (257–366). See also Adam B. Ulam, *A History of Soviet Russia* (New York: Praeger, 1976), 63–64.

72. Alla Kubareva, in an otherwise misguided article, makes some interesting observations, different from mine, on the significance of Trotsky both in the characterization of Shpolyansky and in *The Fatal Eggs.* (See "Mikhail Bulgakov i ego kritiki," *Molodaia gvardiia,* no. 5 [1988], 250–251.)

73. Leon Trotsky, *Literature and Revolution,* trans. Rose Strunsky (Ann Arbor, Mich.: University of Michigan Press, Ann Arbor Paperbacks, 1960), 252.

74. Ibid., 254.

75. Ibid., 225.

76. Quoted in William G. Rosenberg, ed., *Bolshevik Visions: First Phase of the Cultural Revolution in Soviet Russia* (Ann Arbor, Mich.: Ardis, 1984), 366.

77. Trotsky, *Everyday Life,* 33. Originally published in *Pravda,* July 12, 1923.

78. In a diary entry of December 26, 1924 (several months after the completion of *The Fatal Eggs*), Bulgakov quotes George Bernard Shaw: "Quit even discussing international revolution—it's cinema" ("Ia mogu byt' odnim," 155).

79. Bulgakov notes this involvement in "Ia mogu byt' odnim," 146. For a detailed description of the role of the Russian Communists in the German revolution, see Carr, *Interregnum,* 201–242.

80. Bulgakov, "Ia mogu byt' odnim," 147.

81. Ibid.

82. Ibid., 151.

83. Ibid., 149.

84. See Carr, *Socialism in One Country* 1:196–198.

85. Bulgakov, "Ia mogu byt' odnim," 154.

86. Noted by Wright, *Mikhail Bulgakov,* 56; Gudkova, "Povesti," 679.

87. Trotsky, *Literature and Revolution,* 256.

88. For the role of poison gas, see Powell, *"The Fatal Eggs,"* 96–98.

89. McLaughlin notes some similarities in the depiction of these supposed antagonists ("Structure," 272).

90. Gor'ky, who greatly admired *The Fatal Eggs,* regretted that Bulgakov did not allow the serpents to enter Moscow, adding, "just think, what a monstrously interesting picture that is" (letter to M. Slonimsky, May 28, 1925, quoted by Al'tshuler, "A. M. Gor'kii," 159). Levshin recalls that in Bulgakov's telephone improvisation to the *Nedra* editor, the ending was similar to the one Gor'ky preferred ("Sadovaia, 302-bis," 114).

91. Bulgakov, "Ia mogu byt' odnim," 155.

92. A similar observation is made by B. Gasparov, "Novyi zavet," 156.

93. A similar observation is made by M. O. Chudakova, "Posleslovie," Mikhail Bulgakov, "Sobach'e serdtse: povest'," *Znamia,* no. 6 (1987), 135.

94. Bulgakov wrote four more plays in the late twenties, of which two were produced at the time. *Zoika's Apartment (Zoikina kvartira),* written in late 1925, opened at the Vakhtangov Theater in October 1926. *The Crimson Island (Bagrovyi ostrov)* was written in 1927 and began its run at Tairov's Kamerny Theater in December 1928.

95. In the summer of 1925 the *Diaboliad* collection, as well as several stories in periodicals, was published, but by the fall Bulgakov's career as prose fiction writer took a precipitous turn for the worse. Within a short period the printing of *Diaboliad* was confiscated, *Heart of a Dog* was banned, and the journal *Rossiia* closed before publishing the final part of *The White Guard.* In 1926, there appeared a second edition of *Diaboliad* and two slender volumes of Bulgakov's satiric stories and feuilletons, *Rasskazy* and *Traktat o zhilishche,* but the promised separate editions of *The Fatal Eggs* and *The White Guard* did not materialize. In that year most of *Notes of a Young Doctor* was also published, and an occasional Bulgakov feuilleton appeared in *Gudok,* but in 1927 only one story, "Morphine," is known to have appeared.

96. These details and the following account of the aborted attempt to publish *Heart of a Dog* are based upon Chudakova, *Zhizneopisanie,* 245–252.

97. Ibid., 256.

98. Belozerskaya-Bulgakova, *O, med,* 28–29.

99. The novella was first published, with many inaccuracies, in the Russian émigré journal *Grani,* no. 9 (1968), 3–85, and shortly thereafter in book form, in a more authoritative version (Paris: YMCA Press, 1969). The first Soviet edition came out in the journal *Znamia,* no. 6 (1987), 76–135, and has since appeared many times. A stage version, produced at the Youth Theater in Moscow, spawned several interesting reviews, among them the first appearance in print since his rehabilitation of Andrei Sakharov: "Veriu v razum," *Teatr,* no. 8 (1987), 113–115. For a detailed description of this and two other

stage adaptations, see Nadezhda Natova, "Ot teksta k stsene: Povest' 'Sobach'e serdtse' Mikhaila Bulgakova i ee teatral'naia interpretatsiia," in *Transactions of the Association of Russian-American Scholars in the U.S.A.* 24 (1991), 89–131.

100. Chudakova, "Arkhiv," 44.

101. Rydel discusses the influence of *The Island of Dr. Moreau* on *Heart of a Dog* ("Bulgakov and H. G. Wells," 306–309).

102. For a more detailed treatment of point of view, see Helena Goscilo, "Point of View in Bulgakov's *Heart of a Dog,*" *RLT,* no. 15 (1978), 281–291; Diana L. Burgin, "Bulgakov's Early Tragedy of the Scientist-Creator: An Interpretation of *The Heart of a Dog,*" *SEEJ* 22, no. 4 (1978), 494–508. Some of my observations are borrowed from these sources.

103. For a more exhaustive list of literary works with animal narrators, see Goscilo, "Point of View," 290, n. 1.

104. The translation throughout is mine, but I have occasionally consulted the English rendering by Mirra Ginsburg: *Heart of a Dog* (New York: Grove Press, 1968).

105. The last two sentences are omitted from *Sob. soch.*(M), which, according to Viktor Losev, is based on the second variant of the first redaction ("Kommentarii," *Iz luchshikh proizvedenii,* 603). The Ardis edition, like that in *Iz luchshikh proizvedenii,* gives first variant. The second redaction appears in *Izb. pr.* 2:119–208.

106. The dog's omniscience and the blurring of the first- and third-person narrations are noted by Susanne Fusso, "Failures of Transformation in *Soba'e serdce,*" *SEEJ* 33, no. 3 (Fall 1989), 389–390.

107. Fusso notes Bulgakov's "Šarik-like position" in the early 1920s (ibid., 396).

108. Bulgakov, *Izb. pr.,* 2:673.

109. Others have noted the relationship. See Sergei Shargorodsky, "Sobach'e serdtse, ili Chudovishchnaia istoriia," *Lo,* no. 5 (1991), 88–89; Mikhail Zolotonosov, "'Rodis' vtororozhden'em tainym...' Mikhail Bulgakov: pozitsiia pisatelia i dvizhenie vremeni," *Vl,* no. 4 (1989), 164; A. K. Zholkovsky, *Bluzhdaiushchie sny i drugie raboty.* (Moscow: Nauka, 1994), 15.

110. Blok, *Sobranie sochinenii vshesti tomakh,* 6 vols. (Moscow: Izd, Pravda, Biblioteka "ogoneli," 1971), 3: 241. Translation mine. Further page references to this edition will be included in the text, preceded by Blok.

111. Shargorodsky notes this parallel ("Sobach'e serdtse," 88).

112. Shargorodsky sees Preobrazhensky's link to Blok's bourgeois but not to his savior (ibid., 89).

113. Most critics have regarded Preobrazhensky as positive. See, for example, Goscilo, "Point of View"; Wright, *Mikhail Bulgakov;* Proffer, *Bulgakov;* and Chudakova, "Posleslovie."

114. See Belozerskaya-Bulgakova, *O, med,* 23.

115. Chudakova, "Posleslovie," 141.

116. Chudakova quotes from Bulgakov's letter to his sister of January 23, 1923, in which he expresses his desire to set his life on a "normal course." She asserts that such a norm was for the writer an "undeviating reference point in life" (*Zhizneopisanie*, 196).

117. Fusso first noted the connection with Mayakovsky ("Failures of Transformation," 393–395). Losev mentions another possible source, a play by V. Yazvitsky, entitled *Who Is to Blame? (Ruin)* (*Kto vinovat? [Razrukha]*). See "Kommentarii," in Bulgakov, *Iz luchshikh proizvedenii*, 608.

118. The main prototype for the story's hero is said to be Vladimir Evgenievich Komorsky, a barrister whose excellent three-room apartment Bulgakov often visited (see Chudakova, *Zhizneopisanie*, 182–184). Certain important details, however, better fit the writer's uncle, Nikolai Mikhailovich Pokrovsky, who not only lived in a six-room apartment like the barrister in the story but also invited two relatives from the provinces to live with him (see Belozerskaya-Bulgakova, *O, med*, 23). Bulgakov undoubtedly writes of this in "Moscow of the Twenties": "Nikolai Ivanovich recouped his losses with his two nieces. He wrote to the provinces and two nieces arrived . . . Was it clever of Nikolai Ivanovich to hang two nieces around his neck at such a difficult time? Not clever, my dear sir, but brilliant. Nikolai Ivanovich kept his six rooms" (2:444).

119. The symbolic significance of the "hellish" kitchen has been traced by Burgin, "Bulgakov's Early Tragedy," 498.

120. Ronald D. LeBlanc notes that the operations "do little more than cater to the baser instincts of the venal people who can afford them" ("Feeding a Poor Dog a Bone: The Quest for Nourishment in Bulgakov's *Sobach'e serdtse*," *RR* 52, no. 1 [1993], 68). As Natova notes, the musical motif running through the episode—snatches of Don Juan's serenade from A. K. Tolstoy's dramatic poem, *Don Juan*—underlines the "obscenity" of the goings-on ("Ot teksta k stsene," 81–87).

121. Both Vladimir Lakshin, in his introduction to "Sobach'e serdtse" (*Znamia*, 75) and Novikov ("Ranniaia proza," 29) call Preobrazhensky a *spets*.

122. I am indebted here to Natova's informative observations on *Aida* ("Ot teksta k stsene," 85–87).

123. Other critics have noticed this. See, for example, Goscilo, "Point of View," 285; Proffer, *Bulgakov*, 127–128; and Burgin, "Bulgakov's Early Tragedy," 499–500.

124. See especially Proffer, *Bulgakov*, 115, 131.

125. Shortly before he began *Heart of a Dog* (December 23, 1924), Bulgakov noted in his diary Aleksei Tolstoy's jocular description of his own transformation on Soviet soil: "I'm not Aleksei Tolstoy now, but the worker-correspondent and homegrown genius [*rabkor-samorodok*] Potap Der'mov [*der'mo* = shit]. A dirty, dishonorable buffoon" ("Ia mogu byt' odnim," 154). LeBlanc writes

interestingly about Sharik's change for the worse as Sharikov ("Feeding a Poor Dog," 58–59, 67). Gudkova lists various indications of the dog's superiority to Sharikov ("Povesti," 690–691).

126. See Chudakova, *Zhizneopisanie*, 230–231.

127. Novikov relates this question to an issue widely discussed at the time by such writers as Gor'ky, Leonov, and Zoshchenko: the difficulty of overcoming the "dark instincts, more ancient than reason" in the formation of the new Soviet man ("Ranniaia proza," 28, 31–32).

128. A. K. Zholkovsky observes that Sharikov is a "parodic double" of Preobrazhensky. See "Popytki 'Zavisti' u Mandel'shtama i Bulgakova" (*Bluzhdaiushchie sny*, 153).

129. A. K. Zholkovsky mentions the similarity of names. See "O Smerdiakove (O probleme 'Bulgakov i Dostoevskii')," in E. V. Permyakov, ed., *Lotmanovskii sbornik*, 1:576.

130. Burgin, "Bulgakov's Early Tragedy," 501–503. The following interpretation borrows much from her reading.

131. Gudkova also notes the chronological coincidence of what she calls Sharik's "pseudohumanization" with Christ's birth ("Povesti," 692).

132. For other parallels between Sharikov and Smerdyakov, see Zholkovsky, "O Smerdiakove," 568–580.

133. The allusion to "purge politics" is noted by Proffer, *Bulgakov*, 133. As early as April 15, 1924, Bulgakov saw signs of heightened persecution: "There are numerous arrests in Moscow of people from 'good' families. Once again deportations" ("Ia mogu byt' odnim," 150).

134. Zholkovsky notes that Preobrazhensky offers Bormental' as well as Sharik "parental protection" ("Popytki 'Zavisti,'" 152). See also LeBlanc, "Feeding a Poor Dog," 67.

135. Two exceptions are Burgin, "Bulgakov's Early Tragedy," 504, and Zholkovsky, "Popytki 'Zavisti,'" 153.

136. Others have seen this. See Proffer, *Bulgakov*, 130; Natov, *Mikhail Bulgakov*, 45; and Burgin, "Bulgakov's Early Tragedy," 505.

137. There are two versions of the play, the first written in late 1925 and the second, substantially revised, in 1935 for production at the Vieux Colombier Theater in Paris. I discuss the earlier version as published in *Sob. soch.*(M), vol. 3. Two variants of the first version, along with the second version, are included in *P'esy 20-kh godov*.

138. In the later version, Alliluya is renamed Portupeya, probably because of the similarity of the original name to that of Stalin's first wife, Allilueva (see Wright, *Mikhail Bulgakov*, 106). The name of Obolyaninov was also slightly changed to Abolyaninov.

139. Gudkova writes that before giving approval for the Vakhtangov Theater pro-

duction, the censors demanded that Ametistov and Kheruvimov be caught. An insert in the final approved 1926 version has a police agent saying over the telephone that the two were caught by the entrance to the building ("Primechaniia," *P'esy 20-kh godov*, 543).

140. Preobrazhensky, "wonder worker" and "magician," has been called a precursor of Woland (Burgin, "Bulgakov's Early Tragedy," 506; Chudakova, *Zhizneopisanie*, 296). When Burgin states, however, that the professor detests those "whose slavish lives are ruled by asking favors of those more powerful," she fails to see that he himself does not heed Woland's rule that one "should never ask for anything . . . and especially from those who are more powerful than yourself" (5:273). Typical for Bulgakov, Preobrazhensky is an ambivalent figure, whose almost supernatural power allies him to Woland, but who, in his love of comfort and money, foreshadows the fawning Moscow literary establishment.

141. This is noted by Zholkovsky, "Popytki 'Zavisti,'" 160.

Conclusion

1. Bulgakov, *P'esy 20-kh godov*, 423.

2. The evolution of the military commander from "The Red Crown" through "I Killed" to *Flight* has been traced by Chudakova, *Zhizneopisanie*, 280–281.

3. *Kopyto inzhenera (Chernoviki romana. Tetrad' 2. 1928–1929 gg.)*, in Mikhail Bulgakov, *Velikii kantsler: Chernovye redaktsii romana "Master i Margarita"*, ed. Viktor Losev (Moscow: Novosti, 1992), 236.

4. For more on Pilate's military background, see Haber, "Lamp with the Green Shade," 341–343.

5. Several critics have hypothesized that Bezdomny is, in fact, the "author" and narrator of *The Master and Margarita* as a whole. See especially Laura D. Weeks, "In Defense of the Homeless: On the Uses of History and the Role of Bezdomnyi in *The Master and Margarita*," *RR* 48, no. 1 (1989), 45–65.

6. For a more detailed version of my views on Woland, see Edythe C. Haber, "The Mythic Structure of Bulgakov's *The Master and Margarita*," *RR* 34, no. 4 (1975), 384–390.

7. For a detailed description of the love affair between Bulgakov and his third wife, see Chudakova, *Zhizneopisanie*, Chap. 4. For another rather gossipy but well-documented account, see Anatoly Shvarts, *Zhizn' i smert'*, 29–35, 50–55. See also Elena Sergeevna's diary: *Dnevnik Eleny Bulgakovoi*, ed. Viktor Losev and Lidiya Yanovskaya (Moscow: Knizhnaia palata, 1990).

8. For the fullest account of Bulgakov's later life, see Proffer, *Bulgakov*, and Chudakova, *Zhizneopisanie*. Much of my information comes from these sources.

9. Chudakova discusses in great detail the significance of Stalin's call for Bulgakov and his later regret that he did not say all that he should have. Thus the early theme of the intellectual's silence under duress is reinforced by this later instance in the writer's life. (See *Zhizneopisanie,* 340–341, 352, 378, 406–407.)

10. Aside from constantly revising his earlier theater pieces, Bulgakov wrote seven new plays in the thirties: *Adam and Eve* (1931); *Half-Witted Jourdain* (1932); *Bliss* (1934); *Ivan Vasilievich* (1935); *The Last Days (Pushkin)* (1935); *Don Quixote* (1938); and *Batum* (1939). None were produced in his lifetime, although some went into rehearsal. Other theatrical, cinematic, and operatic projects also came to nothing: the stage adaptation of *War and Peace* (1931–1932), the film scripts of Gogol's *Dead Souls* and *The Inspector General* (1934–1935), and several opera libretti. The biography *The Life of Monsieur de Molière* was rejected by Gor'ky for publication in his "Life of Remarkable People" series, and Bulgakov did not even attempt to publish his most important prose works, *Notes of a Dead Man* and *The Master and Margarita.* For a good recent survey of this period, see Milne, *Mikhail Bulgakov,* 189–225.

11. See, for example, Bulgakova, *Dnevnik,* 58, 61, 62, 65.

12. Ibid., 47, 51, 66. Chudakova contrasts Bulgakov's refusal to write on prescribed subjects with the compromises of other talented writers, such as Zoshchenko (*Zhizneopisanie,* 387).

13. Bulgakova, *Dnevnik,* 91.

14. Bulgakov also attempted to write a history of the USSR to place in competition for a high school textbook, which offered a first prize of 100,000 rubles. For the text of his draft, see M. Bulgakov, "Kurs istorii SSSR," in Groznova and Pavlovsky, ed., *Tvorchestvo Mikhaila Bulgakova,* bk. 1, 284–426.

15. Milne also refers to Woland as Bulgakov's alter ego (*Mikhail Bulgakov,* 191).

Index